A HISTORY *of* INDIA
*from the Earliest Times
to Nineteen Thirty-nine*

—

VOLUME II

A HISTORY OF
INDIA

FROM THE EARLIEST TIMES
TO
NINETEEN THIRTY-NINE

Sir George Dunbar, Bt.

VOLUME II

1949

NICHOLSON & WATSON
LIMITED . . LONDON

First Edition   .   .   *January*, 1936
Second Edition   .   .   *February*, 1939
Third Edition   .   .   *November*, 1943
Fourth Revised Edition   *February*, 1949

Printed in Great Britain
by T. and A. CONSTABLE LTD., Hopetoun Street,
Printers to the University of Edinburgh

CONTENTS

VOLUME II

CHAPTER TWELVE

The Later Moguls and the Marathas

CHAPTER THIRTEEN

French and English in the Carnatic

CHAPTER SEVENTEEN

British Supremacy

CHAPTER EIGHTEEN

Consolidation of British Rule

CHAPTER NINETEEN

India under the Crown : Part I. Canning to Ripon

India under the Crown : Part II. Dufferin to Curzon

CHAPTER TWENTY

British Rule and Indian Nationalism

PART I

PART II

ILLUSTRATIONS

Selected and arranged by Winifred Holmes

My most grateful thanks, for their generous help and advice in selecting the illustrations to this book, are especially due to Mr. K. de B. Codrington, Dr. Randle, Sir John Marshall, Mr. Arthur Probsthain, Mr. F. J. P. Richter, M.A., Mr. J. Allan of the British Museum, Mr. V. P. Bhandarkar, Manager of the Indian Railways Bureau, Mr. A. G. Adams, Director of the Parker Gallery, Mr. Mukul Dey, Director of Government School of Art, Calcutta, and Mr. Robert M. Flaherty.

VOLUME II

ix

down to the Deccan to deal with Kam Baksh without enforcing his surrender.

In 1710 the Rajputs again rose, and once more Bahadur Shah invaded Rajputana. The negotiations which were opened with the Rajputs were cut short by the news that the Sikhs were in revolt, and the Emperor, making a peace which left Udaipur, Jaipur and Jodhpur independent in all but name, hurried off to the Punjab.

The Sikh Rebellion. When Aurangzeb died Govind Singh the tenth Sikh Guru sided with Bahadur Shah and was given a command in the Deccan,[1] where, towards the end of 1708, he was murdered by a Pathan. After his death the Sikh scriptures, known as the *Granth*, became the spiritual represent-ative of the Gurus with Govind's chosen disciple Banda the temporal leader of the Khalsa. The Sikhs gathered round him and in 1709 and 1710 Banda succeeded in defeating and killing the Governor of Sirhind, plundered the province and put to death the Hindu betrayer and Moslem assassin of Govind's children. Banda then occupied the country between the Sutlej and the Jhelum and devastated the district of Saharanpur.[2] It was at this point that the Emperor came north to find that the Sikhs had already been defeated and driven into the Jammu hills.

Bahadur Shah died at Lahore in February 1712, at the age of sixty-nine, and the inevitable war of succession immediately broke out.

Jahandar Shah. Of the four sons of Bahadur Shah, the second Azim-ush-Shah had the largest following, and the eldest Jahandar Shah with neither troops nor money appeared to have the poorest chance as a claimant. But Jahandar Shah was joined by the able and unscrupulous Persian Zulfiqar Khan, who (with his father) had no rival in the kingdom either in rank or influence,[3] and soldiers and adventurers flocked to his standard. Zulfiqar Khan arranged an alliance between Jahandar Shah and his brothers Rafi-ush-Shah and Jahan Shah against Azim-ush-Shah who was defeated

----

[1] *History of the Sikhs*, footnote to p. 81.
[2] *Ibid.*, p. 86.
[3] *The Later Mughals*, Vol. I. pp. 9, 10.

and killed in the middle of March. Jahandar Shah then turned upon his brothers and the same fate befell Jahan Shah and Rafi-ush-Shah who were successively attacked. On the 29th March 1712 Jahandar Shah was enthroned as Emperor. Asad Khan kept his former position of Vice-regent and Zulfiqar Khan became chief minister.

Jahandar Shah was the first of the Timurids who could not rule himself, much less govern an empire. He was deposed and murdered by his nephew Farrukh-Siyar, together with Zulfiqar Khan, after a debauched and disgusting career of eleven months. The only notable event in the reign was the reception of a Dutch embassy, which obtained, through "the company's faithful friend" Asad Khan, concessions made useless a few months later by Farrukh-Siyar's successful rebellion.

Farrukh-Siyar entered Delhi as Emperor on the 12th February *Farrukh-Siyar.* 1713 with the bodies of Jahandar Shah and Zulfiqar Khan paraded on elephants in the procession. "Feeble, false, cowardly and contemptible," [1] Farrukh-Siyar was almost entirely in the hands of his chief ministers, the two brothers Sayyid Abdullah Khan and Sayyid Hussain Ali, while the reign of terror which followed the Emperor's accession to power is attributed by Khafi Khan to the influence of Mir Jumla Mutamid-ul-mulk.[2] Mir Jumla, who was a native of Samarkand, was not related to the Persian merchant, statesman and soldier whose adventurous career had ended with honour during the reign of Aurangzeb.

The Sikhs had reunited under Banda during the war of succession *End of Banda.* and continued to give trouble by repeatedly raiding the Northern Punjab until an overpowering force was sent against them. Banda with 10,000 of his men was besieged in April 1715 in the stronghold of Gurdaspur, and for eight months the Sikhs held out until starvation forced them to unconditional surrender. The survivors were executed in batches of a hundred every day for a week and Banda was tortured to death. All save the leaders were offered their lives if they would accept Islam, but the

---

[1] *The Later Mughals*, Vol. I. p. 396.
[2] *Ibid.*, Vol. I. pp. 275-281, with which authority Irvine agrees. But p. 276 footnote offers an alternative, that the Sayyids were responsible.

Sikhs without exception exultantly preferred to die for their faith.[1]
After the defeat and death of Banda persistent persecution drove the
Sikhs into hiding for a generation.

Three other events of the reign may be noticed. In 1714 a
Mission was sent to the Mogul court by the East
*Events of the
Reign.* India Company. In 1717 the *jizya*, which Farrukh-
Siyar had abolished when he proclaimed himself
Emperor, was reimposed. In 1718 Maratha levies came up to Delhi
to take part in the disputes at the court, and their representative
minister Balaji Visvanath negotiated a treaty with Hussain Ali giving
them the *chauth* (one quarter) and the *ser dasmak* (additional tenth)
of the whole remaining revenue of the Deccan. This treaty was
ratified after the dethronement of the Emperor.[2]

Farrukh-Siyar " as irresolute in his actions as he was bold in his
intrigues " had quarrelled intermittently with his
Court Intrigue. Sayyid ministers almost from the day of his accession
and had made more than one attempt to overthrow them. The court
was divided into the factions of the foreign party made up of the
Afghans, Persians, Arabs, negroes and Turks, and the Hindustani
party of Indian-born Moslems (such as the Sayyids Abdullah Khan
and Hussain Ali) with the Rajput, Jat and other powerful Hindu
landowners, groups which were cut across by the opposing cliques
supporting either the Emperor or his ministers.[3] But Farrukh-
Siyar succeeded in alienating most of his adherents, and in February
1719 the Sayyids, " forced into action by regard for their own lives
and honour," [4] seized the Emperor and put him to death on the 28th
April after barbarous ill-treatment.

Three Emperors were placed on the throne in the course of the
next few months, of whom two were already dying of consumption
while the third had been a State prisoner for years. Finally at the end
of September 1719 a fourth descendant of Aurangzeb, Muhammad
Shah, was enthroned by the Sayyids. He reigned in name for twenty-

[1] *The Later Mughals*, Vol. I. pp. 317, 318.
[2] *History of the Mahrattas*, Vol. I. pp. 336–339.
[3] *The Later Mughals*, Vol. I. pp. 272–275.
[4] Shah Nawaz Khan quoted (but not in any way justified as regards the
Emperor's treatment and death) by Irvine, *The Later Mughals*, Vol. I. p. 395.

nine years and lived to see the break-up of the Empire and the invasion of Nadir Shah.

One of his first acts was to abolish the *jizya*, and although two unsuccessful attempts were shortly afterwards made to revive it, this engine of religious oppression was never used again in India.

Muhammad Shah remained completely in the hands of the Sayyid brothers until 1722, when he succeeded in getting rid of them. Hussain Ali was murdered and Abdullah thrown into prison, where he was ultimately poisoned.[1] The Sayyids had ruled with an iron hand, but after their overthrow the Emperor surrounded himself with inexperienced and wholly inept advisers, and what had been the paramount power in India began to drift on the tide of affairs from one generation to the next without exerting the smallest influence upon the history of the country.

Imperial control over the provinces was purely nominal within twenty years of the death of Aurangzeb. Murshid Quli Khan the greatest of the Bengal Viceroys, who died in 1725, combined the posts of Governor and Finance Minister of Bengal, Orissa and Bihar, and after his time the rulership of the richest province in India became hereditary.[2] The Persian, Sayyid Saadat Khan, progenitor of the kings of Oudh, was made governor of that province in 1723,[3] and proceeded to rule it in practical independence, while at the end of the same year the foundations of the great State of Hyderabad were laid by the ancestor of its present ruler.

When Farrukh-Siyar came to the throne Asaf Jah was one of
Hyderabad. the rising men in India. His family, which came originally from Samarkand, had supplied more than one great officer of State, and in 1713 Asaf Jah, already a distinguished soldier and provincial governor, was made Viceroy of the Deccan, as Nizam-ul-mulk. A staunch friend of Farrukh-Siyar, he was relegated within two years to the insignificant Governorship of Moradabad by

---

[1] *The Later Mughals*, Vol. II. p. 96.
[2] *Early Revenue History of Bengal*, F. D. Ascoli.
[3] *The Later Mughals*, Vol. II. p. 135.

the Sayyids. The Nizam[1] began active hostilities against them, from which he issued as Viceroy of the Deccan. Appointed chief minister of the Empire in 1723, the Nizam soon found that his position was intolerable. The young Emperor was surrounded by companions who pandered to his lowest tastes, and he preferred their opinion to the counsel of his minister. "Public business was dealt with as if it were a child's toy. Revenue business was disposed of by the heads of the army, and night-watchmen decided cases instead of the qazi. The Emperor was immersed in pleasure, the nobles drunk with envy, the servants of the State starving." [2]

Thwarted at every turn in his efforts to end these abuses, the Nizam threw up his appointment in the following year and returned to his own province. He had been appointed "Deputy of the Empire," but Muhammad Shah saw that his deputy had every intention of becoming independent of Delhi and sent secret orders to Mubariz Khan, Governor of Hyderabad, to oust him from the Deccan. The Nizam completely defeated Mubariz in the autumn of 1724, and sent his head to court with a congratulatory letter on the victory obtained by the imperial arms.[3] But after the battle of Shakar Khera the Nizam exercised every prerogative of sovereignty except the use of the imperial scarlet umbrella, the recitation of the Friday prayer in his own name and the issue of coinage stamped with his own superscription. The countries south of the Narbada which had been won by the Moguls by more than a century of war were lost to them for ever.

The powerful organization created by the genius of Sivaji disappeared for a time after his death, although the extinction of the kingdoms of Bijapur and Golconda removed the check upon Maratha incursions and swarms of marauding horsemen devastated the Deccan. But the warlike Hindu population of Maharashtra were not united by the

The Maratha Revival.

---

[1] This is actually a misnomer, but it is a simpler description than Nizam-ul-mulk, Mir Qamar-ud-din, Chin Qilich Khan Bahadur, Fath Jang, or Subahdar of the Deccan.

[2] *The Later Mughals*, Vol. II. pp. 131–134.

[3] *History of the Mahrattas*, Vol. I. p. 356.

bond of a fixed determination to throw off a foreign yoke and vindicate their civil and religious liberties. Their guiding star was not patriotism but plunder,[1] and the country administered by Tara Bai, Raja Ram's young widow, was broken into factions all fighting for their own hand. In 1708 Bahadur Shah allowed Sambaji's son Shahu to return to his own people from the Mogul court, and he at once claimed and assumed the kingship, although it was five years before his ascendancy over the Marathas was assured. Unlike his predecessors, Shahu, while he styled himself King of the Hindus, acknowledged the suzerainty of Delhi in his dealings with the Moguls.

Shahu, although he possessed the violent temper of his race, had none of the vices and cruelty of his father. He was *The First Peshwa.* a devout Hindu strongly favourable to the Brahmans, conciliatory in his policy and liberal to all religious establishments. From the first the most experienced Maratha ministers gathered round him, and the ablest of them all was the second minister, or Peshwa, Balaji Visvanath, a Konkani Brahman, who was appointed in 1714. The almost incredible rise of the Maratha people from a state of confusion and anarchy dates from the time when Balaji Visvanath became the trusted adviser of his sovereign, and a common interest was created and for a time preserved among the Maratha chiefs. Shahu, a man of average ability who cared for nothing but hawking, hunting and fishing, strongly disliked the details of administration. The outward show of deference to his position was enough for him, and he did not foresee that he was delegating a power which might supersede his own.

Sivaji's general system of administration was revived, but the *Maratha Administration.* spirit of patriotism which he had inspired was overlaid and smothered by the ruling passion, skilfully stimulated by the Peshwa, which united the Maratha chiefs, the pursuit of plunder. Every leader was encouraged to further activity by a definite share in new conquests, which it was to his own advantage to hold. This entailed an intricate partition of the *jagirs* and provinces which brought about a departure

[1] *History of the Mahrattas*, Vol. I. pp. 303, 304.

from Sivaji's principle of the direct collection of taxes by the central government and the payment of all salaries and military pay by the Treasury. Maharashtra, which had been collectively referred to by Europeans up to the death of Raja Ram as " the Sivajis," [1] now allowed its king a percentage of the revenue (later reduced to a fixed allowance) for his privy purse, while the Peshwa controlled and allotted the remainder.

The financial system introduced by Balaji Visvanath was so complicated that only the most highly educated officials, that is to say the Brahmans, could understand it. The bulk of the revenue came from the levy made upon territories of other powers. The whole authorised *chauth* could never be collected, arrears ran on, and the total claims remained undefined; but, in the words of Grant Duff, " the one system in practice, that of exacting as much as they could, was as simple as it was invariable." A district once overrun by the Marathas was said to be under tribute from usage, and the others were plundered by virtue of letters patent. [2]

The Maratha fleet, under the Angria family, levied their taxation [3]

Maratha Pirates.

at sea, indiscriminately plundering the ships of all nationalities that appeared on the coast. The Angrias, justly notorious as bold and successful pirates, were of mixed Maratha and either Portuguese or Arab descent. [4] Kanoji Angria, who was given ten forts, including Kolaba, Suvarndrug and Gheria (Viziadrug), by Balaji Visvanath in 1713 as an inducement to support Shahu, [5] was a leader of genius and enterprise. He made his position so secure that he was able to defy the efforts of the English government of Bombay, the Portuguese and the Dutch to take his fortified harbour.

In the same way as the Magh pirates of Chittagong had attracted Portuguese desperadoes many of the worst members of the crews of the Maratha ships were Europeans and, as Philip Gosse has remarked, Englishmen. [6] One of Angria's captains was a thorough-paced scound-

---

[1] *History of the Mahrattas*, Vol. I. p. 412 and footnote.
[2] *Ibid.*, Vol. I. p. 342.   [3] *Ibid.*, Vol. I. p. 343.
[4] *Ibid.*, Vol. I., footnote to p. 280.   [5] *Ibid.*, Vol. I. pp. 327–328 and footnote.
[6] *History of Piracy*, 1932, p. 244.

rel named James Plantain, the friend of Mulatto Tom, who was a natural son of the pirate Avery.

Kidd and Avery had both appeared off the Malabar coast at the end of the seventeenth century. The latter, known as the Grand Pirate, by successfully attacking the Mecca fleet of the empire, had caused serious complications between the East India Company and the Mogul government.[1]

It was some time before the East India Company learnt the lesson that the same ship could not reasonably be expected to carry cargo and fight fast piratical craft; and succeeding members of the Angria family continued with the connivance of the Peshwa's government to be the terror of the coast until 1750, when Tulaji Angria disavowed the authority of Poona. This brought down upon him in 1755 a combined attack by the Marathas and a small British squadron under Commodore James, to whose resolute tactics the fall of Suvarndrug was due. A year later a British fleet of twelve warships under Admiral Watson and a force of 800 European and 600 Indian infantry commanded by Clive, then a colonel, co-operating with the Marathas, took Gheria.[2] Tulaji was captured and imprisoned for life. But piracy on the Malabar coast was not finally stamped out by the British until 1820.[3]

Balaji Visvanath died in 1720 and the office became hereditary

Rise of the Peshwas.

when he was succeeded as Peshwa by his eldest son Baji Rao. Bred a soldier as well as a statesman, Baji Rao united the enterprise, vigour and hardihood of a Maratha chief with the polished manners and great ability which frequently distinguish the Brahmans of the Konkan. In the second Peshwa industry and close attention to detail were combined with acute political insight. He had both the head to plan and the hand to execute in his sovereign's name his schemes for the expansion of the Maratha power.[4] While Shahu allowed himself to become, what his successors remained, an ornamental figure-head at Satara,

[1] *History of the Mahrattas*, Vol. I. p. 280, footnote, pp. 288–289 and footnote.
[2] *Ibid.*, Vol. I. pp. 478–485.
[3] *Camb. Hist. British Empire*, Vol. IV. p. 382.
[4] *History of the Mahrattas*, Vol. I. p. 359.

the chief minister Sriput Rao was not so complacent, and struggled for a time to uphold the royal authority. But Baji Rao overcame all opposition, and the most important personages in India, until Dupleix became governor of Pondicherry in 1742, were the Peshwa at Satara,[1] the Nizam at Hyderabad and the Governor of Bengal at Murshidabad.

The Nizam, although at times in alliance with the Marathas, had every inducement to check their growing power and never-ending encroachments. The blackmail which they levied on the Deccan, for the *chauth* was nothing else, was sanctioned on the condition that promiscuous raiding should cease, and this condition was being ignored. The Nizam tried to weaken the Marathas by reviving their old hereditary disputes, but he only strengthened the Peshwa's position and drew the Maratha people more closely together.[2] Active hostilities were equally unsuccessful; he failed to take Poona and his own capital was threatened.

In 1731 the Nizam made a remarkably astute move. He signed a secret compact with the Peshwa by which he was left undisturbed in the Deccan, while the Marathas were given a free hand with respect to the territory still under Mogul suzerainty further north.[3] The Nizam thus averted the danger threatening himself and directed it towards the Rajput States. Nor was this all. Had the Marathas, instead of overrunning these principalities to levy tribute by force of arms, united with the Rajput chiefs of Rajputana and Central India a powerful Hindu alliance might have swept Moslem rule out of India.

The Peshwa Baji Rao established a footing in Malwa in 1734, but two years later he found that, notwithstanding the tribute levied from the foreign districts, the upkeep of the vast army necessary to support his policy was more than the revenue could stand, his troops were in arrears of pay and his finances heavily involved. His demands upon the imperial provinces became even more extravagant and insistent, and in 1736 he made an attempt to extort the Emperor's agreement to them by a demonstration of force. The Peshwa was, however, obliged to retreat from the neighbourhood of Delhi, and a year later

---

[1] Poona did not become the Maratha seat of government until 1750.
[2] *History of the Mahrattas*, Vol. I. pp. 368–370.   [3] *Ibid.*, Vol. I. p. 377.

Muhammad Shah offered the Nizam Malwa and Gujerat if he would drive the Marathas out of these provinces. The Nizam, seriously alarmed by the ever-increasing power of his allies, readily agreed, and moved south from Delhi with 34,000 Mogul and Hindu troops supported by what was considered the most efficient artillery in India.[1]

Baji Rao concentrated all his available forces and crossed the Narbada with 80,000 men in January 1738. The armies met near Bhopal, and the Marathas at once took the initiative, forcing the Nizam to fall back on Seronji. Here he was practically surrounded, and within six weeks of the opening of the campaign he signed a convention giving the Peshwa the whole of Malwa, the absolute sovereignty of the country between the Narbada and the Chambal and an indemnity of fifty lakhs of rupees,[2] equivalent to £500,000 sterling. Baji Rao remained south of the Chambal levying contributions and negotiating for the imperial ratification of the treaty, while the Nizam returned to Delhi, upon which a fearful disaster was about to fall.

Nadir Quli, a Turkman of a poor family in Khurasan, had freed Persia from its seven terrible years of subjection to *Nadir Shah.* the Afghans by his genius as a soldier and his skilful diplomacy, and Shah Tahmasp in gratitude had given to the hero of the Persian people literally half of his kingdom. A few years later Tahmasp was deposed, and Nadir became Regent to his infant son. But the boy died when four years old, and Nadir became King of Persia in 1736 to begin a career of conquest from the Caspian to Kandahar. In 1738 Nadir Shah, then in his fiftieth year, turned towards India and invaded Mogul Afghanistan. Muhammad Shah and his advisers had, in spite of repeated warnings, for years neglected the province and stinted it of money. The administration had fallen to pieces, the troops were "ill-fed, ill-equipped and ill-armed through poverty," and Kabul fell after a five weeks' campaign in the third week of June.[3]

[1] *History of the Mahrattas*, Vol. I. p. 396.   [2] *Ibid.*, Vol. I. p. 399.
[3] *The Later Mughals*, Vol. II. p. 327.

Making use of the diplomatic pretexts which the inept and casual Delhi government presented to him, Nadir Shah moved forward to invade India and passed through Jalalabad on the 12th November 1738. Peshawar was occupied without opposition six days later, and Lahore surrendered early in January 1739. Nadir Shah's invading army, with its cavalry screen 30 or 40 miles in advance of the main body, spread ruin and disorder throughout the Punjab, while the lawless elements in the country, freed from all restraint, took to plunder and pillage; "the whole province was in complete revolution."

Invasion of India.

The Mogul government had not moved a man to protect the frontier when the ominous news of the loss of Kabul reached Delhi in the first week of July 1738; nor were any military preparations made for two months after Nadir Shah came through the Khyber in mid-November. But the occupation of Lahore thoroughly alarmed the court and frantic appeals for help were made to the Nizam, to the Rajputs and even to Baji Rao. The Marathas contented themselves with preparations to defend the line of the Narbada; the Rajput chiefs, hopelessly alienated since the time of Aurangzeb and with the prospect of independence before them, ignored the summons; and the Emperor, influenced by the jealousy and suspicion of the Hindustani party, would not give the Nizam, who had come to Delhi with a small contingent, supreme command of the army.

After more inexcusable delay the imperial troops, which possibly numbered 75,000, including the reinforcements brought by Saadat Khan, Governor of Oudh, began their advance and reached Karnal at the end of January 1739. Here they entrenched themselves in a camp said to have been 12 miles in circumference and awaited the enemy. The size of the camp is explained by Irvine.[1] After pointing out that Lord Lake's camp, during his operations in the same area (1804–06) contained 300,000 souls, of whom only 30,000 were soldiers, he goes on to say: "As the Emperor himself with his harem and the luxurious grandees with their families were present, we shall not be wrong in estimating the population in the camp at Karnal at a million."

[1] *The Later Mughals*, Vol. II. pp. 338–339.

Nadir Shah reached Karnal with a striking force of about 55,000
men. The remainder of his army of 80,000 had
Battle of Karnal. been detached to guard his long line of communications. On the following morning, the 13th February 1739, the
Mogul army moved out from its entrenchments to the attack. The
Persian army consisted of cavalry, mostly equipped with fire-arms,
and a camel corps of swivel guns. The Indian forces with their
almost immobile artillery, their field guns mounted on elephants,
their neglect of musketry and their reliance on the shock tactics of
their heavy cavalry, were mown down by the rapid fire and well-
controlled volleys of the invaders. Muhammad Shah was totally
defeated in less than three hours, and the imperial field treasury,
guns, elephants and baggage all fell into the hands of the victors.

After the battle the Nizam, " the key of the State of India," was
sent to open peace negotiations; and on the 7th March the Persian
king and Muhammad Shah entered Delhi together to settle the terms
of the indemnity.

But while the negotiations were going on a disturbance broke out
in the city in which some Persian military police
Sack of Delhi. were attacked. The mob got out of hand, killing a
number of Persian soldiers, and on the morning of the 11th March
Nadir Shah put the town wards in which the outbreak had occurred
to the sword for five hours. Then he yielded to the prayers of
Muhammad Shah and gave orders for the massacre to cease, an order
which his disciplined troops are said to have immediately obeyed.
The number of people killed in Delhi is estimated by Irvine at 20,000.

In this connection, and as a contrast to modern conditions, a
footnote to p. 93 of Cunningham's *History of the Sikhs* is of interest:
" The defeat of the Delhi sovereign and Nadir's entry into the
capital . . . were not known in London until the 1st October, so
slow were communications and of so little importance was Delhi to
Englishmen " at that time.

Nadir Shah stayed in the capital for about two months engaged
in raising the huge indemnity from the Emperor, the nobles and the
general public, which enabled him to remit the entire revenue of
Persia for three years, in addition to making a lavish award of prize-

money to his troops. Muhammad Shah had to cede to Persia the country west of the Indus " from Kashmir to Sind," and when Nadir Shah left Delhi on the 5th May 1739 [1] he took the Koh-i-noor diamond and the peacock throne away with him. Eight years later Nadir Shah was assassinated, his treasures were plundered and dispersed and with them the Peacock Throne of Shah Jahan.

Timur's invasion of India at the end of the fourteenth century had brought desolation and appalling suffering upon the country from the north-western passes to Delhi, but it did not result in dismemberment. The viceroy whom he left in the Punjab and Upper Sind kept order in these provinces and eventually founded the Sayyid line of Delhi Kings. But Nadir Shah, when he annexed Afghanistan and the trans-Indus provinces, deprived India of her natural defensive frontier on the west and laid her open to renewed attack. As Sir Jadunath Sarkar has pointed out,[2] Timur's destructive work and the threat of further invasion from his country ended with his life. But the Abdali and his dynasty continued Nadir's work in India as the heir to his empire. With the Khyber Pass and the Peshawar district in foreign hands, the Punjab became a starting-point for fresh expeditions against Delhi.

Results of Invasion.

When Nadir Shah entered India, the Punjab, then under an efficient local administration, was peaceful and prosperous. When he left it orderly rule had been exchanged for utter desolation, banditry and anarchy. The Punjab in its state of chaos had passed out of Mogul control more than twelve years before Ahmad Shah Durrani took formal possession of it in 1752.[3] During the invasion of Nadir Shah the Sikhs collected in small bands and impartially plundered their wealthier fellow-countrymen and stragglers of the Persian army. Growing in boldness and strength they began systematically to levy contributions, and to raid farther and farther eastward, plundering, burning and massacring wherever they went.

---

[1] *The Later Mughals*, Vol. II. p. 375 (authority: Hanway).
[2] *Ibid.*, Vol. II. p. 377, in the concluding editorial chapter of Irvine's work.
[3] *History of the Sikhs*, p. 96.

To the east of Delhi the unruly Afghan colonists of Rohilkhand raised themselves by insurrection and hard fighting to considerable importance, although they were not strong enough to resist the Maratha inroads. Rohilkhand was originally the Hindu provinces of Katehr and Sambhala which were colonized in the seventeenth century by Pathans mostly of the Yusufzai tribe, who built Shahjahanpur. The name Rohilkhand is derived from the Afghan *roh*, mountainous, and *ela*, the Hindu word for " a person belonging to a group," Rohilkhand being the district they inhabitated.

In the provinces of the empire to the south of Delhi the Marathas were now established in absolute security and, with the central government entirely powerless, their marauding expeditions began to penetrate repeatedly to Orissa, south-eastern Bihar and Bengal.

Muhammad Shah and his ministers were utterly incompetent and worse. The Nizam was the only able and straightforward statesman left to advise the Emperor, but he was now a very old man, and he was tied to the Deccan where rebellion had broken out among his sons in anticipation of his death. For the Mogul empire no vestige of hope remained.

In 1748 Muhammad Shah and the Nizam both died. The Emperor was succeeded by his son Ahmad Shah, who made Safdar Jang (Nawab of Oudh) his chief minister, and the long-standing rivalry began between the rulers of Oudh and of the Deccan for this office.

The government of Delhi had become a negligible factor, but a first-class Asiatic power had arisen in the kingdom of Afghanistan. When Nadir Shah was assassinated in 1747 Persia was plunged into a state of confusion which lasted fifty years. Ahmad Shah of the Abdali tribe secured control of Afghanistan in 1747 and made the Afghans into the nation which is still ruled by the Durrani dynasty he founded. In the course of his campaigns, which set his frontiers upon the Oxus to the north and almost to the shores of the Caspian to the west, Ahmad Shah Durrani invaded India seven times, and soon forced the Mogul government, paralysed by civil war, to cede the Punjab formally to him.

Ahmad Shah of Delhi was deposed and blinded by his chief

303

minister Ghazi-ud-din, grandson of the first Nizam, in 1754, and was replaced by another Timurid, Alamgir II. Two years later Ahmad Shah Durrani made his third expedition into India. Delhi was sacked and again given over to the horrors of massacre. The Afghan king returned to his own country in 1757, leaving a nominee of his own, the able Delhi noble Najib-ud-daula, as chief minister, while he appointed his own viceroy in the Punjab to keep the road open from Afghanistan.

India at this period was in a state of almost complete chaos and anarchy. The whole country was torn in pieces. The provinces and viceroyalties of the old Mogul Empire had been parcelled out, as Sir Alfred Lyall describes it,[1] " among revolted governors, rebellious chiefs, leaders of insurgent tribes or sects, religious revivalists, or captains of mercenary bands. The Indian people were becoming a masterless multitude swaying to and fro in the political storm, and clinging to any power, natural or supernatural, that seemed likely to protect them. They were prepared to acquiesce in the assumption of authority by anyone who could show himself able to discharge the most elementary functions of government in the preservation of life and property."

The Sikhs had taken the opportunity offered to them by Afghan invasion to rise. Between 1756 and 1758 they were strong enough to occupy Lahore where, under Jassa Singh, a carpenter, they used the Mogul mint to strike rupees with the inscription: " Coined by the grace of the Khalsa in the country of Ahmad, conquered by Jassa the Kalal." [2]

The Maratha bid for Supremacy. There was no organized and settled government in the north, and the Marathas resolved to make a supreme effort to establish their supremacy over all India. They had isolated the Mogul possessions in the Deccan and had every hope of eventually overwhelming them. The future appeared to hold for the Marathas the promise of spreading Hindu authority and preserving Brahman ascendancy throughout the length

[1] *Rise of the British Dominion in India.*
[2] *History of the Sikhs,* Cunningham, Edn. 1918, p. 98.

PLATE XLVII.

(*a*) A " FYL-TCHARNA "
From " Les Hindous "
By permission of the Secretary of State for India in Council

(*b*) INDIAN " GRAB "
From " Les Hindous "
By permission of the Secretary of State for India in Council

PLATE XLVIII.

(*a*) THE FORT, TRICHINOPOLY
By courtesy of " The Times of India " (Copyright)

(*b*) CLIVE

(*c*) DUPLEIX

and breadth of the great Empire where their co-religionists
had for many centuries been a conquered people in their native
land.

But the Confederacy had been founded on the unstable basis of
self-interest and was fed upon plunder. In the time of Baji Rao the
Maratha government had refused the opportunity to ally itself to the
Rajput States and so present a united Hindu front to the Moslem
powers; and the campaigning methods of the Marathas were calculated to arouse the hostility of the peasantry.[1] In their own homes,
tilling their fields and quietly enjoying their hereditary rights, the
Marathas have always been distinguished for their kindliness, their hos-
pitality, their high moral standards and their uncomplaining courage
in adversity. But, as Grant Duff has observed, " the extension of
[the Maratha] sway, carried no freedom even to Hindus, except
freedom of opinion; and it rarely brought protection or improved
the habits and conditions of the vanquished. Destruction, rapine,
oppression and tyranny were their more certain concomitants; and
although entitled to the negative praise of not being blood-thirsty,
they were unfeeling and ungenerous victors."

The Maratha Confederacy had been under the lethargic leader-
ship of Balaji Baji Rao since the death of his father
Invasion of the
Punjab.
Baji Rao, the second Peshwa, in 1740, while the
administration was in the hands of his cousin
Sadasheo Bhao, with Raghunath Rao as the principal general. In
1758, reinforced by the federal contingents of Holkar and Sindia,
Raghunath Rao advanced into Northern India. Delhi was taken
and Najib-ud-daula expelled; Lahore was occupied and Ahmad
Shah's viceroy driven out; and a Maratha administration was set up
in the Punjab. These successes were to mark the highest point of
Maratha achievement. In the words of Grant Duff, " their right to
tribute was acknowledged on the banks of the Coleroon, and the
Deccan horse had quenched their thirst from the waters of the Indus."

This sudden and dramatic Maratha success thoroughly alarmed
the Moslem rulers of the north, and provoked in Ahmad Shah

[1] *History of the Mahrattas*, Vol. I. p. 516.

Durrani the most able Asiatic soldier who appeared in India during the eighteenth century. A Moslem league was formed by Najib-ud-daula, and in the winter of 1759–60 the Afghan king came through the north-western passes to open the campaign. The Marathas were far from their base, their forces were overwhelmed in succession, and Ahmad Shah after reoccupying Lahore swept the confederate troops out of Northern India.

The Peshwa collected every available man, and the Maratha forces concentrated south of the Chambal under the nominal command of Balaji's young son Viswas Rao, *Panipat.* with Sadasheo Bhao as the actual leader. The army which was to renew the invasion of Northern India and make a final bid for Maratha supremacy is estimated by Elphinstone to have amounted to 300,000 men, but these included the usual swarm of camp followers. The backbone of the army, a picked force trained on French lines under the command of Ibrahim Gardi Khan, consisted of 2000 cavalry, 9000 infantry with matchlocks, and 40 guns. The main body was made up of 58,000 Maratha horse, 2000 Rajput cavalry, about 5000 inferior infantry, 200 heavy guns, a number of rocket batteries, thousands of roving freebooters, known in Indian history as *Pindaris*, and a horde of bandits.[1]

Ghazi-ud-din had murdered Alamgir II while the Afghan army was on the march into India, and the young Emperor Shah Alam, who was recognized by Ahmad Shah Durrani, was absent in Bengal trying to make an alliance with the new masters of that province, the East India Company. The Muhammadan defence against the Maratha invasion lay in the hands of Ahmad Shah Durrani and his Afghan army supported by contingents of Indian Moslems.

Ahmad Shah's army, according to Kasi Raja Pundit, who was present at the battle and examined the Shah's muster-rolls, consisted of 41,800 cavalry, 38,000 infantry, including the Afghan musketeers and camel gunners, about 70 guns and a large number of irregulars.[2]

---

[1] *History of the Mahrattas*, Vol. I. pp. 517, 518 with footnote, 521, 522 ; and the account written in 1808 by Saiyid Ghulam Ali, *Elliot and Dowson*, Vol. VIII. p. 400.

[2] *History of the Mahrattas*, Vol. I. p. 521 ; and *Oxford History of India*, p. 464.

The campaign of 1760 began with the occupation of Delhi by the Marathas, who then tried to come to terms with the Afghans. But Ahmad Shah was in no mood to make peace. The Marathas had blundered fatally by abandoning guerilla tactics, and they were trapped in a position from which there was no escape. Desultory skirmishing was deliberately drawn out by the Afghan commander to reduce the Maratha supplies, and by the beginning of the new year the confederate army was on the verge of starvation within its entrenchments at Panipat.

On the 7th January 1761, just before daybreak, the Maratha army left its lines and formed up for battle some little way from the Afghan camp, with Ibrahim Gardi Khan on the left flank, Sindia on the right of the line, and the artillery, according to the tactical dispositions of the time, in advance of the centre. Here they halted and watched the deployment of Ahmad Shah's forces. The engagement began with a furious charge of the Maratha horse upon the Muhammadan centre, and the Afghan cavalry caught at the halt were ridden over and gave way, to be rallied with the greatest difficulty. Ahmad Shah then brought up his reserves and early in the afternoon delivered a strong counter-attack which decided the day. Viswas Rao was mortally wounded and the Maratha army broke into utter rout. Sadasheo Bhao did not survive his defeat though his actual fate is uncertain, and Ibrahim Gardi Khan died of his wounds, a prisoner.[1]

The victorious Afghans showed no mercy to the vanquished. Sindia, who was wounded and taken prisoner, was beheaded, and the number of Hindus killed in action or butchered as prisoners was estimated at nearly 200,000. The Peshwa Balaji Rao, crossing the Narbada with reinforcements, was met by a messenger with a letter from the field, which gave the fatal news: " Two pearls have been dissolved, twenty-seven gold mohurs have been lost, and of the silver and copper the total cannot be cast up." The Peshwa never recovered from the shock of the disaster, and he returned to Poona to die six months afterwards.

[1] Elphinstone's *History of India* ; an almost identical account is given in the *History of the Mahrattas*, Vol. I. pp. 524–529.

Panipat was the greatest battle which had been fought for two centuries between Hindus and Moslems, but its results were quite disproportionate to its magnitude. Babur, when he defeated Ibrahim Lodi in 1526, and Akbar by the destruction of Hemu's army thirty years later, successively established and secured an empire by their victories. But Ahmad Shah, the victor of the third battle of Panipat, gained nothing by his exploit. His troops, who were suffering heavily from disease and who had drawn no pay for two years, became mutinous and insisted on a return to the highlands of Afghanistan, and Ahmad Shah was obliged to retire from India. He left Najib-ud-daula in authority at Delhi and appointed deputies in Sirhind and Lahore, who had considerable trouble with the Sikhs.[1] The Afghan hold on the northern provinces gradually relaxed and the Punjab relapsed into a state of confusion from which it was not restored until the rise of Ranjit Singh at the beginning of the next century.

On the other hand the consequences of the battle were widely felt in India. The Marathas were still the most formidable power in the country in spite of the heavy defeat which swept them for a time out of the north. But Panipat was the death blow to the great confederacy. As Elphinstone [2] has pointed out, " The history of the Mogul Empire closed of itself with that battle and the confederacy of the Maratha princes dissolved when this, their common danger, completely disappeared." Dissensions soon broke out after the death of Balaji Baji Rao, and the government of the Peshwa never regained its vigour. Most of the Maratha conquests were recovered later, but it was by independent chiefs with the help of European officers and trained State troops.

The years 1757 to 1761 were fateful in Indian history. Ahmad Shah, when he retired from India after Panipat, practically closed the line of conquering invaders from Central Asia, and the Maratha confederacy failed disastrously in the bid for supremacy, although its princes had not been crushed.

[1] *History of the Sikhs*, pp. 100–104.
[2] *History of India*, p. 573 (5th Edn.: 1st Edn. 1841).

The destinies of India lay neither with Kabul nor with Poona. But in the east a new and still reluctant authority was taking shape. In 1757 Clive made the East India Company the virtual controllers of Bengal, as the result of Plassey, a power which was manifested by the deposition of the Nawab Mir Jafar in 1760 and the temporary setting up by the Company of Mir Kasim in his place; while on the 14th January 1761, a week after Panipat, the Comte de Lally-Tollendal, representative of France in India, surrendered Pondicherry to the English.

The new era, which opened between the years 1757 and 1761, had its origin in the Carnatic, and the series of events which ultimately led to the establishment of British supremacy are described in the following chapters.

NOTE.—The chronology of events of this period is given at the end of Chapter XIV.

BIBLIOGRAPHY

The Later Mughals, W. Irvine (ed. Sir Jadunath Sarkar), 2 vols., Calcutta, 1922.

History of the Mahrattas, J. C. Grant Duff (ed. S. M. Edwardes), 1921, Vol. I.

History of India as told by its own Historians, Elliot and Dowson, 1867–1877, Vol. VIII.

History of the Sikhs, J. D. Cunningham (ed. H. L. Garrett), 1918.

Cambridge History of the British Empire, Vol. IV.

Rise of the British Dominion in India, Sir A. Lyall, 2nd Edn. 1893.

Early Revenue History of Bengal, F. D. Ascoli, 1917.

CHAPTER XIII

French and English in the Carnatic

THE Carnatic was the most important of the principalities within the suzerainty of the Nizam, who was virtually an independent sovereign in the Deccan after 1724. It lay between the Eastern Ghats and the Bay of Bengal, and extended from the Kistna River south to the Maratha State of Tanjore and the little kingdom of Trichinopoly. On the Carnatic coast stood the three cities of the leading European trading companies, English Madras, French Pondicherry, and Dutch Negapatam. The seat of the provincial government was at Arcot, and the Nizam's deputy, or nawab, who administered it in 1736, was Dost Ali, usually referred to as the Nawab of Arcot.

Ambitious to convert his official appointment as deputy into a hereditary sovereignty, the Nawab determined to extend the territory he governed, and the small States of Trichinopoly and Tanjore seemed an easy prey. In 1736-37 the Nawab's son Safdar Ali and his son-in-law Husain Dost Khan, who is generally known as Chanda Sahib, conquered Trichinopoly, then being ruled by a Hindu princess, the widow of the last Nayak representative of the ancient kingdom of Vijayanagar. Chanda Sahib, who now became its first Moslem governor, combined bold leadership in war with remarkable astuteness in politics. He had a great admiration for the French, whose language he spoke, and in 1739, although his troops had been unable to conquer the Maratha State of Tanjore, he took Karikal and handed it over to the *Compagnie des Indes*.

A year later 50,000 Maratha horse made an incursion into the Carnatic, where they had not been seen for a generation, on the ever-convenient pretext of levying the *chauth*, but probably in reprisal for the Moslem depredations in Tanjore territory. Descending upon the country by an unfrequented route they surprised the Carnatic army in the Dalmacherri Pass, and the Nawab of Arcot was defeated and killed. Safdar Ali then came to terms with the Marathas, buying them off by the payment of a heavy indemnity and making at the same time a secret compact [1] by which the Marathas agreed to crush Chanda Sahib whom his brother-in-law considered too powerful. Trichinopoly was besieged and taken by the Marathas in 1741, and Chanda Sahib was sent a prisoner to Satara.

During the siege the Maratha commander wrote to Dumas, Governor of Pondicherry, demanding the surrender of Chanda Sahib's wife, family, jewels and elephants which had been sent there for safety, with the alternative that the Marathas would take them by force and levy forty years' arrears of *chauth* upon the settlement. Dumas sent back the answer: " The wife of Chanda Sahib is in Pondicherry under the protection of the King of France, my master, and all the Frenchmen in India would die rather than deliver her to you." The Marathas decided that Pondicherry was too strong to assault, and the resolute attitude of Dumas greatly increased the prestige of the French among the Indian princes, and this prestige his successor Dupleix inherited. [2]

Safdar Ali was murdered by a relative in 1742 and his young son, who had been left with the English at Madras for safety, was locally recognized as Nawab and the government was carried on by the Carnatic ministers. These disorders had, however, attracted the attention of the Nizam and, old though he was, he came down in 1743 to the Carnatic with an army of 80,000 men to settle the affairs of the province. He reached Arcot in March, just two months before Robert Clive, about to begin his Indian career as a writer at Fort St. George, sailed from the Thames in the Company's ship *Winchester*. [3] The state of anarchy prevailing in the province is illustrated by the Nizam's remark to his guards at his first levee:

[1] *History of the Mahrattas*, Vol. I. pp. 420, 421.
[2] *Life of Lord Clive*, Forrest, Vol. I. pp. 96, 97.
[3] *Ibid.*, Forrest, Vol. I. p. 8.

" I have seen this day eighteen nawabs in a country where there should be but one; scourge the next fellow who comes with that title." [1]

The Nizam expelled the Maratha garrison from Trichinopoly, appointed an old servant of his, Anwar-ud-din, to administer the government of Arcot, and then went back to Hyderabad. Shortly afterwards the boy Nawab was murdered. The Nizam recognized Anwar-ud-din as his successor, but the new Nawab, surrounded by members of the displaced and highly popular family, who still held the majority of the chief fortresses and *jagirs*, found his position insecure. The political outlook was most uncertain when (in 1742) a master of Oriental diplomacy came to Pondicherry in the person of Joseph Dupleix, to succeed Dumas as Governor and *ex officio* Director-General of the French Trading Company's interests in India. Dupleix had been promoted from chief of the factory at Chandernagore, which he had raised from an insignificant village on the Hooghly to a flourishing colony.

By this time the relative positions of the European trading *The European Trading Companies.* companies had simplified into a commercial rivalry between the French and the English. Portuguese power and prosperity had long disappeared. The Dutch, who had ousted the Portuguese, had been so weakened by their war with France that Great Britain found herself relieved of her most formidable rival at sea, and the Dutch Company began to lose its hold in India and to concentrate upon its valuable interests in Ceylon, Java, Borneo and the Spice Islands. The Danish East India Company, which only existed upon the profits of the carrying trade between India and the Malay Archipelago, had neither money nor influence. A new European competitor had appeared in 1722, when the Austrian-Netherland Company was started at Ostend, with wide military and political powers set forth in its charter. But between the protests of Great Britain, France and Holland in Europe and the eventual hostility of the Indian local authorities, the precarious existence of the

---

[1] *Life of Lord Clive*, Forrest, Vol. I. p. 100.

new-comer came to an end in 1744, and its factory at Bankipore was abandoned.[1]

France was greatly exhausted by the wars which ended in 1713, but the *Compagnie des Indes Orientales*, during the thirty years of peace which followed, made a wonderful recovery from the days of the embarrassed successors of François Martin. This was the more remarkable as they were severely handicapped by their home government. The despotic bureaucracy of France persisted in the policy, when anything seemed to be wrong with their Company, of appointing special commissioners, notwithstanding the Company's protests that all their misfortunes were due to over-interference. The Company was usually heavily in debt to the French government, and its financial aids, apart from grants made by the Treasury, were lottery privileges and tobacco monopolies.

The French Position.

But the Edict of 1719 had given backbone to the *Compagnie des Indes*, the free-trade policy of Law, the Scottish minister of France, had greatly encouraged oversea commerce, and the pacifism of the old cardinal and statesman Fleuri, whose administration in France paralleled that of Walpole in England, had helped this revival. As early as 1715 the French Company had taken possession of the island of Mauritius (Isle de France), which the Dutch had abandoned, and in the islands of Bourbon and France they consequently possessed a connecting link between the now flourishing trade centres in India and the prosperous Breton depot of l'Orient. Bourbon was a rich agricultural colony, and as it was impossible to equip ships anywhere on the harbourless Coromandel coast, the governor of the islands, Admiral Mahé de la Bourdonnais,[2] had, by 1740, converted Port Louis in the Isle of France into a fortified well-found naval base from which the Indian Ocean could be controlled.[3] De la Bourdonnais had brought from Europe a small squadron (which was soon withdrawn) to operate against the English trade

---

[1] *Camb. Hist. British Empire*, Vol. IV. p. 115.

[2] The French possession of Mahé in India and the island of Mahé (Seychelles) are named after him.

[3] *Influence of Sea Power upon History*, Mahan (5th Edn.), pp. 242–243, 273.

in the event of war. But when hostilities opened the French had no men-of-war in Indian waters. The military position in India was also far from satisfactory, for Dupleix found on his arrival at Pondicherry that its fortifications were incomplete, its European garrison numbered less than 450, and the home authorities vetoed the new governor's scheme for military reorganization. Dupleix nevertheless strengthened the defences.

Position of the English Company. The relations between the East India Company and the British Government were in striking contrast to the situation of the French. Far from being in debt to the Treasury, the English Company made annual loans to the Government in aid of war expenses and trusted to their influence in Parliament when dealing with the Crown. Unhampered by interference in their affairs, the responsibility thrown upon their chiefs produced in time a body of capable and experienced administrators, guided by long tradition in the Asiatic trade and with a large reserve of capital behind them.

In 1732 the Company first began to make up regular accounts, and from this date it is possible to trace the fluctuations of their trade.[1]

In spite of the forward policy urged by Sir Josia Child half a century earlier, and regardless of the crisis which arose in 1740 when war between France and Britain seemed imminent, the English Company were content to remain in an even weaker military position than the French. The three Presidencies were entirely independent of each other and responsible only to the Court of Directors in London, Surman's embassy (1714-17) to the Mogul court having been the solitary instance of combined action. The Company's insignificant military establishments were altogether separate, and there was no unity of command. Nor had the British Admiralty any ships upon the Indian station.

By the year 1744 there were in the Company's territory of Madras 250,000 inhabitants nearly all of whom were Indians and, according

---

[1] Tables of exports, imports, duties, etc., are given by Hamilton in *Trade Relations between England and India*, Appendix.

to Orme,[1] the town had risen " to a degree of opulence and reputation which rendered it inferior to none of the European establishments in India except Goa and Batavia." There were about a hundred English civilians in Madras and a European garrison two hundred strong. With the exception of two or three officers none of the troops had seen active service, and they were commanded by an elderly and incompetent Swede who had risen from the ranks. There were hardly any military stores and the fortifications were inadequate.[2]

This was the position of the rival trading companies in the Carnatic when France joined Spain against Great Britain in 1744 in the War of the Austrian Succession. The French had in Dupleix and de la Bourdonnais two representatives to whom no rivals in ability and force of character had as yet appeared among the English officials in India, and had they worked cordially together they might have ruined at least temporarily the English settlements in India.[3] But their views were diametrically opposed, and quarrels took the place of co-operation.

The utter confusion and lack of settled government in India taken in conjunction with the rapid expansion of the Western Powers throughout the world made a European conquest of the country seem only a question of time. Dupleix made up his mind that France should become the suzerain power of an Indian empire of vassal princes; and resolved to bring this about by his own manipulation of Indian politics and alliances as the head of a foreign and independent colony, and by becoming a vassal of the Mogul Emperor and using that position as a lever. But in the first place the English Company had to be driven out. Dupleix had grasped with unerring insight two of the main factors in Indian politics, the utter weakness of the apparent suzerainty of the Empire, and the certainty of eventual European supremacy. But he neglected the overriding influence of sea-power.

[1] *History of the Military Transactions of the British Nation in Indostan*, Vol. I. (4th Edn. 1861), pp. 65–66.
[2] *Life of Lord Clive*, Vol. I. pp. 19, 37.
[3] *Influence of Sea Power upon History*, p. 258.

De la Bourdonnais, whose greatest chance had actually come and gone between 1740, when he was in France trying to raise a fleet, and 1742, when the squadron allotted to him was recalled, aimed at naval supremacy in Eastern waters, and a dominion based, not on the shifting foundations of Indian alliances but upon free and certain communication with the home country.[1] This was, in fact, the essential condition upon which a maritime European power could establish its territorial supremacy in India; and without it the ambitious schemes of Dupleix were doomed to failure. Had it not been for the constant diversion of French policy from the sea to projects of continental expansion this naval superiority was not, even then, unattainable, considering the relative strength of the two navies,[2] and the fact that Great Britain was already at war with Spain. But from 1726 to 1760 the French Government steadily disregarded her maritime interests. Her navy weakened into decay until her commerce and overseas possessions lay at the mercy of Britain when war came, and France had eventually to surrender what Dupleix had actually gained for her, the extent and population of an empire.[3]

Influence of Sea-power.

The influence of sea-power upon the history of India began when the Portuguese secured the trade monopoly of the Eastern seas by the strength of their fleet, while the Mogul empire destitute of a navy was unable to keep its coast inviolate. It became the decisive factor in the middle of the eighteenth century.

When war broke out in 1744 between Great Britain and France Dupleix made an effort to preserve neutrality in India. But the English Company could give no guarantee binding the British Government or the Royal Navy; and in July 1745 a British squadron, which had already taken the French Company's China fleet, appeared off Pondicherry. Preparations were made to besiege the place, but the Nawab of the Carnatic, Anwar-ud-din, informed the Madras Government that he would permit no hostilities within his terri-

---

[1] *Influence of Sea Power upon History*, p. 258.
[2] See Note at end of this Chapter.
[3] *Influence of Sea Power upon History*, pp. 29, 74, 226, 282.

tories by the English, or by the French if they became the stronger,[1] and the operations were suspended.

In the following year de la Bourdonnais appeared off the Coromandel coast with an improvised squadron of eight

Capture of Madras.

ships, and on 25th June fell in with Peyton's four men-of-war, which could, however, out-range and out-sail the French. The action was indecisive, but the British commodore by making for the Hooghly and staying there until reinforcements arrived laid Madras open to attack by the French. De la Bourdonnais with no enemy squadron to face was able to land 2000 Europeans from his ships early in September, and after a two days' bombardment Madras and Fort St. George surrendered on 20th–21st September 1746.[2] The French had suffered no casualties and only four or five Englishmen were killed.[3]

Anwar-ud-din had despatched 10,000 cavalry to enforce his orders as to neutrality when his remonstrances to the French were ignored, but they arrived to find the French flag flying over Madras. The Nawab's troops laid siege to the place in their turn but the French defeated and dispersed them. The accounts of the action do not tally,[4] but as the result a small number of French soldiers defeated a whole army. The superiority of Western field artillery, fire control and discipline over the shock tactics of Indian armies was now evident, and this fact had far-reaching political and military consequences.

The terms by which Madras was to be restored to the English Company after three months on payment of a ransom renewed the quarrel between the French leaders, Dupleix maintaining that the promise to hand back Madras was outside the Admiral's power. De la Bourdonnais had dealt a serious blow to British prestige, but shortly afterwards a hurricane shattered his fleet and he returned to France to be imprisoned in the Bastille for refusing to co-operate energetically in the extirpation of the English settlements. Dupleix

---

[1] Orme, *op. cit.*, Vol. I. p. 61.
[2] *Life of Lord Clive*, Vol. I. p. 38.
[3] Orme, *op. cit.*, Vol. I. p. 68.
[4] *Life of Lord Clive*, Vol. I. pp. 47–49.

denounced the treaty made with the English Company and, having
originally told the Nawab that Madras was being conquered to be
handed over to him, kept the town as a French possession.

De la Bourdonnais had left behind him 1200 well-disciplined
men who were of the greatest value to Dupleix in his future operations, as this brought the Pondicherry force up to 3000 Europeans.[1]
But with the departure of the admiral the command of the sea was
lost to the French. Griffin had arrived in place of Peyton, and the
new British commodore persistently interfered with the efforts of
the French to take Fort St. David, a few miles south of Pondicherry.
Until the Nawab was persuaded that the English cause was hopeless, Dupleix had also to contend with the Carnatic troops, and the
siege of Fort St. David, although its fortifications were on a par
with those of Madras, went on intermittently and unsuccessfully
for eighteen months.

But the siege of Fort St. David is memorable for more than its
resolute defence by 200 Europeans, 100 Indo-Portuguese and Indian
levies armed chiefly with swords and spears.[2] On the 16th March
1747, John Hinde, " Deputy Governor of the United Company of
Merchants of England trading to the East Indies," appointed Robert
Clive ensign of the Second Company of Foot Soldiers at Fort St.
David. Clive had escaped from Madras after the capitulation disguised as an Indian interpreter to avoid giving his parole not to
fight the French. Offered his choice between a writership and
" acting in a Military Sphere (though then at a very low Ebb)," he
decided that the latter " was the most honourable of the two and
most conducive to the Company's Interest." [3] Clive was not quite
twenty-two. The Court of Directors, commenting upon his appointment, remarked, " Be sure to encourage Ensign Clive in his martial

[1] Orme, *op. cit.*, Vol. I. p. 73.
[2] Original garrison. When Major Stringer Lawrence took over command in
January 1748, 100 Europeans from Bombay, 150 recruits from England, 200
Topasses and 500 Indian infantry had arrived to reinforce it. Orme, *op. cit.*,
Vol. I. p. 87. Topasses were Goanese soldiers of mixed descent.
[3] India Office Records, *Miscellaneous Letters*, Vol. 38, No. 120 (*b*), letter
under date 8th March 1755.

pursuits, according to his merit: any improvement he shall make therein shall be duly regarded by us." [1] Ten years later at Plassey, Clive, already the hero of Arcot, gained the practical control of Bengal for the Company and so laid the foundation of the British Empire in India.

One other event was to be a landmark in the development of British power in India. The Court of Directors established the first link between the three independent Presidencies by the reorganization of their combatant forces. One company of artillery was formed in each Presidency and a C.R.A. appointed to command the three units.[2] This was reinforced by a step of greater importance. Major Stringer Lawrence, an officer of Clayton's regiment [3] who had seen service at Fontenoy and Culloden, was appointed Commander-in-Chief of all the Company's forces in India, and landed at Fort St. David on 1st January 1748.[4] It was Lawrence who instructed the military genius of Clive in the earliest stage of his career; and, from the day the "father of the Indian army" took command, the Company's troops rapidly became more efficient. The military establishment, which was entirely separate from the Royal troops, who began to come to India six years later, was both European and Indian. The European units, which were mostly British but included adventurers from almost every country in Europe, were organized in companies, except in Bombay where the battalion system was followed. The Indian troops in 1748 approximated to a body of armed police, commanded by their fellow-countrymen, Indian gentlemen of good birth and position.[5]

The arrival of Admiral Boscawen at Fort St. David at the end of July 1748 with the strongest fleet which had ever been seen in the Indian seas,[6] and with about one thousand infantry on board, altered the situation. The Admiral carried the king's commission as

---

[1] *Life of Lord Clive*, Vol. I. p. 61.
[2] *Evolution of the Army in India*, p. 7.
[3] Later the 14th Foot and now the West Yorkshire Regiment.
[4] *Life of Lord Clive*, Vol. I. p. 61.
[5] *Evolution of the Army in India*, pp. 7, 8.
[6] *Influence of Sea Power upon History*, p. 277.

General and Commander-in-Chief of the land forces in India, although he knew nothing of land operations, and he superseded the able and experienced soldier, Major Lawrence. The reinforcements from England consisted of drafts from different regiments and Scottish Jacobites pardoned on condition of enlistment, together with deserters and criminals released from jail.[1]

It was decided to open the campaign by besieging Pondicherry before the Raja of Tanjore could come to the help of the French. The siege operations were mismanaged and the bombardment by the fleet was ineffective. Dupleix, after his able engineer Paradis was killed, inspired the skilful and vigorous defence, and at the beginning of October the siege was abandoned and the combined forces returned to Fort St. David.[2] It was a conspicuous success for Dupleix and a conspicuous failure for the British.

Before a second attempt could be made to take Pondicherry the news reached India that peace had been signed at Aix-la-Chapelle. One of the conditions of the treaty restored Madras to the English Company in exchange for Louisburg, which the North American colonists had won and had to give up as reluctantly as Madras was yielded by Dupleix.

A speedy revival of trade, after an exhausting war, was essential in the commercial interests of both Companies. But *Anglo-French Relations.* before the English headquarters were moved from Fort St. David to Madras in 1752, the English and French had plunged on opposite sides into Indian politics and all hope of peace and goodwill disappeared in efforts to build up a strong position before war should break out again between the two countries.

Direct open hostilities were not possible, but the indirect method of lending troops to rival Indian princes in order to back their own political manœuvres was an obvious way of extending the influence of the Companies. They had raised forces which were expensive

---

[1] *Camb. Hist. British Empire*, Vol. IV. p. 123.

[2] Clive's criticisms of these operations are given in *Life of Lord Clive*, Forrest, Vol. I. pp. 68–76.

to keep up, but which, on account of mutual jealousy, they were not prepared to disband. On the other hand the prestige of troops trained and disciplined on Western lines made ambitious Indian nobles eager to bid for their services regardless of the consequences of calling in the armed European. This offered to the Companies the alluring prospect of turning the heavy drain of their military establishments to a handsome profit by Indian campaigns, with the added hope of valuable trade concessions and even territory at the expense of a rival. The temptation was too strong to resist and it was taken, to quote Orme's comment, by the English with great indiscretion and by the French with the utmost ambition.

The English Governor Floyer was the first to embark upon this policy. In March 1749 he was approached by Shahji, the dispossessed ruler of the Maratha State of Tanjore, who offered to give the English Devi-Kottai, at the mouth of the Coleroon, in exchange for the help of the Company's troops to reinstate him. The campaign began with half-hearted operations under Captain Cope, but in June (1749) Devi-Kottai was taken by Major Lawrence with Clive as his second-in-command. After the capture of Devi-Kottai a compact was made with the King of Tanjore who ceded the place to the Company in perpetuity and agreed to reimburse the expenses of the war, while Shahji's claims were compounded for a pension from Tanjore State.[1]

The whole affair was a political blunder of the first order, as it gave Dupleix an excellent precedent for taking part in the quarrels of the Indian rulers at the moment when he was meditating similar designs of a much more important and far-reaching character.[2]

The Nizam's death in 1748 had put an end to the period of settled government and comparative peace which he had given to the Deccan. There were two claimants to the succession. While his eldest son remained at Delhi, deep in imperial affairs, the Nizam's second son Nasir Jang, who was at Aurangabad, took the government into his own hands. He was immediately challenged by Muzaffar Jang, son of a daughter of the Nizam, and his claim was backed by some form of authority from Delhi.

[1] Orme, *op. cit.*, Vol. I. pp. 107 *et seq.*
[2] *Rise of the British Dominion in India*, pp. 68–70, 75, 76.

Another political complication arose in the Carnatic. The old Nizam had appointed Anwar-ud-din as Nawab in order to prevent the office from becoming hereditary. But that able representative of the dispossessed family, Chanda Sahib, was released from prison in 1749 and he quickly made common cause with Muzaffar Jang, and opened up negotiations with the French in order to gain for himself the Nawabship of the Carnatic. Dupleix had not forgiven the Nawab Anwar-ud-din for the part he played during the operations against the English Company, and he made an alliance with Muzaffar Jang and Chanda Sahib.

The first objective of the French and their allies was the Carnatic. On the 3rd August 1749 Anwar-ud-din was defeated and killed at the battle of Ambur, and Dupleix received for his help territory round Pondicherry in full right, which more than doubled the French Company's possessions there, and gave them, in addition, the district of Masulipatam and the island of Divi. The English Company at once retorted in kind by seizing St. Thomé, an important point four miles from Madras, in the name of Muhammad Ali, the son and heir of Anwar-ud-din. Issue was now joined, for the English openly backed Muhammad Ali and favoured Nasir Jang. It was clear to Dupleix that he would never be virtual master of the Carnatic, as the power behind Chanda Sahib, while Muhammad Ali was still to be reckoned with; nor could he control the politics of the Deccan while Nasir Jang remained Nizam.

Nasir Jang was slow to realize that the Franco-Indian victory in the Carnatic meant danger to himself. But at the beginning of 1750 he took action, appeared on the Carnatic border with a large army, and formally appointed Muhammad Ali as Nawab. At the end of March Muzaffar Jang and Chanda Sahib, their forces augmented by 2000 Europeans under D'Auteuil, the brother-in-law of Dupleix, moved out from Pondicherry. They were met at Vilnier by Nasir Jang's army, assisted by the famous Morari Rao's Maratha freebooters and 600 Europeans under Major Lawrence. The French contingent behaved badly, Muzaffar Jang's army broke in panic and he himself was taken prisoner by Nasir Jang, who at once retired to Arcot. Here he stayed inactive, while Dupleix disciplined his troops, restored their morale, and then sent the Marquis Charles Castelnau de Bussy, the best general the French ever had in India, to reopen the campaign. De Bussy, in a series of brilliant operations, took Jinji, which had been thought impregnable, and then threatened Arcot. Nasir Jang was killed in action in December 1750 and Muzaffar Jang, released from captivity, returned to Pondicherry to be welcomed as Nizam by Dupleix, while Chanda Sahib was made Nawab of the Carnatic.

Additional grants of territory on the Orissa coast were made to the French by the new Nizam. Dupleix himself was accorded high rank as a Mogul noble and given a *jagir*, while he was recognized as Governor of all India south of the Kistna River. To emphasize the sovereignty which this implied, Pondicherry coinage was proclaimed to be the sole currency of Southern India. In return Dupleix, under the mistaken impression that the English Company would quietly accept the new situation, deprived himself of the services of his one first-rate general by sending de Bussy up to the Deccan to support Muzaffar Jang with 300 Europeans and 4000 Indian troops.

But on the march northwards the French plans were threatened with complete disaster. Three dissatisfied Pathan nobles plotted against the new Nizam and killed him. De Bussy was, however, a master of statecraft. He pressed on to Aurangabad, and in April 1751 proclaimed Salabat Jang, the eldest son of the first Nizam, Viceroy of the Deccan, with the consent of the nobles and the army. Salabat Jang confirmed all the privileges which his predecessors had granted to the French, and de Bussy, with forces which were eventually augmented to 900 Europeans with additional Indian reinforcements, took up his quarters at Hyderabad.

De Bussy was now the real master of the Deccan, and Dupleix the acknowledged ruler of a dominion in the south the size of France with 30,000,000 inhabitants and defended by a victorious army. The French position in India had become so strong that Dupleix even planned to make Salabat Jang, through de Bussy, ruler of Bengal. The prestige of the English was at its lowest ebb.

But while de Bussy succeeded in making his position in the Deccan apparently impregnable by obtaining the personal grant of four districts to pay for the upkeep of his troops and by filling the chief administrative posts with ministers favourable to the French, the position in the south had developed an element of weakness. To win the Deccan, Dupleix had been obliged to divide his forces, and he had no longer the means to support his policy in the Carnatic. His ambitions had lured him into the snare of a double objective.

Major Lawrence had returned to England, disgusted by the perpetual interference of the civil power in military matters and dissatisfied with his position as commander of the forces.[1] But the easy-going Floyer had been replaced at Fort St. David by Thomas Saunders, a level-headed and resolute governor who supported Muhammad Ali in the Carnatic with the troops and the indifferent leaders at his disposal.

In January 1751 an unlucky campaign was opened by the English which led to the occupation of the whole of the Carnatic by Chanda Sahib and his French auxiliaries and the investment of Trichinopoly. The effort made by Captain Gingens, a Swiss officer in the English Company's service, to relieve the place in July, ended in disaster, and the fall of Trichinopoly, whose safety was vital to English interests, seemed only a question of days.

But the hour brought the man. Clive, who had reverted to civil *Arcot.* employ, returned to military service with the rank of captain in January 1751. Although he was not yet twenty-six, he already had considerable war experience, but the plan which he put before the governor was the outcome of his outstanding characteristics, an instinctive insight, quick decisive judgment and dauntless courage. To make certain of taking Trichinopoly, Chanda Sahib and his French allies had left Arcot with an insufficient garrison. Clive's scheme was to make a surprise attack upon Arcot, sixty-four miles west of Madras, and force upon Chanda Sahib the alternative of losing his capital or raising the siege of Trichinopoly. The proposal combined the greatest daring with masterly strategy.

Saunders agreed, and leaving Madras and Fort St. David with

[1] *Camb. Hist. British Empire*, Vol. IV. p. 128.

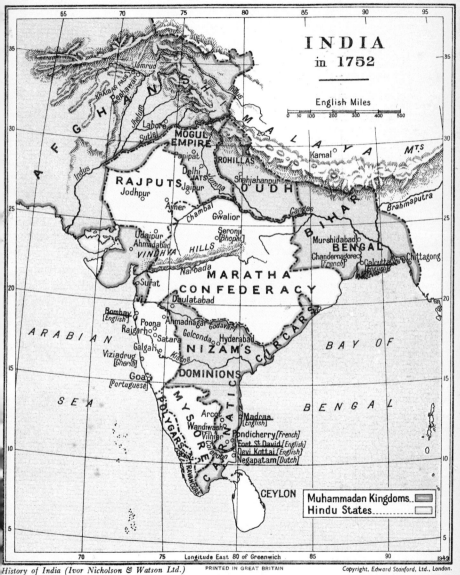

INDIA
in 1752

English Miles

0 50 100   200   300   400   500

AFGHANISTAN

Jamrud
Khaibar Pass
Peshawar
Indus
Jhelum
Lahore
Sutlej
MOGUL
EMPIRE
Panipat
Delhi
JATS
Jaipur
ROHILLAS
Shahjahanpur
Karnal
HIMALAYA
MTS
OUDH
RAJPUTS
Jodhpur
Ajmer
Chambal
Gwalior
Seronj
[Bhopal]
Ganges
Brahmaputra
BIHAR
Udaipur
Ahmadabad
VINDHYA   HILLS
Narbada
MARATHA
Murshidabad
BENGAL
Chandernagore
[French]
Calcutta
[English]
Chittagong
Surat
CONFEDERACY
Daulatabad
Bombay
[English]
Poona
Rajgarh
Ahmadnagar
Godavari
Satara
Golconda
Hyderabad
Galgali
NIZAM'S
Viziadrug
[Gheria]
Goa
[Portuguese]
DOMINIONS
Krisna
CIRCARS
CARNATIC
ARABIAN
SEA
BAY OF
BENGAL
Arcot
Madras
[English]
Wandiwash
Vilhian
Pondicherry [French]
Fort St David [English]
Devi Kottai [English]
Negapatam [Dutch]
POLYGARS
MYSORE
COIMBATORE
TRAVANCORE
CEYLON

Muhammadan Kingdoms
Hindu States

History of India (Ivor Nicholson & Watson Ltd.)   PRINTED IN GREAT BRITAIN   Longitude East 80 of Greenwich   Copyright, Edward Stanford, Ltd., London.

less than 150 men for their defence, Clive marched out from Madras with 200 Europeans, 300 Indian infantry, 3 guns and only four trained officers on the 6th September 1751 [1] to strike the first blow which was to lead to British supremacy in India. On the 12th, having pushed on throughout the previous day in the teeth of a furious monsoon storm, he marched into the town of Arcot and occupied the fortress without firing a shot; the garrison had fled. During the following week he harassed the former garrison which was still in the neighbourhood, and did all that was possible to strengthen the defences for the approaching siege.

All the efforts of the French and their Indian allies failed to retake Arcot, and after fifty days' investment the place was relieved on the 26th November by Morari Rao. When the siege began, after a gallant sortie led by Clive, only 120 Europeans and 200 Indians remained fit for duty.[2] But " inspired by the indefatigable activity, unshaken constancy and undaunted courage " [3] of their young commander they had held the dilapidated perimeter of a fortress a mile in circumference under the stress of fatigue, hunger and disease against the assaults of 10,000 men.

Arcot was a serious blow to French prestige, a factor of vital importance in Indian politics, and the tide of fortune now turned against them in the south.

Jacques Law, nephew of the Regency minister and commander of the French forces, was forced to surrender in June 1752 with 800 Europeans to Major Lawrence, who had returned to India, and Chanda Sahib was beheaded by his Indian enemies. Orme records that he was brave, benevolent, humane and generous, and that his military ability was such that had he been given supreme command of the French troops the catastrophe of the surrender at Seringam, which made Muhammad Ali the undisputed Nawab of the Carnatic, would never have occurred. In ability and character Chanda Sahib was immeasurably a better man than his successful

[1] N.S.: by the old calendar 26th August, *Life of Lord Clive*, Vol. I. pp. 137–138.
[2] *Life of Lord Clive*, Vol. I. pp. 144, 145.
[3] Orme, *op. cit.*, Vol. I. p. 196. The account given in this chapter of the French and English in the Carnatic is based on Orme's *History*.

rival Muhammad Ali, who was shifty in his dealings, extravagant to the extent of hopeless insolvency and an unending source of trouble to the English Company.[1]

Intermittent hostilities, in which the French almost invariably failed and the English gained no great advantage, continued in the Carnatic until August 1754, when the French commissioner Godeheu landed at Pondicherry. The French and British governments had agreed to end the unofficial war between the Companies in India, and Dupleix was recalled to France.

Character of Dupleix.

The career of the great Frenchman was over. He had devoted his talents and his large private fortune with unfaltering courage to the creation of a French empire in India, relying in every move of his tortuous diplomacy on his ambitious, spirited and gifted wife, who was of mixed French and Indian parentage and had been born in Pondicherry. Dupleix had been hampered throughout by lack of support from home, by his own idealism, by his uncompromising attitude towards the English Company, and by the corruption in the administration of the Carnatic due to his Indian agents. But notwithstanding his almost fatal interference in military matters (he superseded five commanders in under three years) and the defects in his character which made it impossible for any official other than de Bussy to work with him, " all his countrymen concurred in thinking that his dismission from the government of Pondicherry was the greatest detriment that could have happened to their interests in India." [2] Dupleix, whose only recognition by the French Government had been the grant of a marquisate while he was in India, died in great poverty in 1763.

The fall of Dupleix seriously shook de Bussy's position in the Deccan. Salabat Jang was weak and irresolute, and his new minister, Shah Nawaz Khan, was hostile to the French. But de Bussy, by his tact and personal prestige, backed by the timely arrival of Law with reinforcements

The French Expedition.

---

[1] See Thornton, *History of the British Empire in India*, pp. 26, 41, 57, 161.
[2] Orme, *op. cit.*, Vol. I. pp. 378, 379.

which brought his force up to more than 1000 Europeans and 5000 Indians, succeeded in foiling the attempts of the minister to get rid of him. He kept his hold over the Deccan until the news of the declaration of war between Great Britain and France reached India towards the end of 1756, when he invaded Orissa and, with Clive engaged in Bengal, seized the English factories and made himself master of much of the coast between Madras and the Hooghly.

The French Government, on the outbreak of the Seven Years' War, determined to drive the English out of India, and after considerable delay despatched 1200 regular troops under Comte de Lally-Tollendal to effect this with a squadron of nine ships, including three first-rate men-of-war, under Commodore d'Aché. On the scale of European operations in India at a time when six field guns generally decided a battle, the force was equivalent to a formidable army, and added to the troops then in the country was sufficient to reduce, temporarily at any rate, the English settlements on the Coromandel coast. The French squadron was superior in numbers to the British on the Indian station, and about equal to it in fighting value.[1]

But the expedition laboured under two fatal disadvantages. In the first place it started too late. Had it sailed from Brest as soon as war was declared, the French forces would have reached India at the critical moment when the English, having lost their forts and factories in Bengal, were about to make their effort to restore their fortunes in that province. By the time Lally landed at Pondicherry in April 1758, Plassey had been won and Clive was able to report that " perfect tranquillity reigns in Bengal."

The second disastrous defect lay in the character of the commander of the expedition. Lally, then fifty-eight years of age, the son of an Irish exile and a French mother, had seen much active service and had gained a great reputation for personal courage. But, as the Directors of the *Compagnie des Indes* were told when they applied for his services, he was a hot-headed, obstinate martinet who was liable to outbursts of ungovernable temper at the least

[1] *Influence of Sea Power upon History*, p. 307.

check or blunder, and would certainly make himself so generally detested that his own officers would be goaded to foil all his operations for the satisfaction of ruining their general. In spite of this unequivocal opinion Lally was appointed syndic of the Company, commissary for the king and commander-in-chief of the French forces in India over the head of de Bussy and superseding Duval de Leyril, Dupleix's successor at Pondicherry. His instructions would have taxed the genius of a Napoleon, for he was expected to reform the whole French administration in India while engaged in a life-and-death struggle with the English.

The voyage ended with the first of several indecisive naval actions between d'Aché and the British squadron under Pocock, while Lally landed his men and took Fort St. David without much difficulty. He followed this up by a futile campaign against the Raja of Tanjore, which damaged his reputation, and by embittered discussions with d'Aché and the council at Pondicherry which weakened his position. He then recalled de Bussy from Hyderabad. Had Lally's purpose been fulfilled this would have been accompanied by a concentration of the French forces in India, a sound strategic move. But de Bussy refused to withdraw a man from the Deccan, and the only results were an immediate quarrel between the two Frenchmen and the final extinction of French ascendancy at the Nizam's court, where English influence took its place.

In the middle of December 1758 Lally laid siege to Madras. Superficially the French fortunes seemed to stand as high as they were when Dupleix was in India. The only places in the Carnatic still in English hands were Chingleput, Madras and Trichinopoly. But in January 1759, while Governor Pigot and Stringer Lawrence were resolutely defending Madras, Clive could accurately forecast coming events in a letter to Pitt [1]: " Notwithstanding the extraordinary effort made by the French in sending M. Lally with a considerable force last year, I am confident before the end of this

[1] Letter to the Rt. Hon. William Pitt, Secretary of State, dated Calcutta 7th January 1759. It is quoted in full by Forrest, *Life of Clive*, Appendix to Vol. II.

they will be near their last gasp in the Carnatic, unless some very unforeseen event interfere in their favour. The superiority of our squadron and the plenty of money and supplies of all kinds which our friends on the coast will be furnished with from this province (Bengal), while the enemy are in total want of everything, without any visible means of redress, cannot fail of wholly effecting their ruin in that, as well as in every other part of India."

On 16th February 1759 the British fleet appeared off Madras and Lally, whose operations had been hampered by the activities of the English forces in the neighbourhood, raised the siege. This reverse was soon followed by another. In October 1758 Clive had sent Colonel Lionel Forde from Bengal to expel the French from the Northern Circars, the districts which the Nizam had assigned to de Bussy for the payment of his troops. Forde was handicapped by shortage of ammunition and a lack of funds which brought on a mutiny of his troops. But he was able to overcome these difficulties, took Masulipatam on the 8th April 1759 after a month's siege, and signed a treaty with Salabat Jang six weeks later which brought the expedition to a successful conclusion and dealt a fatal blow to the French.

The French could still oppose 2000 Europeans to the 1000 of the East India Company in the Carnatic, but Lally's

Pocock and d'Aché.

failure before Madras and the fall of Masulipatam were the turning-point of the war on land. The issue at sea was decided in September. D'Aché returned to the Coromandel coast from the Isle of France, where he had refitted and revictualled under the greatest difficulties at the beginning of the month, and on the 10th September he met Pocock's squadron. The British commodore had nine ships to d'Aché's eleven, but he attacked without hesitation, and after a stubborn and even contest the French broke off the action and took refuge under the guns of Pondicherry. On the 1st October 1759 d'Aché sailed for the islands never to return, and left Pondicherry to the grip of the British blockade.

As Mahan observes: " From that time the result was certain.

The English continued to receive reinforcements from home, the French did not; the men opposed to Lally were superior in ability; place after place fell, and in January 1761 Pondicherry itself surrendered, surrounded by land and cut off from the sea. This was the end of the French power in India, for though Pondicherry and other possessions were restored at the peace, the English tenure there was never again shaken, even under the attacks of the skilful and bold Suffren, who twenty years later met difficulties as great as d'Aché's with a vigour and conduct which the latter at a more hopeful moment failed to show." [1]

In October 1759 Lieut.-Colonel Eyre Coote arrived from England with the 84th regiment (now the 2nd York and Lancaster Regiment) 1000 strong, and after sending a detachment up to Bengal began operations against the French with 1700 Europeans and the Company's Indian troops. After capturing a number of small forts he forced Lally to an engagement at Wandiwash, which the French (strongly against the advice of de Bussy) were trying to retake, on the 22nd January 1760. The French order of battle under Lally and de Bussy consisted of 2250 Europeans, 1300 Indian infantry and 16 guns, and Coote had 1900 Royal and E.I.C. European troops, 2100 Indian infantry, 1250 Indian cavalry and 26 guns. The action was fought almost entirely between the European troops, and resulted in the complete defeat of the French, de Bussy being taken prisoner and Lally wounded. By the first week in April the only places held by the French in the Carnatic were Jinji and Pondicherry. [2]

Wandiwash.

Coote invested Pondicherry a month later, while the British fleet established a blockade, and the end of the last French foothold in India became only a question of how long Lally could hold out. His attempt to retrieve the situation by an alliance with Haidar Ali, the rising general in the service of the Mysore government, had come to nothing; he was on the worst of terms with his own council; there were no

Fall of Pondicherry.

[1] *Influence of Sea Power upon History*, pp. 310, 311.
[2] Orme, *op. cit.*, Vol. II. pp. 577–589.

available funds and hardly any supplies. The gallant defence by the weak and half-starved garrison came to an end on 16th January 1761 and Lally surrendered.

The fall of Pondicherry marks the end of the contest between the French and the English for supremacy in India, for the French incursion during the American Revolutionary War never took hold in the country. The result was due in the first place to the influence of sea-power which enabled the English to receive supplies and money from Bengal and reinforcements from Europe, while the French could get nothing but what came with difficulty to them by land. Another cause was the maladministration of the French financial affairs at home and in India. Lally came out with insufficient supplies and he was continually embarrassed for means to pay his troops, to obtain material, and to pay his workpeople. As Voltaire says, immense sums had been spent during more than forty years to maintain a company equally maladroit in commerce and in war, that had never made any profits, and had paid no genuine dividends either to shareholders or to creditors. There was a third contributory cause in the highly unsuitable character of Lally himself, although nothing could have exceeded his personal courage in the midst of overwhelming difficulties. But none of these considerations was allowed to weigh on Lally's return to France. He was thrown into the Bastille and two and a half years later was executed for betrayal of the interests of his king and the Company of the Indies.

The security of the East India Company's position as regards European rivalry after the fall of Pondicherry is emphasized by an operation which took place in 1762. The successful world war which Pitt had been directing for six years fully absorbed all the resources of Great Britain, and although that minister had resigned in October 1761 his policy was continued when war was forced upon the country by Spain in January 1762. Manilla was to be attacked, and the English Company in India undertook what was to be the last military operation of the Seven Years' War. The expedition sailed from

Expedition to Manilla.

Madras in August, supported by the fleet, and resulted in the whole group of Philippine Islands surrendering in October, and paying a ransom of four million dollars.[1] The colony was, however, restored to Spain at the end of the war.

On the 10th February 1763 peace was signed at Paris. By *Treaty of Paris.* the terms relating to India France recovered the possessions she had held before Dupleix became governor, but she gave up the right of erecting fortifications or keeping troops in Bengal. It was tacitly understood that the English Company should keep all its conquests. The French could still trade in India but the political pretensions of France had been swept away.

The Treaty of Paris marks the point when the maritime powers of Europe finally withdrew from all serious rivalry either in commerce or conquest in India. After 1763 the struggle for ascendancy lay between the British and the Indian powers—" a contest of which the issue was so far from being doubtful, amazing or invisible that it could be and was already foreseen and foretold." [2]

[1] *Influence of Sea Power upon History*, p. 316.
[2] *Rise of the British Dominion in India*, p. 97.

NOTE 1.—THE BRITISH AND FRENCH NAVIES.

In both countries naval discipline and administration had been sapped by the long peace. The British Navy had been reduced from 84 battleships and 40 fifty-gun ships in 1727 to 70 and 19 respectively in 1734. In 1744 the French had 45 ships of the line, but the British first-rates had risen after four years' war with Spain to 90. In 1747, towards the end of the war with Spain and France, Great Britain had 126 battleships ; France had 31 in bad condition, while their dockyards were destitute of material. The French ships built between 1740 and 1800 were better designed class for class than the British, but the British officers and men were superior, and kept this advantage of seamanship by habitually blockading the French ports. Mahan, *op. cit.*, pp. 259, 260.

NOTE 2.

The Chronology of the events of this period is given at the end of Chapter XIV.

BIBLIOGRAPHY

History of the Military Transactions of the British Nation in Indostan, R. Orme, 4th Edn., 1861, Vols. I. and II.

History of the Mahrattas, J. C. Grant Duff, ed. S. M. Edwardes, 1921, Vol. I.

Cambridge History of the British Empire, Vol. IV.

Influence of Sea Power upon History, Captain A. T. Mahan, U.S. Navy, 5th Edn.

Rise of the British Dominion in India, Sir A. Lyall, 2nd Edn., 1893.

Life of Lord Clive, G. W. Forrest, 2 vols., 1918.

CHAPTER XIV

The English in Bengal

THE Anglo-French struggle in India was fought in the Carnatic, but the foundations of British supremacy over the Indian powers were laid in Bengal. This province was the richest in agriculture and manufactures in all India, with a revenue three times as large as that of any other province. Its quota in lieu of further revenue under the feudal system of India according to the *Ain-i-Akbari* was 23,000 cavalry, 800,000 infantry, over 4000 guns and a number of elephants and armed boats. Such resources made the ruler of Bengal as powerful a vassal—or as dangerous an enemy—to the Mogul Emperor as Charles of Burgundy was to Louis XI of France. Consequently its governors after Akbar took over the country were chosen for their devotion to the throne as well as for their eminence in the State. Todar Mal, the great administrator, and Man Singh, Akbar's famous general, were both rulers of Bengal.

But when the empire broke up and Bengal was no longer part of a supremely powerful state, its geographical position made it weaker than any other part of India to withstand foreign aggression. It was the province most exposed to maritime attack and the most valuable in every respect to a seafaring and commercial race like the English. The industries of Bengal included the muslins of Dacca, the silk stuffs of Kasimbazar, jute from its many villages, opium and saltpetre from Patna. The Hooghly gave a far easier entrance to a fleet than the north-western passes to an invading army, while the great rivers of Bengal, the equivalent to the railways of today, led like main arteries up to the heart of India six hundred miles from the sea. As Sir Alfred Lyall has pointed out,[1] whoever holds the great plain stretching from the Himalaya south-eastward to the Bay of Bengal occupies

[1] *The Rise of the British Dominion in India.*

the central position that dominates all the rest of the country. Calcutta was the true centre of government and Bengal the base from which the English between 1757 and 1849 expanded their dominion by wars with the Indian powers.

Akbar annexed Bengal in 1576 and three years later he created the office of finance minister, or *diwan*. This appointment was made by the Emperor, and the minister, who was responsible for the collection of the revenue, the expenditure of public money and the administration of civil justice, was only partly subordinate to the governor. Bengal, Bihar and Orissa, which were administered as two separate provinces after 1607, were re-united under one viceroy in 1697 and shortly afterwards Patna became the seat of the provincial government. After the death of Aurangzeb in 1707 the office of governor, then held by Murshid Quli Khan, became hereditary and to all intents and purposes independent. Murshid Quli Khan, the first and perhaps the ablest of these rulers, combined the civil and military administration with complete financial control, and abolished the check on expenditure which the finance minister had supplied.[1]

The third hereditary governor, Sarfaraz Khan, who had neither ability nor morals, was killed when fighting the Tartar deputy-governor of Bihar, Ali Wardi Khan, in 1740,[2] a year after his accession, and Ali Wardi proclaimed himself viceroy. The new ruler was exemplary in his private life, and a man of outstanding ability. He appointed Hindus to high positions and administered the province exceptionally well.

Ali Wardi's rise to power had, however, seriously alarmed the Nizam of the Deccan, who incited the Marathas to attack him, and his campaigns against these invaders kept him fully occupied until he bought them off and ceded Orissa to the Confederacy in 1751.

Bombay had been taken over by the East India Company with the sovereign powers which had been exercised by the Portuguese. But the real development of British sovereignty in India had its origin in the little group of villages on the mud-flats of the Hooghly over which the Company

The English at Calcutta.

[1] *Early Revenue History of Bengal*, Ascoli, Ch. I.
[2] Orme, *op. cit.*, Vol. II. pp. 27, 29.

acquired in 1690 the rights of a landed proprietor, or farmer of taxes. These villages, which formed the nucleus of Calcutta, yielded revenue from land and local taxation, but the Company in its position as *zamindar* came under Indian jurisdiction in respect to its holdings.[1] The Company's criminal court was not established until the grant of the Royal charter of 1726, when its authority was confined to Europeans.

Murshid Quli Khan had no liking for European trading companies, and his local officials ignored the imperial concessions gained by Surman (1714–17), which granted free trade and additional territory to the English Company in Bengal. Calcutta, however, grew in wealth and importance, and the city whose population in 1704 was about 15,000 increased by the middle of the century to an estimated total of more than 100,000.[2]

In Mogul times there were muslin factories in the chief weaving centres such as Dacca to supply the imperial household and the Nawab of Bengal with the finer grades of muslin, which gave a considerable stimulus to the industry. In 1753 when trade was flourishing the output of the Dacca cloth trade was estimated at about £350,000 in English money, of which the English Company and its servants in the private trade took about a fifth. Reference is made later to the decline in the Indian weaving trade, but it may be said here that, while the production of cotton cloths in Dacca amounted to £300,000 a year in 1766, Rouse, the English chief in the province, reported that in 1776 it had fallen to £200,000.[3] This shrinkage may be attributed to the decline of the Mogul court and to the comparative impoverishment of the provincial government of Bengal.

Economic Conditions in Bengal.

The overseers of a Mogul weaving establishment had uncontrolled authority over the workers, who were liable to corporal punishment if they tried to abscond. Nor did they receive the full pay due to them. In the time of Siraj-ud-daula, a quarter of their

---

[1] *Trade Relations between England and India*, pp. 58, 59.
[2] *Camb. Hist. British Empire*, Vol. IV. p. 112.
[3] *Trade Relations*, p. 198.

pay was said to be deducted by those in charge. Special taxes were also levied on the weavers by the *zamindars* until these were abolished by the East India Company in 1792.[1]

The economic conditions have been described by Orme, the member of council who was collecting materials for his history at least as early as 1757.[2] " The most valuable part of the cargoes returned to Europe consists of silk and cotton manufactures; the weaver of which is an Indian, living and working with his wife and several children in a hut, which scarcely affords him shelter from the sun and rain; his natural indolence however is satisfied in procuring by his daily labour, his daily bread; and the dread of extortion or violence from the officers of the district to which he belongs, makes it prudent in him to appear, and to be poor; so that the chapman who sets him to work, finds him destitute of everything but his loom, and is therefore obliged to furnish him with money, generally half the value of the cloth he is to make, in order to purchase materials, and to subsist him until his work is finished; the merchant who employs a great number of weavers is marked by the higher officers of the government, as a man who can afford to forfeit a part of his wealth, and is therefore obliged to pay for protection, the cost of which, and more, he lays upon the manufactures he has to sell."[3] The full wages of an Indian weaver were from six to eight rupees a month,[4] an average of about three shillings and ninepence a week in English money.

The general state of insecurity created by the Maratha invasions during the governorship of Ali Wardi Khan caused the English authorities to consider with some anxiety the defensive possibilities of Calcutta. Fort William, which had been completed in 1716, was none too strong, and its works, such as they were, had been masked by

---

[1] *Trade Relations*, pp. 199–200.
[2] *Life of Clive*, Forrest, Vol. II. pp. 34, 35, quotes a letter dated 1st August 1757, in which Clive offers Orme " Volumes of Material for (his) History in which will appear Fighting, tricks, chicanery, Intrigues, Politics and the Lord knows what."
[3] Orme, *op. cit.*, Vol. II. pp. 8, 9.
[4] *Trade Relations between England and India*, p. 150.

factories built close to the walls. Had the field of fire been cleared, and the fortress put in a reasonable state of defence, the story of the Black Hole might never have been written. But the military weakness of the European Companies in Bengal, added to the firm policy of the provincial government, enforced a neutrality between the English and the French; and no action was taken.

The loss of revenue resulting from the English trading privileges coupled with the fear that European influence in Bengal would expand as it had done in the Coromandel, where Indian independent authority had disappeared, had for some time been the cause of increasing irritation to the Bengal Government.[1] This came to a head when Ali Wardi Khan died early in April 1756 and was succeeded by his grandson Siraj-ud-daula, a youth of nineteen, of whom neither his Indian nor English contemporaries have a good word to say. The French, who knew him best, considered his chief characteristics to be cruelty, rapacity and cowardice.

Siraj-ud-daula, actuated by his fear of European aggression, resolved to take the offensive against the English.
Fall of Calcutta.
He seized the factory at Kasimbazar on the 4th of June and on the following day began his advance on Calcutta. The regular garrison of the headquarters of the Company in Bengal was only 260 men, with a militia force of about 250 civilians of whom 174 were Europeans and about 1500 Indian matchlock-men. The fortifications were defective, the senior military officer was worse than incompetent and Siraj-ud-daula brought an overwhelming force to the attack. After the first assault crowds of civilian refugees and deserters from the garrison, together with its commanding officer and the majority of the Presidency council, including the Governor Drake, left the city by river during the night. The civil and military control of Calcutta was then assumed by Holwell, the junior counsellor, and one of the few members of council who stayed at his post. Calcutta, and its remaining garrison of 190 men in all, surrendered on the following evening, the 20th June 1756.[2]

[1] *Trade Relations between England and India*, p. 78.
[2] For a detailed account of the taking of Calcutta see Orme, *op. cit.*, Vol. II. pp. 59–73.

After the surrender, Holwell and 145 companions were crowded, in the hottest season of the year, into a cell 18 feet long by 14 feet 9 inches wide, with only two small windows. The prisoners were put into the room at eight in the evening. When the door was opened in the early morning only twenty-three were still living, one of whom was a young married woman whose husband had died during the night and who was taken to the harem of Mir Jafar, Siraj-ud-daula's general.[1]

The Black Hole.

This is Holwell's version of the Black Hole, and although arguments have been put forward to discredit his story the weight of the available evidence bears him out.[2] Orme lays the guilt on Siraj-ud-daula by inference,[3] but the responsibility for the Black Hole cannot definitely or fairly be laid on him. If strong contemporary suspicion was well founded the responsible person was the Sikh banker, Amin Chand, known in history as Omichand. This immensely rich merchant whose interests covered Bengal and Bihar, had for forty years provided most of the English Company's investments; that is to say the supply of goods for export. But he had latterly been shut out from the Company's business. His resentment led him to intrigue against the English with the Bengal government, and shortly before the attack upon Calcutta he was arrested and put in custody, to be released by Siraj-ud-daula.[4] Holwell was convinced that the Black Hole was Omichand's revenge.[5]

Siraj-ud-daula when report was made to him in the morning at once released the survivors, with the exception of Holwell and two other officers of the Company, who were sent to Murshidabad with instructions that they should be well treated.

The news of the loss of Calcutta reached Madras on the 16th of August; and although letters despatched from England in August of the preceding year had warned the Presidencies that war with France was then imminent and

Recapture of Calcutta.

[1] Orme, *op. cit.*, Vol. II. p. 77, and Holwell's account quoted in *Life of Lord Clive*, Vol. I. p. 324.
[2] See Note at end of this chapter.
[3] Orme, *op. cit.*, Vol. II. pp. 76, 77. [4] Orme, *op. cit.*, Vol. II. pp. 76, 77.
[5] See *Life of Lord Clive*, Forrest, Vol. I. pp. 313, 330, 331.

that a formidable French expedition to Pondicherry was being organized at Brest, the Madras authorities decided to abandon their contemplated attack upon the French in the Deccan and send a strong force to Bengal. This courageous decision, which reduced the English forces in Southern India from an equality with the French to half their number in European troops, was completely justified by subsequent events. But it was only reached in the face of considerable opposition in council by the arguments of Orme the historian, Clive then deputy-governor of Fort St. David, and George Pigot the governor of Madras.[1]

The Bengal field force consisted of three companies of the 39th Foot (now the 1st Battalion Dorsetshire Regiment), and about 600 European troops of the Company and 1500 Indian infantry, all picked men. Admiral Watson arranged to act as escort to the expedition with his squadron, flying his flag in the *Kent*, a 74-gun battleship.

The start was delayed for two months by difference of opinion as to the powers to be given to the commander of the force, and by the still more knotty point as to who the commander should be. Clive was eventually given the command with absolute control of all military matters and operations, while the governor of Calcutta and his council were to retain full powers in commercial and civil affairs. Clive was also instructed that if the news of the outbreak of war should reach India while he was still in Bengal he should capture the French settlement of Chandernagore.[2]

The expedition sailed on October 16th from Madras and, skilfully piloted up the almost unknown waters of the Hooghly, began its operations against Siraj-ud-daula. Calcutta was re-occupied on 2nd January 1757 after a bombardment by the fleet, and Admiral Watson replaced Drake as governor.

Siraj-ud-daula with 20,000 horse and 30,000 foot[3] again moved on Calcutta, but his resolution was shaken by a night attack and he came to terms with Clive. By the treaty which Admiral Watson signed on the 9th February the English factories were restored, the

---

[1] *Camb. Hist. of the British Empire*, Vol. IV. p. 144.
[2] Orme, *op. cit.*, Vol. II. pp. 88, 89.
[3] Clive to his father, under date 23rd February 1757.

villages which Surman had obtained, on paper, from Farrukh-Siyar, were handed over, belated sanction was given for the fortification of Calcutta and the Company was granted free trade throughout Bengal, Orissa and Bihar.

Siraj-ud-daula then returned to Murshidabad, swayed on the one hand by hatred of the English and on the other by considerable respect for their military power. On the 10th of March, however, a letter was sent under his seal to Admiral Watson permitting him to attack Chandernagore, and the French factory surrendered after a bombardment by the fleet on the 23rd March.[1]

Irresolute in judgment, Siraj-ud-daula had let the English destroy his natural allies the French, and when *Overthrow of Siraj-ud-daula.* Jean Law,[2] the late chief of the Kasimbazar factory, left Murshidabad in April for Patna, French power and influence vanished from Bengal. At the same time, by his own folly, Siraj-ud-daula aroused general hatred in the province. He incurred the bitter enmity of the great Hindu bankers, the *seths*, whose help had largely contributed to establish Ali Wardi Khan as Nawab, and he alienated his army. Revolution was in the air, and while Omichand entered into the intrigues of the *seths* and at the same time made terms with the Nawab, the nobles determined to overthrow Siraj-ud-daula and make Mir Jafar Nawab in his place.

The English council at Calcutta decided to support Mir Jafar and entered into an alliance with him. But Omichand was let into the secret before his double-dealing was known, and he threatened to reveal the conspiracy to the Nawab unless he received five per cent. on all Siraj-ud-daula's treasure and thirty lakhs, that is to say three million rupees,[3] equivalent to £320,000 at the rate of exchange of the

[1] The story of the commercial ruin of the French settlements in Bengal from the French point of view is to be found in *Three Frenchmen in Bengal*, S. C. Hill (London), 1903.

[2] Jean Law of Bengal and Jacques François Law of the Carnatic were nephews of the Scotsman and French financier John Law of Lauriston.

[3] Clive in his evidence before the House of Commons. The evidence establishing the part played by Omichand in this unsavoury business is to be found in the *Life of Clive*, Vol. I. pp. 417–420.

time. Clive had an exceedingly difficult decision to make on the situation as he saw it. If he allowed himself to be blackmailed by Omichand he had solid grounds for believing that the *seths* and Mir Jafar would refuse to sign the treaty which would bring massacre and ruin upon the English settlements in Bengal. If he rejected Omichand's terms and the conspiracy was revealed to Siraj-ud-daula, the Europeans up country would certainly be murdered and the Nawab with the help of French troops from the Deccan would attack and destroy the English factories. He made up his mind with resolution but, as has been well said,[1] had Omichand sought it he could not have devised a more bitter revenge than the stain which he brought upon the name of Clive. Omichand was completely duped and outwitted, and Clive defended a manœuvre which went the length of forgery by stating before the Parliamentary Committee: "I think it warrantable in such a case and would do it again a hundred times. I had no interested motive and did it with a design of disappointing the expectations of a rapacious man." [2]

Two copies of a treaty with Mir Jafar were prepared by the Council. The main clauses in each confirmed the concessions already made by Siraj-ud-daula, with additions giving the English sovereignty within Calcutta, a grant of land for the maintenance of an adequate military force and compensation for the public and private losses when Calcutta was taken. This was signed by Admiral Watson.

In the copy which was prepared for Omichand to see a stipulation was added that the banker should be given 20 lakhs of rupees, a reduction of 10 lakhs being made to give Omichand, as Clive expressed it, "no room for suspicion." [3] In this version of the treaty with which Watson had nothing to do, the admiral's signature was added by some person, possibly Henry Lushington. After Plassey, Omichand was told how he had been tricked. Orme, as a rule a most accurate authority, gives a painfully dramatic account of the scene, but his statement that Omichand consequently became insane is questionable. He carried on his business and Clive helped him sub-

---

[1] S. C. Hill in *Bengal in* 1756–1757.
[2] *Life of Lord Clive*, Vol. I. p. 421.
[3] *Ibid.*, Vol. I. p. 428.

stantially in the matter of a contract.[1]   Omichand died in 1767, leaving £2000 to the Foundling Hospital in London.

Mir Jafar accepted the valid treaty on the 5th of June, and Clive marched to fight Siraj-ud-daula with his 900 Euro-*Plassey.*   peans, 100 Topasses, 2100 veteran Indian infantry, eight 6-pounder field-guns and two field howitzers,[2] uncertain if his secret ally would co-operate with him.   He met the Nawab's army of 18,000 cavalry, 50,000 infantry and fifty 32- and 24-pounder guns at Plassey on 23rd June 1757, and began the action with little hope of success.   Fighting until about 2 p.m. was confined to an artillery duel in which the small detachment of French artillery with Siraj-ud-daula's army greatly distinguished itself.   The English troops then advanced upon two mounds in front of the Nawab's main position. Mir Jafar and the troops under his command had remained inactive on the right flank of the English line throughout the day, and Siraj-ud-daula, seized with the fear of treachery, fled on a camel to Murshidabad, while his army broke in disorder.   The total casualties among the King's and Company's troops, in the action which cleared the way for British supremacy in India, were 20 Europeans and 52 Indians killed and wounded.[3]

The " whiff of grape-shot " from Clive's guns at Plassey brought the revolution of the Muhammadan nobles, the *Bengal after Plassey.*   Hindu bankers and the officials of the English Company to a successful conclusion.   Mir Jafar became Nawab of Bengal, and when Siraj-ud-daula fell into his hands the ex-governor was immediately murdered.

Clive, who had fought Plassey and installed Mir Jafar at Murshidabad as an officer of the Madras Presidency, had taken full control at Calcutta after the death of Watson in August 1757 and was confirmed by the Court of Directors as governor at Fort William in March 1758, the orders reaching Calcutta in November.   In the meanwhile he had reorganized the Company's forces and the defences of Calcutta.   His position in Bengal in one respect resembled

[1] *Life of Lord Clive*, Vol. II. pp. 7, 8.
[2] Orme, *op. cit.*, Vol. II. p. 174.   [3] Orme, *op. cit.*, Vol. II. p. 178.

de Bussy's situation in the Deccan. Mir Jafar and Salabat Jang were both weak and incompetent, and they were surrounded by nobles who naturally resented the influence of armed foreigners. But while de Bussy never had more than the districts granted to him by the Nizam on which to rely for the maintenance of his troops, Clive's position was incomparably stronger, for the English had now secured effective financial control, as well as a military hold, over Bengal.

Mir Jafar had been invested with the Nawabship by the English under conditions binding him to grant full compensation for the losses due to the seizure of Calcutta and to pay the war expenses of the Company. In addition to this he made enormous gifts to the admirals and to the chief officers of the Company, a practice not then considered immoral, nor was it contrary to King's Regulations and the Company's rules at that time.

Clive received, as a private donation, 1,600,000 rupees in addition to 280,000 rupees as second in the Select Committee and 200,000 rupees as Commander-in-Chief, a total of £243,000 according to the rate of exchange of the Company's bills at the time. The sum eventually paid by Mir Jafar in compensation to the Company, to European, Indian and Armenian private individuals and as presents, after Plassey, amounted to just over £3,388,000.[1] In addition to this the Nawab had to allot a considerable share of his revenue as the price of the annual support given him by the Company.

Mir Jafar in December 1757 signed a further treaty by which he assigned to the Company the *zamindari* rights of the fiscal divisions still called the Twenty-four Parganas, an area of about 882 square miles with a yearly assessment equivalent to about £28,000. This was the first important territorial acquisition of the Company in Bengal. It gave no sovereign powers, as the Company became a landholder under the Nawab who, in theory at least, was the ruler of the province under the Emperor.[2] But the power of the Mogul emperors had gone, and authority in Bengal was divided between the foreign trading

The Twenty-four Parganas.

[1] From the Third Report on . . . the East India Company, pp. 20–23. This is quoted by Mill, *History of British India* (4th Edn.), Vol. III. pp. 367–371.
[2] *Early Revenue History of Bengal*, pp. 19, 20.

company and a governor dependent on its troops for the maintenance of his rule. The quit-rent of £28,000 payable by the Company to the Indian Government was assigned to Clive as a *jagir* in return for his services in defeating a formidable invasion of Bengal in 1759.

At the beginning of that year the Emperor Alamgir II's eldest son Ali Gauhar, who was on the worst of terms with his father's chief minister Ghazi-ud-din, advanced to attack the province, with Shuja-ud-daula the ruler of Oudh and 30,000 men.[1] Clive had been made a Commander of Five Thousand horse and Six Thousand foot after Plassey by the Emperor, and Ali Gauhar summoned him to join with the invaders. Clive answered that his rank as a Mogul noble made him a servant of the Emperor, from whom he had received no such orders, and added that he was "under the strictest engagement with the present governor of the province to assist him at all times."

Invasion of Bengal.

It was a critical moment. Bengal was seething with revolt against the indolence, debauchery and avarice of Mir Jafar, and the Company's forces in the province had been greatly reduced by the despatch of reinforcements to the Carnatic, where the French were besieging Madras. But to fight with the odds against him was Clive's strongest incentive to vigorous and successful action. With about 450 European and 2500 Indian troops he covered 400 miles in twenty-three days, occupied Patna and broke the invading army. The fame of Clive's exploit resounded all over India and gained for him the imperial gift of the *jagir*, which after a lively correspondence between him and the Directors [2] was eventually sanctioned. Clive enjoyed his £28,000 a year until his death in 1774, the whole proprietary right in the land and its revenues afterwards reverting to the Company.

The situation in Bengal during Clive's first administration at Calcutta was one of great uncertainty and difficulty. The revolution which set Mir Jafar on the throne inaugurated a system of masked government in the province. The English had practically conquered Bengal, yet as

Masked Government.

[1] Clive to the Honourable Secret Committee in London 12th March 1759.
[2] *Life of Lord Clive*, Forrest, Vol. II. pp. 197, 198.

representatives of a trading company with no authority to annex territory, they felt unable to assume administrative control and were obliged, therefore, to pretend deference towards an Indian ruler who was really subservient to themselves. As Sir Alfred Lyall has pointed out [1]: " Nothing more surely leads to misrule than the degradation of a civil government to subserve the will of some arbitrary force or faction within the state, and in Bengal the evils of precarious and divided authority were greatly heightened by special aggravations."

The interests of the Nawab and the Company were diametrically opposed at important points. Mir Jafar wanted to remove the Hindu deputy-governors and replace them by his own friends, and he intended to improve his finances by confiscating the property of the *seths*. His policy towards the Company was to evade as far as possible the fulfilment of the financial stipulations of the treaty, and he wished to lessen the power of the English should opportunity arise. It must, however, be said that Mir Jafar had a strong personal liking for Clive, who knew how to deal with an Oriental prince with whom he was firm, candid and courteous but never patronizing.

Clive took effectual measures to protect the threatened Hindus, but the financial relations with Mir Jafar were a continual source of trouble. Both the Company and the Nawab were badly in need of money. The Nawab was being pressed by the English to pay from an exhausted treasury the heavy price for the help which had won him his throne. At the same time he dared not reduce his army to lessen his expenditure. This would have put him completely at the mercy of his foreign allies at a time when he needed troops to quell the disorders in his province and hold the frontiers against the Marathas and other invaders.

The authorities at Fort William were obliged to make large remittances to the Carnatic to carry on the war against the French, while they were expected to send money to Europe to pay annual dividends. To increase their resources the Company, finding themselves irresistible, began to monopolize the whole trade in some of the most valuable products of the country, which caused additional

[1] *Rise of the British Dominion in India*, p. 117.

irritation and led inevitably to intolerable abuses and confusion in Bengal.[1]

Early in 1759 Mir Jafar saw an opportunity to strike at the English through another European power, and entered into negotiations with the Dutch who were contemplating an expedition to India. In June the governor-general of Batavia sent a considerable force of European and Malay troops to Negapatam and, after an indefensible delay, the expedition reached Bengal in November. While Mir Jafar awaited the turn of events before hurrying to the assistance of the victor, Clive faced the crisis with characteristic energy and resolution. With the situation in the Carnatic before him he was determined to prevent the rise of a European rival in Bengal, and he conscripted every available European, Armenian and man of mixed descent in Calcutta which increased his forces by over 700 men. Colonel Forde had by this time been recalled to Bengal and was placed in command of the field force.

The Dutch Expedition.

Great Britain and Holland were not known to be at war with each other when Forde began his advance, and before engaging the Dutch he applied to Clive for the authorization of an Order in Council. Clive, who was playing cards when the letter arrived, took up a pencil and wrote on Forde's letter: " Dear Forde, fight 'em immediately. I will send an Order of Council tomorrow." [2]

The contingent from Batavia and the 600 men stationed at Chinsura were beaten in detail, Colonel Forde winning the decisive action of the short campaign at Biderra (Badarah) on the 25th November 1759. With the complete defeat of the Dutch and the limitation of their European troops in India to a handful of factory guards, all danger of war in Bengal with another European power was at an end.

On 21st February 1760 Clive sailed for England, leaving Holwell as acting governor at Fort William. As his ship came out of the Hooghly he was met by a dispatch from the Coromandel announcing the victory of Wandiwash a month before.

---

[1] *Rise of the British Dominion in India*, p. 118.
[2] *Life of Lord Clive*, Forrest, Vol. II. pp. 160, 161.

The control of the Company's affairs now passed into weaker and
Economic incompetent hands, and there began the one short
Situation, period of Anglo-Indian history which, in the words of
1760-1765. Sir Alfred Lyall,[1] " throws grave and unpardonable
discredit on the English name."

Before dealing with the political events between 1760 and 1765,
reference must be made to the general state of Bengal. In the first
place the whole administration was paralysed by the serious differences existing between the Company, who were virtual masters of the
country, and its ostensible ruler who naturally fought against his
own effacement, was distracted between the fear of assassination by
his own officers and dethronement by the Company, and regarded
any possible intruder, Dutch or Maratha, as a means to shake off the
English. Neither the Nawab nor the English Company could give
Bengal an efficient government; both became equally unpopular and
the province during these years had no authoritative head.

The condition of commerce and industry was equally deplorable.
India was then regarded both in England and by the Company's
servants on the spot as a commercial prize to be exploited. The
English traders came out to Bengal solely to make money. With no law
in the land and no wholesome restraint of public opinion, the ordinary
standards of honour, justice and integrity were generally forgotten in
the pursuit of wealth. Many of the Company's servants returned to
Europe as "Nabobs" with fortunes amassed by methods which fully
deserved the condemnation that has been passed upon them.

For this the Directors and proprietors of East India Company
stock were largely to blame, as they would not sanction what they
regarded as a heavy charge for salaries. Writers were paid £2, 5s. a
month, excluding lodging allowance when quarters were not provided.
The highest salaried officers below the governor with his £2700 *per
annum* were the counsellors who drew £132, 17s. a year, the more
senior officials also receiving gratuities of varying amounts.[2] In the

[1] *Rise of the British Dominion in India*, p. 118.

[2] Extract from dispatch to Bengal 3rd March 1758 (Record Department,
India Office). Writers received 240 rupees and counsellors from 1181 rupees
a year, sums which have been converted in the text into sterling at the contemporary rate of exchange.

opinion of the Directors, however, " The indigence of our Junior Servants, which may too often have been the effect of their Vices and the Imitation of their Seniors, hath not a little Contributed to Increase that load of Complaints . . . urged by the Nabob in regard to the Abuse of Dusticks " (Dustocks, or passes to trade duty free) " a practice we have ever disclaimed and are determined to show in future the strongest Marks of our Resentment to such as shall be guilty of; and do most positively order and direct . . . that no Writer whatsoever be permitted to keep either Palankeen, Horse or Chaise . . . on pain of being immediately dismissed." [1]

With most inadequate means the Company's officials were plunged into surroundings full of infinite temptations to make money in corrupt and dishonest ways. They were in a country where bribes and presents, the customary payments by inferiors to superiors, were an accepted part of the social system; and as the English officials came to be regarded as the embodiment of the real authority of the State they found themselves in a position in which many such doubtful payments were not only voluntarily offered, but could be exacted according to the measure of their power.

Apart from presents and bribes, large sums were to be made by the private trading referred to in the Directors' dispatch. The Company, by its concessions from the imperial government, enjoyed complete exemption from Indian transit dues on the goods being collected for export. But its servants looked upon these privileges as permission to themselves to trade duty free on their own account through the province in such articles as salt, betel and tobacco. Clive had been instructed to place private trading on a legal footing in the negotiations with Mir Jafar, but no authorization for free private trading appeared in the Treaty of 1757. This trade was relatively small during Clive's first administration, and when the Nawab protested against it on the eve of Clive's departure for England a declaration of policy on the question was shelved. But in the following months its volume increased enormously. Illicit trading and the oppression of the industrial workers by local agents which accompanied it spread to English, French, German and American adven-

[1] Ledgers and Journals of the E.I.C. (Record Department, India Office).

turers, as well as to Indian traders, none of whom had anything to do with the Company, and who provided themselves with bought, or forged, free passes.[1]

Warren Hastings, then a junior member of council, sent a strongly worded report to the governor on " the oppressions committed under the sanction of the English name ":

" This evil I am well assured is not confined to our dependants alone, but is practised all over the country by people falsely assuming the habits of our sepoys, or calling themselves our agents. As, on such occasions, the great power of the English intimidates the people from making any resistance, so on the other hand the indolence of the Bengalees, or the difficulty of gaining access to those who might do them justice, prevents our having knowledge of the oppressions, and encourages their continuance, to the great though unmerited scandal of our government. I have been surprised to meet several English flags flying in places which I have passed; and on the river I do not believe that I passed a boat without one. By whatever title they have been assumed . . . I am sure their frequency can bode no good to the Nabob's revenues, to the quiet of the country, or the honour of our nation; but evidently tend to lessen both of them." [2]

Five months after Clive's departure the new governor, Henry Vansittart, arrived from Madras. His political *Political Events.* record in the Carnatic was excellent, but he lacked initiative and was handicapped by the jealousy of all the Bengal officials whom he had superseded.

Vansittart found himself in a sea of troubles. The Treasury at Calcutta was empty, the English troops at Patna were on the verge of mutiny and deserting in numbers for want of pay; Madras and Bombay were entirely dependent upon Bengal for money; the business arrangements for providing goods for shipment to Europe had been suspended; the Presidency income was barely meeting the current expenses of Calcutta; the allowance paid by the Nawab for

[1] *Life of Lord Clive*, Forrest, Vol. II. pp. 225–227.
[2] Hastings to Vansittart, under date 25th April 1762, *Memoirs of Warren Hastings*, Gleig, Vol. I. pp. 107–110.

the troops was several months in arrears, while a large balance was owing on his first agreements; Mir Jafar was old, indolent and voluptuous, estranged from the English and without authority.[1] Vansittart's one consolation lay in the fact that Major Caillaud with a mixed force of King's, Company's and provincial troops had just defeated an invading army under Ali Gauhar, who had now become, after his father's murder, the Emperor Shah Alam II.

The most urgent matter was to restore settled government in the province, and the first problem which Vansittart had to solve was the question of a successor to Mir Jafar.

Mir Kasim becomes Nawab.

The Nawab's son Miran, a profligate and a ruthless murderer, was killed by lightning in July 1760,[2] and this brought Mir Kasim into prominence. He was a son-in-law of Mir Jafar, had great political ability and was liked by the English. The Nawab refused to accept the proposals made to him that he should cede three districts to the English, make Mir Kasim his heir, and give him the office of deputy governor. Whereupon Mir Jafar was deposed by the English, Mir Kasim was set up in his place, and the ex-Nawab retired to Calcutta where he lived on a pension of 15,000 rupees a month paid by his successor.

By the Treaty signed at the end of September 1760 the new Nawab ceded the districts of Burdwan, Midnapur and Chittagong to the English for the maintenance of the Company's troops. This was the first of the " subsidiary alliances " which were a feature of Lord Wellesley's policy later on. In these districts, as in Calcutta and the Twenty-four Parganas, the Company had now the full right of revenue, which they collected themselves, administering the districts through their own agents.[3] But the Treaty was vague in its terms and liable to future misunderstanding. One Nawab had been exchanged for another, but the thorny matter of internal trade had once more been shirked; while the grant of presents which followed,

[1] Mill, *History of British India*, 4th Edn., Vol. III. pp. 305, 306.

[2] *Tamiu-t-Tawarikh* of Fakir Muhammad, and *Chahar Gulzar Shujat* of Hari Charan Das, Elliot and Dowson, Vol. VIII. p. 214 and pp. 428, 429; but M. Jean Law, in his *Memoirs*, stated his belief that Miran was assassinated and his tent burnt to conceal the crime.

[3] *Early Revenue History of Bengal*, p. 20.

although with the exception of Holwell's they had not been stipulated beforehand, as in the case of Plassey, " cast a sordid air over the whole business." [1]

Clive's policy had been to strengthen the English position. He had gone so far as to suggest to Pitt [2] that Bengal should be taken over by the British Government in full sovereignty, with the easily obtained consent of the Mogul Emperor. As he wrote in his letter: " The natives themselves have no attachment whatever to particular princes; as under the present government they have no security for their lives or properties they would rejoice in so happy an exchange as that of a mild for a despotic government."

Vansittart's Policy.

Vansittart's policy was to strengthen the position of the Nawab and, unlike Clive, he withdrew English protection from the Hindu ministers of the province. But he failed to realize that a strong Nawab would inevitably wish to reduce the inequitable privileges which the English claimed and that the question of internal trade would bring on a crisis. In 1763, owing to the aggressive behaviour of the Company's agent at Patna, matters came to a head and the Nawab declared war upon the English.

The Presidency Council put a force of European and Indian troops into the field under Major Adams, which beat Mir Kasim in a series of engagements. They then restored Mir Jafar as Nawab of Bengal by the Treaty of 27th September 1763. Two months later, after his fourth defeat, Mir Kasim fled to Oudh, having put to death at Patna 150 English officials, officers and men, murdered his unsuccessful commander-in-chief, and butchered two of the *seths* who were innocent of any offence against him. [3] The war dragged on until the cold weather of 1764, while Mir Kasim made an alliance with Shuja-ud-daula, the ruler of Oudh, and with the Emperor Shah Alam II, and Major (afterwards Sir Hector) Munro of the 89th Regiment broke a mutiny

Battle of Buxar.

[1] *Camb. Hist. British Empire*, Vol. IV. pp. 168, 169.
[2] Clive to Pitt, 7th January 1759.
[3] An account of the campaign taken from the Powis MSS. is given in *Life of Lord Clive*, Forrest, Vol. II. pp. 236–243.

of a battalion of Indian troops with great but effective severity, and reorganized his army. On 23rd October 1764, at Buxar, Munro with 857 Europeans, 918 Indian cavalry, 5297 Indian infantry and 20 guns completely defeated the Indian allied forces of more than 40,000 men after a stubbornly contested fight. The allies left 2000 men dead on the field, and Munro's losses were 847 killed and wounded.

Buxar was one of the decisive battles of Indian history. Mir Kasim escaped into obscure poverty; the Emperor submitted and came under the protection of the Company; and in February 1765 the fortresses of Chunar and Allahabad were taken and the power of the kingdom of Oudh was broken.

The English had also consolidated their position in Bengal by the Treaty restoring the previous Nawab in 1763. Mir Jafar agreed to limit his forces, to receive a permanent resident at his court, and promised compensation for all losses caused by the war with Mir Kasim. The Nawab died early in 1765, and as his chief minister Nandakumar (Nuncomar) was believed to have betrayed the English plans to the enemy, Mir Jafar's son Najim-ud-daula was only recognized on condition of his appointing a minister nominated by the English, who alone could dismiss him. The Nawab had now lost his last shred of independence and the Company's nominee administered Bengal. A London trading company intent on its dividends had become, by what amounted to foreclosure of a mortgage, virtual master of the richest province of the Great Moguls.

On the 3rd May 1765 Clive, now Lord Clive of Plassey, landed at Calcutta as governor with full powers *Clive as Governor.* to reform the abuses and end the misrule which by this time staggered the Directors. To assist him in the conduct of political affairs he had a select, or secret, committee, the origin of the Foreign Department of the Government of India. With the exception of this reserved subject the general administration remained in the hands of the Council at Fort William.

The first matter awaiting his decision was the political relationship between the Company, the Emperor and the Nawab of Oudh, which had just been complicated by Vansittart's offer of Oudh to the Emperor. Clive solved the problem by restoring to Shuja-ud-daula most of his old dominions on payment of fifty lakhs (5 million rupees), which created on the Bengal frontier a buffer State, whose ruler's every interest was to remain friendly with the English. At the same time he handed over Allahabad and the surrounding districts (formerly within the kingdom of Oudh) to the Emperor, who granted to the Company in exchange what is known as the *diwani* of Bengal, Bihar and Orissa on payment of an annual sum of twenty-six lakhs to the imperial exchequer.

Diwani meant the collection of the revenue of a province and the retention of the surplus after the annual payment had been made to Delhi, as the emoluments and for the expenses of the office. The grant of the *Diwani*, which was the actual starting-point of British revenue administration in India, conferred no sovereign powers, and the general government of the province remained nominally in the hands of the Nawab's deputies. The arrangement had an outward appearance of unreality, but, as Professor Thakore has pointed out,[1] the object of the Company was to secure in this way " not as large a territory as they could seize, nor the position of a sovereign, but something far more modest and serviceable : reliable friends, a stable frontier, an unimpeachable title, and behind these, years of peaceful and profitable trade." The offer of the *Diwani* had been made to the Company as early as 1758; but the Directors of what was still regarded as a purely commercial undertaking were not then prepared to accept any form of administrative responsibility, and the offer was declined.

The Diwani.

Clive appointed Muhammad Reza Khan, deputy of the Nawab after his accession, to collect the revenue for the Company, while the old Mogul subordinate revenue officials were retained. The arrangement proved most unfortunate. The English supervisors appointed in 1769 reported that the revenue officials " exacted

[1] *Indian Administration to the Dawn of Responsible Government*, pp. 26, 27.

what they could from the *zamindars* and great farmers of the revenue, whom they left at liberty to plunder all below, reserving to themselves the prerogative of plundering them in their turn, when they were supposed to have enriched themselves with the spoils of the country." The result of this habitual extortion and injustice was concealment and evasion by the cultivator, and government was defrauded of a large part of its just demands.[1] Three years later, in the governorship of Warren Hastings, the Company determined to "stand forth as *diwan*" and reform the entire system.

The most important administrative question which Clive had
Clive's Administrative Reforms. to settle was that of the Company's covenanted servants. With the general demoralization which had set in, the custom had arisen of expecting large presents, open or concealed, with every change of nawab. The accession of Najim-ud-daula had been a particularly bad case. It was not the result of a revolution backed by armed intervention, but the normal succession of a son to his father, and the precedent of presents from the nawab had been extended to the minister as well. This had been done in the face of specific orders from the Directors prohibiting the acceptance of presents and requiring their servants to sign covenants agreeing not to accept them in future.[2] The council at Fort William pigeonholed these instructions for Clive to deal with, presumedly expecting that his previous practice and present influence would have led him to get the orders quashed before he came out as governor. But they were mistaken in their man. It has been well said that Clive feared nothing, not even his own past; and one of his earliest acts was to require the covenants to be signed by civil and military officers alike.

Clive saw that if illicit gains were to be stopped something would have to be done to increase the income of the Company's officials.

[1] *Fifth Report from the Select Committee of the House of Commons on the Affairs of the East India Company.*
[2] Mill, *op. cit.*, Vol. III. pp. 372, 373.

Accordingly, in addition to allowing liberal salaries to the principal Indian ministers, he introduced a scheme to furnish a good income for the senior servants of the Company out of the inland trade, a method which it is difficult to defend, and which was vetoed by the Directors. The civil administrative reforms, and the reduction of the field allowances of military officers in Bengal to the level drawn in the Madras Presidency under instructions from London, caused insubordination among the civil and military officers of the Company. Clive was quite equal to dealing with this, but the mutiny of the English officers of the three brigades in which he had organized the Company's troops gave him the gravest anxiety. But the European privates and Indian ranks fortunately proved staunch and the mutiny was quelled in a fortnight. The ringleaders, including a brigadier, were court-martialled and cashiered.

Inflexible in resolution in the conduct of affairs there was another side to Clive's character. Before he left India after his second administration he created what is known as Lord Clive's Fund,[1] by devoting a sum of five hundred thousand rupees to provide pensions for servants of the Company, if in poor circumstances, who had to retire on account of ill-health or wounds, and to their widows. The capital was a legacy left to Clive by Mir Jafar, and as it did not come within the Company's prohibition it was invested in trustees and tided over the interval until the Directors began to pension their servants.

A shortage of currency which became acute in 1766 was chiefly *Trade Relations with England.* due to the stoppage of the bullion imports from Europe on which India relied, and partly because the unsettled state of the country had greatly increased hoarding. Nor was the financial situation helped by the steady and continual withdrawal from India of the large fortunes western traders and officials took back with them to Europe. To meet the silver shortage gold mohurs (valued at 14 and 16 rupees)

[1] *Life of Lord Clive*, Forrest, Vol. II. pp. 317, 318.

were minted; and the balance was further improved before the end of the century by silver remittances from China in return for opium and raw cotton, and by large sums received from America.[1]

It must be noted that Indian governments had not then the European facilities of a paper currency and a general system of credit. Prinsep, writing in 1825, refers to this in his financial review[2]: " If a loan is raised or paid off, the whole amount is received or delivered in . . . silver . . . and the most harassing duty the army has to perform is that of providing treasure escorts for the conveyance of cash from place to place. A large supply in hand is indispensable for the current service of the State, and the amount has been estimated at not less than five or six crore of rupees (fifty or sixty million) for the three Presidencies."

Trade between India and England expanded slowly during this period. The commercial policy of the British Government was the protection of home markets, and this had meant to India the exclusion of her silk manufactures and of calicoes for English use if they were printed and painted. Indian cotton manufactures if imported for home consumption paid duty exceeding by more than 100 per cent. the duty on the raw materials for the textile industries of England. These goods were, however, sent to England for re-export, and at the same time the total export of India's textile goods was substantially increased by the Company's flourishing trade with other Asiatic countries, where the rice and sugar of Bengal were equally in demand.

Clive left India for the last time in February 1767 to die by his own hand in 1774. His character stands out
Clive's Character. boldly to be judged by his actions from the day when he began to play a decisive part in Indian history at the age of twenty-six to the end of his second administration as governor when he was not yet forty-two. He had an instinctive grasp of

[1] *Trade Relations between England and India*, pp. 138–144.
[2] *Transactions in India*, 1813–1823, Vol. II. p. 424.

357

essentials; his courage and resolution were as boundless in accepting responsibility when governor as in the field, where he showed himself to be a born leader of men. While some of his acts were quite indefensible as judged by later moral standards, he was above any petty meanness and never vindictive; if he made a huge fortune he was widely generous; though he outmatched Omichand in deception he was trusted implicitly by Indians of every class; and although he shut his eyes to the deplorable effects of masked government in Bengal, "Robert, Lord Clive, did at the same time render great and meritorious services to his country." [1]

During the five years which elapsed before the appointment of Warren Hastings, two governors were in control *Stop-gap Governors.* at Fort William. Verelst, a close friend of Clive's, succeeded him, and Cartier, a worthy man described by Clive as without sufficient confidence in himself, became governor at the end of 1769.

Within a year of Cartier's appointment Bihar and the greater part of Bengal were devastated by a fearful famine, *Famine.* with all the attendant horrors of the earlier famines in India. There were no government schemes in existence for famine relief, but the Company and the provincial authorities contributed large sums and, as is usual in the cause of charity in the East, private individuals of all ranks and creeds subscribed most generously to lessen the distress. It was officially computed that ten million people perished in the year which the famine lasted. [2]

No other event of importance took place in Bengal between Clive's resignation and the appointment of Warren Hastings. But the political situation in Northern India was altered by the move of the Mogul Emperor from Allahabad to Delhi, where he put himself under the protection of the Marathas in December 1771, to spend thirty-two years practically as a State prisoner in their hands, or those of the Afghans.

[1] The last clause is an extract from the Resolution carried without a division in the House of Commons, 21st May 1773.
[2] *The Famine in India*, Forrest, p. 3, pamphlet published in London in 1897.

The Marathas, under the Peshwa Mahdu Rao, had recovered from the disaster of Panipat, the soldier of fortune Haidar Ali had made himself master of Mysore, and these two formidable powers were an active menace both to the Nizam and to the English at Madras. The Presidency authorities mismanaged the political situation. Instead of cementing their understanding with Hyderabad they blundered into hostilities with that State and were later forced into an unsuccessful war with Mysore in which the Mysore cavalry overran the country up to the outskirts of Madras. Peace was made with Haidar Ali in 1769.

Central and Southern India.

But the Madras council were again unfortunate in their policy. They made compacts with Haidar Ali and the Peshwa and also with the Nizam, by which they agreed to go to the military assistance of each. In the following year the Marathas and Haidar Ali again came to blows, both sides called upon the English to fulfil their treaty obligations, and the Madras government having been severely censured by the Directors for the last war, were driven to offend both by refusing to interfere in any way whatever. The Mysore-Maratha war resulted in the defeat of Haidar Ali, who attributed his failure to his faithless desertion by the English and consequently became their persistent and vindictive enemy.[1]

In November 1772, the year of Warren Hastings' appointment, Madhu Rao died at the age of twenty-eight, and his widow, who bore him a remarkable affection, immolated herself with the corpse. The Peshwa had been ill for some time and his death had at first no visible result, " but the plains of Panipat were not more fatal to the Maratha empire than the death of this excellent prince. Although the military talents of Madhu Rao were very considerable, his character as a sovereign is entitled to far higher praise and to much greater respect than that of any of his predecessors. He is deservedly celebrated for his firm support of the weak against the oppressive, of the poor against the rich, and, as far as the con-

---

[1] These events in the Carnatic are detailed by Mill, *op. cit.*, Vol. III. Ch. VIII., and a general summary is to be found in the *Rise of the British Dominion in India*, pp. 136–142.

stitution of society admitted, for his equity to all. Madhu Rao made no innovations; he improved the system established, endeavoured to amend defects without altering forms, and restrained a corruption which he could not eradicate." [1]

Before leaving the subject of Southern India it should be said that the evils of dual government by the Indian provincial administration and the East India Company were at this time at least as great in the Carnatic as they had been in Bengal. The Company's representatives in India had been swept by the tide of events into a situation for which as merchants they were not prepared or, as a rule, fitted. While remote at East India House the Directors, whose business was the prosperity of a great trading corporation, were called upon to face political decisions with which they did not feel competent to grapple. The affairs of the Company, in the words of Mill, excited various and conflicting passions in England, and the attention of Parliament was forcibly drawn towards India.

[1] *History of the Mahrattas*, Vol. I. p. 577.

Note 1.—The Black Hole

Muhammad Ali Khan, who wrote in 1800 what Sir H. M. Elliot has described as one of the most accurate general histories of India, makes no reference to the incident. He merely states that " men, women and children were taken prisoners . . . and all their wealth and property became the booty of the vagabonds of Siraj-ud-daula's army " (Elliot and Dowson, Vol. VIII. pp. 324, 325). But Holwell's account is generally corroborated by the narrative of Cooke (*vide Life of Lord Clive*, Forrest, Vol. I. pp. 314, 316), and the Black Hole is referred to by Clive, Watson and Pigot. Mr. J. H. Little in *Bengal Past and Present* (July 1915 and January 1916) discredits the story altogether on the grounds of numerous demonstrable errors and the lack of contemporary reliable support. But it is not, in the circumstances, altogether surprising that the Calcutta Council— who nearly all disgracefully fled to safety—make no reference to it. If Mr. Little's contentions were correct, Holwell's contemporaries, Watts who strongly disliked him, and Drake who had every incentive to minimize such an incident, would have contradicted the story had it been untrue. They did not do so. The evidence as to whether the story of the Black Hole is substantially true, or a concoction, is reviewed by Professor Dodwell (*Camb. Hist. British Empire*, Vol. IV. p. 156, note), who comes to the conclusion that the weight of evidence supports the accepted version. Lord Curzon in Vol. I. Ch. VII. of his *British Government in India* (London, 1925) also deals with the Black Hole.

NOTE 2.—THE EAST INDIA COMPANY'S ARMY

It is of interest, as marking the beginnings of the British Army in India, to note that after the expedition reached Bengal, Clive reorganized the Company's European troops into battalions from the company system of the Madras forces. The battalion formed by him in December 1756 won their first battle honour at Plassey under the simple designation of " The Regiment." After India came under the Crown this battalion became the 101st (Royal Bengal Fusiliers) to be linked with the 104th, under the Cardwell scheme, as the Royal Munster Fusiliers. [*Hist. Royal Munster Fusiliers*, McCance, 1927 ; MSS. E.I.C. Army Lists (Bombay), 1759–88. India Office Records ; British Army List, 1862–63 ; General Order 70, July 1881.] The question of the relative seniority of King's and Company's military officers which caused so much difficulty in the course of the Bengal expedition was the first of many which gave great dissatisfaction for years to East India Company officers. To improve their status a certain number of King's Commissions were granted to them in 1788 and 1789. [*History of the Madras Army*, Wilson, Vol. II. pp. 168, 169.] But the Company's officers continued to lose their fair share of commands, an injustice which was not removed until 1855. A Horse Guards' Memorandum then gave " the officers of the East India Company's service . . . rank (and) precedence with those of the Royal Army, according to the dates of their commissions, in all parts of Her Majesty's Dominions and elsewhere " (Wilson, *op. cit.*, Vol. IV. p. 434). The point is of interest in view of the decision made during the War of 1914–18, by which Indians became eligible for a King's Commission, instead of only a Commission from the Viceroy. In the establishment of the first Indian battalions, the only European officers were a captain and an adjutant with one sergeant, to each company, and a commanding officer of the unit, who was assisted by an Indian commandant. In 1796 the Indian infantry were reorganized by linking two battalions into regiments with the same number of English officers as in the British Army. Regimental promotion to the rank of major was then introduced. As regards the men, " a jacket of English broadcloth, made up in the shape of his own dress, the knowledge of his manual exercise, and a few military evolutions constituted the original sepoy ; and with this qualification and his English fire-arms, he was found to possess an incalculable superiority over the other natives of India, who, ignorant of the first principles of discipline, were easily defeated."

CHRONOLOGY TO CHAPTERS XII, XIII, XIV

1707. Accession of Bahadur Shah.
1709. The two English Companies become United East India Company.
1712. Accession of Jahandar Shah.
1713. Accession of Farrukh-Siyar.
1714. Balaji Visvanath first Peshwa of the Marathas.
1715. Surman's embassy to Farrukh-Siyar.
1719. Accession of Muhammad Shah.

1719. Formation of new French East India Company.
1720. Office of Peshwa became hereditary on succession of Baji Rao.
1726. Municipal Charters granted to Calcutta, Madras and Bombay.
1731. Compact between Nizam and Marathas.
1738. Invasion of India by Nadir Shah.
      Marathas defeated Mogul army under Nizam.
1739. Nadir Shah defeated Muhammad Shah at Karnal.
      Sack of Delhi.
1740. The Marathas raided the Carnatic.
      Nawab Dost Ali killed.
1742. Aliverdi Khan Nawab of Bengal.
      Dupleix Governor of Pondicherry.
1743. Expedition of the Nizam of Hyderabad to the Carnatic.
1744. War of the Austrian Succession.
1746. De la Bourdonnais took Madras.
1748. Siege of Pondicherry by Boscawen.
      Death of the Nizam.
      Accession of Ahmad Shah as Mogul Emperor.
      Ahmad Shah Durrani began series of invasions of India.
      Madras restored to English (by Treaty of Aix-la-Chapelle).
1749–1754. War of Succession in the Carnatic.
1750–1754. War between French and English Companies.
1751. De Bussy established Salabat Jang as Nizam.
      Seizure and defence of Arcot by Clive.
1752. French defeat at Seringam; death of Chanda Sahib.
1754. Recall of Dupleix.
      Accession of Alamgir II.
      Truce between English and French Companies.
      Mutiny Act (27 Geo. II. c. 9) passed for Indian forces.
1756–1758. Sikhs rise in the Punjab.
1756–1763. Seven Years' War.
1756. Suraj-ud-daula, Nawab of Bengal, took Calcutta.
1757. Clive recovered Calcutta; fought Plassey; and established Mir Jafar as Nawab.
1758. Lally's expedition reached India.
      Capture of Fort St. David.
      Siege of Madras.
      Marathas occupied the Punjab.
1759. Forde took Masulipatam.
      Ali Gauhar invaded Bihar.
      Lally abandoned siege of Madras.
      Dutch expedition failed in Bengal.
1760. Battle of Wandiwash won by Coote over Lally.

1760. Clive left Bengal; succeeded by stop-gap governors and misrule till 1765.
      Ali Gauhar proclaimed Emperor.
      Mir Kasim Nawab of Bengal.
      Marathas took Delhi.
1761. Maratha defeat at Panipat by Ahmad Shah Durrani.
      Lally surrendered Pondicherry.
1762. Haidar Ali usurped Mysore.
      Sikh defeat near Ludhiana by the Afghans.
1763. Pondicherry restored to France by Treaty of Paris.
      Mir Kasim deposed by the English and Mir Jafar restored as Nawab of Bengal.
1764. Munro defeated Mir Kasim at Buxar.
      The Sikhs masters of Lahore.
1765. Clive Governor for second time; obtained grant of *diwani* of Bengal; treaties with King of Oudh and Mogul Emperor.
1766. Grant of Northern Circars to the Company.
      Parliamentary inquiry begins into Company's affairs.
1767–1769. First Mysore War.
1767. Clive finally left India.
1768. Nizam ceded Carnatic.
1770. Famine in Bengal.
1771. East India Company " stand forth as *diwan* " of Bengal.

BIBLIOGRAPHY

History of the Military Transactions of the British Nation in Indostan, R. Orme, 4th Edn., Vol. II.
History of British India, J. Mill, 4th Edn., Vol. III.
Cambridge History of the British Empire, Vol. IV.
History of India as told by its own Historians, Elliot and Dowson, Vol. VIII.
History of the Mahrattas, J. C. Grant Duff, ed. S. M. Edwardes, Vol. I.
Rise of the British Dominion in India, Sir A. Lyall, 2nd Edn. 1893.
Early Revenue History of Bengal, F. D. Ascoli, 1917.
Life of Lord Clive, G. W. Forrest, 2 vols., 1918.
Trade Relations between England and India (1600–1896), C. Hamilton (Calcutta), 1919.

CHAPTER XV

The Expansion of the East India Company

FROM the holding on sufferance of a few scattered trading centres the Company had risen to the control of a great territory and a revenue of £4,000,000, a position which entailed tremendous responsibilities in India, however much these might be neglected, while it raised in England the issue of the relation of the Company to the State. Clive had foreseen the difficulties of Company government and had offered to Pitt the solution, revived later by Warren Hastings, that the British Government should take over the Company's powers. Apart from the relatively small ceded territories, the triple province of Bengal was still technically within the Mogul Empire, and the Home Government refused

But the failure of the Company to face the problems of administration had meant scandalous misrule; the sight of a few commercial agents handling the wealth of a kingdom was scarcely edifying; and from 1766 onwards Parliamentary debates on India became frequent. Something had to be done, and the first action taken was to give the Company a Parliamentary title to their administration in India, and to bring that administration to some extent under ministerial supervision. India House became a buffer between Downing Street and India; and as Sir Courtenay Ilbert has pointed out,[1] the situation created in Bengal by the legislation of 1773 resembled what is now called a protectorate.

The Regulating Act of 1773 was the first experiment at establishing a British Government in India. The early steps were uncertain, many mistakes were to be made, but this innovation was to lead, through the successive stages of Pitt's legislation of 1784 and the Government of India Act of 1858, to Parliamentary democracy in 1935.

[1] *The Government of India*, 2nd Edn., p. 51.

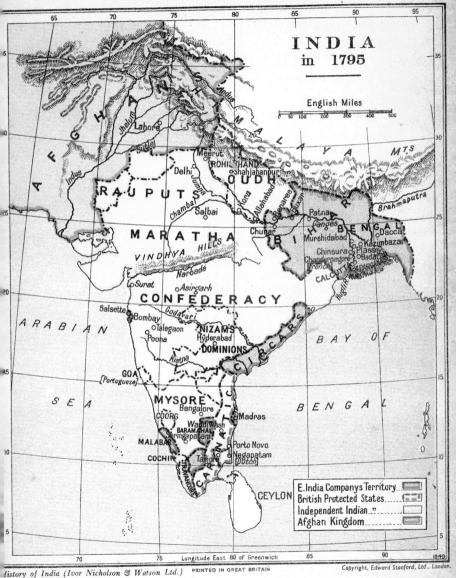

INDIA
in 1795

English Miles

| E. India Companys Territory |
| British Protected States |
| Independent Indian „ |
| Afghan Kingdom |

AFGHANISTAN

HIMALAYA MTS

Lahore

Jhelum

Sutlej

Indus

Meerut

Delhi

ROHILKHAND

Shahjahanpur

RAJPUTS

OUDH

Jumna

Chambal

Salbai

Banares

Allahabad

Buxar

Patna

Brahmaputra

MARATHA

HILLS

Chunar

Ganges

Murshidabad

BENGAL

Dacca

Kazimbazar

VINDHYA

Narbada

BIHAR

Chinsura

Plassey

Chandernagore

Badara

Asirgarh

Surat

CONFEDERACY

Godavari

Frenchng

CALCUTTA

Hughli R.

24 PARGANAS

Salsette

Bombay

Talegaon

Poona

NIZAMS

Hyderabad

DOMINIONS

Kistna

CIRCARS

BAY OF

GOA
[Portuguese]

MYSORE

Bangalore

COORG

Wandiwash

BARAMAHAL

Seringapatam

MALABAR

Madras

Porto Novo

COCHIN

Tanjore

Negapatam
[Dutch]

TRAVANCORE

CARNATIC

CEYLON

ARABIAN

SEA

BENGAL

History of India (Ivor Nicholson & Watson Ltd.)   PRINTED IN GREAT BRITAIN   Copyright, Edward Stanford, Ltd., London.

The transformation of the Company into an organized government was followed by another form of expansion. During the administration of Warren Hastings the struggle for supremacy between the British and the military powers of India began in earnest. Then step by step, from recognition as an equal by the great States to unquestioned superiority, the East India Company increased its dominion until at last all India came to be united under British sovereignty, either directly administered or through the Indian States with their acknowledgment of the paramount Power.

It is confidence in the stability of order, the gift of Great Britain to India, after the series of cataclysms making up her earlier history, which has created among the educated classes of British India in recent years a strong nationalistic feeling best described as political self-respect.

Warren Hastings, who had been second counsellor at Madras since 1769, took up his appointment as governor at Fort William in April 1772. General control was in the hands of the governor and a council of about a dozen members who reached their decisions by vote, and foreign policy was directed by the governor and a committee of two. For the collection of the revenue of Bengal, Orissa and Bihar together with the administration of the civil courts, the Deputy Finance Ministers, Muhammad Reza Khan at Murshidabad and Shilab Rai at Patna, were responsible, and they had under them an exclusively Indian staff of officials. English supervisors had been appointed in 1769 to inquire into the land settlement question and make a report; they had also to prepare a rent-roll which, in the circumstances, was too much to expect. The whole of the provincial administration was under the control of the government at Fort William.

The First Reforms.

The three Presidencies were then completely independent of one another; each was absolute within its own limits and responsible only to headquarters in London. The home administration consisted of the court of twenty-four Directors (who were appointed yearly) and the General Court of Proprietors which included all holders of £500 of Company stock.

The Directors had given Hastings "full powers to make a complete reformation," and he at once began to take measures on the lines laid down by the Directors. He abolished the office of Deputy Finance Minister, and Muhammad Reza Khan and Shilab Rai were tried, and acquitted, on charges of peculation. A Board of Revenue was set up in their place consisting of the governor and members of council; the supervisors became revenue collectors of districts, and the Treasury was moved from Murshidabad to Calcutta. The collectors presided over the civil courts in their districts, and Indian law officers sat in the criminal courts to explain the Muhammadan law, proceedings which were supervised by the district collectors.[1] Chief civil and criminal courts were established in Calcutta, which, in theory at least, derived their authority from the Mogul government in whose name the company administered the revenue.[2]

The dual system of government in Bengal was at an end. But the earliest attempt to collect the revenue, by farming out the estates to the highest bidder, was most unfortunate. This first effort of the Company to manage its revenue affairs resulted in the complete extinction of a skilled, though corrupt, collecting agency and the substitution of an untrained and foreign agency, appointed to collect a revenue that must be, by the very manner of its assessment, excessive.[3] As will be seen, reform, both by the Company and by the British Parliament, had to come by the method of " trial and error."

Hastings effectually stamped out the crying abuse of internal trade by the Company's servants and their local agents. By March 1775 he had abolished the fraudulent use of free trading passes and suppressed the local custom-houses. He substituted instead central custom-houses at Calcutta, Hooghly, Murshidabad, Patna

[1] Fifth Report . . . Select Committee of the House of Commons (pp. 95, 96 of Report as printed in *Early Revenue History of Bengal*).

[2] Fifth Report . . . Select Committee, p. 96 of *Early Revenue History of Bengal*, and Ilbert, *op. cit.*, pp. 43, 44.

[3] *Early Revenue History of Bengal*, pp. 31–33.

and Dacca, and he lowered the duties to $2\frac{1}{2}$ per cent. on all goods [1] (except the monopolies of salt, betel-nut and tobacco), to be paid by all Europeans and Indians alike.

The pay of the Company's senior servants in India had been by this time considerably increased. The governor of Bengal now received in salary and allowances £4800 a year, which, with the fluctuating commission on the revenues granted to him, raised his total pay in 1772–73 to £23,316. The counsellors drew from £342 to £386 in pay and allowances, together with commission which ranged in that year from £2687 for the senior member to £1194 for the remainder. The other servants of the Company drew no commission and their salaries descended from £81 for a senior merchant to £50 for a writer. Salaries for governors and counsellors in the other Presidencies and in Sumatra and St. Helena were considerably less. [2]

A matter which Hastings had to settle on taking over charge was the position of the young Nawab, Mubarik-ud-daula, who had just succeeded. The Nawabs of Bengal had become pensioners of the Company, the prince was a minor, and arrangements had to be made for the management of his affairs, which had been controlled by Muhammad Reza Khan until his dismissal. Hastings cut down the Civil List from thirty-two lakhs to sixteen, and selected as the Nawab's guardian, Manni Begam, the widow of Mir Jafar. To have appointed a woman was, in the East, distinctly unusual, and to have passed over the boy's mother for one who had been a court dancing-girl in early life undoubtedly needed justification. But the arguments in its favour put forward by Hastings satisfied his council, who agreed unanimously. [3] Moreover the Court of Directors approved and the charges levelled by Nuncomar and his English associates might be left without further reference were it not for the dimensions which Nuncomar's case was to assume. The reduction of the Nawab's pension was made by order of the Directors,

---

[1] *Memoirs of Warren Hastings*, Edn. 1841, Gleig, Vol. I. p. 304.
[2] Account of Salaries, etc., dated India House, 11th June 1773 (India Office Records).
[3] Gleig, *Memoirs of Warren Hastings*, Edn. 1841, Vol. I. pp. 269, 270.

but Hastings so reformed its administration that the Nawab actually received more than before for his personal use.[1]

Hastings had become governor " determined to introduce a regular system of protection into the country." It was badly needed. Bengal had been infested for centuries by an extraordinary people called the Sanyasis, hillmen from the Himalaya who roamed mostly naked as pilgrims through the country, were venerated by the Hindus, and kidnapped children wherever they went. In 1773 Hastings organized flying columns of Indian troops and drove the Sanyasis out of the country. But in spite of frontier guards they troubled the northern districts until the end of the century.[2] He also put down with effective severity the gangs of armed robbers who plagued Bengal.

In the same year he reorganized the manufacture and sale of the government monopolies of salt and opium, and for the greater part of a century his regulations were the basis of the system followed by the Government of India.

The tireless energy of Hastings during his governorship of Bengal also included the reform of the coinage by the introduction of what is known as the " sicca " rupee. The standard rupee of the Company was first issued about fifty years later.

Reports reached Calcutta in 1773 of the British Government's

Indian Law and Sanskrit Research. intention to give Fort William a High Court enforcing the penal code of England. Hastings received this news with the comment: " If the Lord Chief Justice and his judges should come amongst us with their institutes, the Lord have mercy upon us! . . . Is it not a contradiction of the common notions of equity and policy that the English gentlemen of Cumberland and Argyleshire should regulate the polity of a nation which they know only by the lacs which it has sent to Britain, and by the reduction which it has occasioned in their land-tax? "[3] His policy was to preserve the Indian laws and make improvements on this foundation.

[1] *Camb. Hist. of the British Empire*, Vol. IV. p. 210.
[2] Gleig, *op. cit.*, Vol. I. pp. 294, 298, 395.   [3] Gleig, *op. cit.*, Vol. I. p. 273.

He was convinced that to rule justly and sympathetically over the peoples of India it was essential to know their laws and customs. These had " continued unchanged from the remotest antiquity," as the Muhammadan government had " generally left their privileges untouched, and suffered the people to remain in quiet possession of institutes which time and religion had rendered familiar to their understandings and sacred to their affections." It would be, he maintained, " a wanton tyranny to require their obedience to (laws) of which they are wholly ignorant " and could not possibly acquire a knowledge. In order that English administrators should know what these Indian laws were, he had, on his appointment as governor, begun, through a body of Indian professors, the translation of the Code of Manu from Sanskrit first into Persian, which he knew well himself, and then into English.[1] This new learning, the knowledge of Sanskrit, was to open to English, French and German scholars the immense wealth of ancient culture enshrined in Hindu literature which had never even been suspected in the West. In 1781 Hastings instituted the Muhammadan College of Calcutta; and later helped Sir William Jones to found the Asiatic Society of Bengal.

The keystone of the foreign policy of Fort William was the maintenance of the kingdom of Oudh as a guard *Foreign Policy.* to the western frontier of Bengal. Shah Alam had come to terms with the Marathas in 1771 and Hastings, with the concurrence of his council and the approval of the Directors, decided to stop the imperial tribute of twenty-six lakhs, and to restore the Allahabad districts to Shuja-ud-daula of Oudh on payment of fifty lakhs. For the Emperor by his move to Delhi had become completely dependent upon the Company's enemies, the Marathas, then a menace to every State in India outside the Punjab. The confederacy under the Peshwa still existed, but it had become more loosely knit, for the different Maratha chiefs were beginning to found separate rulerships.

[1] Gleig, *op. cit.,* Vol. I. pp. 299–304. *Institutes of Menu,* Edn. 1825, Vol. II., gives the English translation by Sir C. Wilkins (who had previously translated the *Bhagavad Gita*) and Sir W. Jones.

Hastings came in contact with the Marathas when they demanded the return of the Allahabad districts to the Emperor (which would have exposed Bengal to attack) and reappeared on the borders of Rohilkhand in 1772 (which threatened the safety of Oudh). The Rohillas asked Oudh for help, Oudh called upon the English, and in 1772 and 1773 the allied forces drove off the Marathas, thanks in the latter year to the revolution in Poona following the death of the Peshwa Madhu Rao.[1]

The operations were straightforward, but the network of intrigue which surrounded them, springing from the desire of Shuja-ud-daula to annex Rohilkhand, eventually brought down a storm of obloquy upon Hastings. A treaty had been signed between Rohilkhand and Oudh, on the advice of the English general Sir Robert Barker, by which Shuja-ud-daula was to receive forty lakhs from the Rohillas when the Marathas retired " either by peace or war." But the Rohillas refused to pay on the grounds that renewed Maratha attack was still possible, and Shuja-ud-daula asked Hastings to lend him troops with which to seize Rohilkhand, offering to pay the Company forty lakhs and the expenses of the force employed. Influenced by the advantages of consolidating Oudh into " a complete compact State shut in effectually from foreign invasions by the Ganges," Hastings finally consented, and the combined forces invaded Rohilkhand in the spring of 1774. The Rohillas fought bravely but they were completely defeated, their leader Hafiz Rahmat Khan was killed, and the country was formally annexed to the kingdom of Oudh.

This action of Hastings is difficult to defend. The political advantage had been gained by an unprovoked aggression upon a State with whom the company had been on not unfriendly terms, and on other grounds the Rohilla war was even less justifiable. Hafiz Rahmat Khan was an admirable ruler, and under him and his brother chiefs it may fairly be said that the mass of the Hindu population were treated with greater consideration and received better protection than was the case in any of the neighbouring provinces excepting those in the

---

[1] *History of the Mahrattas*, Vol. II. pp. 3 *et seq.*

possession of Najib-ud-daula,[1] who was himself a Rohilla, in the Punjab.[2]

Parliamentary Legislation.

In the meanwhile Parliament had intervened in the affairs of the Company. A Committee of the House was appointed in 1766, and this led to a series of Acts regulating the voting at any company meeting and, in the case of the East India Company, the declaration of dividends; while the Company were required to pay an annual sum of £400,000 into the Treasury as the recognition by Parliament of their territorial gains.

These arrangements were based on the assumption that the Company, whose dividends had risen from 6 per cent. in 1766 to 11 per cent. in 1770, could well afford to pay a heavy tribute to the state. The very reverse was the case. The Company's servants might be returning to England with huge fortunes, but in 1772 after declaring a dividend of 12½ per cent. in March, the Directors were driven to confess to the ministry in July that nothing less than a loan of a million pounds could save them from immediate ruin. They were supporting an army of over 30,000 men and their campaigns, however successful, had been expensive, the bulk of the spoils had not been credited to the Company's account, tribute and pensions had to be paid, and a large proportion of the wealth which should have passed into the general exchequer had found its way into the pockets of the Company's servants. The total debt was estimated at more than six million sterling.

The Regulating Act.

Lord North's government took advantage of the situation to alter the Company's system of administration, and in 1773 Parliament passed two Acts, after violent opposition, by overwhelming majorities. One of these Acts met the financial embarrassments of the Company by a loan of £1,400,000 at 4 per cent. and suspended the annual pay-

---

[1] *Hastings and the Rohilla War*, Strachey (London), 1892. Sir John Strachey, however, strongly defends Hastings. Thornton (*op. cit.*, pp. 124, 125) is more critical, while Mill and Macaulay, in the words of Professor Dodwell " wasted a good deal of sentiment and falsified a good deal of history." But the facts were bad enough.

[2] Najib-ud-daula died in October 1770.

371

ment to the government, while it limited the dividend and enforced a half-yearly submission of the accounts to the Treasury. The other, and infinitely more important, was the Regulating Act. By this the Directors were to sit for four years, a quarter of their number being annually renewed, and the qualification for a vote in the court of proprietors was raised from £500 to £1000. But by far the most important clauses referred to administration in India. A governor-general and four counsellors were appointed for the Bengal Presidency, and not only was the government at Fort William given charge of the whole civil and military administration of Bengal, Bihar and Orissa, but it was given control over the presidencies of Madras, Bombay and the still surviving settlement of Bencoolen (Fort Marlborough) in Sumatra.

Warren Hastings was named in the Act as the first governor-general, with General Sir John Clavering, Colonel the Hon. George Monson, Richard Barwell and Philip Francis as his council. These appointments were for five years and their holders could only be removed by the king on the representation of the court of Directors, under whose direct orders the " Governor-general of Bengal in Council " remained. At the end of five years these appointments were to be vested in the Company. The government was under the court of Directors who, in their turn, had to submit to the Treasury all matters referring to the Company's revenue and transmit to a secretary of state all correspondence relating to the civil and military affairs of the country. The governor-general and council were empowered to make ordinances for the administration of the Company's possessions in India provided these did not traverse the laws of England, were registered by the supreme court established by the Act, and were not set aside by the King in Council.

By the Act a supreme court of judicature was established at Fort William, consisting of a chief justice and three other judges to be appointed by the Crown. The jurisdiction of the court extended to all British subjects in Bengal, Bihar and Orissa (with the exception of the governor-general and his council), and to the hearing of actions in which Indians living in the triple province were involved with British subjects.[1] Offences were to be tried by a jury of British residents in Calcutta, and there was the right of appeal to the privy council. The governor-general and council and the judges of the supreme court were to act as justices of the peace and hold quarter sessions. The clause dealing with civil cases between British subjects and " inhabitants " of the country was vague and, even more unfortunately, the relations between the council and the court were left undefined.

The governor-general was to have annually £25,000, the members of council £10,000, the chief justice £8000, and each puisne judge £6000. The other provisions of the Act forbade private trading by the Company's servants, or the acceptance of presents from any Asiatic, excepting professional fees earned by barristers, doctors, and chaplains.[2]

As Sir Courtenay Ilbert has commented[3]: " In 1773 the theory and the experience were lacking which are requisite for adopting English institutions to new and foreign circumstances. For want of such experience England was destined to lose her colonies in the Western hemisphere. For want of it mistakes were committed which imperilled the empire she was building up in the East. . . . (By the Regulating Act) the Company was vested with supreme administrative and military authority. The court was vested with supreme judicial authority. Which of the two authorities was to be paramount? . . . What law was the supreme court to administer? The Act was silent."

Nor was this all. With the boundaries between the executive and judicial powers left to be discovered by in-
The Council. cessant disputes, the chief executive authority at Calcutta lay in the hands of a majority in the council where the governor-general had merely a casting vote. There was no governing head to make instant decision on his own responsibility upon matters

[1] This authority apparently excluded by implication civil jurisdiction in suits by British subjects against " inhabitants " of the country, except by consent of the defendant. *Government of India,* Ilbert, p. 48.

[2] For fuller details of the Act see Ilbert, *op. cit.,* pp. 44–45.

[3] Ilbert, *op. cit.,* pp. 52, 53.

of emergency. Prompt action was impossible where opportunity presented itself for prolonged opposition to any controversial measure.

Given men of reasonable goodwill and moderation, this method of government, faulty though it was, might have worked with tolerable success. But goodwill, moderation, even reason itself were not to be found in the majority of the council. The selection of its members was hardly promising, with two royal favourites of no political capacity, an experienced but not particularly distinguished member of Hastings's former administration and an ambitious minor Whig politician.[1] Only one member, Barwell, had ever set foot in Bengal before his appointment.

Clavering was the type of man quite unfitted to be a general officer and was, if possible, even more unsuitable for councils of State. He was personally brave, but stupid, utterly tactless, quick to take offence and violently hot-tempered. Monson had sense, but he was blindly prejudiced and easily led. Barwell was a prosy official, none too scrupulous in his ways of making a fortune, but he had excellent judgment, was well up in the routine work of administration, and proud to be a steady supporter of the governor-general. The fourth member of council, Francis, after serving on a diplomatic mission to Portugal, had been chief clerk in the War Office. He was a sound classical scholar, and whether he was, as is generally believed, the author of the *Letters of Junius* or not, he appears to have been responsible for a series of political pamphlets which were published anonymously. In character he was unscrupulous, ambitious and bitter, and in the words of Macaulay, he mistook his malevolence for public virtue.

Hastings had been accustomed as governor of Bengal to carry his council with him. He was intolerant of opposition, even when it was honest, and he allowed no consideration of any kind to stand between him and the grasp of full personal power. And now the home government had weighted the dice against him. For two years he was consistently outvoted and over-ruled and, as he said himself, he had been invested with the powers of governor-general

[1] *Warren Hastings, Maker of British India*, A. Mervyn Davies, pp. 148, 149.

by Act of Parliament only to bear his share in the responsibility of measures of which he did not approve.[1]

On 19th October 1774 the three members of council from England landed at Calcutta, the four judges of the supreme court had arrived two days earlier, and the new form of government was established. Its faults were glaring, on the executive side with a governor-general who was powerless to govern, and with a judicial bench undefined in its scope and entirely ignorant of Indian conditions.

Within a week the council were at loggerheads over Hastings' foreign policy and the Rohilla war; and on the insistence of Francis this resulted in a reversal of the policy which had made Oudh a strong frontier State. By the Treaty of Faizabad Asaf-ud-daula, who had recently succeeded his father, was made to cede Benares and Ghazipur, his richest districts, and increase the subsidy paid monthly, as maintenance for the Company's troops, by 50,000 rupees. Oudh was unable with its reduced revenue to meet this expense and the government lapsed into a condition of chaos, which the future did nothing to remedy, and the attempts made by Hastings in 1783 did little to restore order in a country which was then almost without a government.[2]

It is unnecessary to detail the systematic opposition of the majority of the council to Hastings,[3] but from official criticism his opponents descended to charges affecting his personal honour. To such charges Francis was ready enough to listen, and in March 1775 he brought before the council the accusation made by Nuncomar that the governor-general was guilty of gross corruption, one of the charges being supported by a letter said to have been from Manni Begam offering a bribe to secure for her the guardianship of the young Nawab. The facts, as they subsequently emerged when Hastings was impeached, were these. Hastings, when on a visit to Mur-

Hastings and Nuncomar.

---

[1] Forrest, *Selections from the Letters . . . and other State Papers . . . in the Foreign Department of the Government of India, 1772–1785* (Calcutta), 1890, Vol. II. p. 279.

[2] *History of British India*, Thornton, p. 179.   [3] *Ibid.*, pp. 127–129.

shidabad, had accepted from the Nawab's treasury an entertainment allowance equal to £225 a day. In view of the Company's recent orders prohibiting the acceptance of presents, the transaction, as Sir James Stephen admits, " if not positively illegal was at least questionable." [1] But after a trial, lasting seven years, upon his whole administration in India, Hastings was unanimously acquitted upon this charge of corruption, the seventh article of his impeachment.

The majority of the council welcomed the charge against Hastings, and in June and July the case was heard by the judges of the supreme court sitting as magistrates, an unfortunate result of the Regulating Act. In the meantime Hastings, Barwell and Vansittart brought counter-charges of conspiracy against Nuncomar, and a Mr. Fowke who was not then in the Company's service. In the case of these counter-charges Fowke and Nuncomar were found guilty only as against Barwell. Fowke was fined fifty rupees, but no sentence was passed on Nuncomar, as by this time he was lying under sentence of death for forgery. The charges of corruption against Hastings were then dropped in India and the papers sent to England by the council, to be declared by the Company's law officers to be manifestly untrue.

This takes the story of Nuncomar to the point where the venom of Francis, the philippics of Burke and the rhetoric of Macaulay have created in the public mind the impression aptly described by Vincent Smith, that " the Indian Empire rests upon foundations stained by the blood of a judicial murder, planned and executed by the governor-general and the chief justice." It is this which brings Nuncomar's case from its place in the biographies of Hastings and Impey into the pages of history.

At a most opportune moment for Hastings a charge of forgery had been brought against Nuncomar by one Mohan Pershad, the executor of an Indian banker, after failure in a civil suit. The

---

[1] *The Story of Nuncomar and Impey*, Vol. I. p. 72. Sir James Fitzjames Stephen, K.C.S.I., sometime a judge of the High Court (Queen's Bench Division) and a personal friend of Macaulay, examines the whole case with minuteness. He is a strong supporter of Warren Hastings and of Impey, but, as might be expected, his attitude is judicial and his work has been followed to a considerable extent in this account of Nuncomar's case.

trial took place, from the 8th to the 16th of June, before the supreme court. The chief-justice was Elijah Impey who, after a distinguished career at Cambridge, was called to the bar and appointed the first chief-justice in India on the recommendation of Thurlow, then attorney-general. Of the three puisne judges who sat with him, Robert Chambers, a friend of Doctor Johnson and Vinerian Professor of Law at Oxford, had the greatest ability, but he was not a strong judge. Stephen Lemaitre seems to have been narrow-minded, arrogant and violent, and John Hyde was entirely under his influence. The case was tried before a jury of twelve Europeans and Anglo-Indians who found the prisoner guilty; and by the penal law of England to which the court held him to be amenable Nuncomar was sentenced to be hanged. Impey's summing-up [1] laid stress on the points in Nuncomar's favour, but two criticisms must be made on the procedure. The judges severely cross-examined the prisoner's witnesses on the inconclusive grounds that counsel for the prosecution was incompetent; and Impey, through lack of Indian experience, told the jury that if Nuncomar's defence was rebutted the fact condemned him, whereas this rule, as Stephen points out, cannot be applied in the East, where a perfectly good case, should proof be otherwise lacking, is frequently bolstered up by flagrant perjury.

The report of the trial [2] is in itself evidence, as Stephen maintains, that Nuncomar was not the victim of a judicial murder planned by Hastings and carried out by his friend the chief-justice. Sir Elijah Impey was completely exonerated when he was subsequently impeached. Hyde held his office till 1796 when he died, and Sir Robert Chambers afterwards became chief-justice, but no charge whatever was brought against either of them; Lemaitre had died in 1777. The whole bench of judges would have had to be party to the crime and, as Pitt summed up the matter,[3] " the accusation of a conspiracy between Impey and Hastings for the purpose of destroying Nandakumar is destitute of any shadow of proof."

---

[1] Quoted in full by Stephen, *op. cit.*, Vol. I. pp. 139-170.
[2] *State Trials*, Hansard (London), Vol. XX., 1816, 923-1078.
[3] Stephen, *op. cit.*, Vol. II. p. 88.

There can be no doubt, however, that the infliction of the death penalty was so severe as to amount to a miscarriage of justice. Nuncomar was, by the irony of fate, a victim to what Hastings had feared would be the inevitable result of imposing upon India the English law of that day by a court ignorant of the country. By English law there were then no less than two hundred capital offences, and forgery was punishable with death up to 1832. It was looked upon by Indians at that time as a mere misdemeanour, and this was the first instance,[1] and inflicted upon an old man and a Brahman, in which the death sentence had ever been carried out in India for forgery. The governor-general took no steps to reprieve his admitted enemy; and Clavering, Monson and Francis, who had it in their power to save the life of the man they had used as a pawn against Hastings, contemptuously rejected his petition.

The Supreme Court. The clauses of the Regulating Act and of the Charter establishing the supreme court were so vague that collision between the court and the council was inevitable. In their care to avoid proclaiming the King of England sovereign in Bengal, the framers of the Act had established two independent powers and had omitted to define the limits of either. It was impossible to say who really were British subjects, and therefore under the jurisdiction of the court. As Stephen has said: " In one sense the whole population of Bengal, Bihar and Orissa were British subjects. In another sense no one was a British subject who was not an Englishman born. In a third sense, inhabitants of Calcutta might be regarded as British subjects, though the general population of Bengal were not." The jurisdiction of the court over the provincial councils and the landholders was equally undefined. Opposed by the majority of his council, the attempt made by Hastings in 1776 to amalgamate the supreme and the Company's courts ended in failure, and the two authorities drifted into a conflict which reached its height in the Patna case of 1777–79 and the Kasijora case of 1779–80.

In the Patna case the supreme court claimed jurisdiction over

[1] Thornton, *op. cit.*, p. 130.

a Muhammadan revenue farmer for an act done in his official capacity, and found that the local officers of the Company had allowed their functions to be usurped by the Muhammadan advisers on Moslem law and practice. Sir James Stephen makes the following comment on this case: " If the Patna council was a fair specimen of the rest, the provincial councils, considered as courts of justice, were absolutely worthless, and no system for the administration of justice which deserved the name, existed at that time out of Calcutta."[1] The supreme court cast the Muhammadan law officers of the Patna council in heavy damages, a decision which the Directors did not attempt to upset by an appeal to the privy council.

The Kasijora case hung upon the jurisdiction of the supreme court over everyone in the province, the landholders in particular. The court issued a writ against the Raja of Kasijora, the council advised him that he was not subject to the court and sent a detachment of their Indian troops to arrest the sheriff's officers and bring them back to Calcutta. In the opinion of Stephen the action of the council was, apart from the violence of their methods, quite illegal, but the case resulted in practically confining the jurisdiction of the supreme court to Calcutta.

In 1780 Hastings brought the deadlock to an end by offering Impey the presidency of the Company's chief civil court, over which the governor-general had up to this time been the nominal president. The advantage of this arrangement was practical. A real control of a judicial system, which had undoubtedly in the past oppressed the inhabitants of Bengal, was now exercised by a trained and expert judge. But it was open to the criticism that the chief-justice who had been sent out in the king's name to deal amongst other things with complaints against the Company's servants was now at the head of the Company's judicial system, which was largely staffed by those very servants. Impey, moreover, soon after his appointment began to draw a salary of 5000 rupees a month, revocable by the governor-general, in addition to his salary as chief-justice under the Regulating Act. The impression created in England was that Impey had compromised his dispute with the

[1] *Nuncomar and Impey*, Vol. II. p. 178.

council for money in defiance of the Regulating Act. The court of Directors (who had not been consulted) and the House of Commons petitioned the Crown for his recall to answer this charge, and Impey left India in 1783. His impeachment, on this and other charges, completely broke down when it was held four years later.

A Parliamentary inquiry on the administration of justice in Bengal in 1781 led to an amending Act which laid down that the supreme court should have no jurisdiction in matters of revenue and its collection; that no Indian should be liable to the court's jurisdiction simply as a landholder or a farmer of rents; and that the court had jurisdiction over all the inhabitants of Calcutta, Hindu or Muhammadan law being administered according to the religion of the defendant in cases of inheritance, contract and successions. Regulations for the provincial courts and councils made by the governor-general and council were to be subject only to the approval of the king in council.[1] The procedure of the supreme court had been, to quote the petition of the Fort William executive, " the control of a foreign law and the terrors of a new and usurped dominion," and the controversy had ended in a victory for the governor-general and council.

One more Act was passed by Parliament during the administration of Warren Hastings. Fox's India Bill of 1783, with its wholesale transfer of patronage from the Company to nominees of the crown, was defeated in the House of Lords, and Pitt, at the age of twenty-five, came into power after the general election of 1784. His India Act became law the same year.

Pitt's Act of 1784.

The Act put the Company in direct and permanent subordination to a body representing the British Government. A Board of Control was established, consisting of the Chancellor of the Exchequer, one of the secretaries of state and four other privy councillors, and these " Commissioners for the Affairs of India were empowered to control all . . . operations and concerns (relating) to the civil or military government or revenues of the British territorial possessions in the East Indies." A committee of secrecy consisting of not more

[1] *Government of India,* Ilbert, pp. 55–58.

than three Directors was formed to transmit any secret orders from the Board to India without informing the other Directors; and the control formerly exercised by the court of proprietors was abolished. In India the governor-general's council was reduced to three members, one of whom was to be the commander-in-chief of the Company's forces, with precedence next to the governor-general. The governor-general, governors, commander-in-chief and members of council were to be appointed by the court of Directors, but they could be removed from office either by the Crown or by the Directors. The power to make war, except in cases of aggression, was reserved to the court of Directors and the secret committee. In the internal administration promotion was to be as a rule by seniority, and writers and cadets were to be sent to India between the ages of fifteen and twenty-two. Pitt's Act, which established double government in India, though modified in details, remained substantially in force until 1858.[1]

The struggle between Hastings and his council ended in 1777.

Hastings in Control. Monson died in 1776 and Clavering in 1777. Wheler was at first inclined to side with Francis, and Sir Eyre Coote, who became commander-in-chief in 1779 in place of Clavering, proved to be a difficult colleague, but Hastings at last gained control in the council. His strength of character had carried him through, although in June 1777, two months before Clavering's death, Hastings had sent in his tentative resignation, which produced in the council " the convulsion of four days." [2] Finally he rid himself of Francis by a pistol-shot in a duel, and his chief enemy sailed for England in November 1780.

The Rohilla campaign was the only military operation for which

Foreign Policy. Hastings was directly responsible. But from 1776 until 1783 his government was engaged in hostilities, owing largely to the rash policy of the Bombay authorities and to the imprudence and incompetence of the governor and council at Madras. In spite of enemies at headquarters in London,

[1] *Government of India*, Ilbert, pp. 62–66.
[2] Hastings' description of Clavering's " governor-generalship of a day," *Gleig's Memoirs*, Vol. II. pp. 157–164.

opposition in his council, and ever-increasing financial difficulties which led to events most damaging to his reputation, Warren Hastings carried the government in India safely through one of the most dangerous crises in English history; and when he left the country the position of the Company was secure, although its ascendancy had still to be definitely established.

The main factor in Indian politics during the last quarter of the eighteenth century was the Maratha power, a power far too strong and united for any available English force to overthrow. Holding the centre of India the Marathas were in an interior position which enabled them to threaten any one of the three divided presidencies, to intrigue against the Company whenever they wished at Hyderabad and with Mysore, and to communicate with the French by their ports on the western seaboard. To the south lay the formidable State consolidated by Haidar Ali. As Sir Alfred Lyall has pointed out, the balance of power in India then rested upon a triangular equipoise between the Company, the Marathas and Mysore.

The chief actors during this critical period, apart from Hastings himself, were Raghunath Rao (Raghoba), uncle of the Peshwa Madhu Rao, who had died in 1772; Nana Farnavis who by 1778 had secured control at Poona[1]; Mahadji Sindia, guardian of the Emperor and ultimately the dominating Maratha prince until his death in 1794; and Haidar Ali of Mysore. Raghunath Rao, on whose behalf Madhu Rao's successor Narayan Rao had been murdered, was a claimant to the Peshwaship, and the Bombay government, with the object of enlarging their territory and obtaining political ascendancy at Poona, made a covenant with him by which it was agreed that Bassein, Salsette and the islands of Bombay harbour should be ceded to the Company in return for Raghunath's restoration at Poona by English troops.

This treaty led to what is known as the first Maratha war, which the Calcutta government severely condemned. *The Maratha War.* But hostilities had already begun with the seizure of Salsette at the end of 1774. The Bombay forces were commanded by Colonel Keating, who fought a battle at

[1] *History of the Mahrattas*, Vol. II. Ch. XXVIII.

Aras (Adas, in the Gujerat district) in May 1775, at the cost of heavy casualties. The operations were brought to an end on the intervention of the Calcutta government, by the Treaty of Purandhar in March 1776,[1] a treaty which never became effective, as Salsette and Bassein were held by the English while the Marathas refused to cede them.

In 1777 the English authorities were alarmed by the appearance of a French adventurer, St. Lubin,[2] who in his supposed character of envoy from France, with proposals of a Maratha alliance, was ostentatiously received by Nana Farnavis. The Bombay government at once formed a new alliance with Raghunath Rao, and Hastings seeing the vital importance of supporting the Company's cause on the Malabar coast sent a column of 6000 Indian troops across India to the Bombay presidency, in the teeth of violent opposition in his council. These reinforcements, after an unconscionable delay in Bundelkhand under Leslie, were to move from the far side of the Narbada none too soon under a new and energetic commander, Goddard.

The Bombay government had already opened their campaign in November 1778 " by desperately sending a handful of men against the strength of the Maratha Empire," to quote Grant Duff's mildest criticism. These operations were entrusted to a committee of the commanding officer, the civil commissioner Carnac,[3] who actually took charge, and another civilian. The force of 600 Europeans and 3300 Indian troops was further encumbered by a baggage train of 19,000 bullocks, and moved on an average of two miles a day. At the beginning of January 1779 Colonel Cockburn's [4] nominal command, when twenty miles from Poona, was met by a Maratha army of 50,000 men. Carnac lost his head and refused to listen to Cockburn's advice, threw the heavy guns into a tank,

---

[1] See *History of the Mahrattas*, Vol. II. pp. 29–61.

[2] *Ibid.*, Vol. II. pp. 70 and footnote, 71, 72 and footnote, 73, 76, 79.

[3] Carnac had held a commission as colonel in Bengal, but Grant Duff invariably refers to him as Mr. Carnac.

[4] Colonel Egerton, the original commander, had resigned early in the advance owing to sickness, " in which," according to Thornton, " the army probably suffered no loss."

burnt the stores and began an immediate retreat. Two days later, on the 13th January, at Wadegaon, the situation of the column was hopeless and the secretary to the committee was sent to negotiate terms with Nana Farnavis and with Sindia, who was in command of the Maratha army. By this convention all acquisitions of territory made by the Bombay government since 1773 were to be restored to the Marathas, Sindia was to receive the English share of the Broach revenue, and two English hostages were surrendered as security for the carrying out of the terms. Raghunath Rao relieved the committee of the additional disgrace of handing him over to the Marathas by taking refuge with Sindia and personally making the best terms he could get. Sindia secured him a *jagir*, and the Bombay government ultimately allowed him a pension, but after Wadegaon Raghunath Rao disappears from history.

Hastings at once repudiated the convention of Wadegaon, and the Directors in due course dismissed the officers directly responsible for it, but the expedition had been doomed from the start.

Colonel Goddard had crossed the Narbada on 2nd December 1778, and on 26th February 1779 he was at Surat, having covered the last 300 miles in 20 days. His appearance had the best possible effect that circumstances would allow and, on reaching Bombay, he was appointed commander-in-chief. During his advance he had made a firm and valuable alliance with Fateh Singh, the Gaekwar of Baroda. But his negotiations with Sindia and the operations which followed were alike inconclusive.

The history of the English in India now reaches a most critical stage. War had broken out in 1778 between Great *Second Mysore War.* Britain and France on the French recognition of the independence of the American colonies, and the Company began to capture the French possessions in India. Orders were issued from Calcutta to seize the port of Mahé, a likely channel of communication between the French and Mysore, but Haidar Ali objected, maintaining that its inhabitants were his subjects. Taking advantage of Haidar Ali's preoccupation in picking off some outlying Maratha districts, an English detachment took Mahé in March 1779. Haidar Ali made peace with the Marathas, forced the

PLATE XLIX.

FORT WILLIAM, CALCUTTA

From an early eighteenth-century print

By permission of the Secretary of State for India in Council

PLATE L.

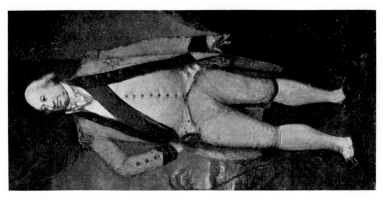

(b) TIPU SULTAN
By permission of the Secretary of State for
India in Council

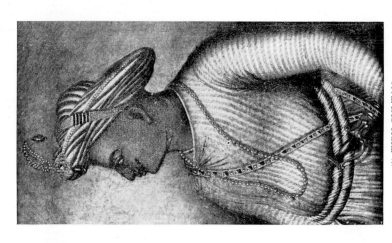

(c) LORD CORNWALLIS
By permission of the Secretary of State for
India in Council

(a) WARREN HASTINGS
Artist unknown
By courtesy of M. G. Dashwood, Esq.

Nizam into a triple alliance against the English and in July 1780 descended upon the plains of the Carnatic with an army of about 70,000 men and a French detachment of 400 from Mauritius. The country was plundered, Sir Hector Munro's force of 8000, which he handled indifferently, was handicapped by want of money, supplies and transport, and on 10th September Colonel Baillie, on the march to join Munro, after a gallant fight, met with overwhelming disaster near Conjeeveram. Munro instead of marching to the sound of the guns retired on Madras, and the place might then easily have fallen if Haidar Ali had attacked it in force.

Hastings rose to the situation with characteristic energy and courage although his treasury was exhausted and his military strength overstrained. His diversion in Central India a month earlier had resulted in the brilliant feat of arms achieved by Captain Popham who took Sindia's stronghold of Gwalior in August (1780) by a night escalade, which raised English prestige enormously. The governor-general at once sent Sir Eyre Coote with 600 European troops and fifteen lakhs of rupees by sea to Madras and despatched a strong force of Indian troops overland. He also succeeded in coming to an understanding with Sindia who agreed, at a price, to mediate between the English and the Maratha government. Sir Eyre Coote began his campaign against Haidar Ali, and won a considerable victory at Porto Novo on 1st July 1781, which he followed up by two more successful actions before the end of September. But Coote was unable to drive the Mysore army out of the Carnatic.

In February 1782 the French admiral Suffren appeared off the Coromandel coast and landed 2000 troops. He was *The French Expedition.* a commander of great ability and always ready to attack his enemy, while his British opponent, Sir Edward Hughes, made up for his lesser skill as a tactician and his slight inferiority in numbers by the superior seamanship and better support of his captains. The Dutch had been drawn into the world war and their Indian settlements as well as those of the French had fallen to the Company. For the first six months Suffren had no harbour nearer than the Isle of France where he could refit after action; and the open roadsteads of the Coromandel coast had to

2 B

answer while he lived off his enemy. In August he took Trincomalee in Ceylon (a late Dutch possession) and until the war came to an end Suffren and Hughes met in their hard-fought actions without any decisive result.[1] In 1783 after peace was declared between Great Britain and France the French admiral sailed back to Europe, to meet with a most cordial reception from a number of Hughes's captains whom he found at the Cape. The French king created a special vice-admiralship for Suffren, to lapse at his death, in demonstration of a gratitude not invariably shown to commanders and administrators, either English or French, when they returned from India after giving of their best for their country.

During 1782 the war on land went none too well for the Company. The year had started badly by the almost complete annihilation in Tanjore of a force of 2000 men under Colonel Braithwaite who was surprised by Tipu Sultan, the son of Haidar Ali. But at the end of the year this disaster was more than counterbalanced by the successful negotiations made by Hastings through Sindia to come to terms with the Marathas; and the treaty of Salbai was ratified by Nana Farnavis on 20th February 1783. Amongst the clauses Salsette was recognized as belonging to the Company. But the importance of this treaty lay in the fact that it placed the political relations of the English and the Marathas on a new and definite footing. " It secured peace with the Marathas for twenty years, and without the acquisition of any fresh territory it established beyond dispute the dominance of the British as a controlling factor in Indian politics, their subsequent rise in 1818 to the position of the paramount power being an inevitable result of the position gained by the treaty of Salbai." [2]

Haidar Ali died on 7th December 1782. He had seen the Nizam detached by Hastings from the confederacy in 1780 and he lived to see the certainty of peace between the English and the Marathas. Before his death he had a remarkable conversation with his minister in which he said: "Between the English and me there were perhaps

---

[1] See *Influence of Sea Power upon History*, Mahan, pp. 427–467.
[2] *Camb. Hist. of the British Empire*, Vol. IV. p. 271. For details of the Treaty see *History of the Mahrattas*, Vol. II. pp. 146, 147.

mutual grounds of dissatisfaction but not sufficient cause for war, and I might have made them my friends. . . . The defeat of many Braithwaites and Baillies will not destroy them. I can ruin their resources by land but I cannot dry up the sea, and I must be first weary of a war in which I can gain nothing by fighting." Thornton estimates his character in the phrase " his ruffian life." Illiterate, brutal and irreligious Haidar Ali unquestionably was, and had he not been utterly unscrupulous his adventurous and successful career for all his natural ability would have been impossible.

After the treaty of Salbai and the death of his father, Tipu Sultan continued the war with the English supported by a strong contingent of French troops under de Bussy, who reached India in April 1783. Tipu, a bold and energetic commander, and de Bussy, old and worn out though he was, were more than a match for the incompetent Stuart who had succeeded to the command after Sir Eyre Coote's death early in 1783. But before a decision was reached the news of peace between Great Britain and France reached India in July of that year.

Tipu's operations had met with considerable success, but he was now without an ally, his resources were almost exhausted, his capital was menaced by Colonel Fullarton, and the Marathas were threatening to attack him. But his good fortune did not fail him here. Lord Macartney, the governor at Madras, was anxious to make peace at any price, and the negotiations which were opened were entirely influenced " by the arrogance and insolence of Tipu Sultan . . . encouraged by the timid subservience of the Madras government." [1] By the terms of the treaty of Mangalore, which ended the long hostilities on 11th March 1784, all conquests on either side were restored, and the surviving prisoners of war held by Tipu Sultan, amounting to more than 2600, including about 1100 European officers and men, were to be released. In spite of orders from Fort William no reference was made in the articles to the treaty of Salbai, but Hastings was most reluctantly obliged to ratify the treaty made at Mangalore.

[1] *History of the British Empire in India*, Thornton, p. 171.

That the English dominion emerged from this prolonged struggle uninjured, though not unshaken, is a result due to the political fearlessness of Warren Hastings. The difficulties which the governor-general had to face apart from the anxieties of the war itself were almost endless. Even after the death of Clavering his own council were not invariably helpful; the two junior presidency governments showed their jealousy of the control of Bengal by frequent and injurious acts of insubordination; the Madras council was supine, and torn by internal dissensions, while "corruption revelled unrestrained." [1] To this there was added the ever-pressing necessity of finding money from a treasury drained by the campaigns against the Marathas to prosecute the war after the outbreak of hostilities with France, against the hostile combination in Southern India. Money was desperately needed in 1778, Hastings was not willing to float a loan, the modern procedure in such circumstances, and he decided to resort to the Mogul method of raising money in cases of emergency —by demand.

His choice of a subject fell on the Raja of Benares, Chait Singh,
Chait Singh. whose tenure and measure of independence as regards the Company was not clearly defined. Hastings felt himself justified in demanding from him a special sum of five lakhs of rupees (over £50,000) in addition to his regular tribute of £225,000, assuming him definitely to be a tributary landholder. The council, eventually including Francis, concurred. Similar sums were demanded in the two following years. Chait Singh delayed payment, and also made difficulties about furnishing 1000 horse which Sir Eyre Coote wanted for the defence of Bihar. Hastings had every reason to believe that Chait Singh had ample resources to meet these demands, though he had much less reason to assume that the Raja was in secret communication with the Marathas.

He resolved to act as if Chait Singh was "a tributary landholder," [2] announced his intention of levying a fine of forty or fifty lakhs, and set off in July 1781 with a weak escort to Benares, which was, and is,

---

[1] Thornton, *op. cit.*, p. 161.
[2] *Warren Hastings, Maker of British India*, pp. 294-297.

the heart of Hinduism and a place of pilgrimage for Hindus from every part of India. When he reached Benares Hastings placed Chait Singh under arrest. The populace rose and massacred a company of the Indian escort with their officers. Chait Singh escaped to his army, now in rebellion against the treatment he had received, and Hastings, who showed the greatest coolness in a highly dangerous situation, found his way to Chunar, concentrated his available forces and drove Chait Singh into exile in Gwalior. The Raja's dominions were sequestrated and given to a nephew, whose annual tribute was raised to £400,000.

The point raised at the impeachment of Hastings was that the Company had, in 1775, definitely bound itself to levy no contribution beyond Chait Singh's tribute of £225,000; and there was the further aggravation that Hastings, after refusing a personal present of £20,000 from the Raja, took the money a few days later to equip an expedition against Sindia, and then went on to attempt to levy the fine of £500,000. But the House of Lords acquitted him by a majority of twenty-three to six on the charge relating to Chait Singh.

Hastings had still to find the money he so urgently needed, and he now turned to Oudh, whose Nawab, Asaf-ud-daula, owed the Company a considerable sum for arrears of subsidy. The Nawab's mother and grandmother, the princesses of Oudh, had inherited from the late ruler Shuja-ud-daula estates and treasure estimated at about two million pounds. Asaf-ud-daula maintained that under Muhammadan law the princesses had no right to so large a proportion of this property and that, while the bulk should have come to him, part of it should have been used to satisfy the Company's claim. On the other hand, in 1775, the widow of Shuja-ud-daula had been induced by the Company's resident to pay her son £300,000 in addition to £250,000 he had already received, on condition that he and the Company guaranteed that no further demand should ever be made upon her. That guarantee was given.[1] But when Asaf-ud-daula at the end of 1781 asked permission to seize the fortune of the princesses,

The Begams of Oudh.

---

[1] *Camb. Hist. of the British Empire*, Vol. IV. p. 300.

Hastings, in the government's desperate straits for money, withdrew the Company's protection from the Begams and instructed the resident Middleton " not (to) allow any negotiations or forbearance . . . until the Begams are at the entire mercy of the Nawab." [1] Hastings was convinced that the Oudh princesses had aided Chait Singh in the Benares affair and he was determined to show no mercy to the " old women . . . who had very nigh effected our destruction." The Nawab himself was more reluctant, but in December 1782 the Begams' treasury officers, under pressure, paid over large sums of money.

These are the chief financial dealings of Hastings with Indian rulers which were brought up at his impeachment. Taking his whole administration the evidence was enough to warrant Pitt and Dundas in their decision to bring Hastings to trial, and the charges look their blackest if the attendant circumstances with which the governor-general had to grapple are not taken into account. But as Sir Alfred Lyall has said, "Allowance must be made for a perilous situation in a distant land [England was six months' distance away by sea], and for the weight of enormous national interests committed to the charge of the one man capable of sustaining them." When the storm had blown over in India and he had piloted his vessel into calm water he was sacrificed with little or no hesitation to party exigencies in England.[2] Burke called Hastings a " spider of hell," and no incident was thought too small if it could be twisted into an accusation against him.

In February 1785, Hastings, whose terms of office had been extended, left India to face the cumbersome and prolonged trial which ended in his acquittal on every count by large majorities. He had come home with £80,000,[3] and his impeachment cost him little short of a hundred thousand, but the Company were as generous as the government of the day would allow. Amidst a circle of devoted friends he lived on, quietly and happily, for more than twenty years

---

[1] *Selections from the . . . State Papers in the Foreign Department of the Government of India*, Forrest, Vol. III. p. 969.

[2] *Rise of the British Dominion in India*, pp. 177, 178.

[3] *Warren Hastings, Maker of British India*, p. 511.

in the house of his ancestors at Daylesford which he had bought back in 1789.

Pending the appointment of a successor to Hastings the senior member of council, John Macpherson, took charge. His experiences even for those days of adventurers had been extensive and peculiar. He had arrived in India as a ship's purser and became secretary to the Nawab of the Carnatic, whose rule was corruption personified, by showing Muhammad Ali a magic lantern and some electrical experiments.[1] The subsequent gratitude of the Nawab secured Macpherson a writership in the Madras government, from which he was soon dismissed for irregularities. Within four years he re-appeared from England, as a member of the Bengal council in succession to Barwell. Macpherson was undoubtedly very able, and he seems to have made advantageous reforms during the twenty months of his administration.[2] But he appears to have fully deserved the intense distrust he inspired at Fort William, and his eventual retirement, with a knighthood, marks the end of the old and evil period in Bengal.

Earl Cornwallis landed in India in September 1786. He had made it a condition of his appointment that he should be empowered to override his council in *Lord Cornwallis.* special cases, and this was embodied in an Act passed in 1786, which enabled him to hold, in addition, the office of commander-in-chief. His powers were again extended in 1791.

Cornwallis was the first of the great dynasty of governors-general to be appointed from England; and with very few exceptions the highest post in India was now closed to the covenanted servants of the Company. The peers selected for the appointment had naturally more weight with the home authorities than was possible to members of the civil service in India and they had the advantage of a wider political experience. Yet none of them proved to be a greater ruler than Warren Hastings.

The chief merchant president of a chartered company had been

---

[1] *Camb. Hist. of the British Empire*, Vol. IV. p. 278.
[2] Thornton, *History of the British Empire in India*, 2nd Edn., p. 187.

exchanged for a senatorial proconsul and Cornwallis came to India with clearly defined and supreme authority over all three presidencies. In the subordinate presidencies of Madras and Bombay, the governors were also selected in England, " among persons of eminence . . . rather than among the servants of the Company " to quote Canning when at the Board of Control. But in point of fact only second-rate men were as a rule willing to accept second-rate posts, and Lord William Bentinck is the only man of real eminence who can be named among them.[1]

Cornwallis had been charged by Parliament to follow a pacific policy and the ministry expected him to concentrate on the reform of the land revenue system, the general administration and the judiciary. But, by the force of circumstances, it was under the first two Parliamentary governors-general, Cornwallis and Wellesley, between 1786 and 1805, that the greatest expansion of British terri-tory in India took place, until the time of Lord Dalhousie more than a generation later ; and under Lord Hastings (1813–23) the treaty map of India was drawn very much as it is today.

The reform of the revenue administration in Bengal was the first matter taken up by Cornwallis. Indian governments have from the earliest times exercised their right to demand a considerable share of the gross produce of the soil, and even today, with such sources as customs, excise and other receipts, land revenue provides 15 per cent. of the total revenue of British India,[2] and the proportion was in earlier times as high as three-quarters of the revenue. Successive governments in India found it convenient to employ a middleman to collect this revenue, known as a *zamindar*. The word *zamindar* has no exact English equivalent, as landholder needs qualification. He succeeded by inheritance, subject to a renewal of title from his sovereign, and the payment of what amounted to succession duty. Under Mogul administration he was not only normally the annual contractor for the public revenue due from his land, but he was

[1] *Camb. Hist. of the British Empire*, Vol. IV. pp. 320, 321.
[2] *Moral and Material Progress of India* (1930–1931), H.M. Stationery Office (1932).

responsible for law and order to the extent of handing over law-breaking tenants to a Muhammadan magistrate for trial and punishment. In Akbar's time he received a commission of about $2\frac{1}{2}$ per cent., as farmer of the taxes, for collecting the revenue. This is the origin of the landlord's rent levied in most parts of India, where freehold tenure (except in Malabar) is extremely rare.

With a system so universally recognized, the English Company, on taking over charge of territory, found the peasants prepared to pay a high proportion of their gross produce in land revenue.[1] But they found great variety in the methods of assessment of land which ranged from immense estates with thousands of tenants down to small peasant holdings well under an acre in size. In the latter case the tenure is called *ryotwari*. At the present day a periodical re-assessment of land values for the purpose of taxation is made throughout the whole of British India, except in Bengal and Bihar and Orissa where the revenue to be paid by each *zamindar* was fixed "in perpetuity" by Lord Cornwallis. A little less than one-half of the area is in the hands of *zamindars*, and these hold their title, however dubious some of the original claims may have been, from the Government of India. The *zamindari* system prevails in Northern India and the *ryotwari* system, speaking generally, in the south.

The earliest problem, which the Company's first attempts, made in Bengal, failed to solve, was to ensure that the assessment was not so high as to throw the land out of cultivation. By the middle of the nineteenth century the great increase in the population created the problem of keeping rents down to a level which would leave the cultivator, who was ready (on such occasions as land might come into the market) to bid extremely high for a holding, sufficient margin on which to live and if possible raise his standard of living.[2] It may here be said that the tendency in the Indian States has been to follow, with considerable caution, the policy of British land administration. Standards of land revenue in

---

[1] W. H. Moreland in Ch. X. of *Modern India*, 2nd Edn., ed. by Sir John Cumming, p. 154, states that in the Moslem period "the ordinary standards ranged between $\frac{1}{3}$ and $\frac{1}{2}$, with a definite tendency in favour of the higher figure."

[2] *Modern India*, pp. 158, 159.

the States have been lowered, but not to the same extent; there has been some reluctance to make binding engagements for so long a period as thirty years; and there has been a definite preference for the " landholder " system.[1]

The Permanent Settlement of Bengal made by Lord Cornwallis has been the subject of lively difference of opinion since the time of the controversy between his chief advisers John Shore (afterwards Lord Teignmouth) and Charles Grant, keeper of the records. Shore maintained that the " rents belonged to the sovereign; the land to the *zamindar*"; while Grant argued that the latter was merely a temporary official and that the right of property in land vested absolutely in the State.[2] The first step taken was to reconstitute the committee of revenue as a board of control over districts administered by collectors who assessed and received the land revenue. The creation of compact districts was the backbone of this reform and was in fact the revival of Akbar's system. This ended centralization of the land revenue administration, with the collectors as mere figure-heads— the fluctuating policy since 1773 which had been strongly disliked by the Directors.

The court of Directors were under the impression that the investigations already made were sufficient for a clear-cut settlement. But Cornwallis found it necessary, in 1787 and 1788, to make annual settlements of the revenue before issuing the more decisive regulations early in 1790, of a ten-year settlement in Bihar and Bengal. This settlement was made final and permanent in 1793 by the approval of the court of Directors and the Board of Control. It confirmed the *zamindars* in the tenure of what was looked upon as their own land, and gave them great and undefined powers which, incidentally, swept away the rights of a large number of sub-tenants and cultivators.

But there is another criticism which the settlement has provoked. Under earlier Indian law a *zamindar* who failed to pay his share of the revenue had been subject to personal pains and

[1] *Modern India*, Ch. X. p. 162.
[2] *Early Revenue History of Bengal*, Chs. V. and VI. This account given above of the land question is chiefly based on Ascoli's work and on the Fifth Report, Cmd. H. of C. 28th July 1812, pp. 1–166.

penalties, but he had not been liable to lose for ever his interest in his property by enforced sale because his agent was late in paying the money due to government. The regulations brought in by Cornwallis authorized forced sales and attachment for default of payment. This caused far more distress to the *zamindars* than the older penalties which the governor-general had abolished, in the belief that he was bettering their conditions and establishing in India a society similar to the landed families of England and Scotland. In order to keep up the level of land revenue, a large number of estates were broken up and sold to recover outstanding balances, and " some of the oldest and most respectable families in the country . . . (were) threatened with poverty and ruin." [1] The auction purchasers of the land under these enforced sales were, as might be expected, greedy speculators utterly regardless of any rights which sub-tenants and cultivators might possess.

The effect of this was most unfortunate, and Vincent Smith, who had considerable experience as a United Provinces district officer, has recorded his opinion that " the effect on the countryside was then disastrous and probably is still felt. A family which has lost its legal rights by an auction sale always regards the transaction as unjust, and usually becomes the centre of agrarian disturbance, frequently resulting in murder." [2]

The Fifth Report of the Select Committee of the House of Commons mentions " the extravagance and mismanagement of some of the principal *zamindars* and a great proportion of the landholders " as a cause of their ruin. [3] But an additional reason was undoubtedly the " no rent " attitude taken up by a demoralized tenantry during Lord Wellesley's administration, and in 1799 a regrettable intro- duction of English law was made to remedy this by giving the *zamindars* the power of distraint.

Had the settlement been considered as an experimental arrange- ment, the policy strongly advised by Shore, all these results could

[1] Fifth Report, as reprinted in the more accessible *Early Revenue History of Bengal*, pp. 213, 214, 218, 219.

[2] *Oxford History of India*, p. 567. First published 1919.

[3] Fifth Report, as given in *Early Revenue History of Bengal*, pp. 216, 217. The Report was published in 1812.

have been remedied before the permanent settlement became regarded as irrevocable.[1]

Code of 1793. In 1793 Cornwallis issued his Code, which covered far more than the permanent settlement, for in addition it dealt with civil and criminal justice, with the police and with commerce. Although it was to be modified in later years this code was the foundation of all subsequent British administration in Bengal.

By these regulations the offices of judge and collector [2] were separated, and a judge was appointed to preside over each district court, responsible for all civil cases. Courts of appeal were established like the criminal courts at Patna, Dacca, Murshidabad and Calcutta. The Muhammadan criminal law, in a slightly modified and less drastic form, was followed, for as yet no penal code had been introduced.

The courts, under the reforms of Lord Cornwallis, and based on the practical proposals drawn up by Sir Elijah Impey, were, however, far too few, and " the accumulation of causes on the judges' file . . . threatened to put a stop to the course of justice. In (Burdwan in February 1795) the number on the file was said to be thirty thousand, and the probability of decision to any suit, estimated to exceed the ordinary duration of human life." [3] Over each of these provincial courts were three English judges, who also presided over the criminal courts at these four towns. The supreme court, sitting as the chief civil court of justice, was the highest appeal court in India.

Commerce. The collectors were given a salary of 1500 rupees a month and the European assistants 500, 400 and 300 rupees respectively, the collectors in addition receiving rather less than one per cent. commission on the revenue collected. All direct and indirect trading by collectors had been forbidden by the directors in 1787. Trade was now to be conducted by the Company's commercial residents, who arranged the prices with the manufacturers, made the necessary advances and supervised the

[1] *Early Revenue History of Bengal*, p. 70.
[2] Called Deputy Commissioner in Upper India.
[3] Fifth Report quoting letter to the Board of Revenue from the Collector of Burdwan in 1795 (*Early Revenue History of Bengal*, p. 230).

carrying out of the work, being paid for their services on a commission basis. Cornwallis held the commercial residents responsible that Indians who supported themselves by weaving were not oppressed, and that the local and foreign traders received just treatment. This was an admirable reform, and lasted as long as the Company remained a trading body.

The Company's trade monopoly was not abolished until 1813, its existence as a commercial body did not end until 1833, but by the time of Cornwallis there had grown up, under the protection of the Company, a small body of free European merchants who held the Company's licence, but only for export trading. These merchants were of considerable service to the country, as they financed the growing number of indigo planters, and were also able to take off the surplus produce not required by the Company and export it to the eastern markets. The increasing importance of the free merchants led to a strong demand for greater freedom of trade with England; and the Charter Act of 1793 introduced by Henry Dundas (Viscount Melville), Pitt's president of the board of control, recognized this private trade by binding the Company to allow three thousand tons of private cargo to be carried annually in their ships.[1]

When Cornwallis arrived in India the Company had become one of the first-class powers in the country, and was at

Political Situation. peace with the Indian States. The Marathas had just joined the Nizam of Hyderabad in an attack upon Mysore, but Cornwallis in accordance with the policy of non-aggression laid down by Act of Parliament refused to join the alliance. He saw, however, as clearly as did Tipu himself, that a collision between Mysore and the Company was only a question of time, and both took steps to strengthen their forces.

In the Punjab a new and formidable power had arisen. From persecuted followers of the reforming teacher Nanak,

The Sikh Confederacy. with no thought of political advancement, the Sikhs had grown into a strong, theocratic, feudal confederacy. There were twelve of these " Misals " or confederacies,

[1] *Trade Relations between England and India,* pp. 188–190.

under independent chiefs, the strongest being the Bhangis of Lahore and Amritsar, who could muster 20,000 men. The total field strength of the Sikhs was then at least 70,000, chiefly horsemen armed with matchlocks. Infantry were looked upon as fit only for garrison duty and artillery only gradually came into use.

Besides the regular confederacies there was a body of fanatics called Akalis, the " soldiers of God," who refused allegiance to any earthly governor, and peculiarly represented the religious element of Sikhism. The Sikhs have a strong feeling that everyone should work, and the Akalis combined abandonment of the world with fighting service, with duty as temple servants or with peaceful occupations for the benefit of the community at large. They inspired awe as well as respect, for they were prepared to plunder those who offended them or injured the commonwealth.[1]

The Sikhs had steadily gathered strength since 1752. In 1763 they heavily defeated the Afghan governor of the Punjab near Sirhind and took that province. A year later they were masters of Lahore. In 1767 the confederacies were united by the common danger which threatened from the invasion of India by Ahmad Shah, the last effort of the old and worn-out Durrani ruler to recover the Punjab. The attempt ended in failure and Ahmad Shah, unable to conquer the Sikhs, retired to Kabul after making Amar Singh of Patiala his military commander in Sind, with the title of Maharaja. In the following year the Sikhs took possession of the country as far north as Rawalpindi. Taimur Shah succeeded his father in 1773, and between 1777 and 1779 tried, and failed, to subdue the Punjab. A Mogul expedition sent up against the Sikhs from Delhi in 1779–80 was equally unsuccessful, but a Sikh invasion of the Doab was defeated at Meerut in 1785 by the imperial army after the forces of the Khalsa had levied their exactions up to the walls of Delhi.

The Sikhs were now masters of the whole country between the Jhelum and the Sutlej, and had, in spite of persecution by the later Mogul emperors and repression and defeat by the Afghan armies of Ahmad Shah Durrani, created what may be termed a revival of Hindu nationality in Upper India. At the same time they had

[1] *History of the Sikhs,* pp. 104–111.

raised a barrier, pushed in later years from the Indus to the north-western passes, which put an end to successful Muhammadan invasion from the north, a series of irruptions which had broken loose upon the plains of India for upwards of seven centuries.

This impenetrable buffer State was, as Sir Alfred Lyall has emphasized, exceedingly serviceable and opportune to the English. The Company's real danger, the only substantial obstacle to their rising ascendancy, lay always in the possibility of some foreign invasion led by some great captain at the head of the fighting tribes of Central Asia. The barrier of Oudh, though effective enough against the Marathas, would have been of little use against the attack of Central Asiatic hordes. But the rise of the Sikhs kept out the foreign Muhammadan, prevented the resuscitation of any fresh Islamic dynasty upon the ruins of the old empire at Delhi or Lahore, and left the existing north-west frontier of the English unmolested for the critical period when the Company were fully occupied with Mysore and the Western Marathas.[1]

Third Mysore War. Although Cornwallis had felt himself precluded by Act of Parliament from a formal alliance with the Nizam and the leading Marathas, Nana Farnavis, Sindia and Holkar in their attack upon Mysore, he was anxious to check Tipu's power. He therefore wrote a letter to the Nizam, which he declared to be as binding as a treaty. In this he promised to fulfil the obligations of assistance to Hyderabad and the Marathas laid down in the treaty of 1768, if the Nizam were to hand over Guntur in the Northern Sircars to the English. Incidentally the district was then part of the Mysore State. Grant Duff,[2] while pointing out the dangers threatening the Company through Tipu's aggressive policy, remarks that the line adopted by Lord Cornwallis was more objectionable than an avowed defensive alliance; and it was looked upon by Tipu as a direct threat to himself. At the end of 1789 Tipu invaded Travancore, which was under the protection of the Company.

The governor-general at once made an open alliance with the

---

[1] *Rise of the British Dominion in India*, pp. 181–183.
[2] *History of the Mahrattas*, Vol. II. pp. 194–195.

Nizam and the Marathas, and declared war upon Mysore in 1790. No important operations took place until the end of the year, when the governor-general took the field in person. Cornwallis was an able general, although he had not the quality of good fortune which Napoleon demanded of his marshals. In the war with the American colonists he had routed Gates and Greene in succession, only to be forced to surrender at Yorktown. He now captured Bangalore. But it took two campaigns which lasted until 1792 before Tipu was driven into his capital of Seringapatam by the allies and forced to make terms, which stripped him of the most valuable half of his territory. The English obtained Malabar and Coorg, and Tipu paid in addition an indemnity of 330 lakhs of rupees. Coorg remained a protected State under its raja until 1834, when it was annexed on account of the misconduct of its ruler. The Marathas and the Nizam divided the rest of the ceded territory between them.[1]

Tipu embarked upon a policy of revenge upon the English. He negotiated with the Marathas and with the Afghan king, and resumed his negotiations with the French, whose soldiers of fortune were serving in Hyderabad and with Sindia. But from France he received no more help than the belated encouragement of a letter in 1799 from Bonaparte in Cairo, during the Egyptian expedition; and the only consequence of his dealings with the French was to expose Tipu to the full weight of English hostility. The rupture between England and France brought about in 1793 by the Revolution made French interference impossible.

Mysore had been heavily hit by the treaty of Seringapatam and the Marathas had become the chief Indian power. *The Marathas and Sindia.* The Peshwa was completely overshadowed by Nana Farnavis, but the most dominant Maratha figure was Mahadaji Sindia, whose policy was to maintain his own independence of the confederacy without dissolving it. He had been appointed vice-regent of the empire by Shah Alam II, made large conquests in the north and defeated his rival Holkar after a desperate battle.

Sindia to a great extent owed his lordship over Upper India to

[1] For a full account of the operations and terms of peace see *History of the Mahrattas*, Vol. II. pp. 195–213.

PLATE LI.

EMBARKING AT MADRAS
From an Aquatint in colour, published 1837
By courtesy of the Parker Gallery

PLATE LII.

IVORY CHESSMEN, 1790
Pieces represent officers and men of the East India Company and
Tipu Sultan's army
By courtesy of Indian Museum, South Kensington

the French soldier of fortune General Count de Boigne. De Boigne's adventurous career [1] led him through service with the English against Tipu and a mission to Afghanistan, to become Sindia's best general. He was an excellent, straightforward soldier who drew into Sindia's ranks European officers of all nations, and organized, trained and equipped his troops on English lines. He left India after Mahadaji Sindia's death and retired to end his days as the public benefactor of his native town of Chambery.

Sindia, a man of great ambition, political capacity and ability as a soldier, died in 1794.[2] His independence had been recognized in 1786, his districts in Malwa were well administered by carefully chosen agents and he occupied the country round Delhi with a large and well-appointed army. Had he lived and succeeded in his policy of alliance against the English, the foreign power which threatened the subjugation of all India, he would have been a serious danger to the Company.

After his campaign against Mysore the aim of the governor-general was to establish peace in Southern India by *Hyderabad.* inducing the Nizam and the Marathas to join him in a treaty guaranteeing against Tipu the territories that each possessed at the end of the war. The Nizam, who was afraid of Maratha aggression, agreed; the Marathas, who meant to attack Hyderabad, refused.

Lord Cornwallis left India in October 1793, his last act before he sailed from Madras being to ensure the annexation *Sir John Shore,* of the French settlements. He was succeeded by Sir *Governor-General.* John Shore, a first-class civil servant who had done excellent settlement work. But he had little initiative and no political foresight and he could see no danger in the alliance just concluded against Hyderabad by the Marathas and Mysore. He maintained an insecure, impolitic and none too honourable peace [3] while the

---

[1] *Op. cit.*, Vol. II. footnote on pp. 160-162, gives the general's story as he told it to Grant Duff.

[2] For an appreciation of Sindia see Grant Duff, *op. cit.*, Vol. II. pp. 227-229.

[3] Thornton, *op. cit.*, pp. 223-224.

Marathas, without the active co-operation of Tipu, defeated the Nizam in the hostilities of 1794 and 1795. These ended in the Nizam's surrender at Kharda, where two battalions of women troops, the Nizam's palace guard, " behaved no worse than the rest of his army."[1]

The Nizam was greatly incensed by what he held to be the evasion by the Company of its engagements to help him. He dismissed the two English battalions which he subsidized, and had been unable to employ against the Marathas, and turned to the French, then ably represented in his army by the Gascon François de Raymond[2] whose men " carried the colours of the Republic . . . and the cap of liberty graced their buttons." Had it not been for the rebellion raised by the Nizam's son Ali Jah, which the English remained long enough in Hyderabad to suppress, the Nizam would have thrown himself entirely on the French side and come into alliance with Tipu.

After Kharda, Nana Farnavis reached the summit of his prosperity.

Nana Farnavis. Sindia's successor, and great-nephew, Daulat Rao, supported him and he had no rivals in the confederacy. But his guardianship of the young Peshwa Madho Rao was so severe that in October 1795 the Prince committed suicide, which led to Nana's fall from power. There were rival claims to the *masnad* to which Baji Rao succeeded in 1796; and the oppression and confusion which the conflicting interests of Sindia and the Peshwa brought upon the State had no hope of remedy until Nana came back in 1798. He died in 1800. His chief defect was ambition, not always restrained by principle, his ill-fortune that, clouded by jealousy and suspicion, he lost his grasp of affairs towards the end. But for over thirty years this great patriot statesman had controlled Maratha policy in opposition to the English, and with him, to quote the resident Colonel Palmer, " departed all the wisdom and moderation of the Maratha government." Its power was, however, already crumbling, and Sindia, who now took control at Poona, was unable to restore it. The end was

---

[1] Colonel Blacker's *Memoirs*, p. 213, footnote.
[2] Grant Duff, *op. cit.*, p. 242 and footnote.

inevitable, with the treaty of Bassein as a signpost on the road to extinction.[1]

Oudh. Oudh had been for years shockingly misgoverned, nor were conditions improved by the so-called supervision of Macpherson, whose own administration of Bengal was described by Cornwallis as " a system of the dirtiest jobbing." The rule of Asaf-ud-daula consisted of squandering in debauchery the revenue wrung from his oppressed subjects; the Company was bound to a policy of non-interference in internal affairs; and the only hope for the country had died in 1794, with its one capable minister Haidar Beg Khan.[2] Only the *jagirs* in Rohilkhand belonging to the Afghan family of Faizulla Khan were in a state of prosperity. These narrowly escaped complete confiscation by the Nawab, and were only partly saved by the prompt action of Sir Robert Abercromby.[3]

The hopeless inefficiency of the Nawab's army to resist foreign invasion was a standing menace to the security of the English northwest frontier which the Company's forces in Oudh were not strong enough to defend themselves; and there was the prospect of invasion from the west. Shah Zaman had ascended the throne of Kabul in 1793, his mind filled with hopes of an Indian empire. At the beginning of 1797 he penetrated as far as Lahore with thirty thousand men, and although domestic disturbances, added to Sikh resistance, obliged him to retreat he was again in Lahore in the following year. The Sikhs with their young leader Ranjit Singh were a strong power in the Punjab, but as the Marathas under Daulat Rao Sindia, who was no friend to the English, occupied Agra and Delhi, the political outlook was distinctly menacing.

Asaf-ud-daula, who was suspected of underground dealings with Zaman Shah,[4] died in 1797. Idle, dissolute and cruel, he was, however, a man of cultured tastes. Three years before his death he built the impressive Imambarah, whose great gate far surpasses the entrance

---

[1] See *Baji Rao and the East India Company*, Dr. P. C. Gupta.
[2] *Sketch of the Political History of India*, Malcolm, 2nd Ed., pp. 127-129.
[3] Thornton, *op. cit.*, p. 225.
[4] *History of the Sikhs*, p. 120, footnote.

to the Sublime Porte at Constantinople, on which it is said to have been modelled.

He nominated as his successor a youth Vazir Ali, whom he recognized as his son, but whom Shore, after sanctioning the succession, discovered to be illegitimate and, moreover, quite unfit to govern. Although the Company's commander-in-chief and the officer commanding the English forces in Oudh represented the danger of reversing his decision, Shore had the courage to depose Vazir Ali, and personally instituted an uncle, Saadat Ali, as Nawab. In January 1798 a treaty was signed between Saadat Ali and the Company which strengthened the north-western frontier of Bengal. In addition to an increase to seventy-six lakhs of the annual payment made to the Company, an English garrison was placed in Allahabad; the Company's troops in Oudh were brought up to 10,000 and made responsible for the entire defence of the country, and the Nawab agreed to have no dealings with other powers without the consent of the Company's government.[1]

Later in the year, in anticipation of invasion by Zaman Shah, the company's forces in Oudh were raised to 20,000. But the invasion never took place. The Durrani king retired from India in 1799, so greatly impressed with the personality of Ranjit Singh who had helped him when in difficulties with his heavy artillery that he bestowed on the Sikh leader the royal investiture of Lahore.[2] The Company's north-west frontier gave no immediate cause for anxiety, but the internal affairs of Oudh threatened to be a source of trouble.

The general policy of Sir John Shore was, in the words of Thornton, essentially quiescent and, apart from his intervention in Oudh, he was only roused to action when he took the Dutch settlements in India and in the Indian Seas. The Dutch had been caught up in the war in Europe in 1795 by the establishment by revolutionary France of the Batavian Republic, and during that year the English sent expeditions to Malacca, Amboyna, Cochin and Ceylon,

Capture of the Dutch Settlements.

---

[1] Thornton, *op. cit.*, pp. 225–229.
[2] *History of the Sikhs*, pp. 119–120.

all of which were taken. Negapatam and Trincomalee had been lost in the earlier war with Great Britain; Cochin was the only Dutch possession to offer any real resistance; and the British flag flew over Colombo for the first time on 16th February 1796.[1]

Sir John Shore, who had been raised to an Irish peerage as Lord Teignmouth, left India in March 1798.

BIBLIOGRAPHY

History of the British Empire in India, E. Thornton, 2nd Edn. 185 8.
Cambridge History of the British Empire, Vol. IV.
History of the Mahrattas, J. C. Grant Duff, Vol. II., ed. 1921.
Baji Rao and the East India Company, 1796–1818, Dr. P. C. Gupta, 1939.
History of the Sikhs, J. D. Cunningham, ed. 1918.
Rise of the British Dominion in India, Sir A. Lyall, 2nd Edn.
Memoirs of Warren Hastings, G. R. Gleig, 3 vols., 1841.
Warren Hastings, Maker of British India, A. Mervyn Davies, 1935.
The Story of Nuncomar and Impey, Sir J. Fitzjames Stephen, 2 vols., 1885.
History of the Trial of Warren Hastings, Esq., with proceedings and debates in both Houses of Parliament and . . . *E.I.C. Courts held in consequence of his acquittal*, Edn. 1796.
The Government of India, Sir C. Ilbert, 2nd Edn. 1907.
Early Revenue History of Bengal and the Fifth Report, 1812, F. D. Ascoli.

---

[1] For the history of Ceylon, a Crown Colony since 1798, and its relation to British policy, see *Camb. Hist. British Empire*, Vol. IV.

CHAPTER XVI

Development of the British Connection

AFTER some hesitation in the choice of a successor to Teignmouth, Richard Wellesley, Earl of Mornington, was appointed, and took over charge in May 1798. Lord Mornington became Marquis Wellesley after the fall of Seringapatam, and it avoids confusion to refer to him as Lord Wellesley throughout his administration. With the exception of Lord Curzon no British statesman came from England as governor-general or Viceroy with a greater knowledge of India. He had been a member of the Board of Control for five years, and had closely studied Indian history and literature.[1]

The political outlook was stormy. Oudh was insecure in the hands of Saadat Ali Khan. Berar was hostile. *Political Situation.* The triple alliance formed by Cornwallis against Mysore had been dissolved. A French party was paramount at the courts of the Nizam and of Daulat Rao Sindia, who was all powerful at Poona. Tipu Sultan in active correspondence with the French, with Kabul, Persia and Turkey, was on the brink of open hostility. To add to the governor-general's anxieties, not only were the revenues of the Carnatic mortgaged to its creditors (some of whom were actually members of the Madras Council) but the finances of the Company were drained by the expeditions against the Dutch colonies, which had stripped the Coromandel coast of troops.[2]

Lord Wellesley's policy was to renew the defensive alliance with Hyderabad and the Marathas, and temporize as far as possible with Mysore. He made a treaty with the Nizam by which the French battalions, totalling 14,000 men, were disbanded; and the

---

[1] *The Marquis Wellesley*, Hutton, p. 17.
[2] Malcolm, *Sketch of the Political History of India*, pp. 229, 230, 233, 234.

force under English command substituted for them was the germ of the Hyderabad contingent.[1] The Peshwa's government did not consent to a similar arrangement, but agreed to join a league against Mysore.

Tipu was requested to disarm and abandon the alliance he had just made with France. The Sultan made evasive replies and Lord Wellesley determined to strike before the French could intervene. In February 1799 he declared war.[2] On 3rd March General Harris crossed the frontier with the main army of Company and Hyderabad troops. A few days later General Stewart with the Bombay division defeated a Mysore army at Coorg; and on 27th March Harris defeated Tipu, who had concentrated his forces at Malavelli to bar the way to his capital. Seringapatam was stormed on 4th May, when Tipu was killed. The governor-general's brother, Arthur Wellesley, then a young colonel of thirty, took command on the following day when the troops were sacking the town completely out of hand. He reported that he hoped " to have gained the confidence of the people " by the rapid and effective measures he took to restore order.

Tipu Sultan was a man of undoubted gifts, but these were outweighed by innate suspicion and diabolical cruelty. He was a good linguist, hard-working and endowed with an imagination which evolved an entirely new calendar, a novel scale of weights and measures and coinage of his own invention. A convinced Muhammadan, who persecuted the Hindu population over whom he ruled, yet he had recourse to the prayers of the Brahmans in times of crisis. England has had enemies more able and more formidable than Tipu, yet never one more bitter or more implacable. But, unfortunately for himself, his " ardent desire to expel the English nation from India " [3] was not guided by a vestige of political insight. It was said in Mysore that " Haidar was born to create an empire, Tipu to lose one," and Tipu Sultan, in

[1] Colonel (Sir John) Malcolm saw the disbandment, as assistant political officer at Hyderabad. For the Hyderabad Contingent see Note 1 at the end of this chapter.

[2] Thornton, *op. cit.*, pp. 233-243, gives full details of the campaign.

[3] Malcolm, *Sketch of the Political History of India*, p. 253.

spite of the plainest warnings, persisted in a policy which could only end in his utter ruin. In a campaign lasting only two months the Moslem power in Mysore was shattered.

Lord Wellesley had not expected so complete a collapse of Mysore and he had now to consider the future of the country. The Marathas, who had taken no part in the campaign and refused to enter into any subsequent covenant, were left out of account. The governor-general decided that the Company and the Nizam should take over the districts which best suited their respective governments and that the old Hindu reigning family, expelled by Tipu's father Haidar Ali, should be restored, to revive, in a limited measure, the ancient kingdom of Vijayanagar. Kanara was annexed by the Company, Seringapatam was retained and the whole of the south-western coast was now under English control. The Nizam was given the north-eastern districts of Tipu's dominions. Mysore State, now completely cut off from the sea, was made over to a minor, Kistna Raja. Purnea, a Brahman of great ability and reputation, who had been Tipu's financial minister, became chief minister of the new Hindu government. The treaties confirming these arrangements were concluded in July 1799. Mysore, which the British Government was obliged to administer, from 1831 until 1881 owing to misrule, is now under its maharaja one of the most modernized Indian States with admirable social services.

The fourth Mysore war annihilated an enemy whose existence in the south had been a constant danger to the Company and, by giving the English complete command of the sea-coast of the lower peninsula, greatly lessened any risk of serious French intervention.

The governor-general was now free to pursue his forward policy, by peaceful annexations of territory and subsidiary treaties with other Indian States. In 1799 Lord Wellesley annexed Tanjore, which had been a Maratha State for about a hundred and fifty years. There had been a dispute over the succession, " native oppression and European cupidity "[1] had brought about endless abuses, and the governor-general took

Annexations.

[1] Thornton, *op. cit.*, pp. 249–251.

over the country, the youthful raja retiring on a pension which was continued until the line died out in 1855. Tanjore had been a source of serious trouble since 1766, when acute dissensions over its affairs broke out in the Madras council, culminating in the arrest of the governor Lord Pigot who died while in confinement.[1]

During the same year internal disputes at Surat induced the Company to take possession of the castle and fleet at that port, an action which Shah Alam II confirmed by authorizing the English to act there as his vice-regent. The imperial standard [2] remained over the castle and on the Company's flagship in the harbour until May 1800, when the failure of the local administration, and communal disturbances between Hindus and Muhammadans, decided the Company to annex Surat by treaty and bring it into the Bombay Presidency.[3]

But by far the most important increase of territory was the annexation of the Carnatic in 1801, which consolidated the Madras presidency substantially as it is today. Muhammad Ali had died in 1795 at the age of seventy-eight. His long life had been a series of intrigues punctuated by financial crises which had made the fortunes of disreputable creditors such as Paul Benfield, who went home to become a member of Parliament.[4] Muhammad Ali was succeeded by his son Umdat-ul-Umara under whom, as in the time of his father, the Carnatic continued to be hopelessly and helplessly misgoverned.

The Carnatic.

Nor had the situation been improved by the treaty made by Cornwallis in 1792. This treaty had set up a form of dual government, the Company taking entire control of the Carnatic in time of war, and restoring it to the Nawab in time of peace. Conditions were added to ensure the payment of the subsidy to the Company and to make a composition with Muhammad Ali's creditors. These arrangements had made efficient administration by the Carnatic

---

[1] Thornton, *op. cit.*, pp. 151–153. The barony (cr. 1765) expired with him.

[2] A note on Indian and English Standards and Colours is to be found at the end of this chapter.

[3] Thornton, *op. cit.*, pp. 251–252.

[4] *Ibid.*, pp. 26, 57, 161, 181, 182 describe the "pecuniary distresses" of the Nawab and the "financial jugglery" of Benfield.

government quite impossible. In order to raise money to meet his obligations the Nawab mortgaged his districts at usurious interest to Europeans. These creditors came to terms with the military authorities who helped them to enforce their claims in the districts, and the peasants had recourse to money-lenders who completed their ruin. Lord Hobart, governor of Madras in 1794, protested against this oppression and represented that the Company's policy of non-interference, under the terms of the treaty, was discrediting the British Government, but the new Nawab, under the thumb of the mortgagees, refused to modify the treaty. The view of the home government was, however, completely changed by the discovery of documentary evidence, on the fall of Seringapatam, that Muhammad Ali and his son had been intriguing with Tipu against the English.[1] In the cipher correspondence the English were referred to as " New comers," the Nizam as " Nothing " and the Marathas as " The Contemptibles." The rulers of the Carnatic had themselves violated the treaty and when Umdat-ul-Umara died in 1801 the Carnatic was annexed by the Company, and the Nawab's heirs were given a liberal pension.[2]

In Oudh Lord Wellesley combined annexations with what may be called a subsidiary treaty. Saadat Ali had been placed on the throne by the English but " the British subsidy was always in arrears, while the most frightful extortion was practised in the realization of the revenue. Justice was unknown; the army was a disorderly mass, formidable only to the power whom it professed to serve. These evils of native growth were aggravated by an extraordinary number of European adventurers, most of whom were as destitute of character and principle as they were of property." [3]

Oudh.

The governor-general saw clearly that the two essentials of military security and civil reform were impossible under the existing vicious and incompetent government and from the first he

---

[1] Summarized by Malcolm, *Sketch of the Political History of India*, pp. 335–338.
[2] Thornton, *op. cit.*, pp. 255–261 ; and *Camb. Hist. Brit. Empire*, Vol. IV, pp. 355–359.
[3] Thornton, *op. cit.*, p. 261.

showed little patience or forbearance in his dealings with Saadat Ali. By the agreement of November 1801 in which Lord Wellesley's brother Henry Wellesley took part, the ruler of Oudh ceded all his frontier provinces, including Rohilkhand, to the Company; the revenue of these territories being taken as equivalent to the subsidy payable for troops. This arrangement to which Saadat Ali only agreed with the greatest reluctance ended the buffer-state policy which had served its purpose for thirty years.

The Company now owned the whole belt of frontier territory and Oudh was encircled by the English dominion. These annexations of some of the richest and most populous districts in the heart of India, along the Ganges and its tributaries above Benares up to the foot-hills of the Himalaya, greatly increased the Company's revenue; Allahabad became a flourishing trade centre and started upon its modern career of prosperity. At the same time the English came in contact with the Maratha chief Sindia along the whole line of his possessions in Upper India.

In the internal administration of Oudh Saadat Ali agreed to introduce, under his own officers, a system of government more conducive to the prosperity and security of his subjects, and to follow in all respects the advice of the officers of the Company's government.[1] In this and the other subsidiary treaties there were grave defects. " The Company was made responsible for the maintenance of a government which it was impossible for its representatives, as foreigners, entirely to control. The Carnatic no doubt had a new and happy future; but in Oudh the snake of oppression was only scotched. . . . But of the great aims, the high conscientiousness, the keen insight and the impressive wisdom of Marquis Wellesley in these, the most characteristic expressions of his statesmanship, there can be no doubt."

In their earliest dealings with the Indian powers the Company had intervened by lending troops to some ruler. *The Subsidiary Treaties.* Later they used their own troops assisted more or less by the ill-trained and undisciplined levies of their allies. A further advance was made when the Indian ally

[1] Malcolm, *op. cit.*, pp. 319–331.

was asked to pay a subsidy with which the English raised, trained and paid the necessary forces themselves. But the subsidies were often in arrears, and the next stage was to adopt the usual practice of Asiatic governments and obtain the assignment of lands upon whose revenue the troops were maintained.

Lord Wellesley's policy of subsidiary alliances, the first of which had been made by Vansittart with Mir Kasim in 1760, was to establish protectorates over the States with which his government had contact. By these treaties the princes agreed to reduce their own military establishments and, while continuing to manage their internal affairs without interference, relied upon the English for external defence and internal security.[1] Cornwallis had tried and failed to bring universal peace to India by a series of treaties of general guarantee. Lord Wellesley hoped to bring about this result by establishing the Company's ascendancy in the councils of the Indian States.

Lord Wellesley concluded a treaty on these lines with the newly restored Hindu State of Mysore. In 1800 a subsidiary alliance was made with Hyderabad. By this treaty the Nizam commuted his military subsidy to the Company by ceding the territories he had gained in 1792 and 1799 from Mysore; and, while putting the control of his foreign policy in the Company's hands, he agreed that in the event of any dispute between his government and another Indian power he would accept the arbitration of the Company.

Mysore, Hyderabad and Oudh were now safe from French influence, and the only powers of importance with *Lord Wellesley's Maratha Policy.* which Lord Wellesley had to deal were the Maratha States. He had raised a barrier against their aggressions by subsidiary treaties with the Moslem rulers, but the general character of the Marathas and the number of French officers in Sindia's service were disquieting elements and he determined to secure a commanding influence in the confederacy councils. Lord Wellesley soon found his opportunity.

[1] *Camb. Hist. Brit. Empire,* Vol. IV. Ch. XXI, p. 354.

The death of Nana Farnavis in 1800 was the signal for a scramble for power among the confederacy chiefs, and fiendish executions and the butchery and confusion of unbridled civil war broke loose between the main rivals, Jaswant Rao Holkar and Sindia. The Peshwa Baji Rao, cruel and vindictive when he had the means to strike, was helpless to assert his personal authority. The civil war went on with varying fortunes until 25th October 1802, when Holkar met the forces of Sindia near Poona. Divisions of both armies were led by Englishmen but Holkar's forces were superior, and after a desperate engagement Sindia was completely defeated,[1] and Holkar established his nominee, Warnak Rao, as Peshwa at Poona.

Baji Rao, whose sympathies had been with Sindia, lost no time in reopening with the English negotiations by which *Treaty of Bassein.* he had already agreed to maintain a force of Company's troops in his territory. On the 31st December 1802 he signed the treaty of Bassein. It was violently criticized by the home authorities on the obvious grounds that it trebled British responsibilities in Western India; and it was to draw the Maratha chiefs together to resist the foreigner. But its far-reaching results have been described by Sidney Owen: " Previously to the Treaty there existed a British Empire *in* India: the Treaty by its direct or indirect operations gave the Company the Empire of India." [2]

By the terms of the treaty a subsidiary force of 6000 infantry with European artillery units was to be permanently stationed in the Peshwa's dominions, and these troops were to act with his own forces in the event of war; no European of a nation hostile to the English was to be entertained; districts yielding 26 lakhs of rupees were to be assigned for the upkeep of the subsidiary force; the Peshwa abandoned his claims on Surat; he agreed to arbitration in his disputes with Hyderabad and Baroda; and he bound himself to engage in no hostilities with other States, nor to negotiate with any power whatever without previous consultation with the Company's goverment.[3]

[1] *History of the Mahrattas*, Vol. II. pp. 316–317.
[2] Introduction to *Selections from the Wellington Dispatches*, p. xlvi.
[3] The nineteen articles of the treaty are quoted by Thornton, *op. cit.*, pp. 279–280.

Up to this point the policy by which Lord Wellesley hoped to establish peace throughout India had developed with unbroken success. The Company's subsidiary troops were stationed at Mysore, Hyderabad, Lucknow and Poona; all disputes between these States were to be submitted to the governor-general for arbitration; while the interference of other European nations was to be excluded.

Arthur Wellesley went so far as to admit that the treaty of Bassein was " the bond of peace to India." It was, however, to be peace through war. The Peshwa had " sacrificed his independence as the price of protection," and he regretted the bargain almost as soon as he had made it. Sindia realized that a life and death struggle with the English was imminent and certain and, while Holkar held aloof, he joined hands with Raghuji Bhonsla the Maratha ruler of Berar.

Baji Rao had been for three months under Arthur Wellesley's protection at Poona when, on the 3rd August 1803, *The Maratha War.* the British agent left Sindia's camp and the Maratha war opened. The governor-general's objects were to conquer Sindia's dominions between the Ganges and Jumna, taking Delhi and Agra; to remove the old Mogul Emperor Shah Alam from Sindia's control; to annex Baroch in Western India; and in the east to join Madras with Bengal by annexing the province of Cuttack. To effect this the Company had nearly 50,000 men in India, and General Arthur Wellesley was able to take the field with 24,000 men, while General Lake in the north had 10,000 under his command.

Sindia and the Bhonsla raja of Berar mustered between them 50,000 cavalry and over 30,000 regular infantry with great strength in artillery, commanded by the Frenchmen Perron (the successor of de Boigne) and Dudrenac; and the Berar levies equipped with matchlocks and rockets brought the Maratha forces up to about 100,000 men. The army of Sindia at this time (and the same remark applies to Holkar) consisted of comparatively few Marathas, being chiefly composed of Rajputs and Muhammadans enlisted in what had been the original Mogul Empire. This, as

Malcolm points out, was a radical cause of Maratha division and ruin.[1]

On the 12th August 1803 General Wellesley took Ahmadnagar, which was supposed to be practically impregnable. On 23rd September with no more than 4500 of his army he met the forces of Sindia and Berar, 50,000 strong with over 100 guns, at Assaye. He attacked without hesitation, the troops advancing under a very hot fire, and won a complete victory.[2] Wellesley displayed in this, his first general action, the same matter-of-fact coolness which distinguished him in his last great battle. A famous incident at Waterloo had its counterpart at Assaye when, at a critical moment, a British cavalry regiment (19th Light Dragoons), with the 4th Native Cavalry,[3] passed through the cheering ranks of a Highland regiment (the 74th) to charge the enemy.[4] In the course of a brilliant campaign through the Deccan Arthur Wellesley went on to win a decisive battle over the raja of Berar at Argaon on 29th November, and in the middle of December he forced that prince to sign the treaty of Deogaon, similar in terms to the treaty of Bassein, and ceding Cuttack to the Company.

Assaye and Argaon.

In upper India General Lake's division was opposed to Sindia's troops drilled on French lines. On 11th September Lake won a victory outside Delhi which gave him the capital of Mogul India. Agra surrendered five weeks later, and on the 31st October Sindia's remaining forces were annihilated after a desperate battle at Laswari. On 30th December 1803 Sindia signed the treaty of Surji Arjangaon, ceding the country

Lake's Campaign.

---

[1] *Sketch of the Political History of India*, pp. 402–403 and footnote.

[2] *Wellesley's Dispatches*, III. pp. 323–326 (ed. Montgomery Martin, London, 1840).

[3] General Sir John Floyd, commanding officer of the 19th Light Dragoons, " had from the day of his arrival in India, laboured to establish the ties of mutual and cordial regard between the European and the native soldiers. His success was complete . . . and the friendship which he established . . . was after his departure consummated upon the plains of Assaye."—*Quarterly Review*, Vol. XVIII (May 1818), p. 392.

[4] Accounts of Assaye and Argaon are given in *History of the Mahrattas*, Vol. II. pp. 340–343, and pp. 358, 359.

between the Jumna and the Ganges, his rights over Broach and other territories.[1]

The Emperor since his move from Allahabad to Delhi had known nothing but misfortune and misery. In 1788, after the defeat of Sindia by a combined Rajput and Mogul army, he had fallen into the clutches of a savage Rohilla, Ghulam Qadir, who blinded him and treated the imperial household with barbarous cruelty. A year later Sindia recovered the capital, together with the provinces of Delhi and Agra, took a fearful revenge on the usurper Ghulam Qadir, and resumed his custody of the Emperor. When Perron became commandant of the fort at Delhi Shah Alam was handed over to the French, from whom as from Sindia he met with neither kindness nor generosity. Old, blind and decrepit, without power, without pomp or state or retinue, the representative of the house of Timur came finally under the protection of the English when Lake entered Delhi.[2]

But the governor-general had not settled with the whole strength of the confederacy. Holkar, who had stayed inactive *Campaign against Holkar.* in Rajputana with a large Maratha horde while Sindia and the Raja of Berar were fighting the English, refused to come to terms. He was pillaging and levying contributions in the country, he had recently put to death three English officers in his service, and in April 1804 Lord Wellesley declared war. At first all went well. Rampura, Holkar's stronghold in the north, was taken and Holkar made a rapid retreat. But Lake, ignoring Arthur Wellesley's advice either to follow him up energetically or withdraw altogether during the rainy season, took half-hearted measures which ended in disaster. A force under Colonel Monson was completely defeated in the Mukund Dara Pass in Rajputana between the 8th and 11th July 1804. Sindia's contingent deserted, and the survivors of the English force had the greatest difficulty in reaching Agra a fortnight later.

The immediate effect of the disaster was to hearten the Marathas,

---

[1] *History of the Mahrattas,* Vol. II. pp. 345–355, 361, 362. But the subsidiary treaty referred to by Grant Duff was withdrawn later.

[2] Thornton, *op. cit.,* pp. 289–290.

PLATE LIII.

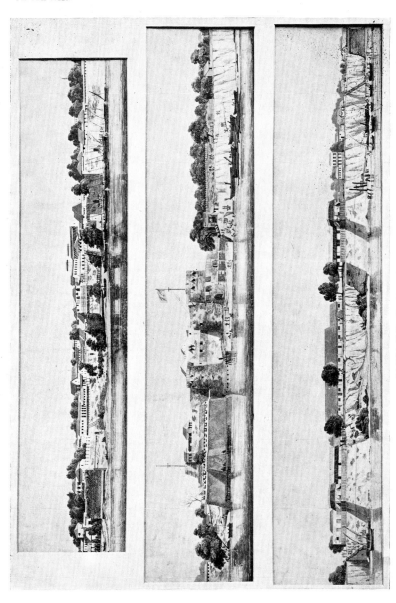

PANORAMA OF SURAT, 1830

By permission of the Secretary of State for India in Council

PLATE LIV.

Maha Raja Ranjit Sing

(b) RANJIT SINGH

By permission of the Secretary of State for India in Council

(a) LORD WELLESLEY

By courtesy of the Parker Gallery

bringing Sindia and the Bhonsla once more into alliance against the English, and it determined the home government to recall Lord Wellesley.

But the reverse was only momentary. Colonel Murray, whose operations had previously been hesitating, captured Holkar's capital Indore, and Holkar himself was unable to take Delhi, gallantly defended for a week in October by a handful of Indian troops under Ochterlony. On 13th November General Frazer severely defeated Holkar at Dig, twenty miles from Laswari, and three days later Lake cut to pieces a force of Maratha cavalry south of Delhi. These successes were, however, counterbalanced by Lake's unfortunate and expensive failure between 4th January and 21st February 1805 to take Bharatpur, whose ruler had deserted the English and joined forces with Holkar.[1] A convention was made with the Raja of Bharatpur in April by which he retained his fortress and the Maratha campaign drifted on without decisive result.

Peace was finally concluded by Lord Wellesley's successor in accordance with a policy of ill-judged concession which failed to realize that Holkar's power had really been broken and that no Maratha prince was left strong enough to withstand the English. Weak allied States like Jaipur which relied on the Company's support were by this policy at the mercy of their rapacious neighbours, and the final reckoning with the Marathas was postponed.

Lord Wellesley's policy had dissolved the last of the European-trained armies possessed by the Indian rulers,[2] and *Lord Wellesley's Policy.* substituted, for these forces under foreign commanders, contingents amounting to 22,000 men paid for by the States and under the Company's control. Arbitration by the English between the Indian powers when inter-State differences arose had been established. British dominion had been almost incredibly increased. Finally, by taking charge of the Mogul

[1] *History of the Mahrattas*, Vol. II. pp. 381-383.
[2] *Sketch of the Political History of India*, Malcolm, pp. 361-363, for French military influence in 1798.

Emperor and his family, Lord Wellesley had inaugurated a change of policy which lasted until 1857. As Sir Alfred Lyall has said: "For at least forty years the imperial sign manual had been at the disposal of any adventurer or usurper . . . who could overawe the powerless court and dictate his own investiture with some lofty office or with a grant of the provinces that he had appropriated." [1] When Lord Wellesley made Shah Alam a State pensioner this was no longer possible.

Lord Wellesley's political horizon was not bound by the shores of India. He saw that if the French were successful in Egypt they would make an attempt upon Southern India. In February 1801 he sent troops under General Baird to co-operate in the Egyptian campaign; and had Admiral Rainier followed his instructions Mauritius would have been captured and the serious losses caused to British shipping by French privateers would have been ended. Ceylon had become a crown colony in 1798, at first under the supervision of the governor-general of India. But the rule of its governor Frederick North (Lord Guilford) was not fortunate, and Lord Wellesley asked, without success, that the island should be brought directly under the Indian government.

Cornwallis had fully realized his responsibility in regard to the condition and treatment of the Company's Indian subjects. When the officers of a court-martial acquitted one of their comrades charged with the brutal assault of a poor Indian in the teeth of the clearest evidence, he reprimanded the offenders in a scathing minute,[2] which might have been written by Lord Curzon.

Lord Wellesley realized a further obligation. The development of the Company had raised its servants from clerks and merchants to magistrates and administrators; they were in fact Indian civil servants in all but name. They came out to India as boys, ignorant of their duties and of the history and languages of the peoples whom they would have to rule. They had no incentive to learn and their incompetence frequently led to idleness and bad habits. Lord Wellesley therefore founded a college

Fort William College.

---

[1] *Rise of the British Dominion in India*, pp. 229–234.
[2] *The Marquess Cornwallis*, Seton-Karr, pp. 112, 113.

at Fort William, modelled as closely as possible on an English university, where Oriental languages and Indian law and customs were taught. The scheme was as warmly approved by Warren Hastings as that great administrator's own proposal to establish a professorship of Persian had been supported by Dr. Johnson, though neither scheme was welcomed by the authorities in London. The Calcutta college was vetoed by the Directors who, however, yielded to pressure and arranged that Indian languages should be taught at the headquarters of each presidency. But it caused the foundation in 1806 of the East India College at Haileybury which gave for nearly fifty years a training upon the lines laid down by Lord Wellesley for the college in India.[1]

The Directors in London had never approved of the governor-general's forward policy, which they felt had led to an increase of territory too great for profitable management. The course of affairs in Oudh, the Bassein treaty, the heavy expenses of the government, and other matters of which they disapproved all urged the Directors to dismiss a governor-general who was as insubordinate as he was brilliant in achievement. They also accused him of abusing his patronage, selecting as instances his employment of his brothers, Henry, afterwards famous as Lord Cowley, British Ambassador at Paris, and Arthur the future Duke of Wellington. Lord Wellesley had sent in his resignation in 1802, but the Directors had refused to accept it; he could not then be replaced. The disaster to Colonel Monson's column in the Maratha war brought them to a decision, and the governor-general was recalled in 1805, in the hope of "bringing things back to the state the legislature had prescribed in 1793." The proposal to impeach Lord Wellesley after his return to England was not pressed.

Thornton [2] takes the view that the one defect in the governor-general's character was "ambition . . . in connecting his own fame with that of the land to which he belonged, and of the government which he administered." But his policy of securing " to

---

[1] Thornton, *op. cit.*, pp. 276–277 (and see Seton-Karr's *Life of Marquis Wellesley*, pp. 117–124).

[2] *Op. cit.*, p. 341.

every State the unmolested exercise of its separate authority within the limits of its established dominion, under the general protection of the British power," [1] was the beginning of the *Pax Britannica* in India.

On the 1st August 1805 the Marquess Cornwallis, in his sixty-seventh year and "drooping under age and infirmities," took office as governor-general for the second time. He came to Calcutta to reverse his successor's policy and he was supported by the alarm which Wellesley's costly and masterful operations had caused in England. Cornwallis died in three months, but he had already laid down the principles on which the Company's government were to act for the next ten years. Sir Alfred Lyall has defined this policy as the experiment of isolation. The consequent renunciations of treaty obligations to allied States and concessions to the Marathas is stigmatized by Thornton as inglorious and dishonourable.

Reaction.

Sir John Malcolm has recorded, with more restrained disapproval, the course of the governor-general's negotiations with Sindia, who had detained the English resident and allowed his camp to be plundered. Lake urged in vain that if Cornwallis persisted in his proposals to withdraw the Company's protection from the small States west of the Jumna they would be overwhelmed by Sindia, or some other Maratha chief, a breach of faith which would dishonour the reputation of England.[2] But the governor-general, old and dying as he was, clung to his policy of peace with the Marathas at any price, even to the "mere point of honour" involved in the release of the resident.[3] He decided to give up Gwalior and Gohad to Sindia, with the districts of Dholpur, Bari and Rajkeri, making the Jumna the English frontier; to abandon the Company's ally Jaipur; and to give the Maratha bandits a free hand.

Cornwallis died at Ghazipur on the 5th October 1805, where

---

[1] Despatch of Lord Wellesley, 13th July 1804, *Wellesley Despatches*, IV. p. 177.

[2] Malcolm, *Sketch of the Political History of India*, pp. 391–408. The author was then the governor-general's political agent.

[3] Thornton, *op. cit.*, pp. 342–343.

he lies in a monument described in the *Gazetteer of India* as
" a domed quasi-Grecian building." Sir John Malcolm says of
Lord Cornwallis: " To a dignified simplicity of character, he
added a soundness of understanding and a strength of judgment which admirably fitted him for the exercise of both civil
and military power; and his first Administration of the British
Empire in India must ever be a theme of just and unqualified
applause." [1]

When Cornwallis died, the first member of council, Sir George
Barlow, acted as governor-general until a new appointment was
made in England. Thornton describes him as " an excellent
revenue officer with none of the qualities of a governor-general."
Like Cornwallis he disapproved of the subsidiary treaties, but to
give him his due he upheld the treaty of Bassein and did not
pursue his policy of non-interference when dealing with the Peshwa
and the Nizam of Hyderabad.[2] But he dissolved the agreement
which had been made with the Sikhs, and he abandoned the Rajput
princes by binding the Company's government, in his treaty with
Sindia (November 1805), to make no engagement with them for
their protection against the Marathas. In regard to this treaty Barlow
made the cynical remark that " the British possessions in the Doab
will derive additional security from the contests of the neighbouring
States." [3] Thus, in the words of Thornton, " did Sir George Barlow
tranquillize India."

In the spring of 1806 symptoms of insubordination appeared
among the Company's Indian troops in the Carnatic;
The Vellore Mutiny. and on 10th July a mutiny broke out at Vellore.
Two English companies with their officers, a total
of 113 of all ranks, were massacred, and order was only restored by
British and Indian cavalry regiments from Arcot. The chief
ringleaders were executed and the other mutineers were dismissed
the service, the battalions which mutinied were disbanded [4] and the

---

[1] Malcolm, *op. cit.*, p. 413.
[2] *Political History of India*, 1784–1823, Malcolm, Vol. I. pp. 373–385.
[3] Thornton, *op. cit.*, pp. 345–348.
[4] Thornton, *op. cit.*, pp. 349–354.

family of Tipu Sultan, who were suspected of complicity, were removed from Vellore to Calcutta.

The immediate cause of the mutiny was to be attributed to the dress regulations issued by the presidency commander-in-chief Sir John Cradock, with the approval of the governor of Madras Lord William Bentinck. These regulations required the men to wear a new pattern of head-dress to which the Muhammadans objected, to train their beards in a particular way, and forbade the Hindus to put caste marks on their foreheads.

Among the peoples of India religion has always been the supremely vital force. They had been accustomed in the past to the violence of conversions to Islam. But as Sir John Cradock, commenting upon " the total absence of [English] religious establishments in the interior of the country," said, " So infrequent are the religious observances of officers doing duty with battalions, that the sepoys have not, until very recently, discovered the nature of the religion professed by the English." [1] Christianity then seemed to Indians in touch with Englishmen to mean wearing hats, eating beef and pork, drinking spirits and neglecting personal purity, rather than a system of lofty theological doctrine. The folly of the Madras government in interfering with the religious susceptibilities of the Indian troops was absolutely wanton, especially as there existed in the districts a strong though utterly groundless fear that a general destruction of caste and forcible conversion to Christianity were contemplated.[2]

The Directors in London recalled the governor who had successfully urged clemency to the mutineers, and the commander-in-chief who advocated sterner measures, while they recorded their views on conditions in India to the President of the Board of Control. Apart from criticism of Lord Wellesley's forward policy they said that the general decline of the fidelity of the army and of the attachment of the people to British rule was due to the fact that a new class of men with little knowledge of India, little interest in its

[1] *History of the Sepoy War in India*, 1857–1858, Kaye, Vol. I. Book II. Ch. I. *The Sepoy Army* (1756–1856), p. 250 and footnote.
[2] Kaye, *op. cit.*, p. 248.

inhabitants, and little toleration for their prejudices had begun to monopolize the chief seats in the government and the chief posts in the army.[1]

In the meanwhile the question of the governor-generalship was being warmly discussed between the Directors and *Appointment of Lord Minto.* the Whig coalition government of Grenville and Fox, which had come in after the death of Pitt. The Directors wished Barlow, who had succeeded in turning a financial deficit into a surplus, to remain, and while Pitt lived, Lord Minto (who had recently become President of the Board of Control) supported the proposal. Lord Grenville, however, exercised the prerogative of the Crown under the Act of 1784 and " vacated " the appointment. After considerable debate in the House of Commons the Directors, who had refused to accept " citizen Maitland " Lord Lauderdale, agreed to Minto's nomination.[2] Minto had, as a friend of Burke, been long interested in India, and had conducted Impey's unsuccessful impeachment. But he had refused the governorship of Madras in 1793, and it was with the greatest reluctance that he accepted the post of governor-general.[3] He reached Calcutta at the end of July 1807, and found the country " in that state of torpor which Sir George Barlow and his friends regarded as tranquillity." [4]

The first event to disturb this calm was a violent outbreak in Travancore at the end of 1808. Travancore was, *Travancore.* at that time, scandalously misgoverned by its chief minister who was actively hostile to the English. The subsidy due from that State to the Company was heavily in arrears and the minister made the pressure brought to bear upon his government to pay this money the pretext for a general rising and an attack upon the residency. Order was quickly restored on the appearance of the Company's troops, the minister committed suicide, and the

---

[1] Kaye, *op. cit.*, p. 251.   [2] Thornton, *op. cit.*, pp. 355–358.
[3] For Lord Minto's Parliamentary interest in India see *Life and Letters*, edited by his great-niece the Countess of Minto (London), 1874, I. pp. 121, 175, 176, 179, etc.; III. pp. 392–397.
[4] Thornton, *op. cit.*, p. 358.

future peace of the principality was placed upon a firmer foundation than it had rested before.

A more serious threat to British security in India than the disturbances in Travancore came from the mutiny of the British officers of the Madras army. Discontent had shown itself in 1807, and when Barlow became governor of the presidency after the arrival of Minto in India, and abolished a tent contract from which commanding officers made money, the smouldering discontent broke into mutiny in 1809. From the garrison in Travancore it spread to Hyderabad, Masulipatam and Seringapatam. Fortunately a sense of duty soon returned, and the mutiny was suppressed. General McDowall, the late commander-in-chief at Madras, whose farewell " offensive and inflammatory " general order had much to do with the outbreak, escaped well-deserved prosecution, the ship in which he sailed to England being lost with all hands.[1]

Mutiny of the Madras Officers.

Although Minto's administration marks an almost stationary period in the growth of British power in India, the governor-general clearly saw, and impressed upon the authorities in England, that it was impossible to remain entirely neutral in India, the policy which they had made up their minds to follow. He paved the way, slowly and deliberately, for the forward policy of his successors. At the same time he began a new phase of British-Indian diplomacy by widespread relations with powers beyond the borders of India.

Foreign Policy.

The treaty of Tilsit in 1807 had made Napoleon master of the continent of Europe, and the French Emperor was pressing upon Alexander of Russia his plan of a joint expedition through Turkey and Persia against the English in India, in order to ruin their commercial prosperity. An imposing French mission was sent to Persia, and the agents of France were busy at other Asiatic courts.

Lord Minto prepared for this possible danger by setting up barriers in the form of alliances with the States on the threatened

[1] Thornton, *op. cit.*, pp. 362–364.

line of invasion. In India itself he sent Metcalfe to Lahore in 1808, and early in 1809 treaties were signed with the Sikhs by which Ranjit Singh's supremacy beyond the Sutlej was acknowledged, and the Sikh confederacies south of that river came under British protection, while their independence was admitted.[1] A mission was also sent to Sind, whose chiefs bound themselves "not to allow the establishment of the tribe of the French" in their country.[2]

A defensive alliance against France was made with the King of Kabul by Elphinstone.[3] But Shah Shuja was deposed soon afterwards and became a pensioner of the Company, to be restored thirty years later by "an ill-fated expedition that eventually cost the English an army and a king his life." A mission to Persia, undertaken by Sir John Malcolm, arrived there about the same time as the plenipotentiary from England, Sir Harford Jones, who concluded a defensive treaty with the Persian government.

The value of these external alliances was shortlived. Napoleon's difficulties in Spain and with Russia soon ended his hopes of conquest in Asia. Within six years the French empire was overthrown, the command of the sea was held by Great Britain and, until Russia carried her frontiers eastwards in 1828 after her war with Persia, all danger of a possible invasion of India disappeared. Napoleon's schemes had, however, widened the British outlook as regards India. The north-west frontier [4] was no longer the kingdom of Oudh and its ceded territories; the buffer State was represented by the Cis-Sutlej confederacies. And, far beyond the confines of India, since the beginning of the nineteenth century the immensity of British interests in India has decisively influenced the relations of the home Government, not only with the Asiatic powers but with any

---

[1] *History of the Sikhs*, pp. 136–141. The Terms of these important treaties are given in full in Appendices XXV. and XXVI.

[2] Thornton, *op. cit.*, p. 379.

[3] Malcolm, *Political History*, Vol. I. p. 421.

[4] The name North-Western Provinces, which disappeared in 1902 when the United Provinces of Agra and Oudh came under one lieutenant-governor, is a reminder of the older boundaries of British dominion.

European State which could in any way affect the British position in the East.[1]

Overseas Expeditions.

While a general peace policy was insisted upon in London, the governor-general, outside India, showed both energy and ability. Public opinion in England influenced Minto to ignore the outrages of the Pindari horsemen of Central India and Gurkha incursions to the Sutlej and the Jumna.[2] But the expeditions he sent overseas were the most brilliant and valuable achievements of his government.

With the co-operation of a British squadron Bourbon was taken in the summer of 1810, and at the beginning of December Mauritius capitulated. This put an end to the enterprise of the French privateers based on these islands which had cost the Company more than two million pounds. Bourbon was restored to the French by the Peace of Paris of 1814.

In 1811 an expedition under Sir Samuel Auchmuty, commander-in-chief at Madras, after heavy fighting took the Dutch settlements in the Moluccas, then under French control, the capital Batavia falling on 28th August. The Moluccas were given back in 1814.

Charter Act, 1813.

An Act of 1807 had given the governors and councils at Madras and Bombay authority to make regulations, subject to the approval of the supreme court, similar to those already vested in the government of Bengal, and the same powers of appointing justices of the peace. But the most important legislation of the period was the Charter Act of 1813. A searching inquiry into Indian affairs by a committee of the House of Commons had produced the famous Fifth Report in 1812. This was a standard authority on Indian land tenures and the judicial and police arrangements of the time comparable to the general survey made nearly a hundred and twenty years later by the statutory commission, under the chairmanship of Sir John Simon.

The House went into committee on the affairs of the East India

[1] See *Rise of the British Dominion in India*, pp. 238–245.
[2] *History of the Sikhs*, p. 134.

Company in March 1813. On the 13th July the Charter Bill was passed in the Commons and was opposed in the House of Lords only by Lord Lauderdale because it did not go far enough.

The Act renewed for twenty years the Company's control of its territories and revenues " without prejudice to the undoubted sovereignty of the Crown of the United Kingdom of Great Britain and Ireland." But subject to certain restrictions, its trade monopoly was abolished, except with China, and the highly valuable tea trade which was preserved to the Company. The powers of the Board of Control were enlarged, although the Company's patronage was continued. It was laid down that 20,000 men should be the maximum of King's troops normally maintained by the Company, the Government in India making its own disciplinary arrangements. Provision was made out of the Company's revenues for a bishop and three archdeacons of the Church of England at Calcutta (an equivalent proposal for the Established Church of Scotland being negatived); and permission was granted to " persons going to India to introduce amongst the natives useful knowledge and religious and moral improvement." [1]

This last clause, which aroused considerable discussion, was, as Professor Thakore points out,[2] the starting point in India of Christian missionary enterprise as licensed by the State, with its twin fruits of Western education and Christian propaganda; and it was safeguarded against interference with the religious convictions of the Indian people.

But the most violent controversy arose over the abolition of the trade monopoly, and the political dangers which were feared from an unlimited influx of Europeans into India.

The House heard the evidence called by the Company to resist these proposals. Their first witness was Warren Hastings, then over eighty, who was received by the members rising in a body and standing until he had taken his seat within the bar. Lord Teignmouth, Colonel (Sir John) Malcolm and Colonel (Sir Thomas) Munro followed. Haworth made a powerful appeal in which he

---

[1] *Government of India*, Ilbert, pp. 72–79.
[2] *Indian Administration* . . . (1765–1920).

emphasized the achievements of the Company supported by its monopoly, while Tierney opposed its commercial policy on the grounds of its injustice to India. Grant reminded the House of its responsibilities in a peroration which may still be recalled, in spite of the intemperance and exaggeration of much of his speech.

" It is not my voice which you hear, it is the voice of sixty millions of your fellow-creatures . . . imploring you . . . not to make them the objects of perilous speculation, not to barter away their happiness for the sake of some insignificant local interests. . . . We are assembled to decide upon the fate of so many millions of human beings. . . . We are to them as another Providence; our sentence is to stamp the colour of their future years, and spread over the face of ages to come either misery or happiness . . . a glorious destiny for this country, but it is one of overwhelming responsibility. I trust that the question will be decided, not upon party principles, not upon trust, not upon vague theories, but upon sound practical policy, and with a view to the prosperity and preservation of our Indian Empire." [1]

Circumstances were too strong for the Company, and the Bill became law. Napoleon had closed the European ports to English merchants by the Berlin decrees. Public opinion was growing in its support of free trade as presented by Adam Smith, and a petition from Sheffield urged that if the trade to the East Indies were thrown open the new and abundant markets would be certain to yield untold wealth to the manufacturers of England.[2] But Warren Hastings, when questioned in the House of Commons on the prospects of trade development, stated that "the requirements of the poor in India, that is to say the preponderàting mass of the people, were confined to their dwellings, to their food, and to a scanty portion of clothing, all of which they can have from the soil that they tread upon."

The financial and economic policy of Great Britain towards India, and the trade relations between the two countries in the

---

[1] Taken from a summary of the debates given by Thornton, *op. cit.*, pp. 381–388.
[2] See *Indian Administration* . . . (1765–1920), Thakore, pp. 45–50.

latter part of the eighteenth century and the beginning of the nineteenth, were influenced by two outstanding events: the industrial revolution in England and the war with France.

Up to this time India with her hand looms and stamps for printing cotton fabrics had supplied the markets of the world with her finer textiles. But the process of textile manufactures in England was completely revolutionized when the power loom was invented and the first steam spinning-mill set up in 1785. Among the English workers these innovations were unpopular to the point of incendiarism, and they led through commercial competition and the callous pursuit of profit to the shameful factory conditions prevalent in England during a deplorable period of the nineteenth century. In India they dealt the weaving industry a fatal blow. By the end of the first quarter of the nineteenth century the markets had been almost wholly captured by the Lancashire manufacturers, while English cottons had found their way even into the bazaars of India. This was an inevitable result of the unequal fight between the handicraftsman and the machine product. At the same time the English mill-owners were afforded the protection of the Acts passed in 1781 and 1785 reinforcing the laws against the export of machines and tools used in the manufacture of textiles, and the sending out of workmen employed in iron and steel manufactures.[1] The Company struggled hopelessly against this competition, importing cottons into England long after this branch of their trade ceased to be profitable. The average loss on piece-goods coming into the Port of London from India between 1789 and 1799 was estimated to exceed 15 per cent.[2]

Commerce and Industry.

Nor was this the only overwhelming handicap. England had followed a policy of protection since the Restoration and import duties had a tendency to increase. But the low cost of production in India allowed a good margin of profit to the Company. Then in 1793 the prolonged hostilities began with revolutionary France and with Napoleon, and from that date until 1815 increasing

[1] *Trade Relations between England and India*, pp. 161–162.
[2] *Ibid.*, pp. 176–177.

duties were levied to raise money for the war. To take an example: the import duties (warehouse and consumption) on bales of Indian plain calicoes rose from £23, 9s. 1d.[1] in 1800 to £85, 2s. 1d. in 1813[2]; while the value of cotton goods exported from England mainly to India rose from £156 in 1794 to £108,824 in the year ending 5th January 1813.[3] The value of Indian piece-goods sold for the Company and private traders fell from £3,215,722 in 1798–99, to a quarter of this total ten years later,[4] and after 1818 this trade was practically extinct.[5]

In October 1813 Francis Hastings, Earl of Moira, succeeded Lord Minto and became governor-general and commander-in-chief. Three years later he was made Marquis of Hastings, the title by which it is more convenient to refer to him. He was nearly fifty-nine, and although he never went to the hills and habitually started work at four in the morning he ruled in India with wisdom and vigour for nine and a half years, a tenure only surpassed by Warren Hastings. The new governor-general found the state of affairs "far from gratifying." Finances were very low, and the army owing to shortage of money was discontented, inefficient and overworked.[6] Outside the Company's ring-fence a large part of India was rapidly reaching a condition of chaos, and the energies of Lord Hastings had consequently to be devoted to external affairs.

The outstanding feature in India was the helplessness of its symbolic head, the Mogul Emperor. However *Authority in the Empire.* ceremoniously the Nawab of Oudh or the Nizam of Hyderabad might obtain from the Emperor a formal confirmation of his accession and parade a conventional homage on his coinage, and in his public documents, there was not a prince in the country who obeyed the Emperor's orders, or paid him tribute or gathered an army in his defence. Mahadaji

---

[1] To which £3 convoy duty was added.

[2] *Trade Relations between England and India*, Table I (Appendix).

[3] Sir Romesh Dutt, *Economic History of British India*, quoting House of Commons Return of 4th May 1813.

[4] *Trade Relations between England and India*, Table III, quoting Milburn (*Oriental Commerce*, Vol. II. p. 235), for the years 1793–1794 to 1809–1810.

[5] *Trade Relations*, p. 175.   [6] Thornton, *op. cit.*, p. 389.

Sindia had used the imperial name to extend his own power; Tipu Sultan had openly declared his independence.

The emptiness of Mogul authority was equally apparent to the English. The Company's servants, when at the head of affairs, had fallen into line with traditional Indian forms. But the dynasty of Parliamentary governors-general came to India with different ideas. Cornwallis would have nothing to do with any such " jargon of allegiance and obedience." [1] After Shah Alam came under the Company's protection in 1803 Lord Wellesley was more courtly in his methods. But while he gave instructions that Shah Alam was to be accorded the forms of respect " due to the Emperors of Hindustan," the Company's resident exercised control in Delhi under orders from Calcutta issued in Shah Alam's name. Lord Hastings definitely and finally extinguished " the fiction of the Mogul government." The inscription upon his seal no longer acknowledged that the governor-general was the servant of the Emperor; and when Akbar II, who had succeeded his father Shah Alam in 1806, desired an interview, Lord Hastings made it a condition that the ceremonial should be omitted which had in the past implied imperial supremacy over the Company's dominions.[2]

Lord Hastings, moreover, encouraged the Nawab of Oudh to assume the title of king; and " terms of equality " between the Company's government and the King of Oudh were used in letters and treaties for many years to come. Sir William Lee Warner quotes a treaty of 1838 which " reads like a leaf taken out of the treaties of the preceding century." [3]

Political Situation. Certain great States such as Hyderabad were under the Company's protection, but British policy had for ten years left almost the whole of Central India to take care of itself. Sindia, Holkar and the predatory leaders had a free hand, and among the Maratha States were

[1] *Correspondence of Charles, First Marquis Cornwallis,* ed. Charles Ross, Vol. I. p. 558.
[2] *Private Diary of the Marquis of Hastings.* These references are quoted in the more accessible *Camb. Hist. Brit. Empire,* Vol. IV. pp. 602–607.
[3] *The Native States of India,* Edn. 1910, pp. 92, 93.

a number of petty feudatories in various stages of independence. The Marathas, whose power rested upon armies maintained by exactions upon their neighbours, were hostile to the English who had defeated them and were busy strengthening their forces. The situation was aggravated by bodies of thousands of Pindari freebooters and by the large number of soldiers who had been disbanded by the Company's government and its allies. These fighting men poured from the pacified districts into the independent territories which Sir Alfred Lyall described as a kind of political Alsatia. The most formidable of the free companies was led by the notorious adventurer Amir Khan, who had given trouble to the Company since 1805, when he sided with Holkar,[1] and had been fortunate to escape destruction four years later by an English force.[2] The Pindari freebooters, mounted on camels or ponies, could move on occasion fifty miles in a day, and they inflicted fiendish tortures to wring money from their victims.[3] In 1814 Amir Khan was living upon Rajputana with a compact and disciplined army of at least 30,000 men and a number of guns.[4]

As some of the Rajput States represented to the British resident in Rajputana: " Some power in India had always existed to which peaceable States submitted, and in return obtained its protection against the invasions of upstart chiefs and the armies of lawless banditti; the British Government now occupied the place of that protecting power, and was the natural guardian of weak States which were continually exposed to the cruelties and oppression of robbers and plunderers, owing to the refusal of the British Government to protect them." [5]

This was perfectly true. A policy of neutrality was totally inconsistent with the position of the Company, which was a continental sovereignty carrying with it the moral responsibility to keep law and order. The home Government, hoping against hope, wished

---

[1] Thornton, *op. cit.*, p. 309.
[2] Malcolm, *Political History*, Vol. I. pp. 403–405.
[3] Thornton, *op. cit.*, pp. 424–426.
[4] *Rise of the British Dominion in India*, pp. 255–256.
[5] Letter from Sir Charles (afterwards Lord) Metcalfe, then Resident in Rajputana, dated June 1816.

for peace and trusted to keep it by alliances with such States as had not as yet become predatory. But they saw that hostilities might become inevitable with the " large hordes of freebooters whose excesses appeared to increase with British forbearance." [1] Moreover the subsidiary treaties had justified the Duke of Wellington's view. They had weakened the feeling of responsibility of the rulers concerned and State government had deteriorated with the assurance of British protection in the event of attack or revolt; consequently in addition to treaty obligations of external defence the Company became increasingly responsible for internal order in the allied States.

Lord Hastings had come to India with a peace policy but his government was involved in an unbroken series of hostilities for the first five years of his administration. The earliest of these wars was with Nepal.

About the middle of the eighteenth century Prithwi Narayan Sah, a chief of Rajput descent, was ruler of Gurkha, a small *The War* hill State on the southern slopes of the Himalaya. In *with Nepal.* twenty years of incessant fighting he became master of the twenty-four States of Nepal; and by 1794 his successors had conquered the highlands between Bhutan and Kashmir and pushed their borders down to the marches of the Company's territories in India. Nepal was essentially a military State, and the government of the country lay in the hands of its warrior statesmen. The army of Nepal was drilled and equipped on European lines and its men, then as now, were born fighters.

Nepalese officers had encroached upon the Company's frontier in the time of Minto, and in 1814 two districts within the Bengal border were seized. Lord Hastings demanded their surrender. The government of Khatmandu made evasive replies and coupled them with further hostile acts. Finally the governor-general broke off negotiations with great reluctance and declared war upon Nepal.

In November 1814 three British columns entered the hills on the first of the frontier expeditions which have intermittently engaged

---

[1] Malcolm, *Political History*, Vol. I. pp. 442, 443.

the Government of India ever since. The strategy as planned by Lord Hastings was sound enough. But four out of his five generals were incompetent and the campaign opened with a series of defeats in one of which General Gillespie was killed. General (Sir David) Ochterlony and Colonel Gardner were the only commanders able to grasp the first principles of mountain warfare. Gardner and Nicolls took Almora, the capital of Kumaon, at the end of April 1815. In May the Nepalese General Amar Singh, who had been driven into Malaon by Ochterlony, was forced to sign a convention surrendering the disputed districts in Bengal, and was allowed to march out from the fortress with the honours of war.

The government of Nepal refused at first to ratify the convention, but after further operations Ochterlony advanced upon the capital and peace was signed at Sagauli in March 1816.[1] Nepal ceded Garhwal and Kumaon with the greater part of the Tarai, evacuated Sikkim and a British resident was appointed to Khatmandu.[2]

This treaty gave the European servants of the Company their first Himalayan hill-stations, and Naini Tal in Kumaon is now the summer capital of the United Provinces. The first Gurkha battalions were then raised, and from the independent kingdom of Nepal, firm ally of Great Britain, the famous regiments of the Gurkha Brigade are still recruited.

During the war with Nepal Pindari outrages in the Company's and the Nizam's territories increased to such an extent that Lord Hastings determined to suppress the freebooters once and for all. In 1816 they raided the Northern Circars and in less than a fortnight plundered 339 villages, killed nearly two hundred people and tortured or maltreated more than four

The Pindaris.

---

[1] Thornton, *op. cit.*, pp. 389–409. Prinsep's account, *Political and Military Transactions*, 1813–1823, Edn. 1825, Vol. I. pp. 81–207, gives maps and sketches.

[2] Brian Hodgson, whose services in the cause of peace on the northern frontier were as great as his pioneer researches in Buddhist literature were distinguished, was promoted resident in 1833. His biography has been written by Sir William Hunter.

thousand peaceful and inoffensive subjects of the Company. This ended the hesitation of the Board of Control under Canning to endorse active measures.[1]

The general situation was not improved by the fact that although the Maratha chiefs openly disowned the Pindaris they secretly encouraged them; and this was to lead, through complications with the Peshwa Baji Rao, to the final extinction of Maratha power in India. Lord Hastings fully realized that the steps he was taking might bring the Marathas into the field against him, and while he mobilized all his available forces he took every political precaution in his power. In the course of 1816 and 1817 treaties were made with about twenty Muhammadan and Hindu states. The most valuable alliance, which Sindia made an ineffectual demonstration to stop,[2] was with Wazir Muhammad (Bhopal) whose successors, most of them princesses, have remained ever since the staunch friends of the British Government. Jaipur, which was threatened by Amir Khan in 1816, was offered an alliance which its ruler refused; and Appa Sahib Bhonsla, the Regent of Nagpur, signed in May 1816 a subsidiary treaty which he afterwards annulled. Amir Khan, after negotiating with the Company and the Peshwa in turn, finally came to terms with Lord Hastings,[3] disbanded his army and was given the Nawabship of Tonk, where his successors still rule.

These diplomatic moves to some extent eased the situation but the keys to the strongholds of the Maratha confederacy lay in the hands of Sindia at Gwalior and the Peshwa in Poona. Sindia's power of offensive was effectually neutralized when Lord Hastings in his preliminary movements against the Pindaris in 1817, marched with his main army to Gwalior and obliged Sindia to sign a treaty which Sir John Malcolm describes as contrary to his inclination but consonant to his interests. By its terms Sindia furnished a contingent for the Pindari campaign under British command, admitted British troops to garrison his country, and agreed to keep his main army

---

[1] Orders received by Lord Hastings at the end of March 1817. For the Despatch of the Board of Control see Malcolm's *History*, Vol. I. pp. 486–488.

[2] *History of the Mahrattas*, Vol. II. p. 454.

[3] Thornton, *op. cit.*, pp. 433–434.

within his own dominions. One of the clauses ran as follows: " If (which God forbid!) the British Government and the Maharajah shall be compelled to wage war with any other State, on account of such State attacking either of the contracting parties or aiding . . . the Pindaris . . . the British Government, having at heart the welfare of Dowlat Row Scindia, will, in the event of success, and of his highness's zealous performance of his engagements, make the most liberal arrangements for the consolidation and increase of his territories." [1]

The Peshwa had remained at peace with the British since the treaty of Bassein ten years earlier, and secure in
The Peshwa.
their support he had steadily strengthened his resources. Baji Rao was bold in intrigue, cowardly in action and depraved in conduct. He was the only Peshwa who had full leisure to devote himself to improving the government, but his administration was notoriously corrupt and he refused to listen to the complaints of his subjects.[2] The Peshwa's attitude towards the Company's government changed in tone, and became noticeably unfriendly, when Trimbakji Danglia became Baji Rao's confidential adviser in 1814. Trimbakji's only qualifications were his vices, and his sole exploit was a highly coloured version of his escape from the Company's prison at Salsette when he was confined there for the singularly atrocious murder of Gangadhar Sastri, the Brahman envoy of the Gaekwar of Baroda in 1816.[3] In 1817 Lord Hastings decided to end the hostile intrigues and unfriendly acts of Baji Rao and Trimbakji either by a treaty which would impose strong British control over the Poona government, or by dethroning the Peshwa. Baji Rao saw his danger and signed the treaty of Poona in June 1817 by which he renounced his headship of the Maratha confederacy, which was dissolved, ceded the Konkan and certain forts to the Company, recognized the independence of the Gaekwar of Baroda and amongst other clauses denounced Trimbakji as the murderer of Gangadhar

[1] Thornton, *op. cit.*, pp. 431–433.
[2] Malcolm, *Political History of India*, Vol. I. pp. 466–468. *History of the Mahrattas*, Vol. II. pp. 429–431.
[3] But cf. *Lord Hastings and the Indian States*, Dr. M. S. Mehta, pp. 107, 108.

Sastri.[1] The Peshwa also transferred his regular battalions to the company as part of the subsidiary contingent which was called the Poona auxiliary force.[2]

In the autumn of 1817 Lord Hastings began operations against the Pindaris, a campaign which became merged in the third Maratha war. A total force of 113,000 men, including 13,000 Europeans with 300 guns, was mobilized, and divided into two armies, the Army of Hindustan under the governor-general and the Deccan Army under Sir Thomas Hislop with Sir John Malcolm as his chief staff and political officer. The strategic plan was to surround the Pindaris in Malwa within a circle 700 miles across and then by a systematic " drive " hunt them down and break up their forces. To prevent the Marathas from joining the freebooters a strong detachment was disposed as a cordon between Poona and Nagpur. The co-ordinated movements of the nine divisions of the " northern " and " southern " armies—the most extensive operations ever conducted in India—were entirely successful, although the troops suffered severely from cholera. By the end of January 1818 the Pindaris were annihilated.[3]

The Pindari Campaign.

The Peshwa, with his new minister Bapu Gokhale, believing that the Pindari campaign offered him the certain opportunity of getting rid of British control, concentrated his army at Poona, and on 5th November 1817 took the field.[4] He burnt the Residency and then attacked the British force 2800 strong under Colonel Burr at Kirkee, with 26,000 men. The Marathas were completely defeated, and Colonel Burr followed up his victory by winning two brilliantly successful actions against equally heavy odds at Koregaon and at Ashti where Bapu Gokhale was killed. Baji Rao, a fugitive after Kirkee, surrendered on 18th June 1818 to Sir John Malcolm, who with misplaced generosity

Third Maratha War.

[1] Malcolm, *Political History*, Vol. I. pp. 479–481.
[2] *History of the Mahrattas*, Vol. II. p. 466.
[3] Thornton, *op. cit.*, pp. 431-455.
[4] The events at Poona during the critical days from the 19th October to the 5th November are vividly described by Grant Duff who was present with the political agent Mountstuart Elphinstone (*History of the Mahrattas*, Vol. II. pp. 471–481).

pledged the Company to grant the Peshwa the excessive annuity of eight lakhs of rupees. Baji Rao went into retirement at Bithur on the Ganges with his adopted son Dhundhu Pant, who was to become known in 1857 as Nana Sahib.

Two of the Maratha chiefs, Appa Sahib, who had succeeded to the throne of Berar, and Holkar, followed the Peshwa's example and began hostilities against the British.

Appa Sahib attacked the small composite force of Indian troops at Nagpur at the end of November 1818, and was severely defeated in the action of Sitabaldi. All was over in less than three weeks. Appa Sahib took refuge with the Sikhs, and the Saugor and Narbada districts of Berar State were annexed by the Company.[1]

The dispositions made by Lord Hastings had effectually prevented united action by the Maratha states, and the campaign begun by Holkar in December (1818) ended in his immediate and total defeat by General Sir Thomas Hislop at Mahidpur. On 6th January 1819 Holkar came to terms, by which he gave up his possessions south of the Narbada, abandoned his claims upon the Rajput chiefs, and agreed to receive a British Resident and to maintain a subsidiary force.[2]

Asirgharh, one of the forts which Sindia had agreed to hand over temporarily, had not been surrendered, and its commandant who had been directly encouraged by Sindia openly helped Appa Sahib.[3] Lord Hastings accordingly decided to take the place; and the siege which began in February 1819 ended in its capture on the 9th April. The fall of Asirgharh ended the war; and Sindia's undoubted treachery was forgiven.

The Maratha confederacy was broken. The Peshwa had disappeared and the descendants of Sivaji were allowed to rule in semi-independence at Satara until 1848 when the British Government, which at that time did not recognize the Hindu law of adoption of heirs, escheated Satara on the ground of lapse and annexed it. Sindia, Holkar and the Bhonsla raja of Berar were definitely bound over to keep the peace of India, and the Maratha States were enclosed

---

[1] *History of the Mahrattas*, Vol. II. pp. 493–498.
[2] *Ibid.*, Vol. II. pp. 501–506.   [3] Thornton, *op. cit.*, p. 454.

within carefully demarcated limits.[1] The existence of the Rajput States, princes of whose race had ruled in India for over thirteen hundred years, was assured.

The year 1819 marks the great political settlement of Central India under British supremacy. It then became recognized that, outside the Punjab and Sind, the foreign relations of every State in the country should be under the control of the British Government of India; that all interstate disputes should be settled by British arbitration; that the British Government would intervene to quell disorder or to remedy gross misgovernment; that the subsidiary forces and state contingents should be under British supervision; and that British residents should be appointed to the more important States to exercise these functions. British ascendancy was absolute.

The policy of Lord Hastings may be summed up as a middle course. It lay between the dream of Cornwallis that the stronger organizations would absorb the petty States and become good neighbours of the British—and the views of Lord Dalhousie, that the good of the people required annexations.

Singapore. The political achievement of Lord Hastings, the result of his brilliantly successful campaigns, was his outstanding work in India, but this was not his only contribution to the building up of British imperial power. The Dutch settlements in Java, taken in the time of Lord Minto, had been unconditionally restored in 1814, and the Dutch at once attempted to exclude all foreign competition in the Archipelago. On the advice of Sir Stamford Raffles, governor of the small British colony in Sumatra, Lord Hastings sanctioned the occupation of the island of Singapore in the Straits of Malacca then inhabited only by a few fishermen. The British flag was hoisted in 1819; and in 1824 an adjustment of territory was made with Holland, which ended all friction with that government.

[1] Prinsep, *Political and Military Transactions in India*, Vol. II. pp. 381–405.

Between 1819 and the end of his term of office Lord Hastings

End of Piracy. sent several expeditions against the pirates of the Persian Gulf and finally stamped out piracy on the Indian coast from the Konkan to Cutch.

Order in the Company's territories was unfortunately disturbed

Internal Disturbances. by two popular outbreaks. The insurrection at Bareilly in 1816 was caused by the injudicious methods of an Indian subordinate, when a new and unpopular police tax was imposed. The tax was denounced as a public grievance and an influential mufti incited the Muhammadans to join in a religious riot. By the middle of April the insurrection became serious. Troops had to be called out but the disturbances were not suppressed until twenty-one Indian soldiers and more than three hundred of the insurgents had lost their lives. British rule in Orissa had unquestionably created a feeling of discontent, as the subsequent official inquiry brought out. The upper classes disliked an administration which, as an Indian of high rank told Strachey,[1] "reduces me to a level with my domestics and labourers." The British courts of justice which were considered a grievance by the upper classes were not looked upon as a blessing by the lower, on account of the expenses and delay of litigation.

The disturbances at Cuttack in Orissa which took place about the same time were due to over-assessment, the raising of the salt tax and the dishonesty of subordinate Indian officials. The riots were quelled and the undoubted grievances were removed by a sympathetic and understanding commissioner.

Lord Hastings, while extending British authority in India, did

Administration. not neglect the administration of the Company's territories, and he paid strict attention to finance. His military operations entailed serious deficits in the budgets between 1818 and 1821,[2] but a surplus was obtained in his last two years without extra taxation, and he gained the confidence of the Indian princes, who began to invest their money in government securities.[3]

---

[1] Thornton, *op. cit.*, p. 412.
[2] Prinsep, *op. cit.*, Vol. II. Statement facing p. 443.
[3] *Life of the Marquis of Hastings*, Sir Lepel Griffin, p. 208.

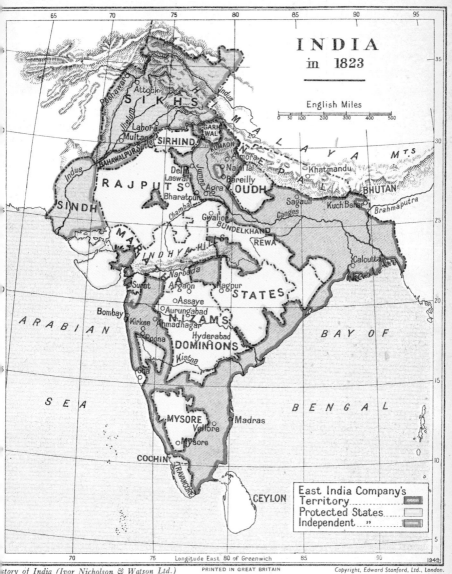

INDIA
in 1823

English Miles
0 50 100 200 300 400 500

SIKHS
Peshawar
Attock
Jhelum
Lahore
Multan
Sutlej
BAHAWALPUR
SIRHIND
GARH
WAL
KUMAON
Almora
Naini Tal
Khatmandu
NEPAL
BHUTAN
Kuch Behar
Brahmaputra
Ganges
Sagauli
Delhi
Laswari
Agra
Jumna
Bareilly
OUDH
Bharatpur
Chambal
Gwalior
BUNDELKHAND
REWA
Calcutta
RAJPUTS
SINDH
Indus
MARA
VINDHYA HILLS
Narbada
Surat
Argaon
Assaye
Nagpur
STATES
Aurungabad
Ahmadnagar
NIZAM'S
Bombay
Kirkee
Poona
Hyderabad
DOMINIONS
Kistna
Goa
BAY OF
BENGAL

ARABIAN

SEA

MYSORE
Vellore
Madras
Mysore
COCHIN
TRAVANCORE
CEYLON

East India Company's
Territory
Protected States
Independent "

ARMALAYA MTS

Longitude East 80 of Greenwich

story of India (Ivor Nicholson & Watson Ltd.)   PRINTED IN GREAT BRITAIN   Copyright, Edward Stanford, Ltd., London.

Agriculture was helped by the reopening of the Hariana and Doab canals, which had silted up, and by the extensive construction and repair of roads. Other public works included the restoration of the old Mogul water-supply of Delhi and the town-planning which gave Calcutta better sanitary conditions, a more beautiful city and a handsome embankment on the river front.

The governor-general's sympathy for the Anglo-Indian [1] community took the practical form of encouraging its members to enter the government service, where their promotion for good work was assured. From the day when Lord Hastings promoted Skinner, descendant of the Scotsman Hercules Skinner and the Rajput girl he married, from captain of Irregulars to lieutenant-colonel, Anglo-Indians have served the government of India loyally and well.

During the administration of Lord Hastings, Sir Thomas Munro, who became governor of Madras in 1820, made a new land survey and assessment in that Presidency. The general system was *ryotwari*, and the holdings ranged from about four acres to over four thousand. Munro rightly kept to that system, but the assessments made were too high, and although the governor did all in his power to modify the local harshness of collection, the assessments were not reduced to a fair level for many years.

The Press. Newspapers in the form of court-gazettes were, at the beginning of the nineteenth century, common in the Indian States. These gave news, as matters of fact, without comment,[2] and Grant Duff makes an amusing reference to the power of publicity under the Peshwa's government. Lord Hastings interested himself in Indian education, founding schools at his own expense; and it was during his term of office that a Bengali news-

---

[1] " A resident British subject (not being pure European) who is of European descent in the male line, or who is of mixed Asiatic and non-Asiatic descent, and whose father, grandfather, or more remote ancestor was born in the continent of Europe, Canada, Newfoundland, Australia, New Zealand, the Union of South Africa or the U.S.A." (*Ind. Stat. Commission Report*, Vol. I. p. 43). The term Anglo-Indian was used by Sir John Malcolm in 1826 (*Political History*, Vol. II. pp. 260–265).

[2] Malcolm, *Political History*, Vol. II. p. 310.

paper first appeared in British India. This was followed by the *Samachar-Darpan*, a periodical edited by the Serampur missionaries; and an Indian-owned press soon developed. For a number of years the Indian press devoted its attention to religious topics, it was not influential in the political sense, and its circulation was not large. Sir Thomas Munro had pointed out that an unrestricted press and an autocratic government were incompatible and that the first duty of a free press was " to deliver the country from a foreign yoke." But although the Indian press grew up under virtually no restrictions, it was not until 1853 that a definitely political paper, the *Hindu Patriot*, appeared. Strong attacks upon the government by Indian newspapers then began, and a censorship was imposed.[1]

It must, however, be said that from about 1790 there had been " in different parts of India a most active circulation of inflammatory papers in the form of proclamations, letters and prophecies, directed to the subversion of the British power . . . in almost all cases . . . addressed to the interests and passions of (its) native troops." [2]

Very different from the earliest Indian publications in British India were the beginnings of the English press in the country. The first English periodical was the *Bengal Gazette*, brought out by Hickey in January 1780, when " the times were favourable for the profit and popularity of an editor prepared to promulgate the acts, the misrepresentations, the calumnies, the public and private scandal, which disgraced the period at which his labours commenced." [3] Hickey spent a large proportion of his time in jail and his paper was suppressed early in 1782. Other enterprising and sometimes seditious journals followed. Lord Wellesley was obliged to take strong measures when the publication of shipping news gave invaluable information to the French privateers; and Lord Minto drew up a revised code of censorship regulations in 1813.

Lord Hastings was prepared to grant a definitely restricted freedom to the press. He substituted a series of regulations for the

---

[1] See *Political India*, ed. Sir John Cumming, *passim*.
[2] Malcolm, *op. cit.*, Vol. II. p. 317, footnote.
[3] Malcolm, *op. cit.*, Vol. II. p. 292.

censorship in 1817, but he forbade criticism of the authorities in India or England, discussion of Indian religious beliefs, and " personal remarks tending to excite dissension in society." [1] This, however, did not deter James Silk Buckingham, the enterprising editor of the *Calcutta Journal*, from launching a widely circulated press campaign against the governor-general, with which his successor, Mr. Adam, subsequently dealt.

It is, unfortunately, impossible to avoid reference to a deplorable indiscretion which marked the close of Lord Hastings'

The Hyderabad Case.

time in India. This was the governor-general's regrettable connection with a firm of bankers whose business dealings with the State of Hyderabad closely resembled the financial operations of Paul Benfield in the Carnatic. A partner of the firm in question, Palmer & Company, had married a connection of Lord Hastings, who was also his ward. The governor-general without proper inquiry granted government sanction to Palmer's application to transact what was in point of fact illegal and dishonest business in Hyderabad. Palmer & Company, with their fees, and charges for interest at an enormous rate, piled up a colossal balance in their own favour, and then applied to the Government of India to recover this sum for them from the Hyderabad treasury. Lord Hastings, who had no financial interest whatever in the transaction, blindly defended Palmer & Company, and this drew down upon him so strong a censure from the Directors that he sent in his resignation in 1821. In the words of Thornton,[2] " the Marquis of Hastings, in this unhappy affair, sacrificed his reputation, which he valued beyond all things, to the passion of others for amassing wealth—a passion in which he did not participate, and by the indulgence of which he was to gain nothing."

Lord Hastings retired on the 9th January 1823. His only known qualification for the appointment of governor-general had been a close friendship with the Prince Regent, afterwards George IV. But Prinsep,[3] writing in 1825, could sum up the results of his adminis-

---

[1] Malcolm, *Political History*, Vol. II. pp. 300–301, footnote.
[2] *Op. cit.*, p. 456.   [3] *Op. cit.*, Vol. II. p. 421.

tration in these words: "The struggle which ended in the universal establishment of the British influence is particularly important. . . . Henceforth this epoch will be referred to as that whence each of the existing States will date the commencement of its peaceable settlement and the consolidation of its relations with the controlling power. The dark age of trouble and violence which so long spread its malign influence over the fertile regions of Central India has thus ceased from this time; and a new era has commenced, we trust with brighter prospects—an era of peace, prosperity and wealth at least, if not political liberty and high moral improvement." The history of India in the nineteenth century and after records the issue of these prospects.

The effect upon India of contact with the West, which first became widespread and insistent at the beginning of the nineteenth century, made its earliest appearance in an attempt at religious reforms. This was to be expected in a country where religion counts more than anything else in everyday life, and where the introduction of Islam had led to the Bhakti movement.

In 1828 the Brahmo Samaj was started, and the ideals of its founder, the Brahman Ram Mohun Roy, may be realized from the titles of his works, *An Abstract of the Sutras* and *The Precepts of Jesus Christ: a Guide to Peace and Happiness*. The Brahmo Samaj, developed by Keshab Chandra Sen, with its encouragement of inter-caste marriage, is today a spent force. Reaction came with the Arya Samaj founded by Dayanand Sarasvati, a Hindu villager whose teaching of the Brahmanic tradition is still a vital movement, especially in the north. Outstanding among these religious revivals is the Ramakrishna movement, as it was named by that Indian saint's follower Vivekananda, the founder of the Order. The movement, which began about the middle of the last century, has been described [1] as the most characteristic expression of Indian nationalism. Centred on the Brahma Sutras, the rock upon which Indian culture is built, it insisted upon selfless service for the masses of the people, with the

[1] *The British Connection with India*, K. T. Paul (London), 1927, which gives the Indian social and philanthropic point of view of the various phases of the Indian national movement.

object of forming a perfect human fellowship. The religious movement soon developed into social reform.

Western ideas were brought in with the English educational system introduced by Lord William Bentinck in 1835; and the writings of Paine and the speeches of the philosophic radicals were read by educated high-caste Indians. Political activity on democratic lines followed the impulse towards social reform. But among the first generation of English-educated Indians and indeed until more recent times when female education began to make some headway, English ideas had no influence among the masses of India. The preponderating influence of Hindu mothers was all against changes affecting family life; the agricultural classes had no use for education; and the Muhammadans stood aloof. Consequently there was brought into existence a small urban class drawn exclusively from men of the higher castes, whose aim was the political liberty to which Prinsep referred in rather dubious terms.

Indian political evolution and the administrative reforms of modern times will be described later, but an indication may be given here of the tendencies of the Indian reformers. Even the earliest had marked political leanings. Ram Mohun Roy, whose interest in the English Reform Bill and in the Indian Charter Act of 1833 took him to England, organized a public protest in 1823 in favour of liberty of the press. A hundred years later Mahatma Gandhi, a student at the bar for four years in London, champion of the " Suppressed " classes, as he has called them, and the leader of the *satyagraha* [1] movement appealed to the Sermon on the Mount as the supreme criterion of private and public conduct.

The era of peace to which Prinsep confidently looked forward in his political review of Lord Hastings' administration was not yet to dawn over India. The government of the Company had still to meet not only the terrible storms of 1857, but the last and most serious challenge made by an Indian power. The Marathas had been weakened by the expansion of their nominal rule beyond their control, and were dealt with in detail. But the Sikhs were concentrated

---

[1] " Non-violent non-co-operation."

within limits which they could fill with their zeal, and were to prove most formidable adversaries.

In 1809 the north-west frontier of British India and the protected *Ranjit Singh.* States had been advanced by the treaty with the southern (Malwa) Sikhs to the left bank of the Sutlej. Beyond that river Ranjit Singh had built up a formidable military State by ruthlessly mastering the rival independent confederacies which when disunited were helpless against an enemy.

Born in 1780, Ranjit Singh was the son of Sirdar Mahan Singh, the enterprising and unscrupulous leader of the Sucharchakia confederacy, and was of Rajput descent. Mahan Singh died fighting in 1792, and Ranjit Singh owed to his wife's mother Sada Kour, a woman of remarkable ability and head of the Karheya confederacy, the early opportunities which led to his later ascendancy.

In Ranjit Singh, who was a born leader of men, unfailing political foresight and indomitable perseverance were combined with the greatest courage and endurance. He was an excellent rider, his love of horses amounting to a passion, he was a keen sportsman and a fine swordsman. Like many other great Indian soldiers and statesmen he was simple in his dress and wore either saffron-coloured Kashmir cloth or plain white muslin without jewels or ornament, except on state occasions. Baron Charles von Hugel [1] saw the Lion of the Punjab when drunkenness and debauchery had prematurely aged him and he was disfigured by smallpox and crippled from a paralytic seizure. He described him as the most ugly and unprepossessing man he saw in the Punjab—except when mounted. The Maharaja was blind of one eye, and a short man with a massive forehead whose head seemed too large for his body. But feeble, blind and paralysed though he became, Ranjit Singh kept his absolute ascendancy over his court of fierce and turbulent chiefs, and until the last day of his life was always instantly obeyed.

Ranjit Singh steadily increased his dominions whenever opportunity offered; and his army was equal to his *The Sikh Army.* ambitions. Very early in his career he realized that the existing Sikh system was unsound. He visited Lord Lake's

[1] *Travels in Kashmir and the Panjab,* 1845.

446

army in 1805,[1] saw the organization and training which had conquered the military races of India, and remodelled the Khalsa army on similar lines. The Sikh horsemen had always been the fighting arm, but Ranjit Singh made his infantry the principal branch of the service, to which he sent the pick of his recruits. In 1812 Ochterlony saw two regiments of Sikhs and several battalions of Hindus drilled by British deserters,[2] and the Maharaja engaged European generals such as Ventura and Allard who had distinguished themselves under Napoleon, and an Irishman, Gardner, who was an able artillery officer, to train his troops. The highest commands in the field were reserved for Indian generals, of whom the best was Hari Singh, who eventually took command on the Peshawar frontier.

The old chiefs disliked the military reforms, but Ranjit Singh gave his regular troops good pay, wore the new uniform and was accustomed to drill his regiments himself. The men of the regular army wore a scarlet uniform, in imitation of the British, and had similar equipment. The feudal levies were mounted, and wore what they pleased. Many of them were country gentlemen of means who paraded in coats of mail, or many coloured silks and velvets, with their swords, their matchlocks and the small round Sikh shields of buffalo hide, and even bows and arrows.

The Sikh administration has been described by Sir Lepel Griffin [3] as the process of squeezing out of the *Administration.* unhappy peasant, Hindu or Muhammadan, every rupee that he could be made to disgorge. The Sikhs, it may be said, were soldiers almost to a man. The revenue officer, who was also the district judge, dared not fall into arrears of payment. His one administrative problem was to maintain cultivation at the highest possible level and at the same time keep the cultivators at the lowest point of depression. Custom-houses covered the country and duties were levied on almost every article of common use, without any discrimination between luxuries and the necessities of life.

The only comment to be made on law and order is that the highways were universally unsafe. But the administration was far

[1] *History of the Sikhs*, p. 172.   [2] *Ibid.*, pp. 172–173.
[3] *Ranjit Singh*, Sir Lepel Griffin, Ch. VII., " Army and Administration."

better than it had been in the days of the confederacies, when government had been nothing more than an organized system of massacre and pillage. The centre and south of the kingdom were firmly and not unjustly ruled, but justice on the north-west frontier, when the Italian general Avitabile governed Peshawar, was symbolized by his portable gallows.

In 1809 Ranjit Singh took Kangra and contained the Gurkhas in the hills to the left bank of the Sutlej. It is un-
Sikh Expansion. necessary to detail the affairs of the two ex-kings of Kabul, Shah Shujah and Zaman Shah and their dealings with the Maharaja, beyond saying that when Shah Shujah was in Lahore in 1813, Ranjit Singh obliged him to give up the Koh-i-noor diamond. This gem was surrendered, on the British annexation of the Punjab in 1849, in token of submission to Queen Victoria. In 1813 Ranjit Singh took Attock, and then turned his forces northwards to fail in his first invasion of Kashmir. In 1815 he began his systematic advance towards what he was to make the existing north-west frontier of India. Multan was taken in 1818, and Ranjit Singh temporarily occupied Peshawar in the same year. The Afghan garrison of Kashmir was overpowered in 1819, and the country annexed, to be followed by the capture of the Derajat of the Indus plain in 1820.

Ranjit Singh now prepared to carry his frontier from the Indus to the north-western passes. Muhammad Azim Khan, who had been the Afghan governor of Kashmir and had recently proclaimed Shah Ayub king of Kabul, was now master of Afghanistan in all but name, and governor of Peshawar. On 13th March 1823 Ranjit Singh crossed the Indus. A religious war had been preached amongst the Khattaks and Usufzais and twenty thousand tribesmen were with the Afghan army which met the Sikhs at Nowshera on the following day. A stubbornly contested action ended in the defeat of Muhammad Azim. Ranjit Singh marched upon Peshawar and sacked it. After plundering the country up to the Khyber Pass, he retired beyond the Indus, leaving Yar Muhammad (Muhammad Azim's brother), who had tendered his submission, to govern Peshawar in the name of the Khalsa.[1]

[1] *History of the Sikhs, passim.*

PLATE LV.

AN OFFICER OF NIZAM'S ARMY
By courtesy of the Parker Gallery

PLATE LVI.

(b) COMMEMORATIVE SATI STONE
To a Brahman woman, Dholpur, 1579
By courtesy of Indian Museum, South Kensington

(a) ANCIENT AHOM TEMPLE, SIBSAGAR, ASSAM
By courtesy of " The Times of India "

Ranjit Singh had now brought under his sway the three Muhammadan provinces of Kashmir, Multan and Peshawar, and he was supreme in the hills and plains of the Punjab itself. Partly by intrigue, but mainly by force of arms, he had created a kingdom which was held together by a strong tie of religion that was wanting in the Pindari hordes and which in the case of the Maratha confederacy was weakened by caste.

No better field than the Punjab could have been selected for the policy of non-intervention by the British Government. The experiment of a strong organization was tried, under every condition of success, in a tract of country where the Company's frontier was defined by a river, and at a time when the house of Delhi and the Marathas were reduced to impotence, while Afghanistan was occupied with its own affairs.[1] But the policy of non-intervention and of avoiding political settlements was to break down in the north, as it had failed in the centre of India. Ten years after the death of the great Maharaja in 1839, the second Sikh war ended in the British annexation of the Punjab.

[1] *The Native States of India*, Sir W. Lee-Warner, 2nd Edn., pp. 98, 99.

NOTE 1.—THE HYDERABAD CONTINGENT

After the disbandment of Raymond's Corps and the substitution of English for French influence in Hyderabad, the Nizam put a subsidiary force at the disposal of the Company; and about 6000 cavalry and 3600 infantry co-operated in the campaign which destroyed Tipu Sultan. This force, whose roll of officers included Spaniards, Portuguese, an East Indian of Dutch extraction, as well as Englishmen, Scotsmen and Irish was " incomplete in numbers, loose in discipline, irregularly paid, badly armed, badly dressed, and subject to (innumerable) frauds and stoppages." It is hardly surprising that mutinies occurred in 1812. In the following year the force was reformed. The famous Russell Brigade was created, and what was eventually called the Hyderabad Contingent came into being, with two infantry battalions and small units of heavy field guns. In 1816 the cavalry were reorganized. General Arthur Wellesley had said in 1803 : " The Nizam's Horse are very useless, which annoys me a good deal "; Lord Gough was to state before the Committee of the House of Commons fifty years later that they were the finest irregular cavalry in the world, a reputation which they afterwards maintained. The strength of the Contingent varied. For some time it consisted of 100 European officers with 60 warrant officers and N.C.O.s, and about 5800

Indian cavalry and 8800 infantry. When the Contingent became part of the Indian Army in 1903 it totalled 126 British officers and 2000 cavalry, 5400 infantry and artillery in Indian ranks and 16 guns. Its almost continuous war service began with the Maratha War in 1817. The Contingent greatly helped in the pacification of the country during the next forty years, it played a prominent part in the Central India operations of 1857–58, and its last engagements as a separate force were in the Third Burma War of 1885 and the subsequent suppression of the dacoits. The *History of the Hyderabad Contingent*, by Major (Colonel) R. G. Burton, from which these facts have been taken, was published by the Government Printing Press (Calcutta) in 1905.

Note 2.—Indian Standards

The *Ain-i-Akbari* gives, as the Mogul Standards, the traditional Indian emblems of royalty, the umbrella, the hand, and various sun standards. By 1800 these were probably purely emblematic of court rank. The six Standards presented to Lord Lake by Shah Alam (after the defeat of Sindia and Perron's battalions) which are now in the India Museum at South Kensington, were the " fish " and the usual flat, gilded emblems the " hand " (*alm*) and the sun standards (*kokba* and *shaban*).

The Marathas had two flags, Sivaji's personal yellow ascetic robe Banner and the Jari Patka, or Golden Pennon, carried before the Bhonsla rajas of Berar. See *History of the Mahrattas*, Vol. I. pp. 283, 297 and note; and *Journal of the Asiatic Society of Bengal*, Vol. XIV. p. 343.

Note 3.—The East India Company's Colours

It is symbolic of the development of the Company that the early device on the Colours of its troops was the trade mark, stamped upon the bales of its goods. This trade mark (and its variants), which were used as early as 1658 (*vide* India Office MSS. Letter Book, Vol. II. p. 69, dated 14th March 1658), was called by the Indian word *nishan*; and the trade " nishan " became, between 1805 and 1813, the soldier's Nishan, the name by which the Colours are known in the Indian Army today.

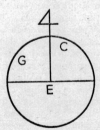

In the Madras Army of 1759 the Company flags were of almost every colour, usually with a red or white cross in the centre. In 1781, under the battalion system, there were two Colours, the Union Jack, and the regimental Colour which bore the union in the upper canton and a wreathed numeral in the centre. In 1797 the Bengal Cavalry, and in 1800 the Governor-General's bodyguard, received Standards. Descriptions of Colours and Standards of the Company's army are given in the authoritative works by Major H. Bullock, *Indian Cavalry Standards* (London), 1930, and *Indian Infantry Colours* (Bombay), 1931, upon which this note is based.

CHRONOLOGY TO CHAPTERS XV, XVI

1772. Warren Hastings Governor of Bengal.
      E.I.C. Directors appealed to Lord North for financial help.
1773. Regulating Act passed.
1774. Warren Hastings first Governor-General.
      Rohilla War.
1775. Benares and Ghazipur ceded to the company.
      Bombay government occupied Salsette and Bassein.
1776. Maratha War.
1778. France declared war (American War of Independence).
      English took French settlements in India.
1779. Triple Alliance of Mysore, Hyderabad and the Marathas against
         the English.
1780. Birth of Ranjit Singh.
1781. Defeat of Haidar Ali at Porto Novo.
      Peace with the Marathas.
      Amending Act passed by Parliament.
1782. Death of Haidar Ali.
      Naval actions between Suffren and Hughes.
1783. French settlements restored by Treaty of Versailles.
      Treaty of Salbai with the Marathas.
1784. Treaty with Tipu Sultan of Mysore; general peace in India.
      Pitt's India Act, establishing Board of Control passed.
1785. Warren Hastings left India.
      Sindia occupied Delhi.
1786–1793. Lord Cornwallis Governor-General.
1789. Tipu attacked Travancore.
1790. Third Mysore War.
1792. Tipu made peace.
1793. War with France.
      Capture of Pondicherry.
      Permanent Settlement of Bengal.
      Act renewing Company's Charter.
1793–1798. Sir John Shore (Lord Teignmouth) Governor-General.
1794. Death of Mahadaji Sindia, succeeded by Daulat Rao.
1795. Defeat of the Nizam by the Marathas.

1796. Ceylon taken from the Dutch.
1797. Shah Zaman invaded the Punjab.
1798. Earl of Mornington (Marquis Wellesley) Governor-General.
    French Expedition to Egypt.
1799. Defeat and death of Tipu Sultan : partition of Mysore.
1800. Death of Nana Farnavis : Subsidiary Treaty with Hyderabad.
1801. Annexation of the Carnatic.
    Oudh ceded frontier territory by Subsidiary Treaty.
1802. Treaty of Bassein and restoration of Peshwa.
    Peace of Amiens.
1803. War renewed with France.
    League of Sindia and Raghuji Bhonsla.
    Treaties of Deogaon and Surji Arjungaon.
1804. Gaekwar of Baroda signed Subsidiary Treaty.
    War with Holkar.
    Colonel Monson's disaster.
1805. Marquess Cornwallis superseded Marquess Wellesley, and died.
    Sir George Barlow Governor-General.
1807. Lord Minto Governor-General.
    Travancore War.
1809. Treaty signed with Ranjit Singh at Amritsar.
    Mauritius captured from the French.
1813. East India Company lost trade monopoly by Charter Act.
1813–1823. Marquess of Hastings Governor-General.
1814–1816. War with Nepal: Kumaon ceded to the Company.
1817. Pindaris exterminated.
    Third and last Maratha War.
1818. Deposition of the Peshwa.
1823. Ranjit Singh master of the provinces of Multan, Kashmir and
    Peshawar.

BIBLIOGRAPHY

History of the British Empire in India, E. Thornton, 2nd Edn., 1858.
Cambridge History of the British Empire, Vol. IV.
The Political History of India (1784–1823), Major-General Sir J. Malcolm,
    2 vols., 1826.
History of the Political and Military Transactions in India (1813–1823),
    H. T. Prinsep, 2 vols., 1825.
The Native States of India, Sir W. Lee-Warner, Edn. 1910.
History of the Mahrattas, J. C. Grant Duff, Vol. II., ed. S. M. Edwardes,
    1921.
Baji Rao and the East India Company (1796–1818), Dr. P. C. Gupta, 1939.

Lord Hastings and the Indian States, Dr. M. S. Mehta (Bombay), 1930.

History of the Sikhs, J. D. Cunningham, ed. H. L. O. Garrett, 1918.

Rise of the British Dominion in India, Sir A. Lyall, 2nd Edn., 1893.

The Marquess Cornwallis (Rulers of India Series), W. S. Seton-Karr, 1890.

The Marquess Wellesley (Rulers of India Series), W. H. Hutton, 1893.

The Marquess of Hastings (Rulers of India Series), Major J. Ross-of-Bladensburg, 1893.

Ranjit Singh (Rulers of India Series), Sir L. Griffin, 1892.

The Government of India, Sir C. Ilbert, 2nd Edn., 1907.

The Economic History of British India, Romesh Dutt (London), Edn. 1902, should be read in conjunction with

Trade Relations between England and India (1600–1896), C. J. Hamilton (Calcutta), 1919.

CHAPTER XVII

British Supremacy

WHEN Lord Hastings left India in January 1823, John Adam, a member of council, acted as governor-general for several months. In deporting Buckingham, editor of the *Calcutta Journal*, for his criticisms of the authorities, Adam showed great moral courage, as Buckingham had the support of the British non-official community in his campaign for the freedom of the Press.[1] Buckingham appealed to the Privy Council against Adam's decision, and lost his case.

Burma.

The new governor-general Lord Amherst came to Calcutta in August 1823 to find the Company involved in difficulties with Burma which made war inevitable.

In the middle of the eighteenth century the State of Ava had overcome its rival Pegu and created the kingdom of Burma.[2] The kings of the Alaungpaya dynasty were strong and aggressive, and they steadily added to their dominions. The Irrawaddy delta and Tenasserim were taken in 1757, Arakan in 1785 and Manipur in 1813; while between 1765 and 1769 a succession of invading Chinese armies had been completely defeated. In 1816 Burmese troops entered Upper Assam, and between 1819 and 1824 they took possession of the country. It was not a difficult undertaking. The Ahom government had broken into four pieces and civil war between

[1] See Malcolm's *Political History*, Vol. II. Appendix VI., for his examination of the advisability of " transplanting English freedom of the Press " into India at that time.

[2] For the history of Burma to the end of the first quarter of the twentieth century see *Burma from the Earliest Times to the Present Day*, Sir J. G. Scott (London), 1924.

the rival factions was spreading chaos and misery through the Brahmaputra Valley.

The English connection with Burma dated from the middle of the seventeenth century when private merchants, abandoning an earlier factory, established themselves at Rangoon to develop the trade in teak and lac. The Burmese were none too friendly, and the efforts of the East India Company to reach an official understanding were consistently ignored by the Burmese government. But when Arakan and Upper Assam were annexed the British and the Burmese became neighbours at two points, as the company had taken over Lower Assam in 1765, with the " Diwani " province of Bengal. This contact created a series of frontier incidents in which the Burmese were the aggressors,[1] and in the negotiations which followed the King of Burma took a very high hand. Self-centred, isolated, and with an unbroken record of conquest, he believed his country to be invincible; and exaggerated estimates of the power of the unknown kingdom were current in Calcutta.

The frontier incidents were succeeded by an act which could only mean war when, in 1823, the Burmese seized the small British island of Shahpuri on the Arakan coast, with a force whose orders were to take Calcutta. At the same time Burmese troops in the north under the pretext of a disputed succession in Cachar invaded that State, and one of the claimants appealed to the British. The occupation of Cachar by the Burmese would have laid Lower Assam open to invasion, and the Company's government, declaring Cachar a protectorate, moved troops to the Sylhet-Cachar frontier. Jungle fighting, with its incidents of attacks upon stockades, followed in January 1824. War was not, however, formally declared until the 5th of March.

First Burma War.

The main operations were based upon Rangoon, which was occupied in May by General Archibald Campbell with a force of 4000 British troops, 7000 Indian infantry of the Madras army and a flotilla of small river gunboats. The escort of cruisers was commanded by Captain Marryat, R.N., the novelist, and one of the

---

[1] Thornton, *op. cit.*, pp. 457–459.

vessels was the *Diana*, the first steamer used in war in the East,[1] which had been built at Calcutta docks and launched in 1823.[2]

The Burmese army of 70,000 men with a number of cannon was mainly a mass levy, and only half the force had muskets. They fought bravely enough and, until he was killed in action, had a capable leader in Bandula. But Campbell's most serious foe was the climate, assisted by the scandalous failure of the medical, supply and transport services. Malaria, dysentery and scurvy accounted for 96 per cent. of the fatal casualties; and including all reinforcements, out of 40,000 men eventually employed, 15,000 died in hospital.[3] A young officer in the Company's service who was invalided on account of wounds was the future founder and raja of the State of Sarawak, James Brooke.

In the north the Burmese were driven out of Cachar and Manipur by June 1825. But the main column, with the auxiliary services hopelessly inefficient and its intelligence branch equally inadequate, could hardly move from its base for the first six months, and suffered severely from sickness during the rains. Campbell's first success was the defeat of the Burmese attack on Rangoon in December 1824; and this was followed, in the autumn of 1825, by an advance up the Irrawaddy.

On 24th February 1826 Campbell dictated the peace of Yandabo, four days' march from Ava. By this treaty King Bagyidaw ceded Arakan, Tenasserim, Upper Assam, Cachar, Jaintia and Manipur to the British, paid an indemnity equivalent to £1,000,000 towards the five million which the war had cost, received a resident at Ava, and agreed to send his own representative to Calcutta. This last condition was never carried out, and with the British resident withdrawn from Ava in 1840, friction with the Burmese government again led to war in 1852.

The Burmese war was not popular in England, for fear of the consequences of this further expansion which brought Avan and

---

[1] Thornton, in his account of the operations ; *op. cit.*, pp. 460–475.
[2] *The Making of India*, A. Yusuf Ali, p. 265.
[3] *Camb. Hist. British Empire*, Vol. IV. p. 560.

Burmese politics within the field of the Company's control. The home Government, however, signified their approval to the extent of giving Amherst an earldom.

A mutiny, which reasonable management should have avoided, occurred at Barrackpur at the end of October 1824. *Barrackpur Mutiny.* The war in Burma which was popular in the Madras army was unpopular in Bengal, and the 47th Native Infantry, when they were mobilized for field service, had other grievances to add to their prejudices against serving overseas. Increased field allowances had been disallowed them while it was granted to the regimental followers, government transport was not provided, and the issue of new knapsacks for which the men had paid was not forthcoming. The 47th Native Infantry mutinied, and the outbreak had to be put down by a column of British troops of all arms and the governor-general's bodyguard promptly sent out from Calcutta.[1]

The earlier operations in Burma, when the failure of the Rangoon expeditionary force was giving the government considerable anxiety, caused a certain amount of unrest in Central India, and trouble occurred at Bharatpur. Raja Baldeo Singh died in 1825 and his infant son was recognized by Sir David Ochterlony, the political agent at Delhi. Durjan Sal, the late raja's brother, who had failed to obtain British recognition of his own claim to the throne when Baldeo Singh succeeded, at once seized the fortress of Bharatpur and assumed what he maintained to be the regency. Ochterlony with equal decision, and on his own responsibility, called up troops and issued a proclamation calling upon the people to defend their rightful ruler. Lord Amherst countermanded these measures, and Ochterlony resigned, dying shortly afterwards. He was succeeded as political agent by Sir Charles Metcalfe.

Bharatpur now became the scene of civil war, and Maratha and other adventurers flocked to the country. The disturbances threatened to spread and the governor-general, who had not

[1] Thornton, *op. cit.*, pp. 447–448. Malcolm reviews contemporary Indian Army conditions in his *History*, Vol. II. pp. 232–236.

originally considered interference in the internal affairs of the State to be justified, now reviewed the situation. He decided that military action would have to be taken and Durjan Sal removed. A strong force with siege guns under Lord Combermere, the commander-in-chief, invested the fortress of Bharatpur, and after a siege of just over five weeks the place, which had defied Lake in 1805, was taken by assault on the 18th January 1826. Durjan Sal was deported and the fortress dismantled.[1]

Great political changes had taken place in India since the days
Paramountcy.
of the supremacy of the Mogul Empire. The Imperial authority had been removed from Delhi. The sovereignty of the Peshwas had disappeared. The ascendancy of the Company had grown by successive stages when " Clive carved out the Province of Bengal by conquest, Lord Wellesley added Madras and the North-Western Provinces partly by treaty and partly by force, and Lord Hastings created the Presidency of Bombay."

Until the end of the eighteenth century the British authorities treated Indian princes, when making alliances with them, on terms of equality, as in the triple alliance against Tipu in 1790. Then by degrees the Company advanced to an assertion of superiority in the treaties which were made, and their Indian allies were now required to surrender their rights of negotiation with foreign powers and with the States in alliance with the Company. At this first stage, however, the government at Fort William disclaimed interference with the internal sovereignty of the States.[2] The system of sub-sidiary forces, a feature of Wellesley's policy, marked not only the pressure of common defence but the contrast between a policy of non-intervention and a policy of union. But changing political, social and economic conditions obliged what had become the paramount Power to exercise these functions of paramountcy beyond the terms of the early treaties.[3]

[1] Thornton, *op. cit.*, pp. 478–485.
[2] *The Native States of India*, Edn. 1910, p. 286.
[3] *Report of the Indian States Committee* (Butler Report), 1929, p. 14.

The growth of British paramount power during the period under review is illustrated by the relations between the Company and Hyderabad. In 1798 the treaty previously made with the Nizam was reaffirmed and the subsidiary force was increased and made permanent. In 1800 a further treaty was made which stated that: " The Honourable Company's Government on their part declare that they have no manner of concern with any of His Highness' children, relations, subjects or servants with respect to whom His Highness is absolute." In 1803 Sikandar Jah obtained the Emperor's confirmation to his accession; and Wellesley at once informed the new Nizam that the British Government considered all treaties made by the late Nizam with the Company remained in full force. In the words of Lee-Warner [1]: " In the first period of British inter-course the prevalent idea in India was that successions needed the confirmation of higher authority; and Lord Wellesley accentuated the principle by delivering a formal instrument to the ruler of the leading State in the country ": a principle which had certainly been recognized by all subordinate States under the Mogul and Maratha governments. In 1804 the Company successfully pressed the appointment of a certain chief minister in Hyderabad. In 1815 the Company had to interfere because the Nizam's sons offered violent resistance to his orders. The administration of the State gradually sank into chaos. Cultivation fell off, famine prices prevailed, justice was not obtainable, the population began to migrate. The Company had again to intervene, and in 1820 British officers were appointed to supervise the district administration with a view to protecting the cultivating classes. [2] These examples are sufficient to show that " from the earliest times there was intervention by the paramount Power, in its own interests as responsible for . . . India, in the interests of the State, and in the interests of the people of the States." [3]

The paramount Power was then the Company acting as trustees of and agents for the Crown, and the Act of 1858 merely changed

[1] *The Native States of India*, p. 324.
[2] *Report of the Indian States Commission*, pp. 14, 15.
[3] *Ibid.*, p. 15.

the machinery through which the Crown exercised its powers.[1] Paramountcy has always been based on treaties, engagements and *sanads* (grants from the Crown to the ruler of a State) made to individual States and supplemented by usage and by government decisions embodied in political practice. In considering this relationship the Indian States Committee concluded (in 1929) that it cannot be maintained that any of the States now in being ever possessed full sovereignty, and so held international status. "Nearly all of them were subordinate or tributary to the Mogul Empire, the Mahratta supremacy or the Sikh kingdom and dependent on them. Some were rescued, others were created, by the British." [2] The Rajput chieftainships, the only ancient political groups surviving in India, were only saved from destruction by seeking shelter within the sphere of the political system of the British.[3]

Lord Hastings brought all India except the Punjab and Sind either directly under British administration or under its control to the extent of foreign policy and the acceptance of British arbitration in interstate disputes. It was also understood that the princes should defer to British advice to cure scandalous misrule.[4]

Amherst in the disputed succession of Bharatpur in 1825 intervened as the paramount Power in the internal affairs of a State "to prevent anarchy and misrule." [5] But the Company after making its precedents returned to a general policy of non-intervention. The Government of India was not then prepared to incur the responsibility of ensuring reasonably good government in the States as an incident of paramountcy. The lesser responsibility

---

[1] *Report of the Indian States Committee*, p. 13.

[2] *Ibid.*, pp. 23–24. But Appendix III. to *Report* (pp. 59–73) should be read in this connexion. It gives the opinion of eminent counsel "that a complete sovereignty was held by the Indian States when they came first in contact with the British power"; a different construction is placed upon "usage and sufferance," and the term "subordinate co-operation" is limited to military matters. This opinion the Committee could not accept.

[3] Sir A. Lyall, *Asiatic Studies*.

[4] For a summary of Lord Hastings' policy see *Rise of the British Dominion in India*, pp. 262, 263.

[5] Sir C. Metcalfe in his Minute of August 1825 to the Governor-General, quoted at length by Thornton, *op. cit.*, pp. 482–483.

was taken of a feudal superiority which simply entailed wardship, escheat and the right of confirming succession. Escheat, an easy method of dealing with inefficient administration on the failure of lineal heirs, involved the repudiation of the Hindu practice of adoption. This created serious discontent among the princes, and was undoubtedly one of the contributory causes of the mutiny in 1857.[1]

Lord Amherst left India in March 1828. His successor Lord William Bentinck had sailed from England a month *Lord William* earlier and took up his appointment in July of *Bentinck.* that year. Bentinck had been governor of Madras from 1803 to 1807, and had been recalled with the Presidency commander-in-chief after the Vellore mutiny.[2] His policy as governor-general can be summed up in the words Peace, Retrenchment and Reform.

The government finances were most unsatisfactory and Bentinck, under definite instructions from London immediately *Retrenchment.* began his campaign of public economy by large and highly unpopular reductions. He carried these out through civil and military committees and by making a tour, early in 1829, to Penang, Singapore and Malacca.

The allowances of the officers of the Company's army were halved, but the cuts were unequally felt, and pressed *The Army.* most heavily on the junior officers, and this at a time when recent reductions in the establishment had seriously affected promotion. The commander-in-chief protested vigorously, but the governor-general had received his orders from the Directors and the decision was final.[3]

On the subject of the army it may here be said that in 1833 Bentinck assumed the appointment of commander-in-chief and issued two orders directly affecting the Indian ranks. He gave

[1] *Modern India*, ed. Sir J. Cumming, 2nd Edn. Ch. II., by Sir W. Barton, pp. 27, 28.
[2] Thornton, *op. cit.*, p. 353.
[3] See *History of British India*, Mill and Wilson, Vol. IX. Edn. 1858, pp. 168–172.

extra pay for long service and he abolished flogging. In abolishing flogging, a humane and excellent measure in itself, Bentinck was before his time. Corporal punishment was not abolished as a peace-time sentence in the British army until 1868, and consequently Bentinck's decision made a highly improper and invidious distinction between the King's regiments serving in India and the Company's Indian troops. Twelve years later Indian courts-martial were again empowered to give corporal punishment.

In 1835 Bentinck wrote a comprehensive minute on the army and the military situation in general, and gave his conclusion that the Indian army was the " least efficient and the most expensive in the world." There was some justification for this sweeping assertion. The Indian units had undoubtedly deteriorated since 1818. They were no longer organized and equipped by their commanding officers, whose control had been lessened; the reorganization of 1824, when regiments were divided, had taken a number of British officers away from their own men; many of the best officers were selected for staff employ; and there was a growing lack of interest and loss of close personal touch by the British officers as regards their men.

In no service in the world is the personal factor of more vital importance than in the Indian army, where sympathetic knowledge of his men is an essential qualification in the British regimental officer. Until the end of the first quarter of the nineteenth century the British officers, out of touch with Europe altogether and without English society, had no interests outside India. Their men were their absorbing interest, the regiment their home. In their private lives the Company's officers had " orientalized " themselves to an extent which taught them the language, the habits and the feelings of the people of the country.

Then came the immense change which steam and the overland route brought to India. Books from England and European news no longer half a year old, and above all English ladies, freely and comparatively rapidly arrived in the country. Indian cantonments began to bear a resemblance to the modern military station, new interests sprang up, and the zenana naturally disappeared.

The British officers with the Indian units were discontented
with regimental duty and embittered by the reduction in pay.
They were as a rule the least efficient officers in the service, and
many of them were too old for their regimental rank.[1] It would
be difficult to imagine a greater contrast to the British officers of the
succeeding generations who have served and are serving with the
Indian Army, an army of the highest efficiency and achievement.

In addition to civil retrenchment, the members of the civil
service were irritated by the governor-general's
The Civil
Service.
institution of confidential reports, to ascertain the
merits, or the defects, of officials.   Thornton
describes this as inquisitional espionage, and confidential reports
were soon dropped.

A source from which the Company had been accustomed to
make large profits was the Bengal opium monopoly.
Opium.
But after the Maratha war, when peace came to the
country, Malwa began to grow the opium poppy to an extent which
seriously threatened the Company's trade.   Malwa opium was
taken through Indian States to Diu and Daman where it was bought
by European and Indian merchants, who then exported it under
the Portuguese flag, to undersell the Company's products.   In
1820–21 six hundred chests were exported from Daman; in 1827–28
the number had risen to four thousand.[2]

The governor-general was not prepared to accept the serious
loss incurred by this private trading free of transit duty.   It was
not possible directly to forbid the growth of the poppy in States
which were internally independent.   But in 1829, after other
measures had failed, most of the princes of Malwa and Rajputana
were persuaded to sign treaties which, " in consideration of annual
payments, and allowing for internal supply, conceded to the British
agent the unnatural privilege of paralysing national industry and

[1] For the Governor-General's minute see *Life of Lord William Bentinck*,
Boulger, pp. 177–201.   For Indian Army conditions see Kaye's *History of the
Sepoy War*, Vol. I. Book I. Ch. II., " The Sepoy Army—its Decline."
[2] Mill and Wilson, *op. cit.*, Vol. IV., footnote to p. 177.

extinguishing native enterprise."[1] This led Bentinck to agree to set free the growth of opium in the States, while the Indian private growers sent their opium direct to Bombay and paid licence duty to the company.

Bentinck, as the whole trend of his policy in India shows, was, for the age in which he lived, a statesman of advanced " Liberal " views. But the policy of the Government of India in regard to opium has undergone a complete transformation since his day. Opium is still a State monopoly, grown only under strict supervision, and with rigid control of the price at which licensed vendors may sell it. But during the twelve years ending with 1931–32 the area under poppy cultivation in British India was reduced by 75·4 per cent., and in 1931 was almost confined to the United Provinces with a total of about 36,500 acres.[2] Much has been done by the Government of India, and also by the Indian States, in recent years to reduce " black spots " (areas where the use of opium is immoderate) and to remedy such abuses as the administration of the drug to babies. The government policy is not the total suppression of the use of opium, except for smoking. Opium is largely used in the malarial tracts, and whatever its real value may be this could not be interfered with at present without causing grave and widespread discontent.[3] The export of opium to China was stopped altogether in 1913.

Two measures were taken by the governor-general which added considerably to the revenue. The first of these was *Land Revenue.* the " resumption," in the permanently settled areas, of land formerly exempt from assessment but whose holders were found on inquiry in 1829 to have illegal or invalid titles.[4] The second was the land settlement made in the north-western provinces by Wilberforce Bird, whose assessments were fair though in some cases rather heavy.

[1] Mill and Wilson, *op. cit.*, Vol. IV. p. 175 (paged incorrectly as 173).
[2] *India in* 1931–1932 (Govt. Printing Press, Calcutta), 1933, p. 205.
[3] *Moral and Material Progress and Condition of India*, 1930–1931 (H.M. Stationery Office), 1932, pp. 437–442.
[4] Mill and Wilson, *op. cit.*, Vol. IX. pp. 179–181.

PLATE LVII

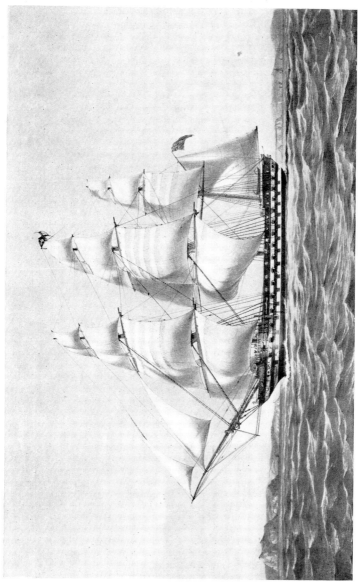

THE "EARL BALCARRES," EAST INDIAMAN, 1417 TONS, BUILT AT BOMBAY IN 1815

By courtesy of the Parker Gallery

PLATE LVIII.

P. & O. COMPANY'S PADDLE STEAMER "PRECURSOR," BUILT IN 1841 FOR THE INDIAN MAIL SERVICE

By courtesy of the Parker Gallery

On his arrival in India, Bentinck found that the civil service
establishment was too small for its duties. Over-
*Administrative
Reforms.*
worked officials were not able to keep in constant
touch with the people, and the provincial courts
were heavily in arrears with accused persons awaiting trial for long
periods.

Cornwallis in his settlement of Bengal had, with only small
exceptions, given the entire control of the civil and criminal administration to Europeans. But gradually it had been found necessary
as well as natural to employ Indians to try their fellow-countrymen
for minor offences, and in 1827 " nearly nineteen-twentieths of
the original suits instituted in the civil courts throughout the country
were already determined by native judicial officers." [1] Just before
Bentinck became governor-general a new and higher grade of Indian
judge was created to hear appeals from these lower courts.

Sir Charles Metcalfe represented that " the best form of
government with a view to the maintenance of British dominion in
India was that which was " most simple and most free from artificial
institutions." His plan may be summarized as: Indian functionaries
in the first instance in all departments; European superintendents,
uniting the local powers of judicature, police and revenue, in all
their branches, through the districts they administered; commissioners over them; and a board over the commissioners,
communicating with and subject to the immediate control of the
government. [2]

For the efficient government of the country a larger body of
officials was absolutely necessary, but the cost of the additional
Europeans, to the number required, was quite prohibitive. Bentinck
therefore decided to employ Indians more extensively and to
introduce reforms on the lines suggested by Metcalfe.

The board of revenue was set up in Allahabad to hear appeals
against over-assessment [3]; commissioners of revenue and circuit
were appointed; the collector became also the district magistrate;

[1] *Life of Lord William Bentinck*, Boulger, p. 64.
[2] Mill and Wilson, *op. cit.*, Vol IX., footnote to pp. 182, 183.
[3] Mill and Wilson, *op. cit.*, Vol. IX. pp. 181, 182.

the provincial courts were abolished; and Indian officers, including "subordinate judges," were appointed on adequate salaries and given responsible judicial and executive functions.

Until the time of Bentinck the supreme government remained in Calcutta through the hot weather. Ootacamund *Hill Stations.* was used as a sanatorium [1] in Southern India, but the Himalayan hill stations did not exist. Although part of Simla had come into the possession of the Company after the Nepalese war it was not until six years later, in 1822, that the first English bungalow was built among its deodars and rhododendrons, and a small European settlement sprang up. The rest of the hill was bought from the Maharaja of Patiala in 1830. Amherst visited the place in 1827, and it was at Simla that Bentinck received Ranjit Singh's mission in 1831.

From this time onwards Simla became the summer capital of the Government of India, the yearly exodus of its departments from the plains to the hills was looked upon as a matter of course, and the secretariat offices on the hillside were gradually built. Bentinck also bought, from the Raja of Sikkim, the site on which Darjeeling now stands.

But over and above the boon of hill stations to Europeans, and beyond his departmental reforms, Bentinck's administration is associated with events which stand as signposts in the evolution of modern India.

An Act was passed in 1832 which repealed the provisions requiring jurors to be Christians,[2] and the Charter *Charter Act,* Act of 1833 introduced changes of the greatest *1833.* importance into the constitution and administration of the East India Company.

Whig principles were in the ascendant; the Reform Bill had just been carried; Macaulay was secretary to the Board of Control; and James Mill, the disciple of Bentham, was examiner of correspondence at India House.

---

[1] Marshman, *op. cit.*, Vol. III. p. 80.
[2] *Government of India*, Ilbert, 2nd Edn., p. 81.

By the Act the Company retained their administrative and political powers for another term of twenty years " in trust for His Majesty, his heirs and successors, for the service of the Government of India " as vested in " the Governor-General of India in Council." [1]   But the tea monopoly and China trade were taken away and the Company, no longer a commercial body, was required to close its mercantile business and wind up its affairs.[2]   The import and export trade had already been abandoned. As the House of Commons committee were told in 1832, the Company had quite enough to do to govern.

The Board of Control remained, and no material alteration was made in the system of the executive government in India, but on the legal side important changes were introduced.   The governor-general in council was empowered to make laws and regulations, subject to reservations which prohibited any law or regulation affecting the prerogatives of the Crown, the authority of Parliament or the rights of the Company.   Parliament maintained the right to legislate for India and to repeal Indian Acts. A fourth member of council, who was not to be of the Company's servants, was appointed, and the first legal member was Macaulay. The confused and sometimes conflicting Presidency regulations were to be codified and an Indian Law Commission, with Macaulay as its most prominent member, was appointed for the first time.

Among other clauses the Act required the Government of India to inquire into and mitigate conditions of slavery, and extinguish it as soon as emancipation should be " practicable and safe." Slavery was made illegal by Lord Ellenborough ten years later.

The change, which was to come a century later, in the status of the provinces illustrates the constitutional development of India. For, by the Charter Act, all executive legislative powers throughout British India were vested in the hands of the governor-general in council.   But nothing in the Act was more striking than clause 87,

[1] The supreme government in India had previously been officially termed the Governor-General of Bengal in Council.

[2] For details of government redemption of stock see Ilbert, *op. cit.*, p. 82.

which declared that " no native of the said territories, nor any natural-born subject of His Majesty resident therein, shall, by reason only of his religion, place of birth, descent, colour, or any of them, be disabled from holding any place, office, or employment under the Company." [1]

In their covering despatch the Directors wrote: " The meaning of the enactment we take to be that there shall be no governing caste in British India. . . . Fitness, wholly irrespective of the distinction of races, is henceforth to be the criterion of eligibility. . . . To this altered rule it will be necessary that you should, both in your acts and your language, conform; practically, perhaps, no very marked difference of results will be occasioned." [2] Nine years before the Act was passed, Sir Thomas Munro, equally distinguished as soldier and administrator, had looked forward to a time when " the character of our Indian subjects would have so far improved as to enable them to govern and protect themselves." [3]

Education. Warren Hastings and Duncan had respectively founded Islamic and Sanskrit colleges in Calcutta and at Benares in 1781 and 1792, but throughout the country education, at the beginning of the nineteenth century, was at a very low ebb. The self-supporting village schools, with their Brahman or Moslem teachers, could not deal with the overwhelming number of boys, while education for girls practically did not exist. There were hardly any printed books either in the classical or the vernacular languages, and western education had not been introduced.[4]

The Directors of the Company, who had most reluctantly allotted a lakh of rupees a year " for the encouragement of the learned natives of India " under the Charter Act of 1813, actively resented the stress laid seven years later on Oriental poetry. They had suggested [5] " any learning that is useful; but poetry is not useful and

---

[1] For provisions of the Act see Ilbert, *op. cit.*, pp. 81–89.

[2] 10th December 1834. India and Bengal Despatch Book, Vol. III. No. 44 of 1834, para. 103 *et seq*. (India Office Records).

[3] Minute of 1824: quoted by Mayhew in *The Education of India*.

[4] *Indian Statutory Commission Report*, Vol. I. p. 379.

[5] *The Education of India*, p. 11, quoting a despatch of 1824.

we suspect that there is little in Hindu or Mohammedan literature that is."

In the meanwhile the watchmaker and secularist David Hare, with a group of Hindu gentlemen, had founded in 1817 the institution which later became known as the Presidency College, and started as "Anglicists" the violent controversy with the "Orientalists." The Orientalists supported the traditional policy of teaching through the medium of the classical languages. The Anglicists were equally determined that the grants of money should be spent on "English education" as the only means of spreading western culture. Ram Mohun Roy, who then knew no English but was deeply read in Sanskrit, was on the side of the Anglicists; and so were the missionaries William Carey, who founded Serampur College in 1818, and Alexander Duff.[1]

When Macaulay arrived in India the education committee at Fort William was equally divided between Anglicists and Orientalists, and the matter came before the council. Bentinck's sympathies were in favour of English education; so were Macaulay's. In February 1835 Macaulay wrote his celebrated minute. He admitted that he had no knowledge of Sanskrit or Arabic, but he took what he described as a parallel case. "Suppose a Pasha of Egypt . . . were to appropriate a sum for the purpose of reviving and promoting literature and encouraging learned natives of Egypt, would anyone infer that he meant the youth of his Pashalic to give years to the study of hieroglyphics, to search into all the doctrines disguised under the fable of Osiris, and to ascertain with all possible accuracy the ritual with which cats and onions were anciently adored? Would he be charged with inconsistency if instead of employing his young subjects in deciphering obelisks he were to order them to be instructed in the English and French languages?"[2]

The parallel between the long-forgotten writing of the priests of Ancient Egypt and the language which has enshrined the living faith and culture of Hindu India for three thousand years is hardly

[1] See *Education of India*, pp. 9–20.
[2] The Minute is quoted in the *Life of Lord William Bentinck*, pp. 152–157.

exact. How far Bentinck, who " wrote more minutes than all the other Governors-General of India put together," [1] but who " read very little " and that " not without pain," [2] was moved by Macaulay's references to farriers and to girls at an English boarding-school, or influenced by a misleading comparison between English and Sanskrit literature, it is impossible to say. But the governor-general had been nearly seven years in India, he believed English civilization to be sound while Hindu civilization had obvious defects, and in the interests of economy Indians with a knowledge of the language of the ruling race were necessary for the administration and development of the country.

On 20th March 1835 Bentinck issued the resolution dated 7th March, [3] which declared that the funds available for education should be devoted " to English education alone," and that English should be the official language of India. The subsistence allowances which had been given to the students at the Indian colleges were consequently withdrawn—to be restored in the form of scholarships by Lord Auckland, the next governor-general.

Higher education in India was now definitely linked with the English language and this, coupled with the declaration made by Parliament in clause 87 of the Charter Act of 1833, made it possible for Indians to enter the higher branches of the government service. This was the direct result of Bentinck's policy, which incidentally had another effect, a bond of unity which Akbar himself had been unable to devise. Educated Indians today, from Peshawar to Cape Comorin, have in English a common language in which they can speak together—a means of communication which no single vernacular tongue could supply.

The Company supposed that by educating the strictly limited literary classes, education would " filter " down through them to the great mass of the illiterate people of India, a theory which ignored the obstacles of caste and class distinction. An educational system was not introduced into British India until Sir Charles

[1] Lord Curzon, *British Government in India*, Vol. II. p. 195.
[2] Lord William Bentinck to James Mill: Boulger, *op. cit.*, p. 54.
[3] See *History of India*, Marshman, Vol. III. p. 64.

Wood, afterwards Lord Halifax, wrote his momentous despatch in 1854.

Sati. If Bentinck's introduction of English as the official language of British India was the feature of his policy which led to the most far-reaching results, the abolition of *sati* was the most striking act of his administration.

The term *sati*, or *suttee*, strictly refers to the person, not the rite. It means a " pure and virtuous woman " and was applied to a widow who sacrificed herself at her husband's death, either by burning, or burial alive. The custom was a survival from a past at least as distant as the human sacrifices of the Druids, which had been stamped out by the Romans in Britain. *Sati* had been discouraged by the Muhammadan rulers and sometimes forbidden, Akbar on one occasion riding out from his palace and rescuing a victim from the flames. It was forbidden in the territories under the personal rule of the Peshwa, and various Hindu princes had from time to time prohibited it.

Historical records give many instances of wholesale *sati*, as in the kingdom of Vijayanagar; and scores and hundreds of women were sometimes burnt, voluntarily or unwillingly, on the death of a king. For more than two thousand years the woman who completed a life of conjugal devotion by *sati* was held in the highest honour. But *sati* was not an essential part of Hinduism. It is not alluded to by Manu, who stated in regard to widows: " A faithful wife who wishes to attain in heaven the mansion of her husband must do nothing unkind to him, be he living or dead. Let her emaciate her body . . . but let her not, when her husband is deceased, even pronounce the name of another man. Let her continue till death, forgiving all injuries, performing harsh duties, avoiding every sensual pleasure and cheerfully practising the incomparable rules of virtue. A virtuous wife ascends to heaven even though she have no child if, after the decease of her lord, she devote herself to pious austerity." [1]

[1] *The Institutes of Menu*, Edn. 1825, Vol. II. pp. 167–168.

471

British governors-general, beginning with Lord Wellesley, had made half-hearted efforts to end a custom which it was impossible to think of without horror, and which the court of Directors urged ought to be suppressed. In 1827 the matter was placed in the hands of the governor-general. Bentinck landed in Calcutta a year later, feeling as he said, " the dreadful responsibility hanging over his head, in this world and the next, if, as the Governor-General of India, he was to consent to the continuation of this practice one moment longer, not than our security, but than the real happiness and permanent welfare of the native population rendered indispensable." [1]

He took the views of the judges, the army (where the custom seems to have been unknown, certainly for a generation),[2] the police, the civil service, and a number of private individuals, including leading Hindus, and found distinct diversity of opinion.[3] Not only did he meet with strong Hindu opposition in certain quarters, he was also seriously warned of the possible consequences by more than one of his higher officials. But the governor-general showed more courage and resolution than Amherst. He was supported by Bayley and Metcalfe, and on the 14th December 1829 he issued his Regulation XVII. This " declared the practice of *sati* illegal, and punishable by the criminal courts as culpable homicide in Bengal." [4] A similar enactment was promulgated in Madras, and legislation to the same effect, but for local reasons in a different form, was carried in the Bombay Presidency. But it took more to end *sati* in the States than Lord Hardinge's pressure nearly twenty years later. Customs and practices, especially any that are interwoven with religion, die hard, and cases of *sati* or attempted *sati* are still recorded, though at long intervals. A case occurred in the Bombay Presidency in 1938.

[1] Marshman, *op. cit.*, Vol. III. p. 53.
[2] Mill and Wilson, *op. cit.*, Vol. IX., footnote to p. 190.
[3] Marshman, *op. cit.*, Vol. III. pp. 54, 55.
[4] *Sati* was then most prevalent in Bengal ; and of the 463 cases in the Presidency in 1828–29, 309 took place in the Calcutta division. Mill and Wilson, *op. cit.*, Vol. IX. p. 189 and footnote.

In his summing up of Bentinck's record in India, Thornton, in
Thuggee. startling contrast to Macaulay's panegyric,[1] considers
 that, excepting the "noble triumph of the aboli-
tion of *sati*, if his administration were obliterated, posterity would
scarcely observe the deficiency, while it is certain they would have
little reason to regret it."[2] It was, however, under Bentinck's rule
that the dreadful secret society of stranglers known as thugs, which
Akbar and Aurangzeb had failed to stamp out, was first systematically
and successfully dealt with, although gangs were known to exist
forty years later. There have been cases of murder since 1877 which
may quite possibly have been perpetrated by thugs; and while it
is never safe to assert that any ancient practice in India has been
entirely suppressed, it may be assumed that the professional poisoner
of today is the lineal descendant and representative of the thug.

Thugs[3] were highly organized gangs of hereditary murderers
who lived on the money and property they took from their victims.
The method of a gang was as simple as it was horrible. The thugs,
with every appearance of a pleasant, cheerful and perfectly innocent
party, attached themselves to likely travellers on the road, won
their confidence, and at a given signal strangled them with handker-
chiefs. The dead bodies were rifled and then buried in pits which
were consecrated to the Hindu goddess Kali, although thugs were
Muhammadans as well as Hindus.

Bentinck created a special department for the suppression of
thuggee in 1829, and to the efforts of Sir William Sleeman above
all others the people of India owed their relief from this fearful
evil. Between 1831 and 1837, 3266 thugs met their deserts. But
the number of their victims in a year had been counted in thousands
and one thug alone is said to have confessed to 719 murders.[4]

[1] On Bentinck's statue in Calcutta. See *Life* (Boulger), p. 203.

[2] Thornton, *op. cit.*, p. 496.

[3] The Hindi word for a cheat : a more expressive term meant " bearer of the
noose." *Confessions of a Thug*, by Meadows Taylor, is more thrilling in fact than
Edgar Allan Poe could be in fiction (first published 1839 ; Ed. Oxford University
Press, 1916).

[4] See *Rambles and Recollections*, Sleeman, 2 vols., first published in 1844.
The 1893 edition, edited by Vincent Smith, has notes which supply the gaps
due to the author's " characteristic modesty."

Towards the Indian States Bentinck pursued the policy of non-intervention which had been impressed upon him by the home authorities; and this brought about a revival of the earlier disorders and consequent misery and desolation in Central India.[1]

The States.

In Oudh the governor-general, who had the power by treaty and the right to dictate the necessary measures to ensure good government, deserted the one minister, Hakim Medi, who could have reformed the administration. In Hyderabad Nazim-ud-daula, who had succeeded Sikandar Jah, was allowed to dismiss the British officials who superintended the State assessments. Injustice and extortion followed and the country relapsed into disorder. But it is unnecessary to detail the " tumult and anarchy " which the policy of non-interference pursued by Bentinck entailed.

There were, however, times when it became impossible to stand aloof " whilst a tributary or an ally was hastening to destruction . . . and the reluctant Government of India was compelled to interpose . . . both with council and with arms, and placed its conduct in constant contrast to its professions. Inconsistency was therefore the main characteristic of the proceedings of the government in its transactions with the native principalities beyond its own borders. . . . The same policy that was disposed to consign Malwa and Rajputana to the renewed horrors of the predatory system, commanded the governor-general to carry his negotiations across the Indus and to establish new relations with Sinde and Afghanistan." [2] The inconsistency was severely punished; but the results belong to a subsequent period.

In 1831 Bentinck was induced by a rebellion in Mysore caused by misrule to act under a clause of the treaty of 1799 and place the country under the direct administration of British officials, leaving the raja only his titular dignity and a liberal allowance. The administration greatly improved, the foundations were laid

[1] See Mill and Wilson, *op. cit.*, Vol. IX. pp. 253 *et seq.*, where his relations with the States are detailed.
[2] Mill and Wilson, *op. cit.*, Vol. IX. pp. 254-255.

for its present prosperity,[1] and it has been admirably governed by its own princes since Lord Ripon restored it in 1881.

Coorg was annexed in 1834 after some hard fighting as a sequel to the defiant hostility of its ruler Vira Raja. This blood-thirsty tyrant had killed all his male relatives, in many cases with his own hands, and after his capital Mercara was taken he was deported to Benares. The Jaintia districts adjoining Sylhet were taken over in 1835 after the ruling chief had refused to surrender men who had kidnapped British subjects and sacrificed them to Kali. British Assam had already been enlarged by the peaceful lapse of Cachar to the government in 1830 on the death of its ruler.

But whatever policy the governor-general might decide to follow there remained only two sovereign powers in India, the English and the Sikh, for the Mirs of Sind scarcely fell within the category of Indian rulers.

Foreign Policy.

Commercial as well as political interests made peace beyond the borders of British India an essential aim of the Company. Bentinck signed treaties with the Mirs of Sind which conceded the opening of the Indus " to the navigation of the world." Diplomatic missions were exchanged with Ranjit Singh, who had suspected that these commercial treaties covered plans for annexation,[2] and a treaty of " perpetual friendship " was signed between the British and the Sikh governments in 1831. But a policy of peace beyond the frontier was hardly encouraged by the " benevolent neutrality " of the Company when Shah Shuja invaded Afghanistan in 1833 to regain his throne from Dost Muhammad, his rival in possession. The immediate result of this invasion was the defeat of Shah Shuja at Kandahar in July 1834 and his return to Ludhiana.

The diplomatic horizon was not, however, bounded by the neighbouring States of the Punjab and Sind. Minto had embarked upon a policy of wider alliances in anticipation of French aggression, a threat which soon dissolved. But since the days of Napoleon another European power had risen in the East and the dread was

[1] Lee-Warner, *op. cit.*, p. 173.
[2] *History of the Sikhs*, pp. 191–198.

founded of a Russian advance upon India. " The British Government at home laid down the principle, big with momentous consequence, that the independence and integrity of Afghanistan are essential to the security of India." [1]

In the opinion of Thornton,[2] Bentinck did " less for the interest of India and for his own reputation than any who had occupied his place since the commencement of the nineteenth century, with the single exception of Sir George Barlow." Marshman takes a contrary view.[3] But it is beyond question that Bentinck's governor-generalship marks the beginning of modern India and that this was largely due to the effects of his policy.

Westernization.

When he laid down his office in March 1835 he had seen many changes. The Company no longer engaged in trade and the great fleet of Indiamen had been dispersed, the members of the civil service and the officers of the Indian army were abandoning their eastern mode of life, and western education had become the official policy.

From the standpoint of the European in India the greatest change in conditions was the spectacular shortening of the time taken to travel between England and India. This improvement has steadily gone on until what once meant at least six months at sea in a sailing vessel was reduced to under a week when Imperial Airways landed mails from London at Karachi on the 5th April 1929.

Steam first " brought England to India " when the *Enterprise*, helped by her sails, reached Diamond Harbour at the mouth of the Hooghly on 8th December 1825, having left England on the 19th August.[4] In 1830 the overland route by Suez was first opened, and in 1836 the Bombay government were able to congratulate the court of Directors on the arrival of despatches from London in forty-five days.[5] The first of the Peninsular Company's steamers was the *William Fawcett* of 206 gross tonnage and 60 horse-power,

---

[1] *Rise of the British Dominion in India*, p. 269. [2] *Op. cit.*, p. 497.
[3] *Op. cit.*, Vol. III. pp. 80–82. [4] *India Gazette*, 12th December 1825.
[5] Mill and Wilson, *op. cit.*, Vol. IX. pp. 215, 216 and footnote.

built in 1829, which traded with the peninsula of Spain. The company became the Peninsular and Oriental in 1840, and sent the *Hindostan* of 1800 tons, its first vessel to go to India, by way of the Cape in 1842.[1]

These were improvements in the conditions of English men and women living in India, and came from the progress of science. But a change of a deeper character was the direct outcome of Bentinck's own policy.

Warren Hastings, who may fairly be described as the first and last governor-general of the Company, had looked at India through the eyes of its inhabitants. A good Oriental linguist, he had a great and wise understanding of their ways and outlook on life, and far from wishing to change the customs of the people he sought to rule them by their own methods. He aimed at a revival of Indian learning, he mixed freely with Indians on the friendliest terms, and he firmly held familiarity with the languages, customs and religions of the country to be essential qualifications for the Company's servants.

Cornwallis, the first of the Parliamentary pro-consuls, knew nothing of the country and could not speak a word of any of its languages. He sincerely wished to benefit India, and from his personal standpoint one of the ways in which this could best be done was to create a landed aristocracy similar to the county families in his own country, out of the *zamindars* of Bengal. This was the first experiment in westernization, and it was hardly a success.

Bentinck revolutionized educated India by the introduction of the English language and western teaching, with the consequent influx of European democratic ideas. For good or for ill the greatest change which the country has seen since the coming of Islam was the westernization of the politically-minded classes in India.

[1] *P. & O. Pocket Book.*

CHRONOLOGY

1823–1828. Lord Amherst Governor-General.
1824–1826. First Burmese War.
1826. Storming of Bharatpur.
Annexation of Assam.
1828–1835. Lord William Bentinck Governor-General.
1830. Annexation of Cachar.
1831. Mysore administered by the Company.
1833. Charter Act. E.I.C. ceased to be a trading body, legislative powers of Governor-General in Council defined.
1834. Annexation of Coorg.
Macaulay appointed Law Member of Council.
Failure of Shah Shuja's invasion of Afghanistan.
Ranjit Singh annexed Peshawar.
1835. Education Resolution.
Foundation of Medical College, Calcutta.

BIBLIOGRAPHY

History of the British Empire in India, Thornton, 2nd Edn., 1858.
History of British India, Mill, continuation by Wilson, Vol. IX. (bound as Vol. III. Edn. 1858).
History of India, Marshman, Vol. III., 1867.
Cambridge History of the British Empire, Vol. IV.
The Government of India, Sir C. Ilbert, 2nd Edn., 1907.
Rise of the British Dominion in India, Sir A. Lyall, 1893.
The Native States of India, Sir W. Lee-Warner (London), Edn. 1910, should be read in conjunction with
Report of the Indian States Committee, 1928–1929, Cmd. 3302, 1929.
The British Connection with India, K. T. Paul (London), 1927.
The Education of India, Mayhew, 1926.
Life of Lord William Bentinck, Boulger, Rulers of India Series, 1897.

Thornton is too prejudiced to give a full account of Bentinck's administration and Marshman is a fairer, if enthusiastic, guide.

CHAPTER XVIII

Consolidation of British Rule

AFTER the retirement of Lord William Bentinck, Sir Charles Metcalfe

Sir Charles Metcalfe. acted for a year as governor-general, and in August 1835 he repealed the press regulations to give journalism in India greater freedom than was then allowed in England.[1] Although this was popular in Calcutta it ruined Metcalfe's chances of having the confirmation of his appointment pressed by the Directors upon a Board of Control which could make political use of the patronage.

Sir Robert Peel, in his short-lived ministry of 1835, appointed Lord Heytesbury to succeed Bentinck. But the Whigs came in again shortly afterwards and Lord Melbourne revoked the appointment and substituted Lord Auckland, who took the oaths at Government House, Calcutta, on the 20th March 1836. Metcalfe resigned the service, and eventually, as Lord Metcalfe, became governor-general of Canada. During the thirty-four years which he had spent in India, since he came as a boy of sixteen to the College of Fort William, Metcalfe had played a prominent part in the political movements of every court from Hyderabad to Lahore, and " no other officer in India enjoyed to the same degree the respect and confidence of the native princes." [2]

George Eden, Lord Auckland, like his father before him, had

Lord Auckland. risen to Cabinet rank in England. He became President of the Board of Trade when the Whigs returned to power in 1830, and First Lord of the Admiralty in Lord Melbourne's ministry four years later. The governor-general elect,

---

[1] Thornton, *op. cit.*, pp. 522–523.
[2] Marshman, *History of India*, Vol. III. pp. 88, 89.

at the farewell banquet given him by the court of Directors, assured his hosts of his " exaltation at the prospect afforded him of ' doing good to his fellow-creatures, of promoting education and knowledge, of improving the administration of justice in India, of extending the blessings of good government and happiness to millions of her people.' " [1]

A quiet even-tempered man of unquestionable ability who made no enemies and cared for nothing but his work, Auckland's appointment seemed safe enough at a time when the Indian treasuries were full and peace reigned over the country. And it appeared at first as if his good intentions might be reasonably fulfilled. But he suffered from the fatal defect of lack of confidence in himself, he was the obedient exponent of the views of the authorities in England,[2] and instead of using his own judgment he trusted to the advice of others, his secretary John Colvin in particular.[3]

With the party manœuvres of the Whig ministry, which palmed " lie upon lie upon the world without one redeeming feature," [4] in defence of its foreign policy, Indian history has nothing to do. But it was the Russophobia of Lord Palmerston and his colleague Sir John Hobhouse, President of the Board of Control, which led to the war with Afghanistan and an overwhelming disaster to the British arms.

Defeat, however disastrous, could be retrieved, as it was retrieved later by Nott and Pollock. But the criminal blunder of the first Afghan war had a result which spread far beyond the defiles leading to Jalalabad. In the words of Sir John Kaye, the war in Afghanistan taught the sepoy " a new lesson and the worst, at that time, which he could have been taught. He learnt then, for the first time, that a British Army is not invincible in the field, that the fortune of the Company might sometimes disastrously fail. He believed that our reign was hastening to a close. The charm of a century of

---

[1] Marshman, *History of India*, Vol. III. p. 112.

[2] Secret Committee Despatch of 25th June 1836 was the guide of Auckland's conduct throughout. *Camb. Hist. British Empire*, Vol. IV. p. 490.

[3] Marshman, *op. cit.*, Vol. III. p. 123.

[4] Sir John Kaye, describing the "garbled " Blue Book of 1839, which he revised and re-edited in the Blue Book of 1859.

conquest was then broken. In all parts of Upper India it was the talk of the Bazaars." [1]

In his internal administration Auckland was sensible and practical.
Internal Administration. Before he had been two months in office his government at the instance of Macaulay removed an undesirable anomaly of judicial procedure. Until then any European might appeal in a civil case from the country [2] courts to the supreme court of the Crown, instead of to the high court of the Company which tried all Indian appeals. This Act, which made an equality in the form of administration of justice between the people of India and European residents, raised a storm in the English press in Calcutta against what was called the " Black Act." But as Macaulay represented: " If [the Company's high court] is fit to administer justice to the great body of the people, why should we exempt a mere handful of settlers from its jurisdiction. . . . If we take pains to show that we distrust our highest courts, how can we expect that the Natives of the country will place confidence in them ? "

In his views on Indian education Auckland was an Anglicist. But he was not prepared to accept Macaulay's extremist policy of purely western teaching; and two years after that enthusiastic reformer's departure from India the governor-general, in 1839, was allowing grants for Oriental publications and refusing to starve existing Oriental institutions. [3] He had substituted the vernacular for Persian in the lower courts of Bengal in 1837, but this had the unforeseen and unfortunate effect of discouraging education among the Muhammadans, a discouragement from which they have not yet completely recovered. Bentinck had founded a reformed medical college in Calcutta for the training of Indian students, which was followed by similar colleges in Bombay and Madras.

---

[1] *History of the Sepoy War in India,* Edn. 1872, Vol. I. p. 274.

[2] The usual term used in India for " country " as distinguished from " urban " is *mufassal.*

[3] *The Education of India,* Mayhew, p. 25. *Hist. British India,* Mill and Wilson, Vol. IX. pp. 213–215.

These were encouraged by Auckland, and "as though to mark India's departure on a westward road a Brahman demonstrator, before a hushed and breathless class of medical students, dissected a human body." [1]

Questions involving religion are always a difficult matter in India, and Auckland's settlement of the Company's official connection with Hinduism showed good judgment. This connection had been for years a scandal and an offence to pious Hindus and professing Christians alike. While reserving the right to take action, should the rules of common humanity or order be broken, Auckland put an end to British official interference in the management of the temples, in the religious proceedings of the priests, and in the arrangement of Hindu ceremonies and festivals. The pilgrim tax was abolished, fines and offerings ceased to form part of the government revenue, and no servant of the Company could any longer be employed in the collection or management of such money. [2]

Irrigation is of vital importance in Indian agriculture, especially in districts where the annual rainfall averages less *Irrigation.* than fifty inches. [3] Systems of irrigation such as canals, storage reservoirs and dams had been known at least in parts of India for a longer period than in any other country, with the possible exception of Egypt and Mesopotamia. But at the beginning of the nineteenth century the Mogul works had fallen into ruin, and modern irrigation in India began in 1819 on the old Delhi canal. In 1836–38 Captain (Sir Arthur) Cotton by his work on the great eleventh-century masonry weir on the Cauvery made Tanjore the richest district in Madras. [4]

These were local improvements, and Auckland must be credited with creating the first large irrigation project which the British undertook. Before he left India he had obtained the sanction of the Directors for Colvin's scheme for the great Ganges canal,

[1] *The Education of India*, p. 19.
[2] Marshman, *op. cit.*, Vol. III. pp. 200, 201.
[3] *Moral and Material Progress of India*, 1930–1931, pp. 227–228.
[4] *Modern India*, 2nd Edn., Ch. XII., by Sir Thomas Ward, pp. 189–191.

and set up a committee to deal with it.[1]   But the Afghan war had drained the treasury, and the works were left to be begun and completed by his successors.

Famine.   The irrigation scheme was planned as a protective measure against a recurrence of the appalling famine of 1837 and 1838 which devastated the Doab from Allahabad to Delhi, following on the drought of 1836.   Private and public effort, where there was no organization for famine relief, could do very little, and 800,000 persons were estimated to have died of hunger or disease.[2]   " In Cawnpore a special establishment patrolled the streets and the river to remove corpses.   In Fatehpur and Agra similar measures were adopted.   Hundreds of thousands died in obscure villages. . . . The dead lay on the roadside unburied and unburnt, till they were devoured by wild animals." [3]

The Oudh Kingdom.   The relations between the Government of India and the Indian States and the immediate and ultimate effects of the policy of non-intervention are illustrated in Oudh, which was consistently misgoverned.   Since Clive created the buffer State British bayonets had kept its rulers secure on the throne.   This had taken from the people of Oudh their one remedy against intolerable oppression—rebellion and deposition— which in a purely Oriental and despotic government was the equivalent to a general election under a modern democratic constitution.

Stipulations made by the Company, as in 1801, that the Oudh administration under its own officers should be " conducive to the prosperity " of the people, had proved futile.   Bentinck's threat had been ineffectual,[4] and in 1837 Auckland entered into negotiations with the kingdom.   With considerable difficulty he induced the king, Muhammad Ali Shah, to accept an alteration in Wellesley's treaty of 1801.   By the new treaty the British Government reserved to itself the right of appointing its own officers to carry out the

[1] *Life of Lord Auckland*, Trotter, pp. 22, 23.
[2] *Ibid.*, Trotter, p. 22.
[3] *Economic History of India*, Dutt, p. 431.
[4] Marshman, *op. cit.*, Vol. III. pp. 27, 28.

necessary reforms, " should hereafter at any time gross and systematic oppression, anarchy and misrule . . . seriously endanger the public tranquillity." Indian institutions and forms of administration were to be maintained " to facilitate the restoration of those territories to the sovereign of Oudh when the proper period for such restoration shall arrive." [1]

The home authorities were not prepared to shoulder this responsibility of paramountcy and the treaty was disallowed, although with considerable lack of candour the king was merely informed that the additional subsidiary force agreed to would not be required. Lee-Warner makes the following comment on the Directors' decision: " This ill-considered opposition to the Indian government bore fruit in due course, and nothing but annexation remained for Oudh and other principalities."

The leading factor in the Asiatic question, starting from the beginning of the nineteenth century, was the eastward advance of Russia, and the points of interest to the British Foreign Office were Persia and Afghanistan.

The ambitions of Russia had led her eastward from Georgia, which she annexed in 1801, to a dominating influence at the Iranian court where in 1834 the Russian agent Count Simonich was urging the new Shah Muhammad Mirza to take Herat; an action which was fully justified by repeated acts of hostility committed by its rulers.[2]

The situation had changed considerably since 1814, when the British home government had concluded a defensive treaty with Persia; a treaty from the fulfilment of which England had shrunk in Persia's hour of need.[3] But in point of fact it did not matter to India whether Persia occupied Herat or not, even if she held that city in dependence on Russia. It was a large assumption for Palmerston, the foreign secretary in London, to maintain that the capture of Herat involved imminent peril to the security and

---

[1] *The Native States of India*, pp. 146–149.
[2] Marshman, *op. cit.*, Vol. III. p. 121.
[3] *The First Afghan War*, Sir H. Mortimer Durand, p. 30.

internal tranquillity of the British dominions in India; while it was a geographical absurdity for him to say that Afghanistan was then the Company's frontier. It was separated from British India by the Punjab, Bahawalpur, Sind and the Rajputana desert, which as Sir Mortimer Durand observed was in itself alone no bad frontier.[1]

Nor had the British Government any quarrel with Afghanistan. Dost Muhammad had risen to power in that country by his own ability in 1826 and he had successfully defeated Shah Shuja's efforts to win back his throne eight years later. He had a grievance against the British for their "benevolent neutrality" to Shah Shuja on that occasion; and Peshawar, which had been taken by the Sikhs, was in the hands of the Company's ally Ranjit Singh. However, in May 1836 the Amir sent a formal letter of welcome to Auckland, referred frankly to his difficulties with the Sikhs and volunteered to be guided by the governor-general's advice.[2]

In July 1837 the Shah of Persia moved on Herat and the first Russian scare began in England, encouraged by an alarmist pamphlet written by (Sir) John MacNeill, the British minister in Persia.[3] In September Captain Burnes, a daring explorer and a staff officer of promise and personal charm, arrived in Kabul as the representative of the Government of India. His mission was ostensibly commercial, but actually it was political.

Dost Muhammad told Burnes that if the British Government would help him to regain Peshawar he would break off his negotiations with Russia and dismiss the Persian envoy then in Kabul. In his anxiety to regain the lost province the Amir assured Burnes that he would be willing to hold it in fief from Ranjit Singh and transmit the customary presents.

"There can be little doubt," Marshman observes,[4] "that if Lord Auckland had boldly faced the question and entrusted the solution to Captain Burnes at Cabul and to Captain Wade[5] at

---

[1] *The First Afghan War*, p. 62.
[2] *Camb. Hist. British Empire*, Vol. IV. p. 491.
[3] Marshman, *op. cit.*, Vol. III. p. 124.
[4] Marshman, *op. cit.*, Vol. III. pp. 125, 126.
[5] The "British frontier authority," resident at the Sikh Court from 1827 to 1839 (*History of the Sikhs*, pp. 183, 225).

Loodhiana, it would have been brought to an early and satisfactory issue. The overtures of Persia and Russia would in that case have been definitely rejected and Dost Muhammad, secured as an ally, would have become an effectual barrier against encroachments from the west."

Auckland rejected the proposal. Dost Muhammad made a final appeal to the governor-general in which he implored him "to remedy the grievances of the Afghans and to give them a little encouragement and power," [1] to which Auckland sent a contemptuous reply. The Amir then turned to the Russian envoy who made with him and with the Kandahar chiefs treaties which were hostile to British interests, and Burnes left Kabul in April 1838.

British policy in 1838 was what it had been in 1809 when Elphinstone's embassy had been sent to Shah Shuja, "to interpose a friendly power in Central Asia between us and any invading power from the west." Auckland proposed to create this power by encouraging the reluctant Ranjit Singh to invade Afghanistan,[2] under certain restrictions, and by helping Shah Shuja to regain his throne. A tripartite treaty was signed in July 1838, by which the Government of India limited its responsibilities to the appointment of a representative at Kabul, to the supply of officers to discipline and command Shah Shuja's army and to make an advance of money to pay it.

First Afghan War. Auckland was soon persuaded that unless the Government of India engaged as principals in the expedition it could only end in complete failure. Sir John Keene was accordingly given supreme command of forces amounting to 21,000 men in an enterprise "universally condemned outside the ministerial circle in Downing Street and the secretaries at Simla." [3] Macnaghten, "long accustomed to irresponsible office, inexperienced in men and ignorant of the country and people of Afghanistan," was appointed chief political officer.[4]

[1] Marshman, *op. cit.*, Vol. III. pp. 128, 129.
[2] *History of the Sikhs*, pp. 219–221.
[3] Marshman, *op. cit.*, Vol. III. pp. 132, 133.
[4] Durand, *op. cit.*, p. 69.

Two months before the field army concentrated in November 1838 the Persians had raised the siege of Herat. The soul of its defence had been a young Bombay artillery officer Eldred Pottinger. He had come to Herat after exploring in Central Asia, and his dispositions successfully foiled all the efforts of Count Simonich and his Russian engineers.[1]

One of the lines of advance of the Afghan Expeditionary Force lay through Sind, with whose independent rulers the company had treaty obligations. The military consideration of safeguarding the line of communications made it necessary to control the country. In order, therefore, to place Shah Shuja on the throne of Afghanistan the Mirs of Sind were made to sign a treaty which practically took away their independence, an independence which had only been preserved from destruction at the hands of Ranjit Singh in 1835 by the determined attitude of Lord William Bentinck.[2]

After terrible hardships the two British columns met at Kandahar, *The First Phase.* which was entered by Shah Shuja in April 1839; and after the capture of Ghazni, Kabul was occupied in August. Sikh troops joined in these operations, but Ranjit Singh died on the 27th June 1839, before the events which " placed the seal of success on a campaign in which he was an unwilling sharer."[3]

An army of 10,000 men was left in the country under a capable *Occupation.* general. But shortly after Dost Muhammad surrendered in November 1840 and was sent to Calcutta with a liberal allowance, Elphinstone, who was too old and infirm for the responsibility, was given command of the army of occupation.

Afghanistan was now under the ostensible rule of Shah Shuja, though it was actually being governed by Sir William Macnaghten. On the strength of his assurance that the tranquillity of the country was " perfectly miraculous," officers were allowed to bring up their wives and families from India. At the same time the Directors in London were urging the governor-general either to withdraw from Afghanistan altogether or strongly reinforce the army of occupation.[4]

[1] Marshman, *op. cit.*, Vol. III. pp. 135-139.   [2] *Ibid.*, p. 114.
[3] *History of the Sikhs*, pp. 221, 222.
[4] Marshman, *op. cit.*, Vol. III. pp. 169, 170.

But Auckland did neither although Persia was now friendly, the Russian expedition to Khiva had failed, Dost Muhammad was a State prisoner, all was quiet in Kalat and Baluchistan, and the western borders beyond British India were absolutely safe from any prospect of invasion.

The Afghans hated the presence of the Company's troops in their country and were irritated by the not invariably *The Second Phase.* tactful control of the political officers. By the end of October 1841 the whole country was up in arms. On 2nd November Burnes and some other British officers were murdered in Kabul by a mob which attacked their house, and the British treasury was sacked. Far from making even an effort to prevent this catastrophe, the British garrison was withdrawn from the Bala Hissar commanding the city, and the whole force encamped in an indefensible position on the plain outside Kabul. Supplies were openly looted, Kabul was in a ferment, but still the authorities did nothing but negotiate. On 23rd December Macnaghten was assassinated by Dost Muhammad's son Akbar Khan outside the gates of the city, and although this took place " within musket-shot of a British army " [1] not a man was moved to avenge him.

On the 1st January 1842 negotiations were reopened with the Afghans. The army under Elphinstone had lost its stores, its morale and, naturally enough, much of its discipline. Nothing was left but to retreat from Kabul. By the convention it was agreed that Afghanistan was to be evacuated, the British forces were to leave behind them their treasure, all their guns except six and the hostages already in the hands of the Afghans, while bills for an indemnity of fourteen lakhs of rupees were drawn on the Government of India,[2] payable after the safe arrival of the force at Peshawar.[3]

On 6th January 1842 the British force—4500 men, 12,000 followers together with women and children—began their retreat through the snow to the death-traps of the Afghan defiles. On 13th January the one survivor, Dr. Brydon, severely wounded and utterly exhausted,

[1] Thornton, *op. cit.*, p. 566.
[2] Thornton, *op. cit.*, pp. 563, 566.
[3] Marshman, *op. cit.*, Vol. III. pp. 191, 192.

rode into Jalalabad. The women and children and the wounded officers, with the married men who remained alive after the passage of the Khurd Kabul defiles,[1] had been transferred into Akbar Khan's keeping. "Elphinstone's army—guns, standards, honour, all being lost—had been itself completely annihilated."

Three months after the British troops left Kabul, Shah Shuja was murdered and his weak and dissolute son Fatteh Jang was set on the throne with Akbar Khan the actual ruler of the country.

On the 28th February 1842 Lord Ellenborough took office in place of Auckland, whose tenure was over.

The new governor-general was just in time to save a second British army from annihilation by reversing the fatal decision ordering Nott to abandon his guns, his supplies and his followers, and retreat from Kandahar.

Ghazni fell to the Afghans on the 6th March, but Jalalabad, Kandahar and Khalat-i-Ghilzai still held out; and *The Third Phase.* on 16th April General Pollock relieved Jalalabad. He then marched on Kabul, which he reached on 15th September. Nott after reducing the country round Kandahar joined up with Pollock at Kabul, and after demolishing a great covered bazaar where Macnaghten's body had been exposed, the British force retired upon Peshawar. Elphinstone had died while a prisoner but the surviving British hostages who had, considering the circumstances, been well treated, came back to India with the army.

The operations which ended in the successful reoccupation of Kabul and the subsequent retirement from Afghanistan were carried out to an accompaniment of proclamations by Ellenborough reflecting alternately his sensitive reaction to a slight reverse and a more resolute attitude. His elaborate reception of the gates of Somnath, which he had ordered Nott to bring back from Ghazni, was distinctly unfortunate. The " return " of the gates did not— even for the Hindus—" avenge the insult of eight hundred years " as the Governor-General proclaimed. They had been made by

[1] Marshman, *op. cit.*, Vol. III. p. 195.

Sabuktigin, had never been in India, and could not therefore have been removed by Mahmud of Ghazni. There was no temple of Somnath to which they could be restored, and the gates eventually found a resting-place in the lumber room of the fort at Agra.[1]

The disastrous business of Afghanistan was ended, not by what Thornton describes as the " masking and mummery " of the military pageant at Ferozepore, at which Ellenborough originally intended to parade the Afghan prisoners, but by the return of Dost Muhammad to Kabul, where he reigned until his death in 1863. At his final interview with the governor-general he said: " I have been struck with the magnitude of your power, of your resources, with your ships, your arsenals, and your armies; but what I cannot understand is why the rulers of so vast and flourishing an empire should have gone across the Indus to deprive me of my poor and barren country." [2]

Dost Muhammad had been " by turns the rejected friend, the enforced enemy, the honourable prisoner, the vindictive assailant " of the British in India. Early in 1857, through Sir John Lawrence and Sir Herbert Edwardes, he finally became a faithful ally. Three months later the Mutiny broke over Upper India. But when the Punjab was so drained of its European and staunch Indian troops " as almost to invite an Afghan invasion, and when the priests of Kabul and the Amir's own sons were calling him to bind on his head the green turban of Islam and sweep the English from the plains of India," [3] he held to the word he had spoken : " I have now made an alliance with the British Government, and come what may I will keep it till death."

The relations of the Government of India with the Mirs of
Sind. Sind during the Afghan war have already been described. Ellenborough went a step further and annexed the country.

Viewed from a military standpoint, Sind was a weak point on the

[1] Marshman, *op. cit.*, Vol. III. pp. 230, 231.
[2] *Ibid.*, p. 233.
[3] *Life of Lord Lawrence*, Aitchison, p. 12.

frontier. It was under the divided control of its mirs and guarded the "most important of imperial interests," the water-way of the Indus. From the political point of view: "If Sind had not fallen to the Company it must have been annexed either by Afghanistan or Lahore." [1] But when the manner in which the annexation was made is considered, no fairer opinion can be quoted than that of James Outram, the Bayard of India, in a letter to his close personal friend Sir Charles Napier: " I am sick of *policy* ; I will not say yours is the *best*, but it is undoubtedly the shortest—that *of the sword*. Oh how I wish you had drawn it in a better cause! " [2] Outram, when political officer in Sind, reported [3] that the " changeable puerile and divided chieftains " were not a source of danger ; and he urged, when pleading their cause in England, that they " never contemplated opposing our power and were only driven to do so from desperation." [4]

In 1842 Ellenborough replaced Outram in Sind by Sir Charles Napier, who was given full military and political powers. He was bent on annexing Sind, and a number of charges against the mirs, such as levying river-tolls contrary to treaty, were soon collected. The pressure brought upon the chiefs caused a popular outbreak on 15th February 1843, and two days later Napier heavily defeated the Sindians at Miani and again routed them, at Dabo, in March. Sind was then annexed with the exception of Khaipur whose ruler had supported the British. Napier became the first governor of the province and ruled it with considerable firmness until 1847.

The Maharaja of Gwalior Jayaji Rao Sindia was a child, and
Gwalior. the regent was loyal to the paramount Power, but in 1843 control of the country had fallen into the hands of the military party. The army, a body of 30,000 men partly officered by Europeans and men of mixed descent, was ill-disciplined, and the state had fallen into serious misrule. In conjunction with the existence of the formidable Sikh kingdom, with its 70,000 troops,

---

[1] Lee-Warner, *op. cit.*, p. 136.
[2] *Life of James Outram*, Goldsmid, Vol. I. p. 331.
[3] Thornton, *op. cit.*, p. 591.
[4] Thornton, *op. cit.*, pp. 596–608, fully describes affairs in Sind.

the unruly forces of Gwalior constituted a danger to the peace of India.

Ellenborough, however, refused at first to intervene. But in December 1843 he was obliged to use force. Sir Hugh, afterwards Lord, Gough, the commander-in-chief, entered Gwalior, accompanied by the governor-general, and beat the State troops at Maharajpur and Paniar.[1] In the treaty signed on 13th January 1844 the governor-general emphasized the principle that the " British Government was bound to protect the person of His Highness the Maharaja, his heirs and successors, and to protect his dominions from foreign invasion, and to quell serious disturbances therein," [2] and he brought to a final issue by limiting the State army, Sindhia's right to maintain forces at a strength which might be dangerous to himself and a threat to his neighbours.[3]

As Lee-Warner remarks: " Beneath the policy of isolation the principle began to be observed that each separate State was one of a family, and that a common defence and a common welfare were objects deserving of attainment."

As regards the outward symbols in the evolution of paramountcy, the British sovereign's image and superscription instead of the Emperor's had appeared on the company's coinage since 1835. Ellenborough wished to go further, and tried to induce the Mogul Emperor to resign his title in the Queen's favour. Had his idea been carried out Victoria would have figured as *Padshah Ghazi*, the Islamic equivalent to the *Fidei Defensor* which Henry VIII had been granted by the Pope for his thesis against the protestantism of Luther.

Ellenborough was almost entirely occupied with external affairs, but during his time in India two important reforms were made.

The organization of the existing police force of British India *Police.*   originated in Sind after its annexation in 1843, a measure due to its governor Sir Charles Napier. This came to maturity in the Act of 1861 which established a purely

---

[1] Lee-Warner, *op. cit.*, p. 39.
[2] *Ibid.*, p. 100.
[3] *Camb. Hist. British India*, Vol. IV. p. 606.

civil constabulary capable of all police duties, and further improvements were made later, notably in the time of Lord Curzon. But at this point, the birth of the present system of law and order, something may be said of the policing of the country up to the time of Lord Ellenborough.

Certain points of similarity in the customs of the Aryan invaders of India and the Saxons who invaded Britain have already been noted. The police systems of the two peoples also bore points of resemblance. Both were based on land tenure. In England the thane in the time of Alfred had to produce the offender or pay the damages. In India the *zamindar* was bound to apprehend all disturbers of the peace and to restore the stolen property, or make good its value. Subordinate tenure holders under the Indian system had their share of responsibility for law and order.

In large towns the police were under an official known as the *kotwal*, but the actual executive police of the country was mainly represented by the village watchman. His responsibilities entailed the detection of thefts and the restitution of stolen property, or in default he and the village community between them had to make up the value. The watchman could call upon the villagers to help him, parallel to the " hue and cry " and the duty of all private persons in England.

Mogul police administration, as given in the edict of Abu-l-Fazul, Akbar's minister, rested, as in Saxon and Norman England, on a system of mutual security. It was reinforced by the obligation to report changes of address to district prefects of police, and the help of all neighbours in cases of theft, fire " or other misfortune," was emphasized.

The system failed as soon as the Mogul power came to an end and all higher control disappeared. When the Company took charge of the provinces, district magistrates were appointed; but this brought no improvement, and efforts were made to strengthen the village police. The first attempt to introduce expert control came in 1808 when superintendents ranking with modern inspectors-general of police were appointed in Bengal. But the select committee of 1832 found the subordinates to be corrupt, inefficient and oppressive.

while the superior officers were too overworked to exercise proper supervision.[1]

The semi-military police force in Sind was a forward step in organization; and at the same time efforts were made to improve conditions elsewhere in a branch of the administration which Marshman has described as " disgracefully neglected and inadequately remunerated. One magistrate was considered sufficient for a population of a million, and the largest scope was thus afforded for the venality and oppression of the native police officers, whose allowances for half a century had been barely sufficient to cover their travelling expenses." [2] Wilberforce Bird, vice-president in council, secured some increase in pay, and established the office of deputy-magistrate to which all castes and creeds were eligible, which greatly improved the efficiency of the department.

Abolition of Slavery. There were then millions of slaves in India, and the question of slavery had been referred to the Law Commission appointed under the Charter Act of 1833. In 1843 a law was passed, through the efforts of Bird, which abolished slavery in British India by a stroke of the pen.

State Lotteries. State lotteries had long since been abandoned in England, but they took place twice a year in India until Ellenborough did away with them in 1843. The proceeds of the lotteries had been used to improve the Presidency towns.

On 15th June 1844 Ellenborough was told that he was dismissed. The court of Directors, remote from the vital problems of the Indian people, had little sympathy with the economic policy of a statesman who, in 1839, had said of the administration in India: " By economy, revenue covers expenditure . . . but we are unable to diminish taxation where its pressure is destroying the power of reproduction and disheartening and alienating the people. We are unable to expend any portion of our income (on) canals and tanks which are essential in many places to prosperity. We diminish salaries until we endanger the character of the (officials). We have

[1] *Report of the Indian Police Commission for* 1902–1903, *passim.*
[2] Marshman, *op. cit.*, Vol. III. p. 268.

an insufficient police, an insufficient establishment for the administration of justice." [1] They disliked his sympathy for the army at the expense of the civil service; and they strongly resented the attitude of a governor-general who never forgot that he had twice been their master on the Board of Control. Ellenborough may have given occasion for unfriendly ridicule but he ended the Afghan war with credit, and his general policy had the support of Queen Victoria, the Duke of Wellington, Sir Robert Peel and Lord Hardinge.

The new governor-general, Sir Henry, afterwards Lord Hardinge, arrived in India on 23rd July 1844, and his journey illustrates the successive stages of progress in travel to the East, with the exception of the air. He came by the overland route in forty-four days; across France, partly by rail; by sea to Alexandria; by river-boat to Cairo; by coach-and-four to Suez; and then to Calcutta by steamer.[2]

Hardinge was a veteran soldier of sixty who had greatly distinguished himself in the Peninsula war and at Waterloo. He had twice been what was then known as " secretary at war " in a Tory ministry, as well as secretary for Ireland, and he had shown his judgment to be sound, his decisions clear-cut and his character to be kindly and generous. He told the secretaries to the Government of India, when he took over charge, that he knew almost nothing of civil administration and even less about India, and impressed upon his officials the extreme inadvisability of trying to mislead him.

Within three months of his arrival in India Hardinge passed a resolution which definitely held out the encourage-
Education.   ment of office and promotion to the successful students of the government colleges and of private institutions; prospects which materialized when the universities of Calcutta, Bombay and Madras were founded thirteen years later, with degrees corresponding to the B.A. and M.A. of the universities in Great Britain.[3]

---

[1] *India under Lord Ellenborough*, p. 3.
[2] *The Making of India*, A. Yusuf Ali, p. 265.   [3] Thakore, *op. cit.*, p. 353.

The Army. After careful consideration Hardinge reintroduced corporal punishment in the Indian Army. Under the old system the yearly number of sentences of flogging had never exceeded 700. Under the new rule introduced by Bentinck, increasing insubordination in the service had substituted 10,000 sentences of hard labour on the roads in gangs with thieves and felons, a punishment which inflicted indelible disgrace on the families of the soldiers concerned. The degrading punishment of flogging still persisted in the British Army and the decision was a difficult one; but, as Marshman says,[1] " It is grateful to record that the punishment was so rarely inflicted that (Hardinge's) order became a dead letter."

Economic and Social. A most important improvement made during Hardinge's administration was the carrying out of the canal schemes projected by his predecessor. Canals have always been of the greatest benefit to India, and the Ganges canal, 525 miles in length, which is still among the greatest irrigation canals in the world, was begun, to be completed in 1854.

In about 1845 surveys were begun on both sides of India for the construction of railways leading from Bombay and Calcutta into the interior of the country. But no construction work was started until the time of Hardinge's successor Lord Dalhousie.

Through British paramountcy the governor-general influenced the Princes to abolish *sati*, female infanticide and slavery within their territories, and before he left India these reforms were active in twenty-four States. The last State observance of *sati* was in 1861.

In his last year of office Hardinge determined to suppress the practice of the primitive tribes of Orissa to make human sacrifices to increase the fertility of their fields. The measures he took in the Hill Tracts were not, however, successful and it was not until 1854 that the persistent efforts of the Government of India brought about the substitution of animals in this magical rite.

[1] *Op. cit.*, Vol. III. pp. 272–273.

But the relations between the Company's government and the
Sikh kingdom are the main features of Hardinge's
administration.

The Punjab.

Ranjit Singh had found the Punjab a waning confederacy broken
into factions, pressed by the Afghans and the Marathas and ready
to submit to British supremacy. He consolidated the petty States
into a great military kingdom, possessing a thoroughly efficient army
of nearly 50,000 regular troops with more than 350 guns, and about
60,000 well-armed yeomanry and militia.[1] He held in check, though
with difficulty, the Pathan tribes with his troops and fortresses at the
mouth of the passes; and as long as he lived the Sikh kingdom was
in friendly alliance with the British.

The situation abruptly changed when the great Maharaja died in
1839. Ranjit Singh's power had lain in the masterful strength of his
personality, he had founded no permanent institutions, and his death
was the signal for anarchy in the kingdom. After a series of murders
in the struggle over the succession, Dhulip Singh the five-year-old
son of Ranjit Singh was proclaimed Maharaja in 1843, with Lal
Singh chief minister. But the supreme power rested with the army.
The Sikh forces, which had been completely out of hand since the death
of Ranjit Singh, had no restraining influence as the foreign officers
had been driven to escape from the country for their lives in 1841.

Neither the military leaders who were constantly in fear of
mutiny, nor the State officials who were obliged to make concessions
to the soldiery they were unable to pay, had any definite scheme of
policy. "They drifted, as more civilized States in modern times
have also drifted, into 'doing something,' and surface currents
decided what that something should be."[2] The Afghan campaign,
and reports of unrest in some of the Company's Indian regiments,
lessened Sikh respect for the British power. Macnaghten writing to
Auckland from Kabul in 1841 had urged the governor-general to
"crush the Sings, macadamize the Punjab and annex the province
of Peshawar to the dominions of Shah Soojah"[3]; and in 1843,

---

[1] *History of the Sikhs*, p. 222 and footnote.
[2] *The Native States of India*, p. 139.
[3] Marshman, *op. cit.*, Vol. III. p. 275.

with the object lesson of Sind before them, the Khalsa had the impression, however erroneous, that the British intended to annex their country.

It was peculiarly unfortunate that at so critical a juncture Clerk, who was Wade's able and wise successor, should have been withdrawn from the Sikh court and replaced in 1844 by Colonel Broadfoot. The new resident had energy and ability, but he was distrusted by the Sikhs, and his appointment was generally held by the English in India greatly to increase the probabilities of war.[1]

At the same time the perfectly natural distrust with which the Government of India viewed the confusion, crime and general restlessness in the Sikh kingdom made a concentration of troops on the Punjab frontier an unavoidable precaution. In 1838 the Company had only 2500 men and a battery of artillery near the Sikh border. Auckland sent up considerable reinforcements, and these were increased by Ellenborough, who saw the political situation " in the light of an armed truce," to about 14,000 men and 48 field guns.[2]

On the 11th December 1845 the Sikh army of 30,000 men at the lowest estimate [3] with 150 guns under the command

The First Sikh War.

of Lal Singh and Tej Singh crossed the Sutlej and invaded the territory of their British allies. In his proclamation of the 13th December the governor-general emphasized the desire of his government that there should be a strong Sikh administration in the Punjab to control its army and protect its subjects. He went on to say that " he had not abandoned the hope of seeing that important object effected by the chiefs and people of that country," but that war was now declared because the " violators of treaties and the public peace " required punishment.[4]

Sir Hugh Gough, with the governor-general serving under him as

[1] *History of the Sikhs*, pp. 279–282 and footnote.
[2] *Ibid.*, footnote to p. 279. *Camb. Hist. British India*, Vol. IV. p. 549, gives the total strength on the frontier, exclusive of hill stations, as 17,612 men and 66 guns, when Ellenborough left India.
[3] *History of the Sikhs*, p. 291 and footnote 1, but see footnote 3 to p. 290, which gives a higher figure.
[4] *The Native States of India*, p. 140.

a volunteer, marched upon the Sikh army near Ferozepore with about 17,000 men and 69 guns. Mudki, on 18th December, was a British success. The Sikhs fought in the "soldiers' battle" of the campaign, as they have always fought—magnificently—and they deserved better leaders. On the night of 21st December, after the first day of the battle of Firozeshah, "the fate of India trembled in the balance." But Gough was a leader of the greatest determination and Firozeshah was won next day after a desperate fight. The British casualties were 2415 killed and wounded, and the Sikh losses were much heavier.[1]

The British victory of Aliwal followed on the 28th January 1846, and an incident which took place when the fight was over is worth recalling. By order of the governor-general a royal salute was fired from the British camp and the bands played the national anthem. The Sikhs on the opposite bank of the Sutlej followed suit and their bands were heard playing "God save the Queen."[2] The decisive battle of Sobraon was fought on 10th February and Lahore was occupied by the British ten days later.

The governor-general was not prepared to annex the Punjab; it *Treaties of Lahore.* would have been contrary to the Company's declared policy and would have meant an army of occupation of prohibitive size. Nor could he support the existing government, which was selfish, intriguing and unstable, by making a definite subsidiary alliance. The treaties of Lahore, signed on 9th and 11th March 1846, were a compromise.

The terms of peace included the Sikh renunciation of all territory south of the Sutlej; the annexation by the British of the Jullundur Doab between the Sutlej and the Beas; the ceding of Kashmir and Hazara in perpetual sovereignty to the Company; the reduction of the Sikh army to 20,000 infantry, 12,000 cavalry, and the surrender of 36 guns in addition to those taken in action; the Maharaja was recognized and the Company disclaimed interference in the internal affairs of the Sikh kingdom. A force was to occupy Lahore until

[1] *History of the Sikhs,* footnote, pp. 296, 297.
[2] *The Sikhs and the Sikh Wars,* General Sir Charles Gough and A. D. Innes, p. 119.

the end of the year to protect the Maharaja and ensure the execution of the terms ; and Henry Lawrence remained as agent at the Sikh capital.[1]

On the 16th March, by the treaty of Amritsar, Hardinge established Raja Ghulab Singh, the Rajput ruler of Jammu, in the subordinate sovereignty of Kashmir,[2] which had been taken over from the Sikhs in lieu of a war indemnity. Kashmir was granted as " the independent possession " of Ghulab Singh and the heirs male of his body. This limitation of tenure bears on the question of adoption and lapse which was already engaging the attention of the Government of India [3] and was to become a prominent feature of Lord Dalhousie's policy. In token of British supremacy the Maharaja was required by the treaty to present " annually to the British Government one horse, twelve perfect shawl goats of approved breed (six male and six female) and three pairs of Kashmir shawls."

Kashmir.

Ghulab Singh had started life as a trooper in Ranjit Singh's army. He had received Jammu as a reward for gallantry, and as a minister of the Khalsa he had taken a leading part in the negotiations after Sobraon. His elevation to the throne of Kashmir was unpopular among the Sikhs,[4] and Lal Singh the chief minister of the Lahore government instigated Shaikh Imam-ud-din the late governor of the country to raise an insurrection in October 1846. This was promptly put down by Henry Lawrence with a British force assisted by 17,000 of the Sikhs who had recently been fighting the Company; and Lal Singh was deported.

The Sikh government, to avoid anarchy in the kingdom, asked for a continuance of British support, and by the revised treaty of 16th December 1846 [5] an arrangement was made which was only short of annexation. The Company assumed administrative control. A Sikh council of regency was appointed to act under a British resident who was given an efficient establishment of assistants to

---

[1] For text of the Treaties see *History of the Sikhs*, Appendices XXXIV., XXXV.

[2] For text of Treaty see *Ibid.*, Appendix XXXVI.

[3] *The Native States of India*, p. 141.   [4] *History of the Sikhs*, p. 319.

[5] *Ibid.*, Appendix XXXVII.

direct and control every department of the government, internal and external, and a British garrison was kept in Lahore. The British resident was Henry Lawrence, and he with the assistants of brilliant promise and fulfilment whom he chose may be called the " shadow administration " of the famous Punjab commission which was to come.

The strictest economy was now a pressing necessity and the governor-general made drastic reductions in the

Army Reductions. army, which had been increased since 1838 by 120,000 men. Hardinge disbanded the police battalions and reduced the rank and file of the Company's forces by 50,000 men. But at the same time he organized three movable brigades of all arms at Lahore, Jullundur and Ferozepore.[1]

On the 12th January 1848 James Ramsay, tenth Earl of Dalhousie, became governor-general. His predecessor left India with the conviction that " it would not be necessary to fire another shot in India for seven years."[2] That Henry Lawrence sailed with him, when he went to England two months later, was as unfortunate as the withdrawal of Clerk from the Sikh capital in 1844. But nothing could have prevented the second Sikh war.

British control over the Lahore government could only have been effective had the Company's authority been universally felt and recognized. But the Sikhs, although they numbered barely one-sixth of the population of the Punjab, were united in the proud memory of their achievements, and they were not yet inclined to settle down as farmers. A signal for a rising could still set the Punjab in a blaze; and that signal was given three months after Dalhousie took office.

Mulraj, governor of Multan under the Lahore administration, had sent in his resignation; and Vans Agnew, a

Multan. civil servant, was ordered down from the Punjab nominally to superintend the installation of the new governor but actually to take over the management of the country and introduce a

[1] Marshman, *op. cit.*, Vol. III. pp. 303–305.
[2] Marshman, *op. cit.*, Vol. III. p. 308.

new system of finance and revenue.[1]   Opposition to this radical change was certain, but Sir Frederick Currie, the resident at Lahore, sent no force with which to support this policy.   An escort of 350 Sikhs and Gurkhas under Lieutenant Anderson was considered enough.   With the connivance of Mulraj the two British officers were murdered at Multan on the 20th April.   Mulraj then issued a proclamation calling upon the people of the province, of every creed, to rise against the English in a religious war.[2]

Lieutenant (afterwards Sir) Herbert Edwardes who was at Bannu covered fifty miles by road and river in twenty-four hours in a gallant though unsuccessful effort to take Multan and crush the insurrection. But the Government of India deferred action during the hot weather, on the advice of Lord Gough.   In September General Whish laid siege to Multan, but the defection of the Sikhs forming the bulk of his force soon compelled him to retire.

By this time the Punjab was up in arms.   The Maharani, a source of widespread intrigue, had been deported, but the Sikh army was burning to fight and there was not " a chief or an officer who was not eager to shake off the yoke of the foreigners and again to enshrine the national idol of Sikh supremacy."

The Sikhs openly gathered under Sher Singh and Chattar Singh, and Gough concentrated his troops at Ferozepore.

Second Sikh War.

On 5th October Dalhousie, before leaving Calcutta for the front, made his pronouncement: " I have wished for peace. . . . I have striven for it. . . . But unwarned by precedent, uninfluenced by example, the Sikh nation has called for war, and on my word, sirs, they shall have it with a vengeance."[3] The governor-general's comment to the secret committee in London on the Multan outbreak was "There is no other course open to us, but to prepare for a general Sikh war, and ultimately to occupy the country."[4]

Gough crossed the Ravi on the 16th November[5] and, after two

[1] Marshman, *op. cit.*, Vol. III. p. 311.   [2] *Ibid.*, p. 313.
[3] *Life of the Marquis of Dalhousie*, Trotter, p. 38.
[4] 7th October 1848, *Parliamentary Papers*, 1849, XLI. p. 374.
[5] Dalhousie to Wellington dated 7th December 1848, *Life of the Marquis of Dalhousie*, Lee-Warner, Vol. I. p. 191.

minor actions, met the Sikh main army of 30,000 to 40,000 men at Chilianwala on the afternoon of 13th January 1849. Sher Singh manœuvred to force an action and Gough advanced to the attack with 14,000 troops and about an equality in artillery. The British losses were 89 British and 43 Indian officers killed, the casualty lists showed more than 2200 killed and wounded, and four guns and the colours of three regiments were lost. The news of the battle made a bad impression in England, and it was decided to supersede Gough by Sir Charles Napier.

But Chilianwala was not a defeat. Better leading by subordinate commanders and the coming of darkness enabled the Sikhs to remain on the field, but their own losses had been heavy and their confidence was shaken. On the 21st February Gough won a brilliant and complete victory at Gujerat on the Chenab. The second Sikh war was over.

On the 29th March 1849 the Punjab was annexed by proclamation and the Maharaja having resigned his sovereignty in favour of the Company was pensioned and required to reside outside the state. By the terms agreed upon,[1] "The Gem called the Koh-i-noor, which was taken from Shah Shooja-ool-Moolk by Maharajah Runjeet Singh, shall be surrendered by the Maharajah of Lahore to the Queen of England."

A board of government was appointed to administer the Punjab consisting of Henry and John Lawrence and C. E. Mansell, who was replaced in 1851 by Robert Montgomery. Under them were the pick of the north-western province, Barnes, John Nicholson, Edwardes, Edward Thornton [2] and many other young soldiers and civilians. The Punjab became known as the non-regulation province and " the accessibility of the officers and the personal influence they gained did more for the pacification of the country than regiments of soldiers."[3] Under Sikh rule the only officers of state had been soldiers or tax-gatherers and the punishments fine or mutilation. Nor had there been a civil court outside Lahore. Instead of the mountains

---

[1] *Dalhousie*, Lee-Warner, Vol. I. pp. 242, 243.
[2] The historian, and author of the *Gazetteer of India*.
[3] *Life of Lord Lawrence*, Aitchison, p. 59.

of regulations piled upon the older provinces Montgomery gave the people of the Punjab a concise manual written on a few sheets of foolscap.[1] Henry Lawrence wanted to help the ruined Sikh court financially for political reasons, Dalhousie intended the money for administration, and Henry was replaced in 1853 as chief commissioner by his brother John, afterwards Lord Lawrence. How the country was disarmed, the frontier defended by the creation of the Punjab Frontier Force, roads and bridges and irrigation canals constructed, may be read in the first Punjab Administration Report.

Second Burmese War. The scene now shifts to Burma. Since the withdrawal of the British resident, trade and the ship-building industry, the business of the small European community at Rangoon, had suffered badly. In 1851 the English merchants complained of incessant acts of oppression and atrocity. Reparation was not forthcoming and Commodore Lambert of the *Fox*, who was " too combustible " to brook the ways of the Burmese authorities, precipitated hostilities.

The governor-general tried, nevertheless, until March 1852 to avoid war. But when the attitude of the court of Ava made hostilities inevitable he took every precaution to ensure success. The medical and supply services were highly efficient, and the campaign, which began with the storming of the Rangoon pagoda on 14th April, ended in November with the occupation of the Pegu province. In the naval escort to the expedition English literature was again represented, on this occasion by Jane Austen's brother, the admiral.

Dalhousie refused to advance to Ava as instructions from London required. The king of Ava refused to sign any treaty and the governor-general thereupon issued a proclamation on the 20th December 1852 declaring the province of Pegu to be henceforth a portion of the British territories. After the annexation Dalhousie made a tour through the new province, as he had done in the Punjab, to organize the administration.[2]

---

[1] Marshman, *op. cit.*, Vol. III. pp. 351–355.
[2] *Life of the Marquis of Dalhousie*, Lee-Warner, Vol. I. Ch. X., Vol. II. Ch. I.

The outbreak of war with Russia in 1854 revived the problem which had been so disastrously misjudged by Auckland. Dalhousie was a statesman of different calibre. *Foreign Policy.* He grasped the plain fact that the Russian Empire, which did not then touch Afghanistan, was beyond striking distance of India, and he set his face against any adventure in Central Asia to assist the operations in the Crimea. At the same time he resisted the strong pressure brought to bear on him to reduce the European garrison in India.[1]

But he took effective diplomatic action. The treaty which he negotiated through Edwardes and John Lawrence with Dost Muhammad was more than a public act of reconciliation. While pledging the Government of India to non-interference in Afghanistan the treaty raised a friendly bulwark against possible Russian aggression, though much of its value was lost in the civil wars which followed the Dost's death in 1863.

In 1854 an engagement of a more lasting value had been made with the Khan of Kalat or Baluchistan, who, like the Amir, promised the East India Company " to be friend of its friends and the enemy of its enemies." The Khan and his successors were admitted into the Indian protectorate on terms of "subordinate co-operation"; he opened his territories to British garrisons and to trade, and the rulers of Kalat were guaranteed an annual subsidy on condition that these terms were faithfully fulfilled. Dalhousie had some difficulty with the Board of Control over an annual subsidy, but the treaty remains to this day the basis of the intimate relations which have existed between the Government of India and Kalat ever since.[2]

Dalhousie had inherited a policy of non-interference with the internal affairs of the Indian States. On the one *The Indian States.* hand the Company exaggerated the risk and the expense of trying to reform abuses in territories not directly under

[1] At the close of Dalhousie's governor-generalship there were serving in India in round numbers 24,000 Royal troops of all ranks. The Company's European military establishment, excluding officers, N.C.O.s and men serving with Indian units, totalled 15,000. The Indian ranks serving with the Company's purely Indian units totalled 223,000, excluding followers. See Kaye, *op. cit.*, Vol. I., Table on p. 626.

[2] *Life of the Marquis of Dalhousie*, Lee-Warner, Vol. II. pp. 102–104.

their rule. On the other hand the princes claimed the right to govern their subjects as they pleased and were under the impression that the surrender of a single attribute of power would entail the loss of all authority.[1] Consequently annexation by the Company was the only alternative to serious misrule. After 1858 annexation was abandoned; and higher conceptions of co-operation and union, coupled with the personal responsibility of rulers, took the place of the more sterile policy inherited and improved by Lord Hastings.[2]

The misrule of Oudh by the king's favourites was scandalous. *Oudh.* But Sleeman the resident, who reported upon the administration of " fiddlers and eunuchs . . . the knaves who surround and govern the king," was opposed to extreme measures and represented to the governor-general and to India House that the country could be brought under British control without appropriating the revenues or wholly superseding local agency. To the chairman of the court of Directors he pointed out that a line of conduct " most profitable in a pecuniary view " might be most injurious in a political one, an opinion emphatically endorsed by Henry Lawrence,[3] and he expressed his conviction that the doctrines of what he described as " the absorbing school " must sooner or later produce a crisis in British India.[4] Dalhousie held that, badly governed as Oudh undoubtedly was, the consistent loyalty to the British of its rulers precluded annexation, but he advised complete British control. The Directors, however, who had rejected Auckland's proposals for reform twenty years earlier, would not listen and, by their orders, Oudh was annexed in February 1856, and its king dethroned.

[1] The safeguarding of the rights of the ruling Princes of India under the paramount Power is instanced in the Butler Report of 1929 (para. 58), where the Committee record their "strong opinion in view of the historical nature of the relationship between the paramount Power and the Princes, that the latter should not be transferred without their own agreement to a relationship with a new government in British India responsible to an Indian legislature." See also report of the Joint Committee on Indian Constitutional Reform [Session 1933–34, Vol. I. Part I., p. 86 (para. 154)].

[2] *Native States of India*, pp. 129–130.

[3] Quoted by Kaye, *Hist. Sepoy War*, Vol. I. p. 137 and footnote.

[4] *Life of Outram*, Goldsmid, Vol. II. pp. 97, 98.

Upon the rejection of these views of the authorities in India by the court of Directors Sir John Kaye makes the following comment [1]: "That the measure made a very bad impression on the minds of the people of India is not to be doubted; not because of the deposition of a king who had abused his powers; not because of the introduction of a new system of administration for the benefit of the people; but because the humanity of the act was soiled by the profit which we derived from it; . . . we had simply extinguished one of the few remaining Mahomedan States of India that we might add so many thousands of square miles to our British territories and so many millions of rupees to the revenues of the British Empire in the East. And who, it was asked, could be safe, if we thus treated one who had ever been the most faithful of our allies?"

But when the influence of India House had been swept away after the shock of the events of 1857, it was the opinion of those wiser administrators in India which was largely instrumental in leading to the grant of "sanads of adoption" by Lord Canning [2] to remove mistrust and suspicion from the minds of the Indian princes.

Dalhousie prepared a careful scheme for the administration of the new province on the lines which had proved successful in the Punjab, and had he remained in India he would undoubtedly have given these reforms the same personal attention. But he did not take action to disarm the province, and Canning who succeeded him in March 1856 took no such precautions and considered one regiment and a battery of artillery a sufficient force to maintain tranquillity in Oudh. The ex-king had not been paid as late as March 1857 any of the allowances conceded by Dalhousie, and the policy of leniency and reconciliation to the change of administration was ignored to the extent of excluding a large number of the Oudh officials from pensions, while sixty thousand disbanded soldiers were in receipt of wholly inadequate allowances.[3]

[1] *Op. cit.*, Vol. I. p. 152.
[2] *Indian States Committee Report*, 1928–1929, p. 15. Lee-Warner, *Native States*, pp. 161–163; *Indian States*, Maharaj Kumar Rhagubir Sin, pp. 33–34.
[3] *Life of Dalhousie*, Lee-Warner, Vol. II. Ch. IX.

Annexation by Lapse.
Another form of annexation, and the one with which Dalhousie's name is generally associated, was annexation by lapse, a policy already explained. But this had been recognized by the Company since 1834 and was not an innovation made by the governor-general. The rule which Dalhousie adopted in at least five of the cases with which he dealt was simple and direct: "In States owing their origin to our grant or gift, if heirs fail, according to the terms of our grant we annex." [1] Satara, Jaitpur, Jhansi, Sambalpur and Nagpur were consequently taken over by the government. The court of Directors entirely approved of this policy.

Common Defence.
The original British schemes for general co-operation in the defence of India included contingents of troops furnished by certain states such as Baroda, Hyderabad, Bhopal, Jodhpur and Gwalior, forces which were commanded, equipped and paid by British officers. With one exception these contingents had to be disbanded. In Hyderabad alone was the experiment successful, and this led to Dalhousie's settlement of the liability of its ruler the Nizam for the common defence. By the treaty of the 21st May 1853 the strength of the Hyderabad Contingent was established, "of not less than 5000 infantry, and 2000 cavalry, with four field batteries of artillery . . . commanded by British officers, fully equipped and disciplined, and controlled by the British Government through its representative the Resident at Hyderabad." For the payment of the Contingent the assigned districts in Berar were handed over to the Company.[2]

Internal Administration.
By war Dalhousie had added the Punjab and Lower Burma to the British Empire, by diplomacy he had secured the western frontier of India, and by his creation of the public works department and by his social reforms he immensely assisted the moral and material progress of the Company's possessions.

[1] *Native States of India*, p. 152.
[2] *Ibid.*, pp. 231, 232.

When Dalhousie went to India there was not a mile of railway
Public Works. in the country. The first line to be opened was
a section of the Great Indian Peninsula Railway
from Bombay, on the 16th April 1853; and when the governor-
general retired three years later 146 miles were open to traffic and
another 150 were under construction.[1] Dalhousie's railway scheme
was the system upon which the great trunk lines of India have
since been built.[2]

At the Board of Trade, under Sir Robert Peel, Dalhousie had
enthusiastically worked for the development of the railways and
telegraphs of England. He was equally energetic in India, and his
scheme for telegraphs, like his plans for railways, formed the basis
of the present system. On the 24th March 1854 the first telegram
from Agra reached the governor-general in Calcutta, and before
he left the country the telegraph line stretched from Calcutta to
Peshawar. Four thousand miles of wire had been erected at a
cost of £217,000 and already a yearly revenue of £23,000 was
being derived.[3]

The Charter Act of 1833 had given the governor-general in
council full executive and legislative powers over the provinces of
British India. But close control was not practicable while it took
at least a week for a dispatch to reach Bombay and Madras from
Calcutta. With the establishment of the telegraph and railway
systems the freedom of action, previously enjoyed by the provincial
authorities, came to an end. The central government was to experience in its turn a tightening up of control by higher authority when
the Red Sea cable was laid.

In 1850 Dalhousie brought in a uniform rate of postage through-
Postal out the country irrespective of distance, by which
Improvement. an ordinary letter was carried for a half-anna stamp,
then equivalent to three farthings. Later he arranged with the

---

[1] *Life of the Marquis of Dalhousie*, Lee-Warner, Vol. II. pp. 191, 196, 199.
[2] In 1938 the total route mileage in India, including State and Company
railways, was 43,128; of this about 100 miles of the suburban lines of Bombay
and Madras had been electrified.
[3] Lee-Warner, *op. cit.*, Vol. II. pp. 191, 194.

home government for a postal rate to England of sixpence for the half-ounce, and in his own words " a Scotch recruit who joins his regiment at Peshawar may write to his mother at John o' Groat's House and may send it for sixpence, which three years ago would not have carried his letter beyond Lahore." [1]   Dalhousie created the post of Director-General of Post Offices, and was long enough in India to see 753 post offices opened and his scheme a financial success.   The present use of the postal service may be realized by the fact that although in India today only about 14 per cent. of the male population and three women out of every hundred can write, professional letter-writers abound, and 575 million letters and 586 million post-cards were carried in the year 1929–30.[2]

The governor-general was a strong advocate of education, in-cluding the establishment of engineering colleges for Indians, and his Diary bears witness to his hope and confidence that the measures being introduced would soon enable the people of India to take a larger part in its administration.[3]

Education.

In 1853 the British Parliament for the first time seriously considered the development of Indian education. The despatch sent out by Sir Charles Wood (Lord Halifax) in 1854 outlined the scheme to be followed by the Government of India. A properly articulated system from the primary school to the university was to be established under the direction of provincial directors of education. Increased attention to vernacular education, both primary and secondary, was prescribed, and a system of grants-in-aid; sympathy was expressed for female education; training institutions for teachers were advocated; and a policy of rigid religious neutrality was emphasized.[4]

Government departments were established in place of the amateur education committees in the Presidencies, and Dalhousie's successor, Canning, set up the universities of Calcutta, Madras and Bombay. The policy emphasized by Wood " of extending far more widely the

[1] Lee-Warner, *op. cit.*, Vol. II. p. 205.
[2] *Moral and Material Progress*, 1930–1931, p. 271.
[3] *Life*, Lee-Warner, Vol. I. pp. 206, 207.
[4] *Modern India*, ed. Sir J. Cumming, Ch. VIII., by Sir P. Hartog, pp. 124–125

means of acquiring general European knowledge " was launched. It created the rigid anatomy of structural uniformity and system essential for the education of India's diverse nationalities in a common spirit.[1] Unfortunately elementary vernacular teaching remained neglected, and the educational system resembled a pyramid with its base in the air.

Finance, forest conservancy and jail conditions were other matters *General Reforms.* which Dalhousie improved. The number of dispensaries was largely increased, the medical service was opened to Indians and a scheme for the reorganization of the medical department was recommended to the court of Directors. But it is impossible to detail all the governor-general's activities.

It may be said, speaking generally of his administration, that he simplified procedure by decentralization (he divested himself of the governorship of Bengal) and he freed the secretariats as much as possible from cumbersome regulations and the " imminent risk of a paper war " of office minutes. In a letter to Hobhouse in 1851 Dalhousie wrote: " The Government of Bombay are like an electric telegraph; they for ever talk at one another on little slips of paper, even when they are collected."

Another great administrator took a similar view of departmentalism. Lord Curzon called that feature of government in India " an intellectual hiatus " in a celebrated minute which described how for fourteen months an important series of papers went " round and round like the diurnal revolution of the earth, stately, solemn, sure and slow, before it occurred to a single human being in the departments that the matter should be mentioned " to the Viceroy. On another occasion Curzon told the Secretary of State that the arrival of a despatch had caused " a sort of literary Bedlam." [2]

Nor was the ability to write a caustic minute the only resemblance between Dalhousie and Curzon. They were the youngest rulers who have ever been sent from England to India; Dalhousie was

---

[1] *Indian Administration to the Dawn of Responsible Government*, p. 343.
[2] *Life of Lord Curzon*, by the Earl of Ronaldshay (Marquess of Zetland), Vol. II. pp. 26, 27, 321.

not thirty-six, Curzon was still under forty. By strength of will each rose above ill-health or bodily suffering to work with volcanic energy, an almost superhuman efficiency and an attention to detail which left their mark on every department of government. They were both determined reformers and they relentlessly pressed incessant changes in an equally " passionate and devoted interest in all that concerned the well-being of India." [1] Autocratic in temperament, neither would brook opposition. The governor-general, when he had decided that he was justified, showed no more hesitation in annexing an Indian State by the exercise of paramountcy, than the Viceroy to intervene to regulate the government of the princes. Dalhousie and Curzon were equally enthusiastic in their admiration for the ancient monuments of the country, and rescued many gems of architecture from decay and ruin. The first restored the Kutb Minar at Delhi, the other recreated the perfections of the Taj Mahal.

The Company's charter was renewed in 1853, not as formerly for twenty years, but "until Parliament should otherwise direct." The most important administrative change made by the Act was the removal from *Charter Act, 1853.* the court of Directors of the right of patronage, which was to be exercised in future by the regulations of the Board of Control. These regulations, which were prepared by a committee under the presidency of Lord Macaulay, threw the covenanted service open to general competition. [2]

On the 29th February 1856 Lord Canning, son of George Canning the statesman, became governor-general, hoping for " a peaceful time of office," but reminding the court of Directors before he sailed that " in the sky of India, serene as it is, a small cloud may arise, at first no bigger than a man's hand, but which growing larger and larger, may at last threaten to burst and overwhelm us with ruin." [3]

---

[1] The words of the quotation are a reference to Lord Curzon in a speech by Lord Morley, Secretary of State for India, in February 1909 (*Life of Lord Curzon*, Ronaldshay, Vol. II. p. 417).

[2] *Government of India*, Ilbert, 2nd Edn., pp. 91, 92.

[3] *Life of Earl Canning*, Cunningham, pp. 36, 37.

PLATE LIX.

BRITISH TROOPS ON THE MARCH, 1857

By courtesy of the Parker Gallery

PLATE LX.

(c) LORD CURZON OF KEDLESTON

(b) LORD LAWRENCE
From the original painting in the
Guildhall Art Gallery, London

(a) SIR ROBERT SANDEMAN

The new governor-general came to Calcutta in the lull before
Conditions in India. the storm. Oudh was neither disarmed, strongly
held nor contented. The dispossessed Peshwa's
son Nana Sahib lived near Cawnpore. The young
widowed Rani of the Maratha house of Jhansi felt she had been
wronged by the annexation of her State under the doctrine of lapse.
To the Hindu rulers as a body the non-recognition of the principle
of adoption seemed an invasion of their ancient institutions.
Dalhousie's intention of bringing the titular sovereignty of the
Mogul emperors of Delhi to an end [1] had roused resentment.
Upper India was charged with forces hostile to British rule and
these were centred in Delhi, Lucknow, Cawnpore and Jhansi.
The generally unsettled state of Indian India was an added
danger.

The general mass of the two hundred and fifty million inhabitants
of the country were passive, as the people of India in the main have
always been in times of disturbance. But the upper classes had lost
their power and influence, and in many cases their livelihood, with
the extension of the Company's administration, and they looked upon
British methods, the pouring of the new wine of the West, however
sound in itself, into the old bottles of the East, with suspicion and
hostility. [2]

On the other hand a distinguished school of statesmen had
newly made their appearance in the Indian States. Ministers such
as Salar Jung in Hyderabad, Dinkar Rao in Gwalior, Sakurni Menon
in Travancore and Madhav Rao in Indore set an example of improved administration. To the support of the Indian princes,
especially the new Nizam Afzal-ud-daula and the Rajput rulers and
their ministers, England was to owe much in 1857.

The foundation of British dominion in common with that of
every other government in the past history of India, was military
power, and the Company had increased its territory in all directions
without increasing its European forces. There was no fear at the

---

[1] *Life of Dalhousie*, Lee-Warner, Vol. II. pp. 134–138. But cf. Kaye,
op. cit., Vol. I. pp. 356, 357.
[2] Kaye, *op. cit.*, Vol. I. pp. 153–155.

moment of danger from without. But within the Indian Empire "contentment was seen in submission, loyalty in quiescence," no thought was taken for internal defence, and the disposition of troops was manifestly unsound.

In the Company's Indian units the almost incredible length of service permitted to the British officers and the inefficiency of many of them had generally reduced discipline to a perilously low ebb, especially in the Bengal army, and commanding officers were out of touch with their men. This danger was accentuated by the fact that Oudh supplied the Company with forty thousand soldiers who were inclined to disaffection and who represented by their family connections nearly one-tenth of the whole population of the late kingdom. Added to this the Presidency systems of army organization with their varied regulations, especially in respect of field allowances, created serious discontent, which had found expression on more than one occasion in mutiny.[1]

These circumstances all tended towards the appalling and tragic catastrophe of the Mutiny. But the immediate cause was the widely circulated report that the cartridges for the rifled musket, with which the army was then being re-armed, were greased with an objectionable mixture which would destroy Hindu caste and insult Moslem ideas of ceremonial purity. In the opinion of Sir John Lawrence the Indian army implicitly believed " that the universal introduction of cartridges destructive to their caste was only a matter of time. They heard (and believed as they heard) that the measure had been resolved on . . . They thought their only chance of escape was to band together, to refuse the cartridges and to resist if force should be attempted by the Government." [2] There was a basis of fact as regards the existence of such cartridges in experimental ammunition which had come from England, but the obvious and necessary re-assurances of the military authorities were outdistanced by the rumours which spread like wildfire through Upper India.[3]

[1] *The Evolution of the Army in India* (Government Printing Press, Calcutta, 1924), pp. 16, 17.
[2] *Life of Lord Lawrence*, Sir C. Aitchison, pp. 74, 75.
[3] Kaye, *op. cit.*, Vol. I. pp. 488–494, 500, 501, 510–524 and pp. 630–631 in Appendix. See also Appendix, pp. 651–654.

In February 1857 there was an outbreak at Barrackpore. On
The Mutiny. 9th and 10th May the Mutiny broke out beyond
control at Meerut, and the mutineers instinctively
marched to Delhi. From there the rising spread through the north-
west provinces and Oudh. Sindia with his minister Dinkar Rao
remained loyal to his engagements, but in June the Gwalior contingent mutinied. The Punjab stood firm, even to Peshawar, and
eventually 70,000 men, of whom one-third were Sikhs of the
Khalsa, were raised by the Punjab government and the chiefs of the
province. Hyderabad sent forces to co-operate with the British
in Central India and Nepalese troops assisted in the operations
further north.

With the promptness and courage [1] which was to save the
situation in India, John Lawrence, on 17th May, sent a force of
3800 British and Indian troops to hold the ridge overlooking Delhi,
already packed with insurgents, and he despatched a stream of
reinforcements as they became available. Delhi was stormed by
British troops, loyal Indian regiments of the Company, Sikhs,
Gurkhas and men from Jammu, led by John Nicholson on the
14th September. Bahadur Shah was captured and exiled and his
dynasty tragically terminated. The fall of Delhi was the turning-
point in the crisis.

Elsewhere the terrible massacre at Cawnpore after Wheeler's
surrender to the Nana Sahib on 26th June was followed on 1st
July by the siege of Sir Henry Lawrence's Residency at Lucknow.
On 25th September General Havelock with Sir James Outram serving
under him fought their way in with reinforcements, and in the middle
of November Sir Colin Campbell at the head of troops from England
raised the siege. The heroic defence of the Residency of Lucknow,
which stands beside the achievements of the Punjab force on the
Ridge at Delhi, was over. Lucknow was finally taken by the government troops in March 1858. By January 1859 fighting in Upper and
Central India was at an end and order was being restored.

[1] There were then in the Punjab 10,500 British troops and 36,000 of the
obviously unreliable Bengal army, with 20,000 Punjab irregulars and military
police. (*Life of Lord Lawrence*, Aitchison, pp. 76, 77.)

The shock felt in England by the events of the Mutiny gave the East India Company its death-blow. It was realized that the system of " double government," with its fatal division of powers and responsibilities, could no longer continue, and a Bill was brought in by Lord Derby's Conservative ministry " for the better government of India," which became law on 2nd August 1858.

End of the Company.

The Act declared that India was to be governed directly by and in the name of the Crown, acting through a secretary of state, who would exercise all the former powers of the court of Directors and the Board of Control. The officials of these two bodies were amalgamated to form the India Office, and the secretary of state was given a council of fifteen members whose decisions he was empowered to overrule but who could interpose a financial veto upon his policy. The property of the Company was transferred to the Crown. The expenditure of the revenues of India was to be under the control of the secretary of state in council, but was to be charged with a dividend on the Company's stock and with their debts, and the Indian revenues remitted to Great Britain were to be paid to the secretary of state in council and applied for Indian purposes.[1] The total Indian debt, after the military operations of 1857–58 had been taken into account, was about 110 million sterling.[2]

Government of India Act, 1858.

As under the Act of 1853, admission to the covenanted civil service was open, by examination, to all natural born subjects of Her Majesty.

Commissions in the army were not then granted by competitive examination and the patronage of military cadetships was divided between the secretary of state and his council. All the forces, naval and military, of the Company were transferred to the Crown by the Act of 1858. The distinction between " Royal troops " and the " Company's European troops," which had existed for more than a hundred years, disappeared. The Company's European infantry

---

[1] *Government of India*, Ilbert, pp. 94–97.
[2] *India in the Victorian Age*, Dutt, pp. 319, 373.

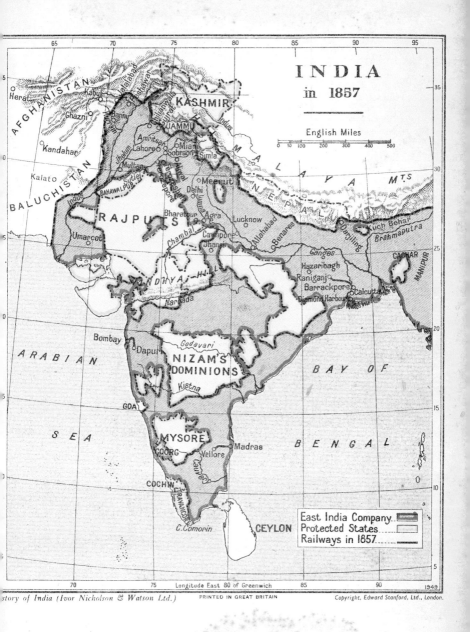

INDIA

in 1857

English Miles

0	50	100	200	300	400	500

East India Company
Protected States
Railways in 1857

AFGHANISTAN

Herat

Kabul

Ghazni

Kandahar

Kalato

BALUCHISTAN

KASHMIR

JAMMU

Jalalabad

Peshawar

Bannu

Attock

Simla

Lahore

Amritsar

Mian

Sobraon

Multan

Indus

BAHAWALPUR

Sutlej

Delhi

Meerut

NEPAL

MALAYA MTS.

RAJPUTS

Bharatpur

Agra

Lucknow

Allahabad

Benares

Chambal

Cawnpore

Jhansi

VINDHYA HILLS

Narbada

Umarcot

Indus

Ganges

Hazaribagh

Raniganj

Barrackpore

Calcutta

Diamond Harbour

Darjiling

Cuch Behar

Brahmaputra

CACHAR

MANIPUR

Bombay

Dapuri

NIZAM'S DOMINIONS

Godavari

Kistna

ARABIAN

SEA

GOA

MYSORE

COORG

Vellore

Madras

Cauvery

COCHIN

TRAVANCORE

C. Comorin

CEYLON

BAY OF

BENGAL

story of India (Ivor Nicholson & Watson Ltd.)   PRINTED IN GREAT BRITAIN   Copyright, Edward Stanford, Ltd., London.

1949

became British line regiments, and the European artillery of the three Presidencies were amalgamated with the Royal Artillery. This reorganization was completed in 1860. The reorganization of the Indian forces was not taken in hand until 1861 and was completed four years later. In this reorganization all the Indian artillery, with some notable exceptions, was abolished. In 1861 the British officers of what was then called the " Native Army " were listed in the Presidency staff corps, and the three Presidency military establishments remained separate for thirty-five years.[1]

The Act laid down that " Except for preventing and repelling actual invasion of Her Majesty's Indian possessions, or under other sudden and urgent necessity, the revenues of India shall not, without the consent of both Houses of Parliament, be applicable to defray the expenses of any military operation carried on beyond the external frontiers of such possessions by Her Majesty's forces charged upon such revenues." [2]

Royal Proclamation, 1858. On 1st November 1858 the transfer of the government to the Crown and the appointment of Canning as the first Viceroy and governor-general was announced in India by royal proclamation, drafted in accordance with Queen Victoria's expressed wishes. The full text is given at the end of this chapter, but, apart from the terms of amnesty which the proclamation contained, the following clauses should be emphasized:

" We hereby announce to the Native Princes of India that all treaties and engagements made with them by or under the authority of the Honourable East India Company are by Us accepted."

" It is Our will that, so far as may be, Our subjects, of whatever race or creed, be freely and impartially admitted to offices in Our service, the duties of which they may be qualified, by their education, ability, and integrity, duly to perform."

[1] *The Evolution of the Army in India*, pp. 18, 19.
[2] Government of India Act 1858, 21 and 22 Vict. c. 108, Section 55.

PROCLAMATION BY THE QUEEN IN COUNCIL TO THE PRINCES, CHIEFS, AND PEOPLE OF INDIA

" Victoria, by the grace of God, of the United Kingdom of Great Britain and Ireland, and of the Colonies and Dependencies thereof in Europe, Asia, Africa, America, and Australasia, Queen, Defender of the Faith.

" Whereas for divers weighty reasons, We have resolved, by and with the advice and consent of the Lords Spiritual and Temporal and Commons in Parliament assembled, to take upon Ourselves the government of the territories in India, heretofore administered in trust for Us by the Honourable East India Company.

" Now, therefore, We do by these presents notify and declare that by the advice and consent aforesaid, We have taken upon Ourselves the said government: and We hereby call upon Our subjects within the said territories to be faithful, and to bear true allegiance to Us, Our heirs and successors, and to submit themselves to the authority of those whom We may hereafter, from time to time, see fit to appoint to administer the government of Our said territories, in Our name and on Our behalf.

" And We, reposing especial trust and confidence in the loyalty, ability, and judgment of Our right trusty and well-beloved cousin and councillor, Charles John Viscount Canning, do hereby constitute and appoint him, the said Viscount Canning to be Our first Viceroy and Governor-General in and over Our said territories, and to administer the government thereof in Our name, and generally to act in Our name and on Our behalf, subject to such orders and regulations as he shall, from time to time, receive from Us through one of Our Principal Secretaries of State.

" And We hereby confirm in their several offices, civil and military, all persons now employed in the service of the Honourable East India Company, subject to Our future pleasure, and to such laws and regulations as may hereafter be enacted.

" We hereby announce to the Native Princes of India that all treaties and engagements made with them by or under the authority of the Honourable East India Company are by Us accepted, and will be scrupulously maintained, and We look for the like observance on their part.

" We desire no extension of Our present territorial possessions; and while We will permit no aggression upon Our dominions or Our rights to be attempted with impunity, We shall sanction no encroachment on those of others. We shall respect the rights, dignity, and honour of Native Princes as Our own; and We desire that they, as well as Our own subjects, shall enjoy that prosperity and that social advancement which can only be secured by internal peace and good government.

" We hold Ourselves bound to the Natives of Our Indian territories by the same obligations of duty which bind Us to all Our other subjects, and those obligations, by the blessing of Almighty God, We shall faithfully and conscientiously fulfil.

" Firmly relying Ourselves on the truth of Christianity, and acknowledging with gratitude the solace of religion We disclaim alike the right and the desire to impose Our convictions on any of Our subjects. We declare it to be Our royal will and pleasure that none be anywise favoured, none molested or disquieted, by reason of their religious faith and observances, but that all shall alike enjoy the equal and impartial protection of the law; and We do strictly charge and enjoin all those who may be in authority under Us that they abstain from all interference with the religious belief or worship of any of Our subjects on pain of Our highest displeasure.

" And it is Our further will that, so far as may be, Our subjects of whatever race or creed, be freely and impartially admitted to offices in Our service, the duties of which they may be qualified, by their education, ability, and integrity, duly to discharge.

" We know, and respect, the feelings of attachment with which the Natives of India regard the land inherited by them from their ancestors, and We desire to protect them in all rights connected therewith, subject to the equitable demands of the State; and We will that generally, in framing and administering the law, due regard be paid to the ancient rights, usages and customs of India.

" We deeply lament the evils and misery which have been brought upon India by the acts of ambitious men, who have deceived their countrymen by false reports, and led them into open rebellion. Our power has been shown by the suppression of that rebellion in the field; We desire to show Our mercy by pardoning the offences of those who have been thus misled, but who desire to return to the path of duty.

" Already in one province, with a view to stop the further effusion of blood, and to hasten the pacification of Our Indian dominions, Our Viceroy and Governor-General has held out the expectations of pardon, on certain terms, to the great majority of those who, in the late unhappy disturbances, have been guilty of offences against Our Government, and has declared the punishment which will be inflicted on those whose crimes place them beyond the reach of forgiveness. We approve and confirm the said act of Our Viceroy and Governor-General, and do further announce and proclaim as follows:

" Our clemency will be extended to all offenders, save and except those who have been, or shall be, convicted of having directly taken part in the murder of British subjects. With regard to such, the demands of justice forbid the exercise of mercy.

Life of Ranjit Singh, Sir Lepel Griffin, Rulers of India Series, 1898.

Life of Lord Auckland, L. J. Trotter, Rulers of India Series, 1905.

Life of Lord Hardinge, by 2nd Lord Hardinge, Rulers of India Series, 1900.

Life of the Marquis of Dalhousie, Sir W. Lee-Warner, 2 vols., 1904.

Life of Sir James Outram, Major-General Sir F. Goldsmid, 2 vols., 1880.

Life of Lord Lawrence, Sir C. Aitchison, Rulers of India Series, 1892.

Life of Earl Canning, Sir H. S. Cunningham, Rulers of India Series, 1903.

The Government of India, Sir C. Ilbert, 2nd Edn. 1907.

India under Lord Ellenborough, ed. Sir Algernon Law, 1926.

CHAPTER XIX

India Under the Crown

I

FROM CANNING TO RIPON

UNTIL 1858 the Government of India rested on the military strength of the East India Company and the garrison of Royal troops, while the general security of the country from invasion was further guaranteed, then as now, by British sea-power. The Act of 1858, which put an end to the greatest mercantile corporation the world has ever known, completely altered the basis of government. This now devolved upon a parliamentary secretary of state for India; the secretary of state was answerable to Parliament; and as Parliament is responsible to the British people, the ultimate power lay with the electors of Great Britain.

From 1858 to 1919 British India was ruled by a civil autocracy in which authority was concentrated at the centre. The whole structure, from the secretary of state, through the governor-general in council, the local governments and the executive officers down to the smallest official, was in theory under the British Parliament. Parliamentary control was, however, in practice limited to alterations in the constitution and the authorization of loans, and its supervision to receiving from the secretary of state his yearly account of Indian administration and the annual statement of receipts and charges. Indian affairs were tacitly held to be outside the range of party politics, and aroused little practical interest in England until Indian nationalism became a disturbing force.

In 1861 three important Acts were passed by Parliament.[1]

[1] *Government of India*, Ilbert (2nd Edn.), pp. 98–104.

523

The Indian Civil Service Act regulated appointments to the *Parliamentary Legislation.* service, abolished the rule of seniority and, with certain safeguards, allowed outsiders to be appointed to any office.

The Indian High Courts Act amalgamated the courts representing the Crown and the Company and established the high courts of Calcutta, Madras and Bombay. The judges of each court, with a maximum of sixteen, were to be appointed by the Crown. One-third, including the chief justice, were to be barristers and another third to be members of the covenanted civil service. Indians could be appointed, and Rama Prasad Roy of the Calcutta High Court was the first of a line of distinguished Indian judges whose numbers since 1919 have considerably increased. In certain cases appeals from the decisions of these courts, the highest courts in India, lie to the Privy Council.

But the most important legislation of the year was the Indian *Indian Councils Act 1861* Councils Act, which modified the executive council and remodelled the Indian's legislatures. A fifth ordinary member was added to the governor-general's council, and Canning distributed the work among the members, placing each in charge of a separate department. This converted the council into a cabinet of which the governor-general was the head.

For purposes of legislation the governor-general's council was reinforced by a maximum of twelve "additional" members, half of whom were to be non-official and nominated, and some of these seats were allotted to Indians. The new legislative council was restricted to making laws, and as there were no private Bills these were initiated by the executive government.

The Act restored to the governments of Madras and Bombay the power of legislation which the Act of 1833 had withdrawn, but with the difference that the governor-general's assent was now necessary; and it gave similar powers to Bengal. At the same time the governor-general in council could still legislate for all the Indian territories under the British Crown.[1]

[1] *Indian Statutory Commission Report,* Vol. I. pp. 115–116, describes the working of these Councils.

Legislation had been entirely in the hands of British officials until 1861, and it is from this date that Indians could take part in making laws for British India. Their earliest representatives came from the aristocracy, the hereditary landed gentry, religious leaders and government pensioners, men naturally reserved and strongly conservative in their instincts. The Indian universities had only been established for four years and Indian leaders and representatives of the modern type had not yet appeared.[1]

The central government now had effective control over the whole of British India, and this was to lead to administrative uniformity, except in the revenue department which dealt with the widely differing habits and conditions deeply rooted in the various regions of the country. At the same time the administration of the district officers lost its earlier personal note under the regulations of a uniform policy.

The Indian States. The assumption by the Crown of the direct government of India and the proclamation of Queen Victoria began the existing relationship between the Indian princes and the paramount Power. In the words of Lord Canning, the first Viceroy of India: "The Crown of England stands forth the unquestioned ruler and paramount Power in all India, and is for the first time brought face to face with its feudatories. There is a reality in the suzerainty of the Sovereign of England which has never existed before and which is not only felt but eagerly acknowledged by the chiefs."

The policy of annexation in cases such as revolt, misrule and failure of heirs was abandoned, and Canning laid down the two great principles which the British Government has since followed in dealing with the States. The first of these was that their integrity should be preserved by perpetuating the rule of the princes, whose power to adopt heirs in accordance with their religious laws and customs was recognized by *sanads* [2] granted in 1862. The second,

---

[1] *Indian Administration*, B. K. Thakore, pp. 137–142.

[2] A *sanad* is a diploma, patent or deed of grant by a Sovereign of an office, privilege or right.

that flagrant misgovernment must be prevented by timely intervention.[1]

The imperial prerogative was exercised in many ways after the
Mutiny by the bestowal of honours, salutes and grants of territorial
possessions, but no manifestation of it was received by the princes
of India with so much enthusiasm as the issue of the eight-score
of *sanads* of adoption or succession. Their influence extended far
beyond those who received them, and a new spirit of co-operation
and union was spread far and wide.[2] The States had " become in
fact part and parcel of the Indian Empire with which their interests
are identified and identical."

The *sanads*, which were to knit the princes to the paramount
Power, were personal concessions to the individual rulers; for, as
Sir Henry Maine said,[3] " While there is only one independent
sovereign—the British Government—there may be found in India
every shade and variety of sovereignty. The mode or degree in
which sovereignty is distributed between the British Government
and any native State is always a question of fact which has to be
separately decided in each case and to which no general rules apply."
About forty of the larger States have treaties with the paramount
Power, a larger number have *sanads*, and the remainder enjoy in
some form or other recognition of their States by the Crown. A
certain number of the States pay tribute.

For half a century political development came slowly. The
paramount Power protected the country, kept peace and order, and
put down organized crime, such as thuggee and dacoity. Such
matters as railway policy, the control of posts and telegraphs,
imperial taxation (such as the salt tax) and the limitation of arma-
ments, became a joint concern between the paramount Power and
the States, but the policy of isolation still lingered. Lytton's
proposal of a consultative body of princes came to nothing and the

[1] *Report of the Indian States Committee*, 1928–1929, p. 15. *The Native States
of India*, p. 163.
[2] *The Native States of India*, pp. 159–162.
[3] Official Minute on the Kathiawar case (1864) quoted by Sir Robert
Holland, *Political India*, Ch. XIV. p. 260, and see *States Committee Report*,
pp. 25, 26.

opportunity to bring the Crown and the States closer together, through the Chamber of Princes, had to wait until 1921.

The importance of the Indian States can be realized from the fact that they cover about three-sevenths of the country (Burma being excluded) with a quarter of its population; an area of 598,000 square miles and 93 million inhabitants in 1941.[1] The States range in size from the highly developed State of Hyderabad, which is 82,700 square miles in extent and has a revenue of £5,000,000, to holdings in Kathiawar of a few acres and "a revenue not greater than the annual income of an ordinary artisan." In this purely Indian India, suzerainty by major States over feudatory lesser States and *jagirs* is recognized by the Government of India. The States are not British territory and their subjects are not British subjects. But as the Indian States have no international life and are unable in any way to communicate with foreign governments, the paramount Power has the duty, by treaty and usage, of protecting Indian State subjects when abroad.[2]

Government in the States ranges from patriarchal feudalism to modern autocracy with enlightened welfare services. The Princes make and enforce their own laws, nor do appeals lie from their high courts to British India or the Privy Council. Each State manages its own internal affairs and spends its own taxes. Most of them levy customs duties at their frontiers. Some mint their own rupee currency. They have their own police, and the more important maintain Indian State Forces for co-operation with the Indian army both in the external defence of India and for purposes of internal order. There is generally a British resident or other agent to offer advice to the ruler. Tribute to the paramount Power is limited to 5 per cent. of a State's revenue.[3]

---

[1] Only States classified in the *Report of the Indian States Committee* are included in this figure. The total area is given as 690,000 square miles, with roughly 600 States. Portuguese Goa has one feudatory State.

[2] *Report of the Indian States Committee*, p. 26. Communication with foreign powers does not, of course, refer to the representative Indian prince who may have been nominated to the League of Nations Assembly.

[3] *East India Budget*, 1938-39, Part II. pp. 4, 5.

Canning's Indian State policy was from the first to create confidence. In 1859, the year before he put forward his general policy, he foreshadowed the closer union about to be established by sanctioning the succession of the illegitimate son of the Raja of Tehri (Garhwal), a case where the British had a clear title to annexation by the doctrine of lapse.[1]

Canning and the Mutiny.

Canning's attitude, in the crisis of the Mutiny, has been described by his biographer [2]: " Lord Canning met it . . . with firmness, confidence, magnanimity, with calm, inflexible justice. On a stage, crowded with heroic personages, he stood—an impressive central figure—too unmoved and too undemonstrative, too completely master of himself to suit the excited tempers and unbalanced judgments of an epoch rife with unprecedented catastrophe; but rising above the onset of ephemeral hostility with a dignity, which, as . . . we are able more justly to appreciate its proportions, places him high on the list of great officers of State."

A measure of this confidence was shown when, in the midst of the staggering events of the summer of 1857, he assembled his legislative council to pass the Act which established the universities of Bombay and Madras on the model of London University. Calcutta University had been similarly founded in January of the same year. The calmness with which the governor-general met the crisis aggravated the European business community into strong hostility, which his subsequent policy of opposition to vindictive repression did not allay. Towards the end of 1857 the European public of Calcutta and Bengal, in a petition to Queen Victoria, alleged that the calamities in India were " directly due to the blindness, weakness and incapacity of the Government." The only notice taken of the petition may be said to have been the Queen's later expressed opinion of Canning's " admirable administration." [3]

[1] *Native States of India*, p. 165.
[2] Sir H. S. Cunningham, *Earl Canning*, p. 13.
[3] *Earl Canning*, Cunningham, pp. 144, 145. *Letters of Queen Victoria*, Vol. III. p. 453.

Oudh. In the case of Oudh, Canning's policy, as a rule most magnanimous, incurred the measured opposition of Outram, then chief commissioner of Oudh, and the outspoken disapproval of Ellenborough and his fellow-members of the Board of Control in England.

The Oudh proclamation of 1858, with a few specified and loyal exceptions, confiscated the proprietary right in the soil to the British Government, who would dispose of such right as might seem fitting; for Oudh had been the centre of rebellion. But Canning was persuaded by Outram to add that " To those who come promptly forward, and supported the Government in the restoration of order, the indulgence will be large, and the Governor-General will be ready to view liberally the claims which they may thus acquire to a restitution of their former rights."

The taluqdars (landed proprietors) of Oudh responded, and at a durbar in Calcutta in April 1861 the Viceroy said to a representative deputation from Oudh: " No part of Hindustan is more flourishing or full of promise for the future. The ancient system of land-tenure has been restored, but has been placed on a new and clear foundation. The preservation of the great families of the soil has been encouraged and facilitated. The rights of the humbler occupants have been protected. Garrisons have been reduced, police diminished. The country is so tranquil that an English child might travel from one end of it to the other in safety; so thriving that its people have been the most prompt and liberal of all the nations of India in responding to the cry of their famishing brethren of the North-West." [1]

Oudh, unlike most of India, is held from government by a relatively small group of individuals. The estates of these taluqdars are only about 260 in number, yet they cover two-thirds of Oudh and pay today one-sixth of the land revenue of the United Provinces. The most powerful of the " barons of Oudh " possess an almost feudal influence over hundreds of villages. Some of them are the descendants of the old conquering Rajput families, with an ancestry going back to the ninth century, and as a body the taluqdars

[1] *Life of Earl Canning,* Cunningham, pp. 155-165.

represent the two great communities. Their common interests consequently cut across the communal divisions.[1]

Canning's allusion to the north-west in his speech referred to

Famine of 1861. the serious famine in Agra, the Punjab, Rajputana and Cutch, due partly to two seasons of poor rainfall and partly to the disturbances in the country. The calamity was most severely felt between Agra and Delhi, where the mortality was estimated at eight and a half per cent. of the population.

The shock of the events of 1857 and 1858, the most critical years in the history of British India, and their inevitable consequences of social and economic confusion, must not obscure the admirable reforms which Canning, nevertheless, was able to introduce. Of these the measure of the greatest benefit to the greatest number was his policy of protection for agricultural tenants.

Before British rule made peace and security a normal condition,

Agricultural Conditions. *zamindars,* their intermediaries and the cultivators were bound together by the necessity of defending life and property from gangs of marauders who habitually ravaged the country. With the establishment of British government this common interest disappeared, and the only bond between the *zamindar,* his intermediaries and the peasant was one of hard cash. As British law and order became taken for granted, the population rapidly increased and the competition for land became a serious problem involving in its turn increasing poverty. It may here be said that the problem created by a rapidly increasing agricultural population has intensified with the years.[2] Nor has land-hunger been lessened by industrialization, the great feature of modern England, which has little appreciable effect in India.[3]

It was clearly necessary to protect the agriculturist from the excessive rise of rents caused by the exactions of landlords who

[1] *Ind. Statutory Commission Report,* Vol. I. p. 64.
[2] The increase between 1921 and 1931 was 34 millions in all.
[3] Not much over 15,000,000 people are associated with these forms of industry the daily average of factory hands being about one-eighth of this total in 1938.

were in the position of monopolists, on the one hand, and by the land-hunger of the peasants on the other.

Canning's difficulty was to find a proper basis of legislation between the classes and the masses. He met it by his Bengal Rent Act of 1859, which has been called the charter of the Bengal cultivators,[1] and was the first of a series of Tenancy Acts.

Tenancy Acts.

The object of these Acts has been to lessen eviction, and limit the increase of rents usually by making the amount dependent on the order of a court or revenue officer; while the right of occupancy has been extended to other cultivators and the rights of tenants-at-will assured.

Oudh, as has been noticed, differed from most parts of the country, as the taluqdars were virtually the proprietors of their estates, a fact which had not been sufficiently borne in mind by the settlement officers when the province was first annexed. On the representations of Outram and John Lawrence the right of property in Oudh was recognized. The first regular settlement of lands was begun in 1860 and completed eighteen years later, the settlement being for thirty years.

When Sir John Lawrence became Viceroy he made an effort, by the first Oudh Rent Act of 1868 (during the process of the Canning settlement), to protect the cultivators of Oudh on the same lines as Canning had protected the Bengal peasantry. But until 1921 the tenants of the great landholders of Oudh had no security of tenure beyond seven years and had to pay very large premiums to obtain renewal. Agrarian trouble on a large scale then threatened and in that year an Act was passed securing a life tenure for the tenant.[2]

The Indian Penal Code, which had been originally drafted by Macaulay and the first Law Commission in 1837, was passed in 1860; and Codes of Civil and Criminal Procedure also came into force.

Law and Order.

---

[1] Romesh Dutt, *India in the Victorian Age*, 2nd Edn., pp. 263–264.
[2] See *India in the Victorian Age*, pp. 264–266, and *Ind. Statutory Comn. Report*, Vol. I. p. 64.

Heavy expenditure had been incurred by the upkeep of a military police to restore and preserve order, and in August 1860 Canning appointed a commission to examine the whole question of police administration. On the recommendations then made the Act of 1861 was passed by the central legislature of the Government of India. The military police, as embodied to keep order in the country, were abolished and a single homogeneous force of civil constabulary was constituted. General control was put in the hands of provincial inspectors-general, but an inspector-general for the Bombay Presidency was not appointed for another twenty years. The police in each district were to be under European district superintendents and assistant superintendents. Until 1905 the higher police officers were recruited entirely from England and joined as assistant superintendents.

One of the weakest points of the system,[1] which was on the whole efficient, was a neglect to make use of the village police; and this, with other defects, was remedied by Lord Curzon's reforms.

The financial position in 1859 was serious. In fifty-nine years only four had yielded a surplus. India's debt, by *Finance.* this time about one hundred million sterling, had added to the burden of the taxpayer an addition of two millions for the annual charge of interest. For four years expenditure had exceeded income by an annual average of nine million pounds.

The remedy adopted in 1859 was to raise the tariff duties to their high-water mark. But a duty of 10 per cent. on the imported cotton piece-goods, upon which Indians had come largely to rely, raised the price considerably; and the duty of 20 per cent. on " luxury " articles imported for European consumption made a heavy addition to the taxation of a limited class. The rates were so abnormal as to defeat the objects of a tariff for revenue, and revision was absolutely necessary.

To deal with the situation Canning obtained the services of James Wilson, financial secretary to the Treasury, who came out to India as the first financial member of council in November

[1] See *Report of Indian Police Commission, 1902–1903, passim.*

1859. Wilson issued a State paper currency, imposed a licence tax on various trades and professions and an income-tax on all incomes above £20 a year. He insisted on the submission of rigid estimates to regulate military outlay (previously a matter of the greatest uncertainty) and also to reduce civil expenditure. Laing, his successor, at the close of Canning's administration, found himself with a surplus and released from an income-tax of 4 per cent. all incomes below £50 a year.

In November 1861 Lady Canning, whose courage and sympathy had supported her husband in his almost overwhelming anxieties, died at Calcutta. Four months later Canning left India, a dying man. But public opinion both in England and in India had already lost its bitterness in a fairer estimate of the unswerving justice and humanity of Charles, Lord Canning, the first Viceroy of India.

Lord Elgin. The new Viceroy, the Earl of Elgin, had been governor-general of Canada, and as special envoy to China had first-hand acquaintance with the Far East. He assumed office on the 12th March 1862, and he died of heart disease at Dharmsala on the 20th November 1863.

The foreign policy of the Government of India was to avoid entanglements in Afghanistan, and this was emphasized in 1862, when the Amir Dost Ali attacked Herat, by the withdrawal of the British Agent from Kabul.

Towards the close of Elgin's short Viceroyalty long-threatened trouble on the north-west frontier came to a head in the Ambela campaign, which before it ended converted a minor expedition into a dangerous war.

The North-West Frontier. Apart from the obligation to keep India safe from foreign invasion the ever-present anxiety of the government has always been that fanaticism may lead the restless and warlike tribes into widespread hostilities. Always present in the minds of the higher command, in a difficult and disadvantageous theatre of war, is the knowledge that failure to hit hard, rapidly and above all successfully, or to

[1] *Life of Earl Canning*, Cunningham, pp. 201–208.

533

show any sign of weakness or hesitation may set the whole border ablaze. The modern policy of transborder roads, the method by which Wade tamed and bridled the Highlands of Scotland after 1745, will be referred to later. But here it may be said that in a frontier expedition the operations of a column, however large, resolve into affairs of small packets; and the loss of one piquet on a height may bring disaster. Mountain warfare is the modern equivalent to Montaigne's example of the chances of war—" dislodging four rascally musketeers out of a barn, pricking out single from a party and meeting adventures alone." Highly disciplined and well-trained troops with good subordinate leaders are essential where, on the march, protective piquets are continually being sent up and withdrawn and the rear-guard is likely to be hard pressed.

The many frontier expeditions which have been made since the British Government took over the border from the Sikh Khalsa cannot be detailed in this History. But the Ambela campaign, the first of considerable importance, illustrates the difficult problems of the frontier.

Early in the nineteenth century a colony of fanatical Moham-
medans, mainly outlaws from British territory, was

The Ambela Campaign. founded by a British subject, Sayyid Ahmad, in the hills above the borders to the north-east of the present military station of Nowshera. He organized a regular propaganda, with its centre at Patna in Bengal, and agencies throughout India collected arms and funds. These bands were a most disturbing element on the frontier in the time of Ranjit Singh, until Sayyid Ahmad was killed in action in 1831. But his death did not disperse the colony, and the British Government inherited this turbulent legacy from the Sikhs. In 1853 and 1858 expeditions were made and Jitana, the chief settlement, was burnt, but in 1862 the " Hindustani fanatics " again gave trouble.

In October 1863 a strong force under Sir Neville Chamberlain was sent up through the Ambela Pass. The Buner tribesmen joined the Hindustani fanatics. The British column had to await reinforcements; and the effect of the prolonged pause was most unfortunate. Enemies multiplied on all sides from Bajaur and

Chamla, and determined attacks on camps and piquets and one or two initial British reverses followed. More troops were sent up and eventually the campaign was successful and the Hindustani fanatics were finally crushed though with considerable loss.[1] But the affair had grown into an entanglement sufficiently serious to produce a political crisis in which even the fundamental duty of loyalty and allegiance came to be gravely discussed among the Moslem subjects of the British Government.[2]

The Ambela campaign was just over when the new Viceroy, Sir John Lawrence, arrived on 12th January 1864 to rule the empire which he had done so much to save.

Sir John Lawrence.

John Lawrence had been gazetted the first lieutenant-governor of the Punjab on the 1st January 1859, a recognition which, in Dalhousie's opinion, the chief commissioner had earned three years earlier. Lawrence held this appointment for barely two months before sailing to England to take his seat in the council of India. His work on a board which had no administrative power was not congenial; and the public personage who most impressed him with his " minute knowledge " of Indian affairs was the Prince Consort.[3]

On 30th November 1863 Lawrence was nominated to succeed Elgin and sailed ten days later. The appointment met with unanimous approval in England. *The Times* said : " It has been happily determined to break through the charmed circle which has so long restricted the office of Governor-General to the peerage, and to send out to the empire which was formed by the exertions of Clive and Warren Hastings, not only a commoner, but a commoner wholly unconnected with any family of the English aristocracy." [4]

---

[1] *Campaigns on the North-West Frontier*, Nevill, 1st Edn. 1912, pp. 50–62, which gives details of the heavy fighting for the famous Crag Piquet. This book should be referred to for N.-W. Frontier Campaigns from 1849 to 1908.

[2] *Life of Lord Lawrence*, Aitchison, p. 13.

[3] *Lord Lawrence*, Bosworth Smith, Edn. 1883, Vol. II. p. 363.

[4] Leading article Dec. 1, 1863.

Lawrence came of a Scottish family which had long been settled in Northern Ireland, and his character showed the patience and self-reliance, the stern morality and the simple faith of the stock from which he descended. He was deeply religious, transparently honest and an extremely hard worker. In his tastes he was homely, in his manner he was outspoken and brusque, but "there was nothing of the bear about him, but the skin." His charity, his sympathy and his kindness of heart were unbounded, and he softened many a reprimand with the simple kindly humour which characterized him.

No political events of any grave importance took place in India *Small Wars.* during Lawrence's Viceroyalty. A small war in Bhutan was undertaken on account of the treatment to which a British envoy was subjected in 1864. The Bhutanese ceded a strip of territory at the foot of the hills for which they were given a small annual payment, and friendly relations with the country have continued ever since.

There were the usual raids on the frontier, and in 1868 a strong force, concentrated from down country with a speed which had great moral effect on the tribes, made a successful promenade through the Black Mountain country without much opposition. The tribesmen very rarely give cavalry an opportunity to charge, but this campaign affords the only example, in the 7th Hussars, of a British cavalry regiment as a body distinguishing itself in this way in Indian border warfare.[1]

When Dost Muhammad died in 1863 a war of succession amongst *Afghanistan.* his descendants plunged Afghanistan into a scene of bloodshed and treachery, while the heir-designate, Shere Ali, struggled for the throne. Lawrence refused to intervene, and declared that the British wished to be on terms of friendship and goodwill " with the nation and their rulers *de facto*."

But his policy was not entirely one of " masterly inactivity." By September 1867 Russia had begun the rapid advance in Central Asia which brought her to the northern and western frontiers of Afghanistan. Samarkand had not fallen when the Viceroy urged that Russia should be told politely, but firmly, that her interference

[1] Nevill, *op. cit.*, p. 63.

536

in Afghanistan, or any other State bordering upon India, could not be permitted; and that friendly negotiations with Russia should be accompanied by help to an established government of Kabul. Consequently, when Shere Ali finally crushed opposition in 1868, Lawrence sent him a present of money and arms. This attitude indicated the policy followed for the next ten years. The Secretary of State had given Lawrence a free hand and his policy was generally accepted at the time. But the practical value of moral recognition without material support in a country like Afghanistan, where no recognized law of rightful succession exists, is another matter.

The outstanding event in India while Lawrence was Viceroy was the terrible famine which swept down the eastern part of the country from Calcutta to Madras, and was so heavily felt in the isolated province of Orissa that the calamity is commonly called the Orissa famine of 1865–66.

Famine.

The south-western monsoon, upon which India depends for her rainfall, was bad in 1865, and the December rice harvest, the most important crop of the year, failed in many districts. Even before the end of September the price of rice in parts of Orissa had risen to famine rates. A month later the whole country was in panic; markets were closed and the poorer classes were reduced to absolute destitution. By June 1866 the state of affairs in the most stricken districts was appalling, for rice, quoted at thirty-five times its normal price in some places, could not be bought at all. "The people of Orissa, shut up in a narrow province between pathless jungles and an impracticable sea, were in the condition of passengers in a ship without provisions."

Relief works and local committees had been established, but grants of money and payment for relief works were useless. Money had no purchasing power; rice was wanted and rice was not to be had. It was only slowly that the authorities realized that food, not money, was required and that the government must supply it. An advance of £200,000 and the promise of unlimited funds was made to Bengal, but by this time the monsoon of 1866 had broken and the landing of the cargoes of rice on the dangerous Coromandel coast was a most difficult operation. In the open roadstead of Puri it took seven weeks to unload one steamer, and up to the end of October only 8750 tons of rice were imported.

September brought another calamity in the river floods which overwhelmed a thousand square miles of country, submerged the homes of a million and a quarter of people, and drowned the young crops to a depth of from three to fifteen feet for more than a month. From the double catastrophe of 1866 it is estimated that one-fourth of the population of the alluvial districts perished. In Orissa alone it has been estimated that more than a million persons died.[1]

The direct responsibility for the failure to take timely steps to fight the famine must be laid upon the government of Bengal. The lieutenant-governor had spent his whole official career in the secretariat, and not one of the officers in Orissa had any special experience of famine. The warnings of the collector of Puri were ignored, and from February to June 1866, while people were already dying of starvation in large numbers, not a single report on the state of Orissa was made by the Bengal authorities to the supreme government. And after that, " on every measure of relief there seemed to be written the fatal words ' too late.' " [2] Lawrence had been in favour of importing rice as early as November 1865, but his opinion was not shared by his council [3] and he allowed himself to be overruled, with fatal results.

The Orissa famine was the starting-point of a concerted policy to prevent a recurrence of such tragedies. In 1874 Lord Northbrook took ample and prompt relief measures, and subsequent inquiries showed that no mortality whatever was due to that famine.[4] But it was not until 1901 and the following years that an effective scheme to deal with scarcity conditions was finally evolved.

The immediate lesson taught by the famine was the vital obligation to irrigate Orissa effectively, control its rivers and improve its communications by land and sea. Schemes of irrigation for the

---

[1] *Life of Lord Lawrence*, Aitchison, pp. 157–161. *History of India under Victoria*, Trotter, Vol. II. pp. 183–187.

[2] *Life of Lord Lawrence*, Bosworth Smith, Vol. II. pp. 482–484.

[3] *Life*, Aitchison, pp. 161–162.

[4] *India in the Victorian Age*, 2nd Edn., p. 258.

improvement of agriculture, and for railways and roads to ensure distribution, were also set on foot throughout India. Lawrence had been an ardent advocate of irrigation works in the Punjab and had spent large sums on canals. But in India generally irrigation had been neglected, and Lawrence urged its importance as a government undertaking upon the home authorities.

In his letters to Sir Charles Wood at Whitehall he wrote with reference to the railway and canal schemes: " Our main object should be to complete the railways . . . which are the great arteries . . . but I doubt if most of them will pay and in our present financial difficulties I am for postponing them all. What seems to me of very much more importance is the question of irrigation. . . . The misery, the loss of life, the poverty which follow a failure of the rain . . . are almost inconceivable. . . . On the other hand well-considered irrigation works are sure to be a profitable investment . . . add to the resources of the State and enrich the people. . . . We are at our wits' end for revenue: any increase of taxation is sure to produce discontent. Is it not a kind of political suicide cutting from under our feet one great source which is available, namely, from the construction of irrigational works? The surplus . . . will enable us to avoid further taxation, or lighten that which exists. Light taxation, in my mind, is the panacea for foreign rule in India." [1]

The secretary of state finally consented that loans should be raised for irrigation works when the surplus revenues were insufficient; and Lawrence created an irrigation department. Twelve years later the total acreage irrigated, by government works in India, was 10,500,000; in 1931 it stood at 31 million acres, representing 12·7 per cent. of the total cultivated area.[2]

Lawrence became Viceroy at a time of great financial difficulty. The budget of 1864–65 showed a deficit of £880,000, and deficits occurred every year but one of his viceroyalty.[3] Apart from famine relief and the cost of two

Finance.

---

[1] *Life of Lord Lawrence,* Bosworth Smith, Vol. II. pp. 493–497.
[2] *India in 1931–1932* (Calcutta, Govt. of India Publication Branch, 1933), p. 108.
[3] *India in the Victorian Age,* 2nd Edn., p. 373.

small wars, salaries of subordinates had to be raised in the government departments; the expenditure on forests and on education was doubled; the cost of the medical services was nearly trebled; decent barracks for the European troops were essential; and just under half a million pounds were required for the site of the India Office in Whitehall.[1]

At the same time the country was convulsed by a commercial crisis. The demand from Europe, following upon *Cotton.* the blockade of the Confederate States in the American civil war, created a tremendous boom in cotton. In 1860 its price was about £44 a ton; in 1864 cotton stood at £189. Enormous fortunes were made, the peasantry in the cotton districts practically coined money, and at the large ports wages almost reached European rates. There were few openings for sound investments and in an orgy of speculation the public, especially in Bombay, plunged into wild-cat schemes, from land reclamation to livery stables. With the collapse of the Confederate States came the inevitable reaction. Cotton fell to about £56 a ton and commercial houses and banks went down in the slump of 1866. A Parsi firm failed for three million sterling, a Hindu millionaire for over two million, and the Bank of Bombay, which had lent itself to a reckless policy of unsecured advances, went into liquidation.[2]

Ten years earlier another distant war had given a steadier impetus to an Indian industry. The first jute mill was *Jute.* started near Calcutta in 1834, but little progress was made until the Crimean war cut off the Russian supplies. Since then the industry has steadily developed. In 1928 it gave employment to 339,000 hands, and jute now heads the list of Indian exports. Originally the capital was in the hands of the Scottish merchants, mostly of Dundee, whose enterprise had founded the industry, but in recent years the number of Indian shareholders in jute (amongst other industries) has greatly increased. Jute is one of the most satisfactory crops for the cultivator, and is frequently the only

[1] *Life of Lord Lawrence,* Aitchison, pp. 165–167.
[2] Aitchison, *op. cit.,* pp. 163–165, and Bosworth Smith, *op. cit.,* Vol. II. pp. 479–480.

" money crop " he can raise. Before the collapse in prices in 1931 about three and a half million acres were under jute, about 90 per cent. being in Bengal.[1]

Disraeli's choice of a successor to Sir John Lawrence was the Earl of Mayo; and there could have been no greater

Lord Mayo.

contrast to the gaunt, austere and weary civil servant than the burly master of hounds radiating health and charm of manner who came out to replace him. Mayo's only political experience had been as Chief Secretary for Ireland, and his appointment raised a storm of party protest in the Press. But Gladstone, who came into power before Lawrence's term was over, did not revoke the appointment, and the Liberal ministry gave Mayo its steady support.

The incoming Viceroy had seen the Suez Canal, then about two-thirds cut, when he passed through Egypt. After landing at Bombay he saw evidences of modern progress in India in the Elphinstone college, the Sassoon hospital, the regimental school of an Indian infantry regiment, listened to Seymour Fitzgerald's plan of making cotton inspectors keep a small garden for experiments in the cultivation of the plant, and inspected the latest type of cotton presses, then in use at Bombay, the centre of the Indian cotton industry.[2] The garden scheme has since expanded into a cotton botanist with an expert staff, Government cotton committees and the assistance given by the Imperial Council of Agricultural Research.[3] In 1851 the first cotton mill had been started in Bombay with British coal; in 1870 there were said to be eleven in the Presidency; in 1875 there were thirty-eight; and the imports of coarse cloths and yarns from England were already appreciably falling off. Fifty years later there were 264 cotton mills in India, run with Indian capital and employing over 300,000 hands.[4]

[1] *Moral and Material Progress,* 1930–1931, pp. 182, 327. *India in 1931–1932,* p. 142.
[2] From Lord Mayo's Diary, quoted by Sir W. Hunter, *Life of the Earl of Mayo,* Vol. I. pp. 165–170.
[3] *Moral and Material Progress,* 1930–1931, pp. 177–182.
[4] *Trade Relations between England and India,* pp. 242–243, and *The Making of India,* A. Yusuf Ali, p. 279.

Mayo took office on the 12th January 1869. Canning had swept away the method of administration by which reams

The Government of India. of official minutes "circulated at a snail's pace in little mahogany boxes from one councillor's house to another."[1] Mayo therefore found himself with a cabinet of seven departmental ministers for foreign, public works, home, revenue and agriculture, financial, military and legislative affairs. Mayo, besides being President of the Council and final source of authority, took over the portfolios of the foreign and public works ministers. "In this oligarchy all matters of imperial policy (were) debated with closed doors."[2]

In view of future political reform the comment made by Romesh Dutt in 1903 on this remark by Sir William Hunter may be quoted: "In this brief but pithy sentence we detect all the strength and all the weakness of Indian administration. The 'oligarchy' comprised the ablest British officials in India, but has never, within a half-century of the Crown administration, admitted an Indian within its body. . . . The people of India have no place within the cabinet; no consultative body of representatives has been organized to advise the cabinet; no constitutional method has been devised to bring the cabinet in touch with the people. The best of governments composed of the ablest of administrators must fail of success when the people are so rigidly excluded from the administration of their own concerns."[3]

Government in India was to travel, since those words were written, an even longer stage than it had advanced in 1870 beyond the military autocracy of the Timurids.

Mayo continued the foreign policy of his predecessor. When he met Shere Ali at Ambala in March 1869 the Amir

Foreign Policy. pressed for a treaty and a fixed subsidy. But the Viceroy made it clear that while the Government of India might be prepared to give him money, arms and ammunition, not a British soldier would cross the frontier to put down rebellion.[4] Although

---

[1] *Life of the Earl of Mayo*, Hunter, Vol. I. pp. 189–190.
[2] *Ibid.*, Vol. I. pp. 189–195.
[3] *India in the Victorian Age*, 2nd Edn., p. 253.
[4] *Life of the Earl of Mayo*, Hunter, Vol. I. pp. 256–262.

Mayo would not support any particular ruler of Afghanistan, he wished to see a chain of friendly, strong and independent kingdoms from west to east beyond the Indian frontier.[1] Negotiations were begun with Russia to create a neutral zone between the Russian and British spheres of influence; the delimitation of the Iranian Baluchistan frontier was carried through; and Mayo succeeded in putting British relations with the King of Upper Burma on a better footing, at least for a time.

In 1870, when civil war threatened in Alwar, Mayo intervened. He called upon the young ruler to accept British *The Indian* arbitration between him and his leading subjects, *States.* which avoided a direct British guarantee to the latter; and the Maharaja's powers were transferred to a council.

Mayo's reorganization of the Political Department " regularized " relations with the Princes by an attempt to apply uniform rules to the varying conditions and relationships of the States.

Before Mayo's viceroyalty all the revenues of British India went into one purse, and the provinces were allotted for *Financial Policy.* their annual expenditure only those sums which the Government of India thought fit, or which it could be persuaded to grant. This resulted in the distribution of the public income taking the form of a scramble in which the advantage went to the most aggressive or persistent of the provincial administrations, without much reference to their real needs. But in 1870 Mayo took the first steps towards financial decentralization in India. The administration of departments such as education, police and medical were transferred to the provincial governments, which were given a fixed annual grant for this purpose, and the provincial authorities were allowed to impose certain local taxes. This limited measure of decentralization, with various adjustments from time to time, proved successful; and Mayo's system remained in force until the introduction of dyarchy with the Montagu-Chelmsford reforms of 1921.[3] By enforcing rigid economy and by reluctantly imposing some

---

[1] *Life of the Earl of Mayo*, Vol. II. p. 271.
[2] *Native States of India*, Lee-Warner, p. 300.
[3] See *Moral and Material Progress*, 1930–31, pp. 357, 358.

additional taxation,[1] Mayo succeeded in turning the annual deficit into a surplus.

The Viceroy also obtained recognition of the principle, for which his predecessor had fought so hard, that unproductive works should be undertaken by loans.

Railways. The earliest policy as regards railways had been to encourage private enterprise guaranteed, and to some extent controlled, by government. In 1868 about 1800 miles of line had been constructed. Mayo began State ownership of railways and introduced the standard Indian gauge of 5 feet 6 inches on trunk lines and the metre gauge for subsidiary lines. Government and private ownership have existed in India side by side from this date.[2]

Lord Northbrook. On 8th February 1872, when on a tour to the penal settlement at the Andaman Islands, Mayo was murdered by a Pathan convict. Lord Northbrook, who was sent out to succeed him, belonged to the great banking house of Baring. His family had a long official connection with India and his father had been born in Calcutta. Northbrook himself had been Under-Secretary under Sir Charles Wood (Lord Halifax) at the India Office, where his influence had made a strong impression.[3]

The principles of government in India were summed up by Northbrook in the following terms: " Our dealings with the native princes must be strictly governed by the treaties and agreements which we have made with them; we must show our sympathy with the nobler and educated classes and associate with them as much as we can in the government of their country; we must cherish and reward our native soldiers and officers; we must rule the people with patience, remembering how far they are removed from ourselves in education; and we must be cautious and deliberate in the introduction

---

[1] *Life of the Earl of Mayo*, Hunter, Vol. II. pp. 90, 91.
[2] *Ibid.*, Hunter, Vol. II. pp. 277–290.
[3] *Earl of Northbrook*, Sir B. Mallet, p. 57.

of changes in their institutions and habits. Above all we must keep India at peace." [1]

These words sound like a succession of platitudes only when the history of India through the centuries which had gone before is ignored.

Finance, as might have been expected, was the strong feature of Northbrook's administration. But his viceroyalty marks an important stage in the evolution of British government in India. The use of the telegraph cable, a new invention in 1872, inevitably increased the amount of control which the home authorities could exert, added to which were the democratic tendency of the times and the growing interest shown by Parliament in all executive matters. [2] A new relationship consequently sprang up between the Government of India and the India Office, which was emphasized by the friction between the strong personalities of Lord Northbrook in India and Lord Salisbury in London.

Only one event of importance took place in British India during Northbrook's administration. At the end of October

Famine.
1873 the reports which reached the Viceroy on the crops in Bihar and part of Bengal foreshadowed another great calamity. Relief measures were promptly taken, with the energetic support of the Bengal provincial government; and in 1874 " for the first time in Indian history a great failure of crops such as hitherto had produced famine was met in such a way as to save the lives of the public."

The case of Baroda, with which Northbrook had to deal, is an

Baroda.
important landmark in the relationship between the supreme government and the Indian States. [3]

Baroda was, of course, much in the same position as other leading Indian States with reference to the paramount Power. Its government, which had previously been none too good, rapidly became worse when Malhar Rao succeeded in 1870.

---

[1] *Earl of Northbrook*, Sir B. Mallet, pp. 134, 135.
[2] *Ibid.*, pp. 113, 114 quoting Sir Evelyn Baring (Lord Cromer).
[3] For a statement of British policy see *Indian States Committee Report*, pp. 16, 17.

Three years later the Government of India was obliged to appoint a commission of inquiry. On its report the Gaekwar was warned that if certain reforms were not carried out he would be relieved of his authority.

But before the end of the probationary period an attempt to poison the resident Colonel Phayre was reported and the Gaekwar was suspected of complicity. This added the more serious charge of disloyalty. The extreme step was taken of trying the Gaekwar in 1875 by a commission of the chief justice of Bengal, three British high commissioners and three Indians, the Maharajas of Gwalior (Sindia) and Jaipur and Sir Dinkar Rao, minister of Gwalior. The commissioners were not unanimous. The Government of India consequently dropped the charge of disloyalty, but deposed Malhar Rao from the sovereignty of Baroda on the grounds of notorious misconduct, gross misgovernment and evident incapacity to carry into effect the necessary reforms. Malhar Rao's issue were barred from the succession by proclamation in April 1875, but the widow of Khande Rao, his predecessor, was permitted to adopt a son selected by the British Government from the Gaekwar family.

A large staff of British officials administered Baroda during the long minority of the young prince; and when the new Gaekwar was entrusted with full powers and privileges no new treaty or conditions were necessary.[1] Since then Baroda has been admirably ruled.

Northbrook had not been long in India before he decided that what he described as an "uneasy and dissatisfied feeling" might be due to "increased taxation and certain improvements in the laws, etc., which have perhaps been pushed forward a little too fast."[2]

Finance.

Income-tax more equitably adjusts the incidence of taxation between the rich and poor, and alone could reach the Indian and European trading classes and the wealthy landlords; and this led Wilson to advise and Mayo to impose this form of taxation. But Northbrook, after careful consideration, decided not to renew it.

---

[1] *Native States of India*, pp. 168–171, etc. [2] Mallet, *op. cit.*, p. 65.

He had already, in 1873, vetoed the Bengal Municipal Bill, which would have increased local taxation, and so gave financial relief which, in the words of a leading Indian newspaper, had "a most soothing effect on the popular mind." For Northbrook's policy was to ease financial pressure by strict economy, particularly in the military department and by inaugurating in the public works a system of cheap irrigation based on local requirements and knowledge. His budgets, however, all showed a deficit.[1]

Tariff Policy. In the tariff controversy which took place during Northbrook's administration the Viceroy, in the words of his biographer, was the champion of India as against British prepossessions and interests.[2]

In 1874 a duty of 5 per cent. existed on Manchester cotton piece-goods. The manufacturers strongly pressed Disraeli (afterwards Earl of Beaconsfield) to remit this, on the grounds that the Indian cotton mills, whose output was now greatly increasing, used duty-free raw Egyptian and American cotton, and so could compete unfairly with higher-grade English goods. Previous to this the Indian mills had only manufactured coarse goods from Indian cotton.[3] Northbrook, backed by his tariff commission, decided that the then firmly held principles of free trade were not violated by a duty levied for revenue purposes only, and that the Government of India could not possibly forgo a duty which brought in £800,000 a year. In August 1875 the Viceroy passed a Tariff Bill in the Legislative Council abolishing all export duties with the exception of those on rice, indigo and shellac, and reducing the general scale of import duties from 7½ to 5 per cent. A concession was made to Manchester cotton goods by imposing an import duty on raw cotton coming to India from foreign countries.

The India Office was distinctly taken aback by the news of a tariff change of which it knew nothing, and Salisbury cabled his strong disapproval on the grounds of the right of the secretary of

---

[1] *Earl of Northbrook*, Mallet, pp. 65–73. *India in the Victorian Age*, p. 373, taken from *Parliamentary Statistical Abstracts*.

[2] Mallet, *ibid.*, pp. 107–108.

[3] *Trade Relations between England and India*, p. 236.

state to be consulted about proposed legislation.[1] Nothing came of the vigorous exchange of despatches which followed and the controversy died away with the visit of the Prince of Wales, afterwards King Edward VII, and the announcement of Northbrook's resignation.

The Central Asiatic question began when the British crossed the
Afghanistan. Indus and the Russians reached the Oxus. By Northbrook's time the problem had resolved itself into the relationship of these two empires with Afghanistan. British interests required a barrier between India and Russia, whose policy for many years to come was to " keep England quiet in Europe by keeping her employed in Asia." [2] Afghanistan was the only independent State left on the Russian line of advance, and it was therefore peculiarly unfortunate that British diplomacy should have alienated the Amir.

Shere Ali had been disappointed by Mayo's award in the Afghan-Persian boundary commission. He misinterpreted Northbrook's subsequent proceedings as attempts to weaken his power and to interfere in the internal affairs of Afghanistan. He was, moreover, irritated by the Viceroy's refusal to recognize his younger son, Abdullah Jan, as heir to the throne.

The critical phase in the Amir's relations with the British was reached in 1873, when Shere Ali sent his envoy to India. The Amir decided that he must either obtain definite and practical British protection or he would have to accept the unsolicited patronage of Russia. Northbrook cabled to England his recommendations to help the Amir with money, arms and, if necessary, troops to repel an unprovoked invasion. But the Liberal Government refused its sanction to the agreement, a decision which involved very serious consequences. Shere Ali turned to Russia, and while there was no accredited British representative in Afghanistan, a succession of Russian agents found their way to Kabul.

[1] The tariff controversy as seen from different standpoints can be read in Mallet, *op. cit.*, pp. 107–112 ; *Trade Relations*, pp. 236–245 ; and *India in the Victorian Age*, 2nd Edn., pp. 402–409.
[2] *Life of Lord Curzon*, Ronaldshay, Vol. I. pp. 297–298.

At this point Disraeli came into power, and Salisbury, now secretary of state for India, being thoroughly dissatisfied with the position, urged the Viceroy in 1875 to establish a British agency at Herat, and possibly at Kandahar.[1]

Northbrook was fully aware of the value of a British representative in Afghanistan, but he considered that Shere Ali was so much opposed to allowing British officers in his country that to force agents upon him would " subject us to the risk of another unnecessary and costly war in Afghanistan before many years are over." [2]

In September 1875 Northbrook asked to be allowed to resign in the following spring " for domestic reasons." [3] The Prime Minister appointed Lord Lytton, then British Minister at Lisbon, and chiefly known as a man of letters under the name of Owen Meredith, to succeed him.

The new Viceroy took office in April 1876 with what may be described as sealed orders defining the policy to be followed in Afghanistan, but his instructions gave him considerable freedom of action. As the Amir's attitude was still uncertain, he was to be asked to receive a British Mission. If he refused the situation would at least be clear. If he accepted the Viceroy was empowered to promise help in case of an unprovoked attack upon Afghanistan and to grant what amounted to the requests which had been denied to the Amir three years earlier. In 1873 this might have made Shere Ali a firm and friendly ally, but now it was too late.

From April until October a correspondence which led nowhere passed between Simla and Kabul. But in December 1876, thanks to the remarkable local influence of Major (Sir Robert) Sandeman, a treaty was signed with the Khan of Kalat and chiefs of the Baluchistan clans which substantially strengthened the British situation on the frontier. Quetta was occupied, the Bolan Pass secured and a strategic position was gained on the road to Kandahar.

In January 1877 an Afghan mission to India continued the indefinite negotiations for three months. But it was now obvious

---

[1] Lord Lytton's Indian Administration, Lady Betty Balfour, pp. 5–24.
[2] Dispatch of 30th September 1875, Mallet, op. cit., p. 105.
[3] Ibid., p. 114.

that British influence was extinct in Kabul, and after March communications with the Amir came to an end.

A month later war broke out between Russia and Turkey. In January 1878 a Russian army was before Constantinople, and Disraeli's ministry, faced with the prospect of war with Russia, made the imperial gesture of garrisoning Malta with Indian troops. Russia's reply was to move troops towards Afghanistan and to send General Stoletoff on a mission to Kabul, the policy of weakening British protection of Constantinople by stabbing at India.[1] The mission left Tashkend on 13th June (the date on which the Berlin Congress held its first sitting), and was received by Shere Ali, with considerable hesitation, on 22nd July.[2]

Lytton, with the consent of the home authorities, then made his final effort, and requested the Amir to receive a British Mission, the letter reaching Kabul in August on the day of Abdullah Jan's death. The Government of India, relying entirely on moral influence, sent Sir Neville Chamberlain with only a small escort, and the mission was curtly refused passage through the Khyber Pass in September.

The Amir ignored the ultimatum then sent to him, and war was declared with Afghanistan on 21st November 1878.

Second Afghan War. General (Sir Sam) Browne advanced through the Khyber, General (Lord) Roberts up the Kurram and General Biddulph from Quetta. After Roberts' victory at the Peiwar Kotal, Shere Ali fled to Russian territory.

In May 1879 the treaty of Gandamuk was signed with Yakub Khan, the new Amir, by which Afghan foreign affairs were to come under British control, the passes occupied, and a British envoy accepted by Afghanistan. Sir Louis Cavagnari was appointed, and on the representation of Yakub Khan, the Viceroy, against his own inclinations, sanctioned his residence at Kabul.

On 3rd September 1879, within six weeks of his arrival, Cavagnari

---

[1] *Life of Lord Curzon*, Ronaldshay, Vol. I. p. 143.
[2] *Lord Lytton's Indian Administration*, pp. 247, 248. For details of the treaty by which Shere Ali gave Russia control of the foreign policy of Afghanistan and free and exclusive commercial access to the country, see *ibid.*, p. 370.

and his escort of seventy-five Guides cavalry and infantry were murdered by Afghan troops. The Amir made no effort to save the British mission but the subsequent Kabul commission exonerated him of complicity. Stewart at once reoccupied Kandahar, and on the 8th October, Roberts, advancing by the Kurram, appeared before Kabul. Yakub Khan, by this time a refugee in the British camp, abdicated at the end of the month and Roberts took over military control of the country. The deportation of the ex-Amir to India was the signal for a religious rising and Roberts had to fight hard at Sherpur in December before the country subsided into the dangerous tranquillity of a volcano.

At the best of times Afghanistan is a peculiarly unstable kingdom. Its people, many of them nomads, are grouped in a number of tribal republics, whose allegiance to the Amir is often hardly more than nominal. But it was impossible for the Government of India to prolong the military occupation indefinitely, and Lytton could not in the circumstances restore Yakub Khan. He decided, with the sanction of the Conservative ministry, to divide up the country. He proclaimed that the British would recognize a friendly ruler at Kabul chosen by the people themselves; and he made Wali Shere Ali Khan ruler of Kandahar, supported him with troops and established a strong advanced frontier post at Pishin.

This was the situation when Abdur Rahman Durrani, a nephew of Shere Ali, emerged from his retirement at Samarkand and with a hundred followers and two thousand pounds borrowed from the Russian governor-general rode south to win the throne of Afghanistan. He at once got in touch with the British authorities and was negotiating for his recognition as Amir when, on 26th April 1880, the Conservative government went out and Gladstone became Prime Minister. The Liberals had violently attacked Lytton over Afghanistan and the Viceroy resigned, to be replaced by the Marquess of Ripon.[1]

Ripon went out pledged and eager to reverse his predecessors'

---

[1] For details of the events in Afghanistan see *Lord Lytton's Administration*, the *Official Account of the Second Afghan War*, and the descriptive narrative given by Earl Roberts in *Forty-one Years in India*.

policy. But circumstances were too strong for him. In June 1880 Shere Ali's younger son Ayub Khan, who had kept his hold on Herat, set out towards Kandahar. On 27th July he completely routed a brigade under General Burrows at Maiwand, and invested Kandahar. Roberts marched from Kabul, covering the 313 miles between 11th and 31st August, and relieved Kandahar after a hard and well-fought engagement in which Ayub Khan was decisively defeated.

Shere Ali Khan resigned in November, leaving Kandahar without a ruler, and Ripon recognized Abdur Rahman as *Settlement with Afghanistan.* Amir of Afghanistan. Although he abandoned Lytton's demand for a British envoy Ripon's policy was otherwise in accordance with the aims of his predecessor. He secured control of the foreign relations of Afghanistan and he retained Pishin. Ripon's own party were furious and the immediate abandonment of Pishin was announced in the Queen's Speech in 1881. But the Viceroy saw clearly that these means of controlling the Amir were essential to avoid another Afghan war later on; and he let it be known that he would resign rather than withdraw from Pishin. Gladstone accordingly let the matter drop. It took Abdur Rahman eighteen months to expel Ayub Khan and establish himself firmly upon the throne of Afghanistan.

With Afghanistan under the iron rule of an Amir friendly although aloof in his attitude towards the British *Lord Lytton's Administration.* Government, we can return to Lytton's administration in India.

By the proclamation to the Imperial Assembly at Delhi on 1st January 1877, when Queen Victoria was declared *Kaisar-i-Hind*, Empress of India, the Crown became formally identified with the hopes, the aspirations, the sympathies and interests of a powerful native aristocracy. In the words of Holkar: " India has been till now a vast heap of stones, some of them big, some of them small. Now the house is built and from roof to basement each stone of it is in its right place." [1]

[1] Letter from Lord Lytton to Queen Victoria (23rd December 1876 to 10th January 1877), Lady Betty Balfour, *op. cit.*, p. 123.

The most serious domestic event with which Lytton had to deal
was famine in the southern provinces of India. The
Famine. failure of the monsoon in 1876 affected an area of
about 200,000 square miles with a population of thirty-six millions
and was most severely felt in parts of the Madras Presidency, Mysore,
the southern half of Hyderabad and the Deccan districts of the
Bombay Presidency.

Sir Philip Wodehouse, governor of Bombay, promptly organized
large public works. The Madras government misjudged the situation
and made hopelessly inadequate arrangements which the Viceroy
was obliged to remedy by a personal visit to Madras. The famine
lasted until 1878, spreading northwards in the second year, and the
mortality due to famine alone in one year in British India was
estimated at over five million. The foresight of the Bombay government kept the relief expenditure down to four million pounds in that
Presidency, as against ten millions in Madras, where a million acres
went for a time out of cultivation.[1]

The policy put forward by Lytton for famine relief is the backbone
of the existing system. He saw that there were only two effective
means of fighting it and mitigating its effects. These were railways
and irrigation works; the third method—emigration—not being
feasible.[2] As a first practical measure he started the famine
insurance grant, by which an annual allocation is made from general
revenues, and this fund is available for famine relief, protective
works, and for the relief of debt.

Protection was then looked upon as an exploded theory, and
Salisbury, the secretary of state for India, gave his
Tariffs. opinion that " it is difficult to overstate the evil of
permitting an industry so large as the cotton manufacture of India

[1] *India in the Victorian Age*, 2nd Edn., pp. 427, 496. *Lord Lytton's Indian
Administration*, p. 225.

[2] *Ibid.*, p. 228. For emigration difficulties see *Moral and Material Progress*,
1930–1931, pp. 47–60, where Indian Government action, to remove disabilities
met with by Indians within the British Empire, is described. In 1931, including
800,000 in Ceylon, there were 2,305,000 Indians overseas in the British Empire,
and about 100,000 permanently settled in foreign countries.

is likely to become to grow up under the influence of a system which a wide experience has proved to be unsound." [1] It was, moreover, strongly held in England that the duty of 5 per cent. levied in India on imported goods was a serious hindrance to the trade of Manchester, and that any form of protection was against the interests of the consumer.

Lytton, an ardent free trader, wished to see all import duties swept away, and having " convinced himself that the essential interests of India required the measure," [2] he brought forward a Bill in 1879 exempting coarse cotton goods from customs duty. Only two members of his council supported him. The majority urged the existing budget deficit, and reflected the objections of the Indian merchants and the chambers of commerce of Madras and Calcutta.[3] But Lytton, exercising his powers under the Act of 1870, overruled the majority of his council. In the course of the discussion of the cotton duties the secretary of state refused to admit the claim made by the Government of India that measures affecting the customs tariff should be left entirely to them. Salisbury insisted that the consent of the home Government had to be obtained before important changes were made.[4]

The tariff policy for the next fifty years was an adjustment between the principles of free trade, the representations of the Lancashire cotton industry, and the necessity of raising revenue in India. In 1882, with a good budget, Ripon abolished the remaining import duties, except those on salt and liquors. In 1894, when the Government of India was faced with a deficit of two million pounds, import duties were reimposed. The tariff consisted of a general *ad valorem* duty of 5 per cent., to which there were certain exceptions. By Indian legislation in 1896 an import rate of $3\frac{1}{2}$ per cent. on cotton goods was counterbalanced by a $3\frac{1}{2}$ per cent. excise on cotton goods made in the Indian mills; a special measure in the interests of Lancashire. All that can be said for this excise duty is that it gave

[1] *Lord Lytton's Indian Administration*, pp. 479–480.
[2] *Ibid.*, p. 482.
[3] *India in the Victorian Age*, pp. 412–415.
[4] *Trade Relations between England and India*, pp. 227, 228.

to the hand-loom weavers (who were exempt from it) the same measure of protection, as against the Indian mill-owners, which the British manufacturers enjoyed.[1]

This measure, as the Joint Select Committee on the Government of India Bill pointed out in 1919, created the belief that India's fiscal policy was dictated from Whitehall in the interests of England, and that the sooner this idea was eradicated the better for the good relations between both countries. Theoretically the excise duty was within the strictest tenets of free trade. It raised the necessary revenue whilst keeping the import duty on imported cloth at a low level, and so mitigated the rise in its retail price. But when the suggestion had been made, in 1876, that the removal of the cotton import duties might make it necessary to impose an excise duty upon Indian cottons, Salisbury observed in his despatch: " I can hardly conceive a course more injurious to a young and rising industry in the natural growth of which India has the deepest interest." [2]

In 1916, under the stress of war, the general tariff of 5 per cent. was doubled; and an additional 1 per cent. was levied in the depression which came later. The reforms of 1919 brought a new influence into play which will be referred to later, but it may be mentioned here that the excise duty imposed on cotton in 1896 was abolished in 1926.

A feature of Lytton's administration which without doubt or controversy benefited the consumer was his action *Salt.* in regard to the salt tax. Reference to this tax, which is as long established as any in India, has already been made; and although Akbar made an unsuccessful attempt to abolish it, salt has remained an inevitable source of revenue to every government in succession. Before the days of British rule transit dues, added to the local cesses, were liable to raise the price of salt in inland districts to an exorbitant figure.

The government monopoly established by Warren Hastings was attacked in 1845 on the grounds that the tax was high and the salt neither good nor cheap. The monopoly was consequently relaxed, to disappear altogether in 1862 and be replaced by excise; but the

[1] *Trade Relations between England and India*, p. 253.   [2] *Ibid.*, p. 244.

government continued, and still continues, to make salt. The inferior Indian product was gradually superseded by imported white salt in Bengal, where salt cannot be made locally, as in Madras and Bombay. The inland customs houses had been abolished in 1834, and a customs barrier set up round British Indian territory inside which the manufacture of salt was prohibited.

In his budget speech in March 1877, Sir John Strachey described this customs barrier, which stretched for 2472 miles and was guarded by 13,000 men [1]: " Along the greater part of this enormous system of inland customs lines . . . a physical barrier has been created comparable to nothing that I can think of except the Great Wall of China. It consists principally of an impenetrable hedge of thorny trees and bushes, supplemented by stone walls and ditches across which no human being or beast of burden can pass without being subjected to detention and search. . . . Owing to the levy of the export duty on sugar, the same obstructions are offered to the traffic passing in the other direction." [2]

Another point about the salt duties was their inequality, the amounts levied varying considerably in different parts of the country. By giving compensation to manufacturers whose salt works were suppressed, and by treaty with the Indian States, to whom annual payments equivalent to the duty were made, Lytton equalized the salt duty throughout India, and the " hedge " was removed. At the same time the price of salt was greatly cheapened in Northern India by railway construction.[3] Since 1924 the tax upon salt has been fixed at a rate working out at about fourpence a head *per annum* throughout British India. Of the salt now consumed in the country about 35 per cent. is manufactured by or for government, and the rest is either privately manufactured or imported.

Lytton extended Mayo's scheme of decentralization, and
Administrative Reforms. further developed the system of provincial assignments. In his last year of office he gave a new impulse to the employment of Indians in government service.

---

[1] *Modern India*, 2nd Imp., p. 247.
[2] *Lord Lytton's Indian Administration*, p. 465. [3] *Ibid.*, pp. 469–470.

Indians had found it almost impossible to take advantage of the
Charter Act of 1833 and the rules as first applied in
*Indians and the
Civil Service.* 1853 of open competition for the covenanted civil
service. The expense of the journey to England
prevented many good scholars from going to London to sit for the
examination. In 1878 only nine Indians held posts in the covenanted civil service of their own country. Lord Lawrence's scholar-
ship scheme, favoured by the Conservative government, had been
dropped by the succeeding Liberal ministry, in which the Duke of
Argyll, as secretary of state, held the opinion that Indians could be
best employed in judicial posts, and their selection made in India
without competitive examinations.[1]

All parties were agreed that the pledge first made in 1833 must
be kept, but to honour it effectively in the observance more favourable
conditions were necessary. In 1878 Lytton put forward a scheme
which, in collaboration with the secretary of state, was put into
force in 1879. A maximum of one-fifth of the total number of civilians
appointed by the secretary of state in any one year to the covenanted
civil service were to be Indian probationers selected by the local
governments and approved by the governor-general in council. At
the end of two years, after passing the necessary tests, these probationers would enter the new class of statutory civilians, on two-thirds
of the salary payable to English civil servants of corresponding rank.
In addition to this several branches of the uncovenanted service
were reserved exclusively for Indians. These rules did not, of
course, prevent Indian candidates from competing, as before, at the
examinations held in London. No legislation was needed to carry
out these reforms, which were continued by Lord Dufferin, who
substituted a provincial service for the statutory civilian system.[2]

The policy of reducing the proportion of Europeans in the
administration was pursued, and in 1904 Lord Curzon pointed out
that to rule over 230 millions of people under 6500 Europeans were
employed and 21,800 of the inhabitants of India itself. In the posts
carrying pay of over £800 a year, 1263 were Europeans, 92 were Indians

---

[1] *India Under Victoria*, Trotter, Vol. II. pp. 391, 392.
[2] *Lord Lytton's Administration*, pp. 524–534.

and 15 were Anglo-Indians.[1] The systematic "Indianization" of the services was still to come, but it is interesting to compare this proportion with the purely Indian personnel in the public service under Akbar.[2]

The differences between the civil service in England and in India need some explanation. In England government officials are collected in large offices aloof from the general public. Their work is specialized and seldom technical. But although there are big secretariats in India the total number of officials employed in them is relatively small. The civil servants are mainly distributed over the face of the country to do their work as individuals. The Statutory Commission report describes their varied duties: "Lecturing in universities or bridging rivers, fighting epidemic disease or dealing with widespread riots, excavating a prehistoric city or installing a water supply for a new one."

From East India Company servants, whose duties were little more than revenue collecting, the district officer was evolved, with the whole administration in practice depending on him. The British official touring his district had become, in the eyes of the people under his charge, *the* Government of India "at once autocrat, counsellor and friend." Lord Curzon, speaking of the British officials who died at their posts at Jubbulpore and at Nagpur during the famine of 1896, touched upon an aspect of British rule in India which is too often forgotten: "These men did not die on the battlefield. No decoration shone upon their breasts, no fanfare proclaimed their departure. They simply and silently laid down their lives, broken to pieces in the service of the poor and the suffering among the Indian people; and not in this world, but in another, will they have their reward."[3]

In 1857, when the vernacular press had little influence, a short-lived Act was passed directed principally against the papers published in English. But by 1875 the vernacular newspapers were printing articles which the Secretary of State described as "not only calculated to bring the

The Vernacular Press Act.

---

[1] *Modern India*, 2nd Imp., p. 88. [2] See p. 200.
[3] *Life of Lord Curzon*, Ronaldshay, Vol. II. p. 81.

Government into contempt, but which palliate, if they do not absolutely justify as a duty, the assassination of British officers." [1]

The Second Afghan War gave rise to very outspoken criticisms of the Government by vernacular newspapers, in Bengal especially. These had become much more open since 1874. Supported by the opinion of all the local governments (except Madras, where the Indian press was negligible) and with the sanction of the Secretary of State, the central government introduced and passed the Vernacular Press Act on 14th March 1878. The Act was preventive rather than punitive, and amounted to the provision of guarantees by publishers and printers. But the council of India were not unanimously in favour of the measure, there were debates in the House of Commons,[2] and in 1882 the Act was repealed. It had not, in point of fact, ever been fully enforced.

Before dealing with the events of Ripon's Viceroyalty, reference *Sir Syed Ahmad* must be made to the renaissance of Muhammadan *and Aligarh* education. This was due to the exertions of one man. *College.* For what Raja Ram Mohun Roy had done for the moral and intellectual rejuvenation of the Hindus Sir Syed Ahmad Khan accomplished for the Moslems. " There would be no educated Muhammadan community existing and flourishing today but for the heroic pioneer efforts and far-sighted vision of this great man, who did not see in the utter collapse of the Mogul empire an argument for racial estrangement and enmity." [3] The Syed had shown conspicuous courage and loyalty to the British Government in 1857, and while he was not favourably inclined towards the Indian National Congress, he saw clearly enough the need for harmonious co-operation between Hindus and Moslems.

Syed Ahmad came back from a visit to England convinced of the supreme importance of progressive education as a civilizing influence, and began the efforts which led to the establishment of

[1] Lord Salisbury to the Government of India, *Lord Lytton's Indian Administration*, p. 504.
[2] *Ibid.*, pp. 502–523.
[3] *India's Nation Builders*, N. D. Bannerjea (1919), p. 95.

the Muhammadan Anglo-Oriental College at Aligarh, with the object of combining Islamic culture with the education necessary for success under modern conditions. Primarily for Moslems the college is, however, open to students of other religions, and the first graduate was a Hindu.[1] The foundation stone was laid by Lytton in January 1877[2] and it has proved a successful and vigorous institution. It became a university in 1920, and in 1931 there were 1914 students in the university proper and its dependent institutions.

Mysore.

Except for the concluding stages of the Afghan War, and a Mahsud expedition in 1881 when some valuable survey work was done, Ripon's term of office was a period of peace. The only political event of importance was the rendition of Mysore.

Lord Wellesley had recreated the Hindu State in 1799, but the condition of good government had not been kept by its rulers. In 1831 the country was placed under direct British administration, when the foundations of its present prosperity as an admirably ruled state were laid. After the death of the deposed Maharaja in 1868 the Government of India recognized his adopted son as his successor. The heir to Mysore was carefully educated, and the State, with good laws, competent law courts and a sound system of revenue settlement was handed over by Ripon in 1881.[3]

Local Self-Government.

Mayo's decentralization scheme of 1870 had greatly increased the number of urban municipal bodies although very little was accomplished in the rural districts. In 1882 Ripon passed a series of Acts giving municipal and districts boards a high proportion of elected members.[4] But general apathy and the innate disinclination of the elected members to take responsibility combined to disappoint the expectations of

---

[1] *Moral and Material Progress,* 1930–1931, p. 468.

[2] *India's Nation Builders,* pp. 111, 112.

[3] For the deed of transfer, which fully describes the general position of the States, and of Mysore in particular, to the paramount power, see *The Native States of India,* pp. 174–179.

[4] For the resolution which gives Ripon's policy, see *Report of Indian Statutory Commission,* Vol. I. pp. 299–300.

Government except in a few large cities. The extension of local self-government did not "very soon manifest itself . . . as the instrument of political and popular education" which, in the words of the resolution, Ripon had hoped. Even in many of the towns the municipality continued to confine its activities to approving the decisions of the official chairman, and in the districts, with few exceptions, local self-government continued to be, as in the past, one of the many functions of the district officer. This state of affairs was recognized by the authors of the Montagu-Chelmsford Report in 1918.[1]

The Census. The first Indian census was taken in 1881, and since that date this has been repeated every ten years. While the statistics showing the birth and death rates and the relation between them are of the first importance, a comprehensive survey was included until 1941 of every custom and activity of the people and every conceivable matter concerning them, from the rainfall to the age of marriage.

The Ilbert Bill. After 1870 successful Indian candidates began to appear as members of the civil service. They were mostly appointed to the judicial branch, and by 1883 some were senior enough to be shortly eligible for appointment as district and sessions judges. But by the existing law no Indian-born judge or magistrate, except within the Presidency towns, could hear charges against European residents. Consequently, unless the law were amended, Indian-born judges would have less power than European members of the same service. Courtenay Ilbert, then law member of the Governor-General's council, accordingly introduced a Bill to abolish "every judicial disqualification based merely on race distinctions."[2]

The Bill aroused the strongest opposition amongst Europeans in out-stations, such as the indigo-planters and managers of tea-gardens, who were afraid of unfair decisions. Their cause was taken up by the European residents of Calcutta; and it was strongly supported in England, where public meetings of protest were held

---

[1] See also *Indian Statutory Commission Report*, Vol. I. p. 302.
[2] *Political India*, p. 37.

in St. James's Hall and in Limehouse. At the same time a counter-agitation began among educated Indians, who resented these demonstrations as an undeserved slur upon their judicial probity. *The Times* pointed out [1] that the introduction of the Criminal Jurisdiction Bill had caused widespread agitation and excitement, had evoked antipathies of race, and produced a vast amount of reciprocal irritation; and asked whether it were desirable to do so much evil that so small a good might accrue. The Government of India withdrew the Bill and substituted an amendment of the Code, which reserved to European alleged offenders the right to claim trial by jury.

BIBLIOGRAPHY

I. From Canning to Ripon

A Sketch of the History of India (1858–1918), Professor H. Dodwell, 1925.
Life of Earl Canning, Sir H. S. Cunningham, Rulers of India Series, 1892.
Life of Lord Lawrence, Sir C. M. Aitchison, Rulers of India Series, 1905.
Life of the Earl of Mayo, Sir W. W. Hunter, Rulers of India Series, 1892.
Thomas George, Earl of Northbrook, Bernard Mallet, 1908.
Lord Lytton's Indian Administration, Lady Betty Balfour, 1899.
Government of India, Sir C. Ilbert, 2nd Edn., 1907.
Indian Administration to the Dawn of Responsible Government, B. K. Thakore (Bombay), 1922.
Native States of India, Sir W. Lee-Warner, 1910.
Report of the Indian States Committee, Cmd. 3302, 1929.
Trade Relations between England and India, C. J. Hamilton (Calcutta), 1919.
India in the Victorian Age, Romesh C. Dutt, 2nd Edn. 1906, a work which has had a wide circulation, especially in India. It contains many statistics and is carefully documented, but the author makes certain challenging assertions which are not borne out by historical fact, and the book must be read with caution.

---

[1] Leading article, 26th June 1883.

India Under the Crown

II

FROM DUFFERIN TO CURZON

THE appointment of a Catholic Viceroy, Ripon being a convert to the Church of Rome, had raised a storm of disapproval in English Protestant circles. He left India amidst enthusiastic demonstrations of the affection of the Indian people, and Lord Dufferin, who became Viceroy in December 1884, confessed later to Ripon that this " made the position a little difficult for your successor." But Dufferin, who was deeply impressed by his courage, conscientiousness and ability, made it clear from the first that there was to be no change of policy.[1]

The new Viceroy had excellent judgment and a remarkably firm will, and his infinite tact enabled him to carry his point with the minimum of friction. He had held appointments in the Liberal Government, including the post of under-secretary of state for India, and he had represented his country abroad as commissioner in Syria and in Egypt, as ambassador at St. Petersburg and Constantinople, and governor-general of Canada.

His first business was to pass the Bengal Tenancy Bill, which had *Land Acts.* been taken in hand by Ripon. The landlords opposed legislation affecting rents and fixity of tenure as an infringement of the permanent settlement. Actually it was a continuation of Cornwallis's policy, and the Bill, an improvement on the Bengal Tenancy Act of 1859, became law in 1885.

Dufferin saw that in Oudh the position of the tenants was much the same as upon large estates in Ireland where he was a landed proprietor. The evils of great insecurity and incessant competition had to be guarded against, and the Viceroy succeeded in overcoming the natural reluctance of the taluqdars to an amendment of the

---

[1] *Life of the Marquis of Dufferin and Ava*, Sir A. Lyall, Vol. II. pp. 75, 76.

law of 1868 in favour of the tenants. The Oudh Rent Act of 1886 enabled the 1,800,000 tenants-at-will to improve their holdings, entitled them on eviction to compensation for improvements, and provided a seven years' tenure.

In 1887 a Punjab Tenancy Act was passed. The Punjab is mostly a land of small landowners and peasant proprietors, and the Act regulated the relations between these owners and their tenants as regards rent and compensation for improvements.

Land legislation is never an easy matter, and it is exceptionally difficult in India. But with the co-operation of able and experienced local officers Dufferin's policy may fairly be said to have materially benefited agriculture in Bengal, in Oudh and in the Punjab.

Affairs in Afghanistan and the annexation of Upper Burma are the chief events of Dufferin's Viceroyalty, but *Domestic Affairs.* before dealing with these a word should be said on domestic matters. Finance was made difficult by the fall in the price of silver, a serious economic event to which India is particularly vulnerable. In 1886 legislative councils like those in the Presidencies were set up in the North-West Provinces. A commission in 1886 to brighten the prospects of Indians in government posts led, in 1892, to the creation of the provincial and subordinate civil services.[1] The Moslem pilgrim traffic was much improved. Viceregal visits to the States began a closer understanding with the princes.

In December 1885 the Indian National Congress held its first meeting of Hindu, Muhammadan and Parsi delegates *The National Congress.* at Bombay. Controversy over such measures as the Vernacular Press Act and the Ilbert Bill had much to do with its birth, but concerted All-Indian action for social and political reform had been advocated by Alan O. Hume late of the Bengal Civil Service and by other Englishmen, and Dufferin was in favour of a means of expressing political opinions in what would be purely theoretical debate.

[1] See *The I.C.S.*, Sir Edward Blunt (1937), pp. 49-51.

Starting from the British Indian Association in Bengal in 1851, Indian interest in politics had deepened since 1860. But political life really began with Congress. It opened by advocating an administration on Western parliamentary lines, the inclusion of more Indians in the Civil Service, prevention of the economic exploitation of the country; and in denial of hostility to British rule for many years ended its annual sessions with cheers for the British Imperial Sovereign. From the first the Parsi political reformer and Member of Parliament, Dadabhai Naoroji, was associated with Congress; and, until the organization was finally captured by the left wing, Surendranath Bannerjea enthusiastically fostered the growth of Indian nationalism in what was an urban middle-class body unaffected in its early years by communal feeling.

In 1884 the Russian advance in Central Asia had reached Merv,
Russia and Afghanistan. a threat to Afghanistan and an ultimate menace to India which could only be met by diplomatic means. Ripon had suggested an Anglo-Russian boundary commission under Foreign Office arrangements to set a limit on Russian expansion, and when Dufferin came to India the commission was at work. But the general feeling in England, although described in some quarters as " Mervousness," was one of not unreasonable alarm and, in March 1885, the Government of India was instructed to mobilize an army corps to move on Herat should Russia attack that Afghan fortress and make war inevitable.

At this juncture the Viceroy invited the Amir to meet him at Rawalpindi, and Abdur Rahman entered India on the same day of March 1885 on which his troops were attacked by the Russians at the disputed frontier post of Panjdeh. The informal hostility of the incident was not looked upon by the Amir with the feelings which it excited in England, where frontiers are regarded in the light of international law as immune from border skirmishes. Abdur Rahman's chief concern was the exclusion at all hazards of British and Russian officers and troops from Afghanistan, a policy to which he resolutely held for the whole twenty years of his subsequent reign. He asked from the British Government no more than money and arms. These Dufferin willingly promised him and the Amir returned well satisfied to Kabul.[1] The Panjdeh incident was smoothed over, and the boundary commission satisfactorily delimitated the Russo-Afghan frontier.

Third Burmese War. While affairs beyond the North-West Frontier were giving the Viceroy grave anxiety, serious trouble had arisen in the east. British imperial policy, following the practice of Rome, has been to see that bordering States have been so far protected, whether they wished it or not, as to prevent powerful neighbours from meddling with them. The prosecution of this policy has been one of the leading motives of wars, annexations and alliances.[2]

Since 1879 the resentful attitude of the Burmese Government of Ava had necessitated the withdrawal of the British resident from Mandalay. British commercial rights were being disregarded, and British subjects such as members of the Bombay and Burma Trading Company were being exposed to grave injustice and injury. This was the situation when, in February 1885, the Viceroy learnt that King Theebaw had made a treaty with the French Government under which special consular and commercial privileges were accorded to France.

With the sanction of the home authorities, Dufferin sent an ultimatum demanding a settlement of all matters under dispute, requiring Theebaw to receive a permanent British resident at his court, and laying down the principle that the Burmese king must in future defer to British advice in regard to his foreign relations. At the same time about 10,000 troops were concentrated at Rangoon.

No satisfactory reply was received from Burma and war was declared in November 1885. Eighteen days later Theebaw surrendered and was deported to India. The country was formally annexed on 1st January 1886. Guerilla warfare, however, protracted hostilities for about five years and called for the employment of 30,000 troops

[1] *Life of the Marquis of Dufferin and Ava,* Lyall, Vol. II. pp. 85–109.
[2] *Ibid.,* Vol. II. p. 116.

before it ended. In 1897 Upper and Lower Burma were united into a single province under the Government of India.

Lord Dufferin left India in December 1888 leaving an unclouded sky behind him, and taking with him the re-
Lord Lansdowne. membrance of " universal kindness and goodwill which he had received in all parts of India and from every section of its inhabitants." He was succeeded by another ex-under-secretary for India and governor-general of Canada, in the Marquis of Lansdowne, whose administration, except for several of the inevitable minor frontier expeditions, was one of profound peace.

The zone running southwards from the Hindu Kush to the Arabian Sea, known as the North-West Frontier,
The North-West Frontier. involves two problems—the international and the tribal. There is the possibility of invasion by a foreign power and the constant problem of the control of the border tribes.

The frontier may be divided into two parts, Baluchistan and the country to the north.

The only definite advance before Lansdowne's time had been to extend the British sphere of influence from the Sind
Baluchistan. border into the highlands of Baluchistan, and to occupy Quetta in 1876. Peace among unruly hill tribes like the Maris and the Bagtis was due to the wonderful personality of Sir Robert Sandeman, who dealt " with the hearts and minds of the people and not only with their fears." The earlier incessant raiding into British India had ended when Sandeman, as a young district officer, had won the confidence of the local chiefs and persuaded them to keep order themselves. Sandeman took advantage of the Baluchi oligarchic organization, and local and inter-tribal disputes were settled by the assemblies known as *jirgahs*, over which govern-ment officers presided; there were no revenue or criminal courts. His right-hand man for twenty years, until Sandeman's death in

1892, was Rai Bahadur Hittu Ram, C.I.E., who had started life in a government office on five rupees a month.[1]

In December 1889, at the request of the Zhob Valley chiefs and with government sanction, Sandeman took over that district. Apozai, where the durbar took place, became Fort Sandeman, and this singularly remote military station, and Jacobabad in Sind with its Indian record-breaking temperature of 126 degrees in the shade, rather unfortunately commemorate two of the most famous names on this frontier.

The problem of the frontier from Waziristan northwards was not so easy to solve. The Amir claimed a shadowy superiority over the tribes up to the Indian frontier, and the Pathans were consequently able to play off the British official against the Afghan. To this was added the turbulent character of a people who hate authority, and whose young men have always been more inclined to listen to their fanatical Moslem priests than to the cautious advice of their chiefs and the older men amongst them. The semi-nomadic tribesmen in a country as hard and grim as themselves spend much of their time in fighting, raiding the plains, and carrying on family blood-feuds. Fine natural shots, of splendid physique for the most part, the Pathans rank among the finest fighting men in the world; and as private trading in arms has enabled them to keep abreast to an appreciable extent with modern improvements in rifles, only picked and highly-trained troops can hold their own with them on their native hills. Even today the tribes can find some reply to aeroplanes in infiltration tactics and movements by night.

The Pathan Problem.

To gain some measure of political control over the border tribes and so end a situation which was always liable to cause trouble, Dufferin sent Sir Mortimer Durand to Kabul, in 1893, to settle the spheres of influence of the two countries. In the course of the next few years the boundary commission demarcated the " Durand Line " from Chitral to the Zhob Valley.

[1] *Life of Sir Robert Sandeman*, T. H. Thornton, 1895. *Sandeman in Baluchistan*, Hittu Ram (Lahore), 1907, gives a vivid account of Sandeman's work on the frontier.

PLATE LXI.

Central Press Photos Ltd.

THE KHYBER PASS

Two years earlier the Hunza-Nagar expedition had resulted in the strengthening of a weak point in the line of the North-West Frontier. The little hill states of Hunza and Nagar, bordering on Russian Turkestan and China, acknowledged the suzerainty of Kashmir to the extent of an annual tribute amounting in all to a handful of gold-dust, a couple of horses and hounds, and two baskets of apricots. But in May 1891, Hunza, with Nagar as a reluctant ally, invaded the Kashmir frontier. A British force was sent into the country, the ruler of Hunza fled into China, and the two States have been consistently loyal to their obligations ever since.[1] But as regards the relationship between the Pathan tribes and the British Government the situation remained far from satisfactory.

After the Persian and Afghan invasions and conquest of the eighteenth century, no Indian government was concerned with the Pathan tribes until Ranjit Singh expelled the Afghans. Then for a quarter of a century a purely local situation arose in the collisions between the Sikhs and the trans-border tribes, but this in no way affected the rest of India. In 1849 the British annexed the Punjab kingdom, and the North-West Frontier became the concern of the Government of India, and this created an entirely new problem. The policy Dalhousie adopted is known as the close-border system. The tribes raided, kidnapped, and harboured outlaws until the patience of the British Government was exhausted, when a punitive expedition was sent against the offending tribe.

When contact was first made it might not have been impossible to " Sandemanize " the Pathans by using their tribal assemblies to settle disputes, by creating tribal police and so transferring responsibility for their own political, social and economic development to the people themselves under British supervision. But the only form of tribal responsibility attempted was the seizure of men and property of the tribe to which offenders belonged; and the criminal code enforced on Pathans under British administration was the criminal law of England, modified to some extent, but holding murder as a capital offence. The Pathan, with his universal blood-feuds, takes a lenient view of murder, and his tribal law aims at redress instead

[1] *Campaigns on the North-West Frontier*, pp. 130–149.

of punishment. The imposition of standards looked upon as imperative in western civilization on a people who have never understood them and who might otherwise have been controlled through their own tribal law and procedure, created the outlaw who escapes from British India over the border, and has been the direct or indirect cause of numerous expeditions in reprisal for border crime.

The close border system definitely ended with the demarcation of the Durand Line. Between 1893 and 1895 advanced posts were built on the Samana ridge above Kohat, and in the Gumal, the Tochi and the Kurram valleys, while garrisons were placed in the Malakand and in Chitral. In many cases tribes were paid large allowances for protecting the roads.

The Indian States.

In 1891 there was serious trouble in the remote State of Manipur over the succession. The chief commissioner of Assam and others of his party who went to deal with this were murdered. The rebellion was suppressed by British troops, the leaders were tried and executed for murder, and measures were taken to ensure necessary reforms. The State was not annexed and the importance of the incident lies in the principles laid down in this case; namely:

The repudiation by the Government of India of the application of international law to the protected States; the assertion of the right to settle successions in case of rebellion against a chief; the doctrine that resistance to imperial orders constitutes rebellion; and the right of the paramount power to inflict capital punishment on those who had put to death its agents in the lawful discharge of their duty.[1]

The Government of India had also to intervene in Kalat, where the Khan began grossly to misgovern after Sandeman's death. The leading men in the State were consulted, and they recommended that the Khan should be deposed and his son made ruler. The Government of India agreed, and the succession was facilitated by the voluntary resignation of the reigning Khan in 1893.[2]

[1] *The Native States of India*, pp. 179–183.
[2] *Administration of Lord Lansdowne*, p. 51.

In the last two years of Lansdowne's administration the earlier
Internal Affairs. budget surpluses were changed into deficits, largely
on account of the increasing burden of the home
charges caused by the fall in the price of silver, and consequently
in the exchange value of the rupee. The value of the rupee
fluctuated between 1s. 6d. in 1890 and 1s. 2½d. in 1893.[1] This
seriously affected trade and led to the formation of the Indian
Currency Association which was joined by members of all classes.
The international conference convened at Brussels in 1892 to consider
the monetary question failed to agree, and the Government of India
accordingly took its own measures. In 1893 the Indian mints were
closed to the free coinage of silver; the value of the rupee in relation
to gold was fixed at 1s. 4d.; and currency notes were issued in Calcutta
and Bombay on this basis. Gold was not made legal tender.[2]

The peace of the country was broken for a time by communal
disturbances. A laudable Hindu movement for the protection of
cows from cruelty degenerated into a high-handed and illicit
agitation to suppress the slaughter of kine for food or sacrificial
purposes. Riots amounting to anarchy broke out in Bombay between
Hindus and Moslems, and heavy casualties were caused by similar
disturbances in Bengal and the North-West Provinces. The riots
were suppressed by prompt and vigorous government action, a duty
which the Viceroy emphasized was due to the whole community
" to secure to both great religious denominations freedom from
molestation or persecution in the exercise of their religious observances." On Lansdowne's suggestion the popular leaders in the disturbed districts formed conciliation committees to go into the question
of custom as to the slaughter of kine and to take steps to prevent
these outbreaks in future.[3]

The state of Indian education at its weakest point, for girls and
Position of women, is seen in the fact that Lansdowne's efforts
Women. to improve it, which included technical instruction,
were hailed as a great advance. In female education the number of

---

[1] *India in the Victorian Age*, p. 583.
[2] *Administration of Lord Lansdowne*, pp. 35–39.
[3] *Ibid.*, pp. 20–23.

571

girls rose from 214,000 to 270,000; thirteen women graduated as bachelors of arts and one took the degree of master. A large extension was made to Lady Dufferin's scheme for supplying medical aid education to the women of India through special hospitals and dispensaries.

In passing an Act raising the age of consent from ten to twelve Lansdowne encountered strong Hindu opposition; in 1930 the Sarda Act penalising the marriage of girls under fourteen had the strong support of many Indians of both sexes. But while the Hindu fire ceremony infers age of discretion in the bride, and Islamic law gives women a voice in choosing a husband, the marriage age is in practice ruled by popular consent.[1] As an instance, in twentieth-century Baroda, where fourteen is the marriage age for girls, the law is broken yearly by thousands who cheerfully pay the consequent fine. To quote the Aga Khan: "Sati, infant marriage, the compulsions of permanent widowhood and the enervating restrictions of the purdah, are so many hateful caricatures of the teaching of the Prophet, and indeed of the earliest and finest writings of Hinduism, namely, respect and honour for women by protecting the persons of the bearers of the race from risks of violence. These and other social evils have so handicapped India that it is impossible to conceive of her taking a proper place in the midst of free nations until the broad principle of equality between the sexes had been generally accepted by her people." [2]

But the second quarter of the twentieth century can claim not only an industrial revolution but the awakening of Indian womanhood. Female education increased, plurality of wives, Moslem as well as Hindu, grew rare, and purdah, even among Moslems, lessened. Girls of eighteen began to go to the cities as factory hands, typists and clerks, thus loosening the traditional Joint Family tie, and highly educated Indian women joined the learned professions and, with the franchise, entered politics with success.

The best mind and thought of the country has for many years seen the need for improvement in the position of women; and the

[1] See Report, Age of Consent Committee, 1928-29, passim.
[2] India in Transition, H.H. Aga Khan (1918), p. 256.

All-India Women's Conferences which have been held since 1926 have done much to promote the social as well as the educational welfare of the women of India.[1]

Parliamentary Legislation. The India Councils Act of 1892 increased the size of the legislative councils and allowed limited discussion of the annual financial statement.[2]

Army Reform. In 1893 the office of commander-in-chief in the Madras and Bombay armies was abolished by Act of Parliament. This enabled the Government of India to carry out a reorganization scheme with one commander-in-chief, a reform which four successive Viceroys had urged and which had been originally recommended by Lord William Bentinck in 1833.[3] The Presidency system was abolished in 1894 and the whole army in India was reorganized in four separate commands, with an additional line of defence in the Imperial Service troops raised by the States. The term " Indian Staff Corps " was not abolished until 1903, when British and Indian officers and men of Indian units became the Indian Army.

Lord Elgin. In 1894 Lord Lansdowne was succeeded by the Earl of Elgin, whose father had died in India as Viceroy in 1863. Unlike his immediate predecessors, Elgin had held no great offices, and he was called upon to grapple with a highly critical situation on the frontier and with two serious domestic calamities, bubonic plague and a devastating famine. In foreign politics he improved relations with Russia, completed the Afghan boundary line and the marking out of the frontier between Burma and China and Siam, all of which had been begun by Lansdowne. The work of the Durand commission was interrupted in 1894 by the rising of the Waziris, who felt that their independence was threatened, and a strong force was required to reduce them.

---

[1] *Moral and Material Progress*, 1930–1931, pp. 459–461 ; and *Education Report of Auxiliary Committee of the Ind. Stat. Commission*, p. 181.

[2] *Government of India*, Ilbert, 2nd Edn., pp. 107–108.

[3] *Ibid.*, p. 108 and footnote.

Trouble over the succession brought on, in 1895, a revolt in
Chitral. Chitral, where the British agent and his escort
were besieged, until their relief by a remarkable
feat of mountain warfare conducted by Colonel Kelly. Elgin wished
to hold Chitral; the Rosebery government vetoed its retention;
but the Conservative government came in before the troops could be
withdrawn and reversed the decision.

In 1897 occurred the most formidable outbreak that the British
Tirah Campaign. arms had up to that time been called upon to suppress on the North-West Frontier of India. The
more critical nature of the operations in Waziristan in 1919 and 1920
was due to the fact that India had been drained of her best troops,
and the campaign had to be fought with raw and inadequately
trained forces.[1]

The military operations of 1897–98 are known as the Tirah
campaign, but the frontier was involved from the Mohmand country
in the north to Southern Waziristan; and at one period the command
of the Khyber was completely lost. The rising had its origin in
the unrest caused by the demarcation of the boundary line, which
brought the tribes within the sphere of British influence and gave
rise to a fear of annexation. The flame was fanned by their religious
leaders and it was not lessened by a pamphlet issued by the Amir
urging the true believers " to stand firm when ye meet the unbelievers
marching in great numbers against you." [2] It is only fair to add
that in the subsequent operations Abdur Rahman preserved a
strictly neutral attitude. More than 40,000 men had to be employed, including Imperial Service troops under the Indian princes,
before the tribesmen submitted, paid their fines and surrendered
rifles.

Plague entered India through Bombay, probably from China,
Plague. in 1896, and rapidly spread through the Presidency.
Strict quarantine regulations were issued and search
for infected houses rigidly enforced; later, inoculation was introduced.
The clash between modern sanitary ideas and ancient Hindu custom

[1] See *Waziristan 1919-1920*, H. de Watteville (1925).
[2] Nevill, *op. cit.*, p. 212.

574

caused great antagonism to the plague campaign, and this was further inflamed by certain local Indian newspapers with regrettable results in the riots of 1897. By 1899, to quote Lord Curzon, " science and compulsion and evacuation at the point of the bayonet " were replaced by " conciliation, persuasion, the employment of volunteer agency, the relaxation of former rules." [1] The plague reached the Punjab in 1902 and a little later the United Provinces were infected. The greatest number of deaths from the disease occurred in 1907 (1,160,000) and 1911 (over 700,000).[2] The death-rate from plague has now fallen to less than 30,000 in the year.

The number of deaths in India from " preventible diseases "
Effects of Disease. is an economic factor of serious importance, for this amounts to five or six millions every year. A fourth of this mortality is due to malaria, and 10,000,000 annual admissions to hospital may be taken to occur on account of this disease alone. These are staggering figures, but it must be remembered that very nearly one-fifth of the human race live in India. The All-India Conference of Medical Research Workers stated in 1926 that the percentage of loss of efficiency of the average person in India from preventible malnutrition and disease was not less than twenty per cent., and that the percentage of infants born in India who reached a wage-earning age was about fifty.[3] This terrible enervation is largely responsible for the poverty of the masses, and the best efforts of government are powerless to do more than palliate it.[4] Unhygienic habits and an apathy generally based on a religious conviction of the unalterability of fate, added as these are to poverty, are handicaps that only education, finance, time and individual effort can remedy.

In 1937, a "good year," about 560 British soldiers and 390 Indian respectively per 1000 were admitted to hospital. In 1920 it had been 1071·5 per 1000 British and 762·3 per 1000 Indian troops.

[1] *Life of Lord Curzon*, Ronaldshay, Vol. II. p. 84.
[2] *Moral and Material Progress*, 1930–1931. Diagram facing p. 418.
[3] *Ibid.*, 1930–1931, pp. 161–162, 424.   [4] *Ibid.*, pp. 413–436.

Famine.

Failure of the monsoon in 1896, followed by a disastrously bad harvest in Western, Central and Southern India caused a famine of intense severity over an area of 570,000 square miles with a population of 130 millions. The number of starving people being kept alive by the public relief works rose at one time to nearly five millions, and in spite of the distributing facilities given by railways, government organization, and private charity, great numbers died of starvation and disease. This famine, the most widespread of any in the nineteenth century, cost the Government of India about ten millions sterling, and but for the funds raised throughout the British Empire the cost in life and in money would have been far heavier.

Lord Elgin was succeeded by Lord Curzon of Kedleston, who became Viceroy on 3rd January 1899, eight days before he was forty.

The new Viceroy was a man of high courage and great ambition.

Lord Curzon's Personality.

He had made his name in politics as under-secretary of state for India, and had piloted the Indian Councils Bill through the Commons in 1892. He had travelled in Central Asia and discovered the source of the Oxus, he had visited Persia, in Kabul he had impressed the Amir and his son Habibullah Khan by his personality, he had seen the North-West Frontier and toured eastward from Siam to Peking ; and he had written important books on Persia and the Far East.

His biographer has recorded the generous impulses, the exuberant affection, the deep humbleness of heart fully realized by an intimate circle. But to the official world of Simla Curzon presented a front of haughty and chilling reserve, a brusque lack of consideration which did not even spare the lieutenant-governor of a province and, at times, a ruthless animosity.

Viceroy of India "at the height of his own powers, he dominated the administration in a way which few, if any, of his predecessors had done and in which it will never again be given to any governor-general to do. The history of British rule in India for seven years is the story of Lord Curzon's daily life and work."[1] Since

[1] Lord Ronaldshay in *Life of Lord Curzon*, Preface to Vol. II.

the days of Warren Hastings, Dalhousie alone equalled him in dynamic energy and passion for work, in attention to detail, in zeal for efficiency.

In 1900 a famine of extreme severity swept the country and was most intense in Bombay and the Central Provinces, to add to the horrors of plague. Over twenty-five million people in British India and thirty millions in the Indian States were affected, and in British India alone there were approximately one and a quarter million deaths from starvation. It was, as Curzon stated, " not merely a crop famine, but a fodder famine on an enormous scale, followed in many parts by a positive devastation of cattle—both plough cattle, buffaloes and milch kine. It affected and may almost be said to have annihilated the working capital of the agricultural classes." The Viceroy travelled through the famine districts organizing and superintending relief. Generous help was given by the Indian princes, notably the Nizam of Hyderabad and the Maharaja of Gwalior, and large sums were subscribed throughout the Empire for the starving people. The expense of relief was enormous. In 1896 there had been a million and a quarter of persons receiving relief, and in 1900–01, when the numbers were five millions, the estimated cost was about eight and a half million sterling.[1] Speaking generally the effects of the famine were more serious in the Indian States, while the death-rate in the majority of the famine districts in British India was hardly more than normal. But the cultivators had been hit so severely that the Government of India remitted large arrears of land revenue.

Famine.

The famine commission of 1901, the third since 1880, reported that relief organization could be considerably improved both in efficiency and economy. But, as the Viceroy observed, " to ask any government to prevent the occurrence of famine in a country the meteorological conditions of which are what they are here, is to ask us to wrest the keys of the universe from the hands of the Almighty." [2] All that could be done was to lessen its effects. The irrigation committee of 1901–03 laid down the policy of expenditure on famine

[1] *Life of Lord Curzon*, Vol. II. pp. 86–87.
[2] *Ibid.*, Vol. II. pp. 283–284.

protection works, such as reservoirs, which could not be constructed from loan funds on account of the cost; and works of this nature were constructed later, more especially in the Bombay Deccan and in the Central Provinces where the risk of scarcity is always great.[1]

The central government had now, humanly speaking, perfected famine relief measures, and could see any danger signal in the weekly reports on rainfall and the crops. If the monsoon failed the provincial plans would set up relief circles and assemble plant without delay, while revenue collection would be suspended. Extra officials, engineers, doctors (to guard against outbreaks of disease) and grain would be hurried to the stricken districts from every province untouched by famine. When the rains came the villagers would be moved from the larger relief works to smaller ones near their homes to cultivate their fields, with loans to restock their holdings.[2]

On his arrival in India Curzon had at once taken up the frontier question. He saw that the Punjab government, *The North-West Frontier.* in addition to the normal administration of a province, was unable to deal with the exacting and imperial responsibility of the North-West Frontier. He therefore made a separate North-West Frontier Province in 1901, directly under the Government of India, with a chief commissioner, and a judicial commissioner's court at Peshawar instead of the chief court at Lahore. The old North-West Province was renamed the United Provinces of Agra and Oudh.

The frontier was at that time protected by large bodies of troops in isolated positions, an expensive method which was also unsound from the military standpoint in the event of mobilization against Afghanistan or Russia. The Viceroy, whose policy had its origin in the Khyber agency established about thirty years earlier, made a compromise between the " close border " and Sandeman systems. The regular troops were withdrawn to their bases, tribal militia under British officers were substituted, and the tribesmen were paid

[1] *Moral and Material Progress*, 1930–1931, pp. 227–234.
[2] See *Modern India*, pp. 187, 188 and Ch. XII. by Sir Thomas Ward.

to protect their own country. There was no occupation of tribal territory and no attempt at administration, however indefinite, up to the Durand Line except in the Wana, Tochi and Kurram valleys.

Curzon was opposed to frontier expeditions and preferred the action of blockade. But the Mahsud blockade, which began in 1900 and lasted a year, employed a considerable force, and before it ended involved the troops in hard marching and sharp fighting indistinguishable from a recognized frontier campaign.

Afghanistan. The consistent policy of Abdur Rahman to avoid contact with the British was continued by his son Habibullah, who succeeded in 1901. This position was complicated by Russian intrigue and by the quantities of modern arms which were coming into Afghanistan. In 1904, when Curzon was absent in England, the acting Viceroy, Lord Ampthill, sent a mission to Kabul under (Sir) Louis Dane, and a treaty was signed which accepted the claims of the Amir to arrears of subsidy and free admission of munitions.

The Persian Gulf. British supremacy in the Persian Gulf, a matter of vital importance to India and to the Empire as a whole, was being undermined by the naval activities of Russia and by the avowed intention of Germany to secure with the help of the Turks a terminus for the Baghdad railway at Koweit. Curzon urged the cabinet to take a strong line, and at the close of the South African War the Conservative government declared the application of a Monroe doctrine to the Persian Gulf. The Viceroy made this declaration effective by a tour to the chief ports in 1903, when he established satisfactory relations with the chiefs on the Arabian and Persian coasts.

The Teheran government was then far too weak to control its sheikhs, who were, in actual fact, as independent as the tribal leaders on the Arabian coast. The only power which could exercise control, police the Gulf, and deal with the gun-runners whose cargoes frequently went to the Pathan tribes, was the British.

In subsequent years Persia developed a strong government policy which asserted itself along its own coast to Mohammerah, and British control became limited to the Arabian littoral. Great Britain made treaties of friendship with the sheikhs from Koweit to Aden ; and Bahrein, where a British naval station and airport were established, became the most important centre on the coast. In Curzon's day the British buoyed and beaconed the waters of the Gulf ; by 1935 Imperial Airways, the modern link between Europe, India, Singapore and Australia, had made the Persian Gulf the Suez Canal of the air.[1]

At another point of the compass the extension of Russian influence led to a further demonstration of the forward policy.
Tibet. Tibet is under the suzerainty of China, a suzerainty which was more than once manifested, until the Chinese Republic, by invasion. In theory ruled by the Dalai Lama, Tibet was governed throughout the nineteenth century by regency councils under whom the spiritual head of the country hardly, if ever, reached an age when he could assume power. But about 1898 the incarnate Dalai Lama, thanks to the watchfulness of the Russian Buddhist, Dorjieff, reached his majority and overthrew his council.

Not unnaturally guided by Dorjieff, the Dalai Lama sent three missions to Russia between 1898 and 1901. Tibet was a closed country to the British, and as all indirect means through the Chinese to make effective commercial agreements with the Tibetan government had failed, Curzon decided to send a mission to secure direct access to Tibet by a conference held within its borders. The mission under Colonel, afterwards Sir Francis, Younghusband, after an unfortunate attack by the Tibetans on the way up, reached Lhasa at the beginning of August 1904, and a treaty was signed a month later.[2] Its terms were practically annulled by a later Convention with China and Russia by which Russia and England agreed to treat with Tibet only through China, send no representatives to Lhasa, and obtain no concessions such as mines, roads and telegraphs in the country.

[1] *The Times* (London) Articles, 12th and 13th June 1935.
[2] See *Lhasa and its Mysteries*, L. A. Waddell, 1905.

Curzon had come to India determined to strengthen the relations between the paramount power and the ruling princes. He announced at Gwalior that "the native chief has become, by our policy, an integral factor in the Imperial organization of India. He is concerned not less than the Viceroy or the Lieutenant-Governor in the administration of the country. I claim him as my colleague and partner."[1] To make this aim more practical he revived Lytton's idea of a council of princes, after a conference of rulers at Ajmer in 1904; but the home Government did not approve.

The Indian States.

In his speech at Gwalior the Viceroy also emphasized the obligations of the princes to their own people, and foreshadowed the active interest which he was to show in keeping them to "the stern seat of duty." In 1900 he issued a decree that in future permission to Ruling Chiefs to visit countries outside India would be granted by the Government of India alone.[2] Largely owing to the financial difficulties of the States brought about by famine, Curzon made his authority felt to a considerable extent in their internal affairs, an active interest which had a perturbing effect.

Two years of famine had brought Hyderabad into serious financial difficulties, and the Viceroy visited the Nizam in 1902 to make a new arrangement that would ease the burdens imposed by treaty on the State. By the Curzon agreement the Hyderabad Contingent was absorbed in the Indian Army, and Berar (assigned to the paramount Power to satisfy the military charges) was leased in perpetuity to the Government of India, the Nizam receiving Rs.2,500,000 a year as rent. In 1936 the Berar question, a trouble of more than eighty years' standing, was settled. The Crown reaffirmed the Nizam's sovereignty over Berar,[3] while the Nizam agreed that this territory should be administered under the Government of India Act (1935) as if it were part of the Central Provinces.

Hyderabad and Berar.

---

[1] *Life of Lord Curzon*, Ronaldshay, Vol. II. p. 89, Speech at Gwalior, 29th November 1899.
[2] *Ibid.*, Ronaldshay, Vol. II. pp. 90–92.
[3] The rent (£187,500) was continued under the settlement.

Berar in its anomalous position as non-British territory, and consequently outside the Government of India Act, was then absorbed into the Central Provinces as an annex under the Governor-General in Council, to be represented in the Central Provinces legislature in due course.[1]

To provide increased opportunities for the military aspirations of Indian gentlemen and princes, Curzon founded the Imperial Cadet Corps. The chiefs' colleges at Ajmer, Lahore and Rajkote and the Daly College at Indore, were the recruiting grounds, and after a three years' course those who passed the final tests became eligible for the rank and status of a British officer in staff or other extra-regimental employment.[2]

Imperial Cadet Corps.

To the initiative of the Viceroy was due the assembly of the princes of India at the durbar held at Delhi on 1st January 1903, to celebrate the accession of King Edward VII in 1901 to the Emperorship of India. In urging his proposals on the home Government, Curzon declared: "The one thing most needed in India is the sense of common participation in a great political system of fellow citizenship of the British Empire. The opportunities that exist of creating and fostering this feeling are few." [3] For the elaborate ceremony, when the King-Emperor was represented by the Duke of Connaught, and at which a hundred ruling chiefs and about 173,000 people were present, the Viceroy was to a great extent personally responsible.[4]

The Delhi Durbar.

Nor did the Viceroy, who could evoke the stately magnificence still to be found in India, forget the splendours of the past. An archæological department, mainly for research, had been in existence since 1862, but Curzon, when he came to India, was horrified at the desecration and neglect of the priceless architectural heritage of the country. Some

Ancient Monuments.

---

[1] *Indian Statutory Commission Report*, Vol. I. pp. 72–73.
[2] *Life of Lord Curzon*, Vol. II. pp. 126–128.   [3] *Ibid.*, Vol. II. p. 231.
[4] The detail personally considered by Lord Curzon is illustrated by his rejection of " Onward, Christian Soldiers " for the British Parade Service on the grounds that two of its lines " would not be particularly appropriate " (*Life*, Vol. II. p. 230).

of the finest Mogul monuments in India were either in a state of ruinous decay or, whitewashed and plastered, degraded into use as post-offices, petty courts and private houses. In 1902 Curzon appointed a trained classical archæologist in Sir John Marshall as director-general, to preserve the ancient monuments and to explore important sites. Curzon's inspiration alone made possible the work which his able director-general carried out in India. The excavations at Taxila, in the Buddhist sites of Bihar and Orissa, and the remarkable discoveries at Harappa and Mohenjo-daro are of world-wide interest.[1] The second director-general was an Indian, the department is staffed by Hindus and Moslems, and more than three thousand monuments are under the care of the archæological survey.

On the recommendations of the Indian Currency Committee an Act was passed in 1899 making the British sovereign legal tender in India and fixing the rupee at 1s. 4d.

Finance.

Famine made remission of taxes impossible in the early part of Curzon's Viceroyalty, but the Budget of 1903 gave considerable concessions. Middle-class wage-earners received a remission of income-tax and the cultivators found relief in a reduction in the salt duty. Two good harvests and wider markets for cotton and tea increased national prosperity, and this was reflected in the seventh and last Budget of Curzon's administration. Taxation to the extent of £1,371,000 was remitted, a million pounds were spent on administrative reforms, better postal facilities were provided, and in spite of heavy expenditure on the army and the railways, there was a surplus of over £900,000 on an eighty million budget.[2]

"The peasant," to quote the Viceroy's own pronouncement, "has been in the background of every policy for which I have been responsible, of every surplus of which I have assisted in the disposition." He was determined to

Land Policy.

---

[1] A very good summary is to be found in *Moral and Material Progress,* 1930–1931, pp. 481–495.

[2] *History of India,* Trotter, Edn. 1917, pp. 451, 455.

vindicate the British land settlement and revenue policy in the eyes of the world,[1] and his resolution of 1901, a document of the greatest impartiality and amazing insight, stands as a landmark in the history of the land revenue policy of India under British rule. Curzon carried his aims into effect by constant legislation, and he relieved the stress in time of famine by the suspensions and remission resolution.

However thrifty an Indian small-holder may be, his lack of capital and the fact that he has to wait some months for a return for his labours and expenditure—apart from the expense of religious and social festivals—forces him into debt. The Punjab Land Alienation Act of 1900 aimed at preventing money-lenders and shopkeepers from buying land from hereditary cultivators, or from holding such land on mortgage for more than twenty years without government consent. There was similar legislation later for some other parts of India. But it was difficult to make these provisions effective, and the problems of rural indebtedness and the " fragmentation " of holdings, which is especially prevalent in the Punjab, had to be tackled in other ways.

The reports of the Famine Commission of 1901 and of the Irrigation Commission of 1903 were acted upon by Curzon with the far-sighted statesmanship which, coupled with strong financial aid, the vast agrarian problem demands. The debt question was met by the Co-operative Credit Act of 1904. Eight years later the Co-operative Societies Act encouraged the extension of the village credit societies to replace the money-lenders whose activities have also been checked by other legislation.

In 1901 Curzon appointed an inspector-general of agriculture. In 1903, with the generous donation of £30,000 made by Mr. Henry Phipps of Chicago, he was enabled to submit to the secretary of state the scheme which founded the admirably equipped Agricultural Research Institute, where the experimental farm and the college have a government grant. In 1929 a Council of Agricultural Research

---

[1] Specifically in answer to Romesh C. Dutt whose challenges were made in his open letters to the Viceroy, and later in his *Land Problems in India* and in *India in the Victorian Age*.

was formed to promote provincial co-ordination. But its income was inadequate, the provinces, autonomous after 1935, did not co-operate and the Departments of Agriculture were fatally understaffed and lacked trained men. Research seemed of secondary importance with farming methods still primitive and many culturable areas waste, while over a million tons of rice, India's most important food-grain, had to be imported yearly.[1]

Education. Curzon's view of the policy of education was summarized in his remark: " Ever since the cold breath of Macaulay's rhetoric passed over the field of the Indian languages and Indian textbooks the elementary education of the people in their own tongues has shrivelled and pined." Three out of every four country villages had no school, and more than four-fifths of the boys of school-going age were without even primary education. He determined to put elementary education on a sounder footing and to begin his reforms in the high schools and colleges.

The Universities Act of 1904 gave these bodies new powers of government, and laid down the policy of supplementing examinations by thorough general teaching in order to raise the standard of higher education. The university senates were remodelled and affiliated colleges were placed under regulation and inspection. These reforms were good in themselves but they aroused considerable opposition from those who were affected by them. Later Acts led to the transference of the control of education to Indians, but in elementary education Curzon secured a large permanent annual grant which made it possible to open thousands of new schools.

Partition of Bengal. The Bengal Presidency has had more changes of boundary than any other British political unit, and at different times it has included Bihar, Orissa, Assam and Agra. Until 1911 Calcutta was the capital of British India. A quarter of a century later Bengal stood fifth in

[1] See *Food-grains Policy Committee Report* (G. of I. Press, 1943), pp. iv, 2, 21-28, 29, 30, 128.

585

provincial areas with 82,955 square miles, though its population of 60,314,000 headed the Census of 1941. But its size at the beginning of this century, the isolation of its eastern districts, and the consequent difficulties of effective control and police supervision decided Curzon to divide the province. In 1905 the short-lived province of Eastern Bengal and Assam was created with the commercial and educational centre of Dacca as its capital.

The announcement of the partition in the face of strong opposition to its original proposal raised a storm of bitter Hindu resentment which swept over its politically-minded classes throughout India. It had its origin in the fear of Moslem preponderance in the new province, and it was strengthened by the belief that the partition was aimed at weakening the national movement by dividing the province which had begun to take its leadership. The agitation was unlike anything previously known in the country. Its originators, such as Surendranath Bannerjea, in entire good faith denied that the movement was anti-British: they wished to use constitutional means to awaken public opinion in England to the seriousness of the situation.[1] But the campaign involved a boycott of British goods which was enthusiastically supported by the student community and the younger generation of the politically-minded classes. It brought into the nationalist movement the unbalanced and explosive element responsible for terrorism, a criminal form of protest most damaging to the national cause. Congress in 1905 no longer regarded British rule, which had admittedly created "a sense of national existence," in the earlier light of "a merciful dispensation of Providence," and self-government "similar to what exists in the self-governing colonies of the British Empire" was proclaimed to be the essential remedy.[2]

The Congress Left Wing.

The conduct of the anti-partition campaign alienated Moslem sympathies from the Congress movement, and in 1906 the All-India Moslem League was founded to safeguard their own interests.

[1] *A Nation in Making*, Sir Surendranath Bannerjea, pp. 187–189.
[2] G. K. Gokhale at the Twenty-first Indian National Congress; *Report*, p. 13.

Curzon, in England on leave in 1904 on the understanding that

The Military Controversy.

his term of office was to be extended, found the cabinet highly critical of his forward foreign policy and positively hostile to the view of his commander-in-chief, Lord Kitchener, that military considerations should govern their prospective agreement with Afghanistan. The Viceroy, who reacted to opposition as strongly as Warren Hastings and Dalhousie, returned to India to be plunged into further controversy.

Kitchener, whose thorough reorganization for the speedier concentration of an efficient field army on the North-West Frontier was a striking achievement, now pressed for the abolition of " dual military control," by fusing the executive functions of the commander-in-chief and the administrative functions of the military member of council in one person. Curzon, backed by weighty military opinion, maintained that this would in practice substitute, without any check, a military autocracy for the Government of India. Moreover, to add to the existing responsibilities of the commander-in-chief a heavy load of administrative and quasi-military duties, as well as the preparation of the military budget, would be to impose " an impossible burden for one man to assume." The decision of every other member of council when the question came up in March 1905 was against the commander-in-chief. The home Government, standing between the masterful personalities and great public services of Curzon and Kitchener, offered a wavering compromise in the form of a military supply member. But as the cabinet would not accept safeguards which to Curzon were essential, he resigned in August 1905 and Lord Minto was appointed in his place. The military supply member and his department duly appeared, to be absorbed in 1909, after a rather ineffective existence, into the Army department.[1]

That the burden laid upon the commander-in-chief was impossible for one man to assume was proved in 1915, when the breakdown of the military administration under the test of war brought

[1] For the opposite views in the controversy see *Life of Lord Curzon*, Ronaldshay, Vol. II. pp. 373–389, and *Life of Lord Kitchener*, Sir George Arthur, (1930) Vol. II. pp. 199-223.

disaster in Mesopotamia ; an inexorable result to which the financial restrictions of the Indian Government upon military requirements appreciably contributed.

The dramatic departure of the last of the great proconsuls
whose personal authority impressed itself over all India closed the
era which had opened under Canning. For a time the efficient
machinery of British bureaucratic administration continued to work
as before. But the claim for immediate independence was to rise
uncompromisingly beyond the policy of a succession of secretaries
of state, whose declared aim came to be the achievement step by
step of a Dominion government of the Indian people by Indians
themselves.

BIBLIOGRAPHY

II. From Dufferin to Curzon

Life of the Marquis of Dufferin and Ava, Sir A. Lyall, 1905 (2 vols.).
Administration of the Marquis of Lansdowne, G. W. Forrest (Calcutta),
    1894.
Life of Lord Curzon, Earl of Ronaldshay, 1928, vols. I. and II.
A Nation in Making, Sir Surendranath Bannerjea, 1927.

CHRONOLOGY

1858.   Indian Government transferred from the Company to the Crown.
        Lord Canning Governor-General and first Viceroy.
1861.   Indian Councils Act.
        Famine in Upper India.
1862.   Grant of Sanads of succession to Indian States.
        Lord Elgin Viceroy.
1863.   Death of Amir Dost Muhammad.
        Ambela Campaign.
1864.   Sir John Lawrence Viceroy.
1865–1867. Orissa Famine.
1868.   Shere Ali, Amir of Afghanistan.
1869.   Lord Mayo Viceroy.
1872.   Lord Northbrook Viceroy.
1873–1874. Bihar Famine.

1875. The Prince of Wales (afterwards King Edward VII) visited India.
1876. Lord Lytton Viceroy.
Royal Titles Act.
Occupation of Quetta.
1876–1878. Famine in Southern India.
1877. Foundation of Aligarh College.
1878–1880. Second Afghan War.
1879. Indian Civil Service Reform.
1880. Lord Ripon Viceroy.
1881. Restoration of Mysore.
First Indian Factory Act.
1882. Local Self-government Acts.
1884. Lord Dufferin Viceroy.
1885–1887. Tenancy Acts.
1885. Panjdeh Incident.
Third Burmese War.
Indian National Congress held its first meeting.
1886. Annexation of Upper Burma.
1888. Lord Lansdowne Viceroy.
1891. Manipur Massacre.
1892. Indian Councils Act.
1893. Army reorganization.
Durand Line Demarcation Commission; forward policy on North-
West Frontier.
1894. Lord Elgin Viceroy.
1895. Chitral Expedition.
1896–1897. Appearance of Plague; Famine in Western, Central and
Southern India.
1897–1898. Tirah Campaign.
1899. Lord Curzon, Viceroy.
1901. Creation of North-West Frontier Province.
Famine Commission Report.
1903. Agricultural Legislation.
1904. Tibet Expedition reached Lhasa.
Universities Act.
1905. Russo-Japanese War.
Partition of Bengal: political unrest.
Resignation of Lord Curzon.

CHAPTER XX

British Rule and Indian Nationalism

PART I

BEFORE the British supremacy, two empires, the Maurya and the Mogul, had approached universal stabilized sovereignty. The Mauryas sprang from the soil of India, and in their ancient realm, whose North-West Frontier was the Hindu Kush, sectarian strife was unknown. The Mogul domination of the sixteenth and seventeenth centuries was Moslem, and alien to the peoples of India; and only the toleration of Akbar and his immediate successors brought a truce to religious enmity which had split the country for five hundred years.

The administration of both empires involved an enormous body of officials, but there was always personal contact between king and people—that visible and direct exercise of supreme authority associated with Oriental rule. The greatest of the Mauryas had heard the causes of his people during his daily massage; Akbar's day began at sunrise with his first appearance to the crowds eagerly awaiting the arbiter of their destinies; the most tyrannical of the Moguls would sit among his subjects granting petitions with a smile, or ordering an instant execution.

Asoka's " drum of piety " and Akbar's military power tempered with mercy gave security to a sub-continent whose history for the eighteen intervening centuries had been largely a stark record of invasion and conquest. Chaos returned on the disruption of the Mogul Empire. Then, with the opening years of the nineteenth century, a new era began in which there were to be two Indias, the

Indian India of the princes, and the European administration of British India, both within the security of the British Empire.

British dominion was founded by traders turned soldiers and administrators. There was at first no feeling of racial superiority but, unlike the earlier conquerors, the English did not settle in the country and identify themselves with its peoples. In British India, as it expanded, the live contact for good or ill of an Oriental despot was replaced by a form of crown colony government in which no Indian had a voice.

European Bureaucracy. For the last seventy-four years of the East India Company supreme authority over British India lay between its court of Directors of merchants and retired Company servants, and the "Board of Commissioners for the Affairs of India," consisting of the Chancellor of the Exchequer, a secretary of state and four privy councillors. This board of control in practice meant its president, who was virtually secretary of state for India, although the Board was not normally an originating but a revising body.[1] Though called a "board of interference" by Dalhousie, the authorities in London rarely imposed a policy upon the administration at Calcutta. In the background, after 1773, Parliament gradually increased a rather spasmodic supervision.

Supreme authority was taken over by the Crown in 1858, but until the Red Sea cable was laid in 1870 the Government of India was remote from control. From then onwards, when it came to the point, decisions depended upon whether the Viceroy or the secretary of state was the stronger, with the odds steadily increasing in favour of the secretaries of state, none of whom visited India until 1917. But it was an ex-Viceroy—and that statesman Lord Curzon—who added "responsible government" to the scheme for reform.[2] This meant Parliamentary democracy, a method of government new to the country, and bound sooner or later to affect the Indian States.

Under the Indian Civil Service Act of 1861 the pick of the Civil Service examinations—the successors of the early revenue-collecting agents and the later Haileybury cadets—came out to serve their time

[1] *A Constitutional History of India*, A. Berriedale Keith (London, 1936), p. 98.
[2] *Life of Lord Curzon*, Vol. III. pp. 167, 168.

ⁱn India with impartial justice, sympathy and integrity, but from an inevitable European standpoint. Handicapped by the regulations there were only four Indians in the I.C.S. in 1871,[1] and in 1904 only 92 held posts in their own country worth over £800 a year in a total list of 1370 higher officials. This hardly bore out the promise of 1833. The exclusion of Indians from high responsible appointments—both civil and military—in British India for a succession of generations could not fail to have a deteriorating effect upon their manhood and self-respect. It entirely disabled Sir Thomas Munro's hopes in 1824 that the peoples under British rule would be trained " to govern and protect themselves."

There were, on the other hand, 21,700 Indians in subordinate posts in the Government of India, in a list of 28,300. This *bloc* of educated men, chiefly Bengalis, thankfully accepted things as they were until saturation point was passed in posts open through the matriculation examination of the Indian Universities and the serious lack of employment and discontent among these graduates began.

Every five years a new Viceroy landed at Bombay to fill the most splendid of imperial appointments and represent a supreme authority which was unapproachable, impersonal and aloof from all religious differences. His council, until 1909 brought the first step in constitutional reform, was entirely European.

The whole system was a guardianship, unparalleled in its magnitude and efficient control, of Asiatics who had neither responsibility nor influence in the conduct of their own affairs. Whatever else British dominion may or may not have done, it set up a standard of absolute justice between Indian and Indian and guaranteed internal peace, and security from invasion. But to Hindu leaders of thought like Rabindranath Tagore the rule of earlier foreign conquerors was " a mere drift on the surface of her life. This time it was the Nation of the West driving the tentacles of its machinery deep down into the soil." [2] This machine-like administration reached the height of its efficiency under Curzon.

---

[1] Under the Act of 1935 the I.C.S. cadre at the end of 1938 was 599 Europeans and 587 Indians, on a rising proportion of the latter.

[2] *Nationalism* (3rd imp. 1918), p. 8.

But another factor was coming into play. In the security of
Growth of the British power and with English as the common
Nationalism. medium of expression among the educated classes,
small groups in British India, influenced by western
thought and action, were awakening to political ambitions which
found their voice in the Indian National Congress. They could
trace the development of responsible government in England which
began with the Reform Bill of 1832. They could study the " passion
for self-government . . . the riot of new constitutions . . . the force
of the gale that swept the Continent in 1848 [and] ended the age
of Metternich." Nor, in the twentieth century, could an ever-
widening circle of politically minded Indians fail to be impressed
by the sequence of events in Ireland.

For half a century British rule in India had not been violently
challenged. The Home Rule movement of Indian Liberalism,
which was on strictly constitutional lines, had effected no change
in the form of government. But left-wing Nationalists were of
different temper. They meant war to the knife for complete independence, and they took full advantage of the discontent which
sprang from various causes.

Curzon, whole-heartedly devoted to improving the conditions of
the silent masses of rural India, was frigidly uninterested in the
political opinions due to English education. In his whirlwind drive
to improve the government by greater centralization, he openly
declared that the efficiency he demanded was only possible by reserving the higher posts for Englishmen. Moreover, he could see
nothing in the national leaders but the personal ambitions of a few
men to gain place and power. His remodelling of the Calcutta
corporation, his university policy and, above all, his partition of
Bengal, fanned the political discontent which was becoming increasingly evident when Lord Minto succeeded him in 1905.

There were other causes of unrest. One of the most galling to
Indians whose outlook had been widened by education and travel,
were the rigid restrictions of the Arms Act passed by Lord Lytton,
which applied to pure-bred Indians only. Another was the system of
indentured emigration, which gave an impression that Indians had an

inferior status among the subjects of the King-Emperor. Far from being responsible for this, the Government of India as represented by Lord Hardinge, supported the Indians in South Africa—a cause championed by Gandhi with his " potential *satyagraha*," non-violent passive resistance; and some remedial measures were eventually taken.

There were also, among those ignorant of India's history, art and philosophy, disgraceful manifestations of the attitude that " the average Englishman considers himself to be superior to the average Indian, and the latter is generally content to be so considered " [1]; an inflated racial estimate not limited to " natives " but reinforced by colour prejudice that was much in evidence in Victorian England. The feeling of racial superiority over Indians may have begun when steam " brought England to India " in 1825 and Englishmen abandoned those ways of the country that they had previously followed. It was fostered by the British policy of excluding Indians from positions of authority in the services, and it was encouraged by the domination of the materialist ideas and achievements of the West over the ancient civilization of India.

But, on the other hand, the startling victories in 1904-5 of Oriental Japan over Russia—the bugbear of British foreign policy for seventy years—helped to adjust an Indian inferiority complex and strongly encouraged the Nationalist movement. The educated classes began to dwell upon the past greatness of Asiatic peoples and to assert the superiority of Indian culture over that of Europe at a time when the mechanical inventions brought in by the British were losing their earlier impressiveness.

Gokhale, a statesman of rare ability and insight, urged that the educated classes could only be conciliated by associating them more and more with the government of their own country, a policy to which England was pledged.[2] Minto sympathized with these views. In 1906 a committee considered such questions as a council of princes, an Indian member of council, and greater scope in Budget debates.

---

[1] *Mahatma Gandhi, Life, Writings and Speeches* (2nd Edn., Madras, 1918), p. 180.

[2] G. K. Gokhale, in the Budget debate of 1906.

The King's Speech at the opening of Parliament in 1907 gave the first hint of Indian reform.

Unrest. By this time grave disturbances were breaking out in different parts of the country. At the beginning of the century the system of gymnastic societies, which had started in Bombay, was taken up in Bengal. Hindu middle-class lads—for the movement included neither Moslem nor peasant—were enrolled to become compromised, after an initial training in the highest standards of moral purity, in revolutionary conspiracy.

The degeneration betrayed in the gangster methods of the terrorists is as deplorable as it is tragic. For a protest against excessive westernization and a revival of the soul and the ancient culture of Hindu India—the ideals of Tagore and of Gandhi—lay at the root of the revolution in Bengal. It was largely to counter what had become a dangerous threat to public order that Curzon partitioned that province. But the storm burst in 1907 with aggravated fury, and the revolutionary wing of young political India sought to justify cold-blooded murder as the warfare of a legitimate government and robbery with violence as tax-collecting.[1] Inflammatory meetings became frequent in Calcutta, where an attempt was made to assassinate the lieutenant-governor—a prelude to the attempts upon Minto and Hardinge. There were riots in Madras. In the Punjab the local government had handled the Chenab canal colony with less than its usual wisdom and something distinctly like a breach of faith. A number of anti-British meetings were held; and in April and May of 1907 serious riots occurred at Lahore and Rawalpindi. The Government met the situation with the Seditious Meetings Act.

Communal feeling was running high in Eastern Bengal. The Moslems of the new province had viewed the partition from a very different angle than the Hindus. They were against the violent agitation and the boycott of British goods, and vigorously opposed intimidation and terrorism. In May 1907 there was a general rising of the Moslem peasantry in Mymensingh district against their Hindu landlords and creditors.

[1] See *Young India*, Lajpat Rai (New York, 2nd Edn. 1917), pp. 187–189, 211, 212.

The formula " Swaraj " had been adopted in 1906 to keep Congress united. The Liberals meant by this Home Rule by constitutional means, while the left wing meant a fight for independence. This led to a violent split at the election of a president in 1907. The moderates then kept control of the organization, and Tilak led the extremists into the wilderness, where they remained until 1916, after Gokhale's death.

Congress and Extremists.

Bal Gangadhar Tilak had been the most determined opponent of the unpopular segregation regulations during the plague epidemic of 1896–7 in Bombay. A Chitpavan Brahman, as were the Peshwas, he used the cult of the Maratha Sivaji against two alien civilizations by recalling past Moslem defeats and by inflaming public opinion against British rule. His weapons were his newspaper the *Kesari* and the youth movement. Though defeated in Congress, his campaign in the Deccan for " national schools " and temperance, combined with anti-government propaganda, attracted hosts of followers. This ended with his trial and imprisonment for an article published in the *Kesari* on political murder.

Confronted with widespread defiance of authority, the Government resorted to deportation and the enforcement of the Regulation of 1818, equivalent to the suspension of the Habeas Corpus Act in Great Britain. Minto also passed the Indian Newspapers Act in 1908, which was followed in 1910 by the Press Act, legislation which emphasized Sir Thomas Munro's views nearly a century earlier.[1]

A comparison between 1878 and 1938 shows the growing influence of the Press in modern India. In 1878 the largest circulation of any Indian newspaper was 5000 copies.[2] In 1938, to take two examples only, the Bengali daily *Ananda Bazaar Patrika* averaged over 65,000 and the Madras *Hindu* (printed in English) about 35,000 copies ; figures that bear to the number of readers alone at the least the same proportion that British broadcasting licences bear to the number of listeners.

---

[1] See p. 442.
[2] *Proceedings of the Council of the Governor-General of India*, Vol. XVII. (1879), p. 177.

Before the Indian Councils Act brought in the Morley-Minto

Moslem Representation. reforms, Moslem deputations claimed separate representation. They urged that communal tension would make it impossible for a genuine Moslem representative to be successful in a mixed constituency, as they were in a minority [1] in all except two provinces; and that riots at the polls could only be avoided by separate electorates, as adopted by municipalities and district boards. To this they added the political importance of their community and its contribution to Imperial defence.

Replying in 1906 to the deputation led by the Aga Khan,[2] the Viceroy made the first official acknowledgment of the Moslem claim for separate representation, a statement held by that community as a definite pledge.[3] The Government of India accordingly proposed, and in this they had Gokhale's support, that except where special protection was unnecessary, Moslems should have separate electorates. This did not appeal to the democratic instincts of the Secretary of State. But the insistent claims of the largest minority unit in India could not be denied.[4] After hearing a deputation of the All-India Moslem League in January 1909, Morley accepted the Moslem claim, a recognition of communal representation which has survived intense and unremitting Hindu disagreement.

The Indian Councils Act of 1909 began constitutional reform.

The Morley-Minto Reforms. But it was in no sense democratic, for Morley had said he would have nothing to do with Parliamentary government,[5] and the secretary of state, with his constitutional responsibility to the British Parliament, was still the controlling authority. Nor was the new Indian element large enough to make their position in the councils more than advisory. But it was a genuine attempt to bring educated Indian opinion in

---

[1] In British India Moslems formed 24·16 of the population (*Census Report*, 1901).

[2] Aga Sultan Sir Muhammad Shah, whose grandfather was given the title by Fateh Ali Shah of Persia (1795–1834). The Aga Khan is head of the Ismail Moslems of East Africa, Central Asia and India.

[3] *Life of Lord Minto*, pp. 243, 244, John Buchan (Lord Tweedsmuir).

[4] *The Indian Horizon*, The Maharajadhiraja of Burdwan, p. 16.

[5] House of Lords, 17th December 1908.

touch with the Government; and this bore fruit in the work done by Indian members to improve legislation.

In the provincial legislative councils the official majority disappeared under the " additional " members who were chiefly the selected representatives of local authorities, large landowners, trade associations, universities and special Moslem members.

The central legislative council was greatly enlarged, noticeably by non-official election from the provincial councils. But the secretary of state justified retaining an official majority on the grounds that the governor-general's council " should continue to be so constituted as to ensure its constant and uninterrupted power to fulfil the constitutional obligations that it owes, and always must owe, to His Majesty's Government and to the Imperial Parliament." [1]

Morley, who had already admitted two Indians to his own council, agreed to the appointment of an Indian to the governor-general's council, and S. P. Sinha,[2] a distinguished Hindu barrister, was made legal member.

Minto's policy was to bring the princes into a united front against political discontent and violence. His revival of Lytton's scheme for an advisory council of rulers and great landowners presented difficulties and came to nothing, but he consulted the leading princes on the spread of sedition in some of the States. In reaffirming their relations with the Paramount power, he pointed out that in Imperial matters, such as railways, telegraphs and other services, the Government had to safeguard the whole of India.[3]

The Indian States.

Minto's viceroyalty, which ended in November 1910, was summed up by Mrs. Besant, the left-wing Nationalist: " He tried to draw the two nations together in spite of the difficulties. He inherited many sad traditions, and the wave of life sweeping over India showed itself in many objectionable forms. He rightly struck down violence, but did not refuse the gift of self-government. . . . In the midst

[1] *Indian Statutory Commission Report*, Vol. I. pp. 117–119, 183–187.
[2] Afterwards 1st Lord Sinha ; made governor of Bihar and Orissa in 1920.
[3] Speech at Udaipur, Nov. 1909 (*Report of the Indian States Committee*, 1928–1929, p. 19).

of danger and criticism . . . (with) flawless justice and perfect courage (he) laid the foundations of self-government within the Empire. Of his own initiative, taking full responsibility, he set free the deportees." [1]

The Imperial Durbar. During Lord Hardinge's viceroyalty the King-Emperor George V and Queen Mary visited India. Their Coronation Durbar was held at Delhi on 12th December 1911, when the ruling princes did homage. The occasion was marked by grants of land, a large gift for education, release of prisoners, extra pay to the Indian Army ranks and the lower grades of the civil service, and the Indian Army was declared eligible for the Victoria Cross.

The opportunity was taken to announce two momentous decisions reached by the Viceroy, the secretary of state (Lord Crewe) and the Asquith cabinet, decisions which came as a surprise to Parliament, whose sanction it had not been thought necessary to ask. The first was to make a new capital at Delhi with an enclave free from provincial pressure. The other decision was a rearrangement of the eastern provinces which reunited the two Bengals. To the Hindu left-wing politician " the annulment of the partition helped to assuage public feelings, and anti-Government agitation subsided to a large extent " [2]; while Moslem opinion bluntly expressed itself at Delhi in the penetrating comment " No bombs, no boons." [3]

The War of 1914–1918. The World War broke out in August 1914. The magnificent response of British and Indian India was a total of 1,302,000 combatants and non-combatants to the Imperial forces. Indian troops acquitted themselves gallantly in the mud and cold of Flanders, in East Africa, in Palestine, and faced the disasters of the earlier mismanagement in Mesopotamia.

In recognition of her services in the war, India's representatives were treated on an equal footing with the Dominions in the Imperial War conferences, the Imperial War Cabinet of 1917, in the peace

---

[1] *Life of Lord Minto*, p. 320.
[2] *The Indian Struggle*, Subhas C. Bose (London, 1935), p. 22.
[3] A widely circulated remark quoted by Keith, *op. cit.*, p. 234.

negotiations and in separate membership of the League of Nations. By this the Home Government " virtually, though not technically, bound itself to the task of creating a self-governing India which would be entitled on the same basis as the Dominions to vote freely in the business of the League." [1] In 1916 Congress had called upon Great Britain to announce that a " self-governing India is the goal of her policy, and grant us a substantial instalment of reform after the war as a step towards that goal." [2] This resolution was moved by Surendranath Bannerjea and supported by Tilak, now restored to the fold, and by Mrs. Besant.

The entry of Turkey on the side of the Central European Powers greatly disturbed the Moslem community. Until *Moslems and the Great War* 1914-18. about the close of the nineteenth century the average Indian Moslem had at least subconsciously " looked upon himself as a member of a universal religious brotherhood, sojourning in a land in which a neutral government, with a neutral outlook, kept law and order and justice. His political and communal pride was satisfied by the fact that his co-religionists in Turkey, Persia, Morocco and (nominally at least) in Egypt, enjoyed independence and national sovereignty. While his allegiance was to the British Crown, his political self-respect was satisfied by the existence of the Sultans at Constantinople and Fez and of the Shah and Khedive at Teheran and Cairo. . . . (Moreover) the British Government was the mainstay and support in the diplomatic arena of the independent Mahomedan States. . . . Within a generation the whole Mahomedan world-outlook changed. Forces beyond Moslem control led to the disappearance of Mahomedan rule and independence in North Africa. Persia gradually drifted into being a mere name for spheres of influence between Britain and Russia. Turkey herself, the last of the independent Mahomedan dominions, was drawn into the Teutonic orbit, first through economic and semi-political causes and finally by her participation in the Great War on the German side." [3]

---

[1] *A Constitutional History of India*, see pp. 460–476.
[2] *Growth and Development of National Thought in India*, Ishwar Nath Topa (Hamburg, 1930), pp. 170, 171.
[3] *India in Transition*, H.H. The Aga Khan (1918), pp. 22, 23.

To continue the story. When the helpless Sultan Mehmed V signed the treaty of Sevres in August 1920 the whole of Turkey that was not occupied by the Allies was in the hands of Mustapha Kemal, leader of the Grand National Assembly at Angora. In November 1922 the Sultanate was abolished, and just under a year later Turkey became a republic with Mustapha Kemal (Ataturk) as its first president. Represented by one transient figure after another, the Khalifate survived until the 31st March 1924 when, by vote of the Assembly, there was no longer a Commander of The Faithful and Shadow of God upon Earth. In 1928 Islam ceased to be the State religion of Turkey.

The peace conditions and the part taken by the British Government (Montagu dissenting) were deeply resented by Moslem India. The Khilafat movement, which grew in strength with its organized agitation against the peace terms with Turkey, was unfortunately responsible for the tragic attempt to find a new home under Islam in Afghanistan for some 18,000 Moslems from Sind and the North-West Frontier Province. But its position was soon weakened as regards political Hinduism by communal outbreaks, and was completely undermined when the Khalifate was abolished. The All-India Moslem League then emerged from temporary eclipse.

In 1916 a spirit of compromise hovered over political India.
Communalism. Moderates and extremists appeared on the same platform; and what meant more to the Nationalist cause, an alliance was made between Congress and the All-India Moslem League. In December 1916 the Lucknow pact settled the proportionate representation of Hindus and Moslems on the provincial and central legislative councils.

But this did not end communal trouble. In 1915 and 1916 there had been serious rioting in the Patna district over cow-sacrifice at the Bakr-id festival. In 1917 there was a bad recurrence in a neighbouring district, when large Hindu mobs wrecked Moslem villages. Order was only restored by calling out nearly 2000 police and troops. After a savage outbreak in the United Provinces in 1918 a religious truce lasted for about four years.

Until commerce became the absorbing interest of Europe, wars on account of religion were not uncommon. In England the Pilgrimage of Grace, in Scotland the Covenanting movement, were born of the strength and sincerity of religious convictions. In India religion is still the strongest influence in the lives of the people—quiet, hard-working, naturally law-abiding folk, in whose villages Hindu and Moslem are seen living peaceably together. But the curse put on India by Mahmud of Ghazni, and quickened by the bigotry of Aurangzeb to the doom of an empire, has hung through the centuries over the land. Nor is it laid yet. Communal disturbances led Shah Alam II to appoint the East India Company as his vice-regent at Surat; and such outbreaks remain to this day a serious problem to responsible authority. In the cities the clash of movable Hindu and Muhammadan festivals, the music of a Hindu procession passing a mosque, disputes about religious buildings and, above all, the Moslem killing of the Hindu sacred animal, the cow, are all fertile causes of trouble. It is the absolute impartiality between warring creeds of the stolid British soldier on which the local authorities still rely when some provocation has caused religious riot and bloodshed.

In August 1917 Edwin Montagu, who had become secretary of state for India in July, announced in Parliament that the Government policy was "the increasing association of Indians in every branch of the administration and the gradual development of self-governing institutions with a view to the progressive realization of responsible government in India as an integral part of the British Empire." The Home Government and the Government of India were to be judges of the time and measure of each advance.

Reform and Political Unrest.

There followed the secretary of state's visit to India to confer with Lord Chelmsford; and when the Montagu-Chelmsford Report [1] (with emphasis on the secretary of state) was published in July 1918 the parliamentary stage was set for the new Government of India Act.

Meanwhile, unrest in India had grown far more serious than at the time of the Morley-Minto reforms; and events conspired to make the situation still more critical. The moderate party dis-

[1] Cmd. 9109 of 1918.

satisfied, Moslem feeling perturbed by the weakening of Turkish power in Europe, and their confidence in the Government shaken by the reunion of Bengal, terrorism rampant—such was the situation when war broke out in Europe.

New dangers soon threatened from the east to the west of India. In February 1915 a shipload of Punjabis, with a grievance against the Canadian immigration laws, and inflamed by the Ghadr party,[1] were sent back to Calcutta. A collision with the local police was followed by abortive attempts at revolt in the Punjab and at Benares, while Ghadr agents tampered with the loyalty of Indian troops and military police in Burma. Across the North-West Frontier members of the Moslem Khilafat organization were plotting with the Turco-German mission in Kabul.

In the extremist view the " First War of Independence " had been in 1857 and the terrorism of 1907 opened the Second.[2] Strong measures, however unpopular, were in the circumstances unavoidable, if the Government were to carry out its most elementary duty, and the Defence of India Act (1915) was passed to bring revolutionary offenders to trial, without appeal, and to intern suspects.

In 1916 Mrs. Besant left her religious and educational work in Madras for a " raging and tearing " Home Rule campaign in support of Tilak. Throughout the country a deep mistrust in British promises was created " despite earnest effort to redeem them." [3] And this at a time when it was no longer possible to say that educated India exercised no influence on the masses whom Gandhi hopefully believed " were widely penetrated with the desire for Home Rule." [4]

When the Montagu-Chelmsford report reached India in 1918 its outline of immediate provincial reform with " responsible government " as the end in view was welcomed by the Liberals, who looked

[1] *Ghadr* (mutiny), the name of a newspaper started in San Francisco in 1913 to attack the Government of India.

[2] *The Indian Struggle*, pp. 20, 30, 31, 33. But see *Autobiography: Jawaharlal Nehru* (London, 1936), p. 315, for what is the responsible Congress view on the wrongfulness, futility and harm of terrorism.

[3] *A Nation in Making*, p. 333.

[4] *My Experiments with Truth*, Vol. II. pp. 460–461, and *Mahatma Gandhi, Life, Writings and Speeches*, pp. 365, 366.

upon opposition as "treason against the Motherland." But the scheme was greeted with angry disappointment by the left wing. They "captured the machinery," the moderates disappeared from Congress [1] and the extremists embarked, as the Nationalist party, upon what had become the stormy sea of Indian politics.

With the revolutionary movement clearly gaining ground a committee advised what are termed, after its chairman a British judge, the Rowlatt Bills, to counter it. One of these, the Anarchical and Revolutionary Crimes Act, was passed in 1919, when the war period was over, and led to the most serious situation India had known since 1857. On the one hand was the Government responsible for law and order, and determined to enforce it. On the other, nationalist feeling was expressed in Gandhi's outburst that, on the published evidence, the Bills were "unwarranted and such that no self-respecting people could submit to them." [2] Gandhi headed the opposition with his non-violent passive resistance.

The Coming of Gandhi.

But its author had made his "Himalayan miscalculation" of the behaviour of an excited mob, which observance of the old Indian *hartal*, or day of fasting and abstention from business, did nothing to allay. In March and April 1919 there was much rioting in Western India, where industrialism was notorious for outrageous profiteering and the shocking condition of the workers, and in the agricultural Punjab, where the pressure of recruiting had been especially severe; while in April relations with Afghanistan became so strained by the Amir's instigation of the frontier tribes that war came in May and the wave of border unrest broke in Waziristan in the most determined and critical fighting ever seen on the North-West Frontier.

The internal situation had come to a head in the Punjab when a meeting held in the Jallianwalla Bagh, Amritsar, on 13th April, in defiance of General Dyer's orders, was broken up with the loss of 379 killed and over 1200 wounded, casualties irrefutably beyond the action necessary to disperse the assembly. What was, to any observer, practically a state of war in the Punjab, instantly subsided, order

---

[1] *A Nation in Making*, pp. 312–314, 305–308.
[2] *My Experiments with Truth*, Vol. II. p. 478.

was restored and mob atrocities ceased. But the shock of the action taken aroused amongst Indians throughout the country a feeling of horror and of racial bitterness unknown for sixty years.

In this atmosphere the Montagu-Chelmsford reforms were made law, and came into force two years later.

The Act classified the departments of government as central and provincial, and divided provincial subjects into *Government of* "reserved" and "transferred," a distribution of *India Act*, 1919. responsibility labelled dyarchy. It ended "one-man government" in the provinces and established an elected majority in the central legislature.

The governor-general's executive council was unaltered and the Viceroy, with his foreign secretary, and his political secretary for the Indian States, continued a principle of control over these affairs begun under Warren Hastings.

The Indian legislative council was divided into two chambers, the council of state and the legislative assembly. In each the elected members outnumbered the officials and the nominated non-official representatives.

In the provinces [1] the governor was given an executive council of four (or two) members appointed by the Crown, half of whom were in practice Indians. This council dealt with the "reserved" subjects and was not responsible to the provincial legislative council. Ministers appointed by the governor and responsible to the legislative council dealt with the "transferred" subjects such as education, health and local self-government. The governor could veto measures or certify and pass Bills in spite of an adverse vote.

Less than one-third of the legislative council were British or Indian civil servants appointed by the governor and his nominations to represent minorities and special interests, such as the depressed classes and labour. The other members were elected, originally, by

[1] Madras, Bombay, Bengal, the United Provinces, the Punjab, Bihar and Orissa, the Central Provinces, Assam, Burma (1923) and the North-West Frontier Province (1931); other areas being under commissioners responsible to the Government of India.

limited enfranchisement of the adult male population. Although all the provinces gave votes later to women, and the Madras legislature elected a lady deputy president, the masses in general and most women were debarred by the property qualification.

The governor-general, as an over-riding safeguard, could certify measures and expenditure, withhold consent to central and provincial Bills, and in a case of emergency could rule by ordinance for not more than six months. If, in fact, he judged the safety of British India to be involved, his personal decision became that of the Government of India. But he remained statutorily answerable to the British Parliament through the secretary of state, whose orders he was required (and through him the provincial governors) to carry out.

As a stage towards self-government the Act gave Indians their first opening since 1773 to take a responsible share in the administration of British India, and justify further reforms by their wisdom and capacity. But the time was out of joint. Indian politicians, the Moderate Hindu Liberals excepted, dwelt on the restrictions of the safeguards rather than the new freedom to adopt policies wholly in India's interests, limited though these might be at this stage. Dyarchy proved a disappointing constitutional compromise. But, what was more unfortunate, both Hindus and Moslems saw the Act as a golden, and perfectly legal, opportunity to dominate the other, and this inflamed the communal tension existing in British India.

In 1921 the Chamber of Princes was established. The individual relations between States and the Paramount power

The Indian States.

were no concern of the Chamber, nor had it any executive powers. But it gave the Viceroy a recognized advisory body on Indian State matters generally and on those affecting all India, while it brought the princes into consultation on Imperial affairs.

This was a promising link between the princes and the Paramount power. But the smallest States were entirely unrepresented, the most important cold-shouldered it, other rulers began to withdraw, and within fifteen years what could have been the one common platform for the princes had practically collapsed.

British Rule and Indian Nationalism

PART II

Nationalist aspirations had grown with the years. They began with self-government within the Empire. Then left-wing views gained ground and "Swaraj" with its different interpretations was accepted by Congress. To Gandhi it originally meant "self-government within the British Empire if possible and without it if necessary."[1] This was eventually to quicken, when Japan was at the gates, into a demand for immediate freedom in which, Britain having "quitted" the country, India would frame her own constitution; an aim which became the key to Congress policy and action. Meanwhile communal antagonism had culminated in the equally uncompromising policies of the Moslem League (in 1940) for a "national homeland" in Pakistan and of Congress for an undivided India. In 1905, the Indian Liberal demands for self-government might have formed the basis for agreed constitutional reform, but "*post est occasio calva*" and now it was too late.

While all parties in India, and eventually in Britain, were agreed that self-government was the objective, the British Government was weighted by its responsibilities towards the country as a whole; and the spectacle of the Indian political arena came with increasing force to impose the question whether Britain had the moral right to leave India to so grave a risk of civil war and anarchy. But to Congress an advance by stages to the freedom of Dominion status seemed only to be an insincere and reluctant policy of appeasement conceded under pressure; and British guardianship of minority interests, specifically of the Moslem community, and the Crown obligations to the States, were stigmatized as the old device, "Divide and Rule," displayed upon the Union Jack.

The transformation in Indian politics was seen in the Amritsar Congress of 1919. Pandit Motilal Nehru, representative of the finest type of Hindu politician, and previously a moderate, was elected

[1] *My Experiments with Truth*, Vol. II. (1929), p. 585.

president.   But the inspiration of the Congress party, now predominantly Hindu, was Gandhi, its masterful leader for the years to come.

Mohandas Karamchand Gandhi was just fifty when he became
the greatest and at times the most perplexing figure in modern India.
He belonged to a Vaisya family of Kathiawar and had qualified for
the Bar in England.   His future was foreshadowed in his champion-
ship of his fellow-countrymen in South Africa.   On his return to
India he resolutely took up the cause of the indigo peasant-cultivators
in Bihar.   The outbreak of the World War saw him enthusiastically
conducting a recruiting campaign for the British; within a year of
the armistice he was the outstanding leader of nationalist India.

The main influences on a character to the highest degree autocratic,
unworldly in its idealism, and incapable of selling the truth to serve
the hour, were the strict Vaishnavist rules of his home, the spirituality
of the *Bhagavad Gita* which he studied as a young man, and the teaching of Christ on poverty and riches.[1]   With a personality that could
inspire almost overwhelming reverence, the strength of his religious
convictions and the abandonment of everything save the practice
of what he preached gave the Mahatma his power ; a power over
the masses which no political mistakes or inconsistencies could
undermine.

His outlook is shown by his views on caste.   As Gandhi saw it,
the right of the higher castes to wear the sacred thread and the
tuft of hair symbolic of spiritual regeneration could only come
" after Hinduism has purged itself of untouchability and . . . removed
all distinctions of superiority and inferiority." [2]   He told his fellow-
countrymen, " We are guilty of having suppressed our brethren;
we make them crawl on their bellies; we have made them rub their
noses on the ground; with eyes red with rage we push them out of
railways' compartments—what more than this has British rule done?
What charge that we bring against Dyer and O'Dwyer,[3] may not

[1] *E.g.* " On Economic versus Moral Progress," *Life, Writings and Speeches*,
pp. 223–225.

[2] *My Experiments with Truth*, Vol. II. p. 329.   Vaishnavism, which is strong
in Bengal, has done much to lessen rigid caste distinctions.

[3] Sir Michael O'Dwyer, Lieutenant-Governor of the Punjab during the
critical years 1913–1919.

others, and even our own people, lay at our doors? . . . It is idle
to talk of ' Swaraj ' so long as we do not protect the weak and the
helpless. . . . But I have faith in me still. . . . I have realized that
the spirit of kindness . . . which forms the corner-stone of the Jain
and Vaishnava religions . . . is slowly but steadily gaining ground
in the hearts of the masses of this country." [1] But to safeguard their
political rights the Depressed Classes can rely only on their own
leaders.

In 1920 Gandhi, carrying his followers with him, coalesced with
the Khilafat movement in which Maulana Muhammad Ali, the
younger of the Ali brothers, was the leading spirit. The opposition
to British government was now united. Non-co-operation, used as
a political and not a personal protest against the visit of the Prince
of Wales in the cold weather of 1921, brought matters to a head.
Violent meetings—instantly declared illegal—were held, there was
much rioting, and before December all the important leaders, with
the exception of Gandhi, were in jail. Tilak, with all his learning and
ability, his uncompromising aims and his immense popularity, had
died the year before.

Nevertheless, the end of the year found Congress, under Gandhi's
leadership, a well-organized body engaged in a widespread campaign
against established authority. The party had its flag of red, white and
green in horizontal bands, the red being changed later to saffron [2] ;
and congressmen wore as a uniform the coarse hand-woven cloth
known as *khadi*, an industry that Gandhi had made his own. The
situation, so far as Congress itself was concerned, was a boycott of
the Government and of foreign goods in which every province took
part, while it was most determined in Bengal.

But the weakness of a Hindu-Moslem alliance had already betrayed
itself. The Moplahs—part-Arabs of Malabar and stout-hearted
army recruits since 1902—rose in August 1921 and made victims not

[1] Speech at the Suppressed Classes Conference, Ahmedabad, 1921, *The
Bleeding Wound* (2nd Edn., Ajmer, 1932), pp. 11, 12.

[2] Saffron to represent courage and sacrifice; the white, peace and truth; green,
faith and chivalry; and the spinning-wheel in blue on the white ground, the hope of
the masses.

only of government officials, but of a number of Hindus, including women.[1] The sequel was inevitable; and on Gandhi's arrest and imprisonment early in 1922 the artificial coalition fell to pieces. Communal rioting, particularly serious in 1923 at Multan and Amritsar, in Calcutta in 1926, and at Cawnpore in 1931, has broken out at intervals ever since.

After the Moplah rising Gandhi's Hindu followers began to distrust his political wisdom, and their confidence was further shaken by the failure of his promised " Swaraj by the end of the year." Then in February 1922 the National Volunteers murdered twenty-one police officers at Chauri-Chaura by burning the police station, an outcome of his own teaching which overwhelmed the Mahatma with horror. He suspended the civil disobedience movement throughout India and confined Congress activities to village industries, removal of untouchability, the promotion of communal unity, education and the suppression of the drug traffic—peaceful constructive work which made less immediate appeal to the extremists; and this caused a split in the Congress party.

Religious disturbance in another form occurred in the Punjab. In 1920 the reforming Sikh sect of the Akalis agitated to bring their religious shrines, then controlled by the reactionary Mahants, under popular committees. Pathans employed by the Mahant of Nankana Saheb were guilty of a horrible massacre in 1921; there was tension between the rulers of Nabha and Patiala; and this matter was only set right, with the help of moderate Sikh influence, by provincial legislation in 1925.

Before describing the steps leading to the reforms of 1935, something should be said about other matters affecting the people of the country. The abnormal influenza epidemic reached India in 1918 and caused the death of thirteen million people. Four years later floods inundated four large districts in Bengal, destroying the crops and doing a crippling amount of damage. On 15th January 1934 there was a tremendous earthquake in North Bihar, in which 7253

---

[1] For a vigorous indictment of Gandhi and his policy see *Gandhi and Anarchy*, Sir Sankaran Nair (Madras, 2nd Edn. 1922).

people were killed, and had it occurred at night the death roll would have been enormous. The Quetta earthquake, on the night of 31st May 1935, was an even more terrible catastrophe, in which at least about 35,000 people lost their lives and the military and air force cantonments were practically destroyed.

Financial Conditions. The Third Afghan War of three weeks' rapid action had been, in its limited scope, successful, but it had cost the Government over £16,000,000. The expense of countering revolution kept rising. World conditions were neurotic and helped to influence the fall of the rupee from three shillings to about half that figure. In 1927 the rupee was stabilized at 1s. 6d., although strongly opposed by the western Indian cotton manufacturers, who wanted a 1s. 4d. rate. The Indian commercial magnates at once went over to Congress and began to give that party their influential support.

Without money, nation-building was impossible. Although Congress had boycotted the 1920 elections, about one-third of the electorate had gone to the polls. But with little to allot to the newly-appointed ministers for social services, and with weak departmental control, this first stage towards responsible government was disappointing.

Agriculture. The agrarian problem of India is as great as the number of her peasantry, whose sixty million families represent more than three-fourths of the whole population. Nothing could be less economical than the traditional methods of farming, ploughing with oxen and harvesting with sickles the scattered fields which make up a holding averaging barely six acres. Even these are liable to reduction by "fragmentation"—the custom for each heir to take a share of every field wherever situated. Nothing could be more ominous for the future than the rapidity with which the population continues to multiply; it rose from about 305,700,000 in 1921 to 389,000,000 twenty years later. Nor have the closely restricted conditions under which Indians have been permitted to emigrate to other parts of the British Empire, nor the policy of foreign governments, made it possible to relieve by these means the ever-rising pressure upon the land. The only practical large-scale relief for land hunger was to be found in government irrigation schemes, the Lloyd barrage being the largest work of its kind in the world, which had added by 1935 nearly 32 million to the acres cropped in British India, an increase of about 15 per cent.

The Indian peasant—he can hardly be called a farmer—grows food crops primarily for his own needs and sells the surplus. Consequently it is from the narrow margins of millions of small peasant growers that the impressive totals of India's agricultural production are derived. Living as he has done through the centuries on the verge of destitution, he is too often forced to sell a portion even of his bare subsistence needs to meet his land revenue and salt tax, pacify the inevitable money-lender and find cash for sheer necessities. Harder still is the lot of the village Untouchables, working as farm hands on land they may not hold, or earning their daily bread in some employment which spells pollution to the caste Hindu.

To improve peasant conditions an Act was passed in 1904 which started co-operative societies. The practical value of this self-supporting and self-controlled movement can be measured by its growth, notably in the Punjab and, among the larger States which took it up, in Gwalior and Bhopal.[1] The co-operative societies opened savings banks, encouraged cattle and mule breeding, began to reassure a suspicious peasantry with the object of merging fragmented holdings into "pool" farms, sank numerous wells and converted previously waste land. But rural indebtedness, frequently inherited, continued to increase, and a generation after the Act was passed it was estimated that 90 per cent. of the credit of the country was being supplied by the money-lenders.

By the famine relief organization which a strong central government could rapidly set automatically in motion throughout British India prior to provincial autonomy, the people had at length been safeguarded from the appalling disasters that famine used to bring. But no administration can guard against floods, or prevent acute

---

[1] By 1937 there were 94,243 societies in British India, of which 81,427 were purely agricultural; and 16,985 in the Indian States, 14,481 being agricultural. For the Punjab see *Report on Co-operative Societies in the Punjab* (Lahore, 1938).

agricultural depression such as occurred with the slump of 1929. It can legislate and, in times of distress, help with money. The Agricultural Research Institute was founded in 1903; and the Imperial Council of Agricultural Research, formed in 1929, offered such benefits as a yearly income of under £130,000 could furnish.[1] But the difficulty of radically improving farming methods when the grants of money available have to benefit so colossal a number of peasants can be gauged by an annual expenditure of $1\frac{1}{4}$d. per head of the population on agricultural and veterinary services.

While the number of people living on the land is far more than required for proper cultivation, there are various ways in which the peasant can add to his slender and precarious cash earnings. The most obvious are the age-old cottage industries. Weaving for individual and locally needed designs in particular [2] (hand-spinning cannot compete with the mills), glass-ware and handmade paper, bring money into the homes, and many suitable occupations were encouraged by the rural reconstruction campaigns courageously started by Mahatma Gandhi and F. L. Brayne of the Indian Civil Service.

Farming is at a standstill for at least four months in the year, and peasants by the hundred thousand flock to the factories for temporary employment, especially in seasonal industries such as cotton ginning, cotton and jute pressing and rice milling. Time-honoured customs and conventions as to women do not encourage enterprise, while the traditional organization, which is the bed-rock of village life, restricts cultivators who wish to make money in other employments. Agriculture must inevitably remain the predominating industry of India, although with the economic expansion of the twentieth century [3] the people of the country became more factory-minded. But the develop-

[1] *Foodgrains Policy Committee Report*, 1943, p. 27.
[2] In the year 1913-14 60 per cent. cotton piece goods were imported, 20 per cent. from Indian mills, 20 per cent. hand-loom production ; in 1936-37 13 per cent. were imported, 61 per cent. were from Indian mills and 26 per cent. from the hand-looms. (Authority, S. Lall, Deputy High Commissioner for India).
[3] For an authoritative survey of India's industrial development see Vol. II. *Indian Economics*, by G. B. Jathar and S. G. Beri (Oxford University Press, 5th Ed. 1939).

ment of India's internal trade greatly depends on the systematic extension of her arterial and feeder roads as well as upon the installation of cheap and abundant electricity. More than this: it is only by the planned development of India's resources, agricultural and mineral, by the increasing technical skill of labour and by the efforts of her experienced business men, in fact through the full use of her great economic assets in the world markets, that the immense and mainly agricultural masses of India can be raised "from poverty to security; from ill-health to vigour; from ignorance to understanding." [1]

Income tax has never, since it was introduced in 1860, been the great source of revenue which it is in western industrialized countries [2]; and it is the overwhelming predominance of agriculture and the prevailing poverty of the masses that explain why Indian revenues are so largely derived from land and from taxes on consumption, the chief sources of State revenue from time immemorial. An Indian village is nearly self-supporting, and internal excises are limited to such things as salt, kerosene oil and alcoholic liquors, for which the people depend on outside supply. Tobacco, a lucrative item in British budgets, is grown in many villages, which has made the levy of an excise upon it impracticable. Agricultural incomes are exempt, but since 1886 the income-tax rate with growing industrialization has varied with budget requirements.

The British liquor policy since 1790, as restated by the Committee of 1906, was to discourage its excessive use by as high taxation as possible without stimulating illicit production. Since the Montagu-Chelmsford reforms brought excise under Indian ministers there has been a leaning towards prohibition—the policy strongly advocated by Gandhi. Liquor shops have been greatly reduced and duties raised. But, apart from the reliance of the provinces for 12 per cent. of their revenue upon the £8 millions derived from liquor excise, total prohibition seems hardly more practicable than it was in the

[1] Address by the Viceroy, Lord Wavell, to the Central Legislature, 17th February 1944.
[2] 1938-39 Central Budget estimate of £64,440,000 revenue yielded £11,250,000 in income-tax. *East India (Budget)*, 1938.

days of Aurangzeb. Illicit traffic has notably increased, and an effective prohibition policy would require the co-operation of the autonomous provinces and of the Indian States.

India presents an extreme contrast between incomes in the different classes and a grave inequality in the distribution of taxation. Large landowners in the Permanent Settlement areas of Bengal pay to the State what amounts to a rent-charge representing about a twenty-fourth of the gross value of the produce, while their agricultural income pays no income tax. There are, moreover, no death duties in India. But the much criticized settlement made by Cornwallis in 1793, considered no longer " sacrosanct," has been reviewed with the object of reform.

At the other end of the scale, the small farmer not only pays over to the State a considerable proportion of his income from land, but he bears the added burden of the duties on certain absolute necessities of life. Nor, the sugar-cane industry excepted, has the Indian tariff policy helped the agricultural interest.

Labour Conditions. The villager lives in a mud hut or bamboo shack which he and his family may share with the cattle, and ideas of sanitation and hygiene, in spite of the efforts of various local bodies, have hardly dawned on him. But in referring to the poverty and wretched conditions to be found in the country, it is impossible to leave out the appalling state of affairs that can be allowed in an Indian city, where wealth made in cotton, or jute, has built its palatial residences. An example recorded by Gandhi in November 1932 will serve.

Vile Parle is a Bombay suburb of about 1700 villas or houses inhabited by well-to-do Hindus and others. The Municipality spends 31,000 rupees of its income of Rs. 70,000 on conservancy.

" The scavengers are accommodated in quarters where there are no roads, no arrangement for water supply and no sanitary convenience. The land itself is low-lying. The huts are hovels constructed from dilapidated tins which were once used for conservancy work. There is no lighting. Near by is the dumping ground for the suburban rubbish, which gives an eternal stench.

Next to it is a structure for housing conservancy motor-lorries. Attached to this is a water-pipe for washing dirty tins, and if the overseer is well-disposed, he would allow the scavengers to help themselves to water from this pipe. On the other side is a row of carts that receive the buckets collected from the privies of householders. . . . These quarters are surrounded by fields which are often under water, breeding mosquitoes, harbouring scorpions, snakes and field rats. Thirty-one families live in this condition." [1]

The first Factory Act was passed in 1881. With the industrial expansion since 1922 legislation greatly improved conditions for factory and mine workers,[2] as for example by the Workers' Compensation Act (1923)—the first legislation in social insurance in India—and the Trades Disputes Act (1929). Conditions are often foul in small disorganized industries, and Government policy is to bring these more under supervision. But legislation has not always succeeded in raising the worker's standard of living. It has been represented that when the hours were reduced from ten to nine the cotton-mill owners of Ahmedabad promptly lowered the wages of their workers.[3] Labour conditions in the textile factories were still so intolerable in 1927–28 that violent strikes, due to the spread of communist ideas, amounted to a loss of thirty million working days.

Fiscal autonomy, always to the fore in nationalist programmes, came at the Montagu-Chelmsford stage of progress. *Tariff Reform.* The secretary of state broke away from the policy of his predecessors and conceded to the Government of India the right to make its own tariff arrangements in the interests of its own citizens.[4]

Before the World War, imported piece goods held the field in

---

[1] Pamphlet on Untouchability: *My Soul's Agony* (Bombay, 1933), pp. 57, 58.

[2] In 1894 there were 815 " defined " factories in India and Burma, employing about 350,000 ; in 1922, 5144 factories with over 1,350,000 hands.

[3] *Autobiography : Jawaharlal Nehru*, p. 589.

[4] Reply to a Lancashire deputation, 3rd March 1921, and dispatch, 30th June 1921 (*Ind. Stat. Commn. Report*, Vol. I. p. 356).

the Indian markets. But since then the policy of " discriminating protection " has increased the output of piece goods from the Indian-owned mills towards meeting home requirements.

In 1923–4 a tariff board was set up, and in 1926 the special protection given to Lancashire cotton was abolished. Four years later the cotton duties on both British and foreign goods were raised to save the Bombay mills in the world-wide trade depression. The immense interests of the Tata Iron & Steel Company at Jamshedpur have been protected from outside competition by successive Acts; and the heavy duties levied on foreign sugar from 1930 onwards have rapidly developed the cane-sugar industry in the Punjab, the United Provinces, and Bihar and Orissa. But, speaking generally, the height of existing tariffs is for revenue to balance the Budget.

Representatives of Indian commerce and industry attended the Ottawa conference called to encourage Empire trade by preferential reductions of customs duties. But the legislative assembly has remained strongly protectionist, and the Congress party is against preference.

In a country where religion, in one form or another, is a *Christianity in India.* practical reality, and to be without faith a scorn and a reproach, something must be said about Christian missions and the influence of Christianity upon Hinduism.

It is a strong tradition that Christianity came to India with St. Thomas the Apostle, and that he was martyred in Travancore in A.D. 72. About the middle of the fourth century some four hundred Syrian refugees from Persian persecution settled in Malabar, and the Christian faith has been kept alive in Southern India ever since. In 1348 the papal legate to Pekin found both Catholics and Nestorians at St. Thomé. When Vasco da Gama came to Calicut, and eight Franciscan fathers followed in 1500, there were about 20,000 Catholic families scattered along the south-west coast. This closed the Syrian period. Today the Malabar Christians belong to three different Churches. More than half a million with their Syriac liturgy are in communion with Rome; there are about 370,000 of the Orthodox Church under a bishop consecrated by the Patriarch of Antioch; and about 150,000 Reformed Syrians follow certain practices of the Anglican Church.

The sixteenth century saw the great effort to make Mogul India Christian. St. Francis Xavier of the newly-formed Society of Jesus came out to devote the last ten years of his life to missionary work in India and the Far East. A Jesuit college was founded at Salsette. Akbar, and after him Jahangir (whose reasons were material rather than spiritual), invited a succession of Jesuit fathers to live at the Imperial court. Many converts were made on the Malabar coast; and a Jesuit missionary in the depths of the country won a high place in Tamil literature by his poems.

Religious toleration was not a characteristic of the sixteenth century, as Queen Elizabeth's quietly effective measures and Alva's unforgettable atrocities each in their own way bear witness. The Portuguese in Diu confiscated mosques and diverted their revenues to Catholic institutions; they pulled down temples and built churches with the stones; they proscribed public acts of Hindu and Moslem worship in Portuguese India; and they reserved all posts and dignities to Christians. But their missionaries were devoted, a number suffered martyrdom, and before Akbar's death Christian centres were established in Agra, Delhi and Lahore which still survive. Generally speaking, Christianity was then confined to the coasts.

With the collapse of Portuguese power and influence the vision of a Christian India faded. But one point should be noticed, for it directly bears on the future of Christianity in the country. In 1637 Pope Urban VIII created vicariates independent of the Portuguese patronage, and the first of a succession of Indian bishops, the Brahman Oratorian Matthew de Castro of Goa, was made vicar apostolic of Bijapur and Golconda. In 1705 the Portuguese Viceroy gave the number of Indian secular priests on his territory as 2500.

Up to A.D. 1500 Christianity in India had been non-missionary. Since then it has been vitalized and extended by western endeavour. When the Catholic missions were sinking for a time into stagnation,

Protestant missionaries were enthusiastically entering the field. But when the position of Christianity in twentieth-century India is considered, Pope Benedict XV's words, written in 1919, should be borne in mind: " Wherever there exists an indigenous clergy, adequate in numbers and in training, and worthy of its vocation—there the missionary's work must be considered brought to a happy close; there the Church is founded."

The first Protestant mission was Lutheran, and started in Danish Tranquebar in 1706. But the " father of the Protestant Churches " in Southern India was the Lutheran Frederick Schwartz (1750–98), whose large congregations were taken over later by the German Leipzig mission. In 1793 came the preacher William Carey, who on account of the East India Company's policy had to register himself as an indigo planter. It was in Danish Serampur that he founded his college, and set up his printing-press in 1818.

Five years earlier the Charter Act had given an official status to the Church of England, though similar claims for the Established Church of Scotland were then disallowed; and Parliament, when it abolished the trade monopoly, allowed Christian missionaries into a country which the East India Company, with an eye upon its dividends, had closed to a general influx of Europeans.

Missionary societies eagerly responded. The Wesleyans came to Southern India, the English Baptists to Benares in 1816, the Anglican Society for the Propagation of the Gospel was in Tanjore by 1825, the Church Missionary Society began its work in different parts of the country, Alexander Duff of the Church of Scotland came to Calcutta in 1829, and the Basel Missionary Society and the American Congregationalists went to Mangalore and Madura in 1834.

The first Hindu religious reformer influenced by Christianity was the Brahman friend of Carey, Raja Ram Mohan Roy. To a knowledge of Islamic culture and the study of Vedic literature in Sanskrit he added the Old and New Testaments in the original Hebrew and Greek before he published *The Precepts of Jesus : a Guide to Peace and Happiness*. In 1828 he established the Brahma Samaj. Later the Ramakrishna order was founded with its aim of selfless service in "a cult of humanity more or less loosely connected with the original ideals of the New Testament or the Tripitakas." [1] In the twentieth century Gandhi was preaching recognition of Christ's teaching as the test of the actions of men. These instances are not an acceptance of Christianity. As the Mahatma has said: "There are thousands of men and women like me who cling to Hinduism because they believe there is in it the amplest scope for mental, moral and spiritual expansion."

Certain features of Christianity have been cited as absorbed by different forms of Hinduism.[2] But the real contribution made by the Christian religion was described by Sir Narayan Chandavarkar, judge of the Bombay High Court and Hindu reformer who died in 1923: "The ideas that lie at the heart of the Gospel of Christ are slowly but surely permeating every part of Hindu society and modifying every phase of Hindu thought."

The British Government of India has never swerved from strict religious neutrality. But it supports social services of the Christian missions both Catholic and Protestant, such as hospitals,[3] leper work, the admirable Salvation Army settlements for the wandering criminal tribes, and cottage industries.

Educational establishments, for example the Jesuit College at Calcutta with its important observatory attached, make known the science, philosophy and art of the western world as a complement to the teaching of Sanskrit literature and ethics at Benares Hindu University and the traditional Islamic culture of the Moslem University at Aligarh.

To turn to the growth of Christianity in modern times.

[1] Art. in *Prabuddha Bharata* (publication of the Ramakrishna movement), April 1927, quoted by K. T. Paul in *British Connection with India* (London, 1927), footnote to pp. 50, 51.

[2] *India, Census Ethnography*, 1901–1931, p. 89. Referring to the Lingayats (a reforming non-Brahmanist twelfth-century sect founded by Basava), an obvious slip is made here and in *Census Report*, 1931, Vol. I. Part I. p. 380, in stating that they have " a doctrine of immaculate conception " ; this should read, the Hindu concept of a Virgin Birth.

[3] The (Protestant) Christian Medical Association of India *Report* for 1937 shows their hospitals to have 19,000 beds, while in all India the hospital beds are stated to be only 57,000. (*Christianity in India Today*, Rev. J. C. Houpert, S.J., Trichinopoly, 1938.)

Christianity came fourth at the 1931 census in numerical order with 6,297,000,[1] of whom 5,991,000 were Indians. This represented an increase of 238·1 per cent. since 1881.

Christianity meets with various difficulties, but by far the greatest among educated Hindus is the dread of social ostracism which to a high-caste convert means the loss of all this world has to offer him. The children of converts, however, if they are the right type of Christian, are met by their Hindu fellow-countrymen with toleration, respect and even affection. At the other end of the social scale the Untouchable has nothing to lose and something definite materially to gain. It is not, therefore, surprising that the overwhelming majority of converts—and they are yearly increasing—come from the victimised masses of the scheduled classes of Hindu India, who find in Christianity their refuge.

The number of these conversions is a problem in communal politics. Gandhi—championing the "suppressed" classes—took up the question on religious grounds, urging that this "ineffaceable blot" must be removed by reform inside Hinduism,[2] a policy Congress endorsed in 1920.[3] But views of a different character have been put forward. Maulana Muhammad Ali, when president of Congress, proposed a mass conversion of the Untouchables to Islam, an increase of the Moslem community which was not welcomed in other quarters. In 1937 a similar political consideration produced the equally unpopular scheme to turn the depressed classes into Sikhs.

This brings us to the present position of Christianity in a country where *swaraj* is the strongest mundane factor. All bishops of the Catholic Church, with her supernational organization, are appointed by the Holy See, and in an Indian hierarchy which includes British

---

[1] Catholics and Romo-Syrians, 3,083,000 ; Anglican Church of India, 747,000 ; other communions, 2,467,000—approximately. There are in addition the Christians in French and Portuguese India recorded as 314,000 Catholics. *Indian Census Report*, 1931 (Delhi, 1933), Vol. I. Part II. p. 520; *Christianity in India Today*, pp. 28–31 ; *The Healing Church*, 1938–39 (Church House, Westminster, 1938), p. 52.

[2] Speech at the Y.M.C.A., Madras, 1916. *Life, Writings and Speeches*, p. 191.

[3] *My Experiments with Truth*, Vol. II. p. 568.

and Basque, Belgian and German, one archbishop and six bishops were Indian in 1938. The Catholic missionaries—priests, nuns and brothers—come from almost every country in Europe. Nearly all the 2600 secular priests are Indians and about one-fifth of those in religious orders, which means that two-thirds of the Catholic priests are of the country.[1]

The Church of England in India became the Church of India, Burma and Ceylon by the Act of 1927, which took effect in 1930. The Anglican communion in India then became autonomous, with a general council as its supreme governing body. There is one Indian diocesan bishop and two assistant bishops, and in the twelve dioceses (excluding Ceylon and Burma) 532 out of 884 clergy are Indian. Union between the Anglican and other Protestant Churches in Southern India has been under negotiation since 1920.

The Presbyterian and Congregational Churches of Southern India united in 1907, and those of Northern India in 1924, the latter representing Presbyterians of Scotland, England, Australia, Canada and America. Indians have been Moderators of the General Assemblies governing these communions. The Federation of Evangelical Lutheran Churches in India, which includes the Danish mission, was in 1926 also formed as an indigenous organization.[2]

The Government of India Act of 1935 continued the nomination of chaplains of the Established Churches of England and Scotland by the secretary of state on the advice of the ecclesiastical authorities concerned. These services are a federal subject, and their cost to Indian revenues is limited to £315,000 a year, exclusive of pensions.

There has been Communist propaganda in India since 1920, the *Communism.* Comintern section aiming at a united front with Congress to establish a " Soviet regime." But, under Lenin's policy, their economic ideas hardly appealed to Congress

---

[1] *Christianity in India Today*, pp. 32–34, and *Catholic Directory for India*, 1938.

[2] (*Anglican*) *Ecclesiastical Year Book for* 1938, and *India and the Christian Movement*, by the Anglican Bishop of Dornakal (V. S. Azariah), Madras, 1936, pp. 85–87, 103.

leaders, while an anti-God campaign was abhorrent to the deeply religious masses. By 1938, however, Communist influence, with the sympathy of some members of Congress Working Committee, had become appreciable, especially in Bombay and Cawnpore.

With Gandhi in prison and temporary eclipse for some years, *Political India.* Congress in 1922 was led by C. R. Das at the head of the new anti-Gandhi Swaraj party. They were out to wreck by obstruction a form of constitution they would have none of, and they succeeded in forcing the governors of Bengal and the United Provinces to take the administration into their own hands. Nor were they alone in believing dyarchy to be no solution of the constitutional problem, for among its various critics were the statesman Sir Tej Bahadur Sapru, and the British Conservative party. At the same time C. R. Das had thrown his great personal influence into the scale in favour of Dominion status as against independence, and pressed for a Round Table Conference to establish it. His untimely death in 1925 dashed the prospects of responsive co-operation. The effect of his loss upon Congress was to break the party into discordant fragments.[1]

The restlessness and discontent of 1927 and 1928 cast the shadow of coming events. The Indian Trades Unions began to use their newly-gathered strength. Communism increased its activities after British relations with Russia were broken off in 1927. The peasants of the United Provinces, Oudh and Gujerat, were openly discontented with local conditions. But more important politically was the rise of the Students' Movement, which included both semi-religious and revolutionary-minded groups. The movement was strongly supported by Congress at the suggestion of Jawaharlal Nehru who, having been sent to Harrow and Cambridge by his father, had in return taken Pandit Motilal Nehru to Moscow to witness the tenth anniversary celebrations of the Soviet.

In 1927 the British Government appointed a Statutory Commission from the three political parties at Westminster, with Sir John Simon as chairman, to report upon the working of the 1919 Act. No Indians were included, which, though constitutionally correct,

[1] *The Indian Struggle*, Subhas C. Bose, pp. 117, 128–132, 136.

made an unfortunate impression in India. The proposal for a joint conference between the British representatives and Indian members of the central legislature was coldly received. Congress was openly hostile ; and although the Commission received help from all the provincial legislatures save one, it was boycotted by political India generally, and local branches of Congress openly condoned the campaign of political murder which started in Bengal.

Their report [1] condemned dyarchy, advocated genuine responsible government in the provinces, advised the separation of Burma and hoped for the future federation of British India and the States. It failed to satisfy the Indian extremists and was considered by the British Conservatives as positively dangerous, but many of its findings appeared in the Act of 1935.

Three other bodies were considering constitutional problems. The All-Parties Conference of Indian Nationalists appointed a Committee [2] in 1928, under Motilal Nehru, to report on constitutional reform. This was a frank statesmanlike attempt to face the obstacle of communalism and, with a hardening attitude towards the States, the question of federation. But its findings,[3] which included provincial autonomy, joint electorates, federation with Dominion status "as the next immediate step" without banning future complete independence, split the Conference into three hostile camps, Mahasabha, Moslems and Sikh, and no practical results followed.

Early in 1929 an All-India Moslem Conference at Delhi, under the presidency of the Aga Khan, stated that in the ultimate Indian constitution only complete autonomy in a federal system would be accepted by the Moslems. Maulana Muhammed Ali, a "leftist" member and ex-ally of Gandhi, died in London in 1931, and the Round Table Conference lost a strikingly forceful delegate.

The Indian States Committee, under Sir Harcourt Butler, indicated ways in which " political and economic relations between

---

[1] *Indian Statutory Commission Report,* Vol. II.

[2] Including Sir Tej Bahadur Sapru, with Jawaharlal Nehru (General Secretary of Congress) as Secretary.

[3] See *Report, All Parties Conference,* 1928. (Allahabad, 1928.)

British India and the States " might be adjusted [1]—but not to the satisfaction of the princes, who, however, lost the advantage of a united front in 1930 by dissension.

Revolt and Conference.

In October 1929 the Viceroy, Lord Irwin (afterwards Lord Halifax), announced the decision of MacDonald's Labour Government that Indian political leaders would be consulted at a Round Table Conference to secure " the greatest possible measure of agreement " in the next Reform Bill. Gandhi's demand for full dominion status as the basis for the conference could not be entertained, and Congress launched, in the Civil Disobedience movement, a most determined attack upon the authority and prestige of the Government.

It opened on 6th April 1930, when Gandhi defied the unpopular monopoly of the Salt Law on Dandi beach. Once again the Mahatma, and with him the leading Congress politicians, failed in all sincerity to realize that non-violence and an excited Indian mob are a contradiction in terms. Before the authorities grasped the extreme seriousness of the movement revolutionary disturbances, with strong Hindu popular support, broke out from Chittagong to Peshawar, from Karachi to Vellore. Some of the towns came for a time under mob control; there was a commercial boycott with the inevitable struggles between pickets and the police; bomb outrages occurred in many places; agrarian unrest was stimulated in the United Provinces; rebellion was attempted in Burma. On the North-West Frontier the political-religious Red Shirt movement under Abdul Ghaffar Khan of Uttmanzai, while backed by Congress, was enlisting thousands of Moslems in the Peshawar district with the avowed aim of creating an independent Pathan State.

In the face of disorder flagrant and widespread enough to create an impression that the Government of India was ceasing to govern, the authorities took the measures referred to as " rule by ordinance." A large number of congressmen, including Gandhi, were arrested, martial law was locally applied, Congress Working Committee was

---

[1] See *Report, Indian States Committee, 1928–29.* The privately circulated *Indian States and the New Regime,* by Maharaj-Kumar Raghubir Sinh (Sitamau, 1937), is an interesting analysis of States politics.

declared an unlawful association, the property of unlawful associations was made liable to confiscation, and Abdul Ghaffar Khan, leader of the " Servants of God " and disciple of Gandhi, was arrested.

At the same time Irwin warned Indian politicians of the danger of preaching defiance of the law as a patriotic expression of political dissatisfaction with lawful authority, in view of any ministerial responsibilities that might shortly be their own.[1] In October 1929 he had made the first clear official declaration that Dominion status was "the natural issue of India's constitutional progress." Gravely impressed by "the webs of mistrust" clogging the relations between India and Britain, Irwin's extreme reluctance to take repressive action against Congress brought moderate Indian opinion to his side; and it may be said that the strong measures taken by his successor, Lord Willingdon, which defeated the Civil Disobedience movement, were the logical development, and not a reversal, of Irwin's policy.

On 12th November 1930 the Round Table Conference opened in London. Congress was not represented, but the delegates from the States included the Maharaja of Bikaner and Sir Akbar Hydari, from British India Sir Tej Bahadur Sapru, and the British members represented all three political parties.[2] The principle of federation, under safeguards, was accepted by the States.[3]

Before the second session MacDonald's National (coalition) ministry was in power and there had been an important development in India. Gandhi and the Congress Working Committee were released in February 1931, and conversations began between " the tall thin Christian " statesman and the khadi-clad Hindu ascetic, which ended on the night of 4th March in the Irwin-Gandhi agreement. By this pact all political prisoners whose offences had not involved violence were released, the emergency ordinances were withdrawn and Civil Disobedience, which had been ruinous to trade and finance, and an almost unbearable strain on the civil administration, was discontinued.[4]

[1] Address to the Central Legislatures, 9th July 1930.
[2] Burma had its own Conference at the second session.
[3] Proceedings of First Session, Cmd. 3722 of 1931.
[4] The Government statement on the conversations is given in full in *The History of the National Congress*, pp. 738–744.

Gandhi accordingly entered the Conference in September as the sole representative of Congress, which in view of the divisions in the Nationalist ranks was perhaps unfortunate.[1] The Conference was confronted with the communal controversy, intensified by the shocking Hindu-Moslem riots in Cawnpore earlier in the year and the general renewal of these disturbances. Gandhi returned dissatisfied to India, and Congress was not represented at the final session which closed the Conference in December 1932.

There could be no more serious obstacle to constitutional progress than communalism. Numerous conferences of Indian leaders to solve communal representation had proved as abortive as the Round Table Conference.[2] Finally appeal was made to the Prime Minister (MacDonald), who announced the British Government's decision in the Communal Award of 17th August 1932 as regards the provincial legislatures. Included in this decision the depressed classes were given separate constituencies for twenty years in addition to a vote in the general Hindu constituencies.

When the award was published Gandhi was in jail, as a result of his ineffectual revival of Civil Disobedience [3] on his return from England. With dramatic suddenness he startled India by beginning a fast to death unless the communal separation of the outcastes was altered. A week of feverish negotiation with Hindu and outcaste leaders produced the Poona pact, which gave the depressed classes more seats, but at the cost of bringing them under the virtual control of Congress by joint electorates. On 26th September 1932 the British Government modified the Communal award accordingly, and Gandhi's waning political prestige was re-established.

Events on the North-West Frontier can be shortly summarized. In 1931 the Red Shirts and Congress activities, added to border unrest, created a situation from March to December that might at

---

[1] Compare *The Indian Struggle*, pp. 248–250, 256–260, with *Jawaharlal Nehru, an Autobiography*, pp. 291, 294, *The History of the National Congress* (Sitaramayya), pp. 784–785, and the official *India in 1931–32*, p. 32.

[2] Speech by Sir C. P. Ramaswami Aiyar in the Legislative Assembly, 5th Sept. 1932.

[3] Convictions falling from 17,818 in February 1932 to 1545 in December. *India in 1931-32*, pp. 54, 55.

any time have caused a disaster of the first magnitude. Eventually 47,000 troops had to be employed. Abdul Ghaffar Khan had been released by the Irwin-Gandhi pact (regarded by the Khan as merely a temporary truce), and his recruiting campaign for Red Shirts, which began in March, won enthusiastic response. The movement, which threatened to extend into the tribal areas, demanded decisive action. The Khan and other leaders were arrested by surprise on the night of the 24th December, and the Peshawar district was occupied by six mobile columns. The general situation then came under control, but the ban on Red Shirt associations, as revolutionary bodies, remained. That the North-West Frontier Province was given the prestige of a governor's province under the new reforms, had also a salutary effect.

The constitutional reforms of 1935 were based on the conclusion reached by a Joint Select Committee of Parliament *Government of* (excepting the extreme right wing) to which delegates *India Act,* 1935. from British India, the Indian States and Burma, representative enough to include Anglo-Indians and the depressed classes, were invited for consultation.[1] The Bill received the Royal Assent on 2nd August 1935 and came into force as regards the provinces, partly on 3rd July 1936 with the electoral provisions, and completely on 1st April 1937. On 2nd August 1858 the Act had been passed which brought India under the British Crown and Parliament.

If the Act fell short of Dominion status it was a considerable advance towards it. That status, as defined by the Statute of Westminster (1931), means the right of the self-governing colonies to an equal measure of autonomy in external affairs while united by a common allegiance to the Crown, with the right to leave the Commonwealth. In practice it has varied from the position the Irish Free State attained by armed rebellion to the complete absence of individuality in external relations and to the parliamentary control of its financial affairs instanced in Newfoundland. Nevertheless the British Commonwealth presents, in Great Britain

[1] See *Joint Committee on Indian Constitutional Reform*, Session 1933-34, Vol. I. Report and Proceedings, Vol. II. Records (H.M. Stationery Office, London, 1934).

and the Dominions, the most effective association of free nations ever devised.

While Burma was separated from India and Aden became a Crown colony, as regards British India the Act with certain restrictions gave autonomy to the eleven provinces.[1] The provincial governors continued to be appointed by the Crown. They retained safeguards mainly to ensure " law and order "; in emergencies they were empowered, with the consent of the governor-general, to issue ordinances and permanent Acts; and if the constitution should break down they could take over as much of the administration as might be necessary. In using these special powers, the governor would be answerable to the governor-general and through him to the secretary of state and Parliament.

Apart from these reservations, the machinery of provincial administration was transferred to Indian hands. The council of non-official ministers appointed by the governor became answerable to the elected provincial legislatures of one or two chambers.[2] The governor was no longer responsible for the financial stability of his province, and, although their financial resources were restricted, no important subjects were reserved from the control of the ministers.

The provincial electorate was widened to include 29 million men and 6 million women, an increase from 3 to 14 per cent. of the population, with separate electorates for Moslems, Sikhs, Indian Christians,[3] Anglo-Indians and Europeans, and special seats for women, landlords, industry, universities and labour.

In British India the Act was, as an experiment in democratic government on British lines, a far-reaching development of the Montagu-Chelmsford reforms. As regards the sub-continent as a whole it was designed to maintain by federation the unity which British dominion had achieved.

---

[1] Orissa and Sind became provinces in 1937 under the Act.

[2] Bengal, Bombay, Madras, the United Provinces, Bihar and Assam were given Upper and Lower Houses.

[3] Among the critics of communal categories the Anglican Bishop, V. S. Azariah of Dornakal, has urged as " tragic that the representatives of the Christian churches . . . should have consented to use their numerical strength for obtaining political power," *India and the Christian Movement*, pp. 106-107.

The keystone of the new constitution was to be a central federal government of the provinces and States, the relations between the States and the paramount Power being defined by the treaties, engagements and *sanads*[1] which had brought Indian India into "subordinate union." Federation, therefore, could only come by the voluntary accession of the Princes; and the Act provided that rulers of States representing at least half the total population of the States and entitled to at least half the seats allotted to the States in the federal Upper Chamber would have to sign instruments of accession. Federation would then be established by Royal Proclamation. As the rights of paramountcy over the Indian States could not be exercised by any federal authority (outside the subjects voluntarily surrendered by the Princes to federal legislation) the States relations with the Crown would stand as before, the Viceroy exercising the powers of agent to the Crown.

These reforms gave the Viceroy appointed by the Crown in his separate capacity as governor-general the executive power and authority of the central government, including supreme military command. For the "key" subjects, among which were included defence, tribal areas and foreign affairs, the governor-general continued to be responsible to the secretary of state and Parliament. To administer these reserved subjects he was given three independent counsellors and could co-opt a financial adviser. Dyarchy had been weighed and judged to be unavoidable in the central government.[2]

The federal legislature would be the governor-general representing the King-Emperor, the council of state and the federal assembly[3]; British Indian delegates being almost all elected, those from the States being nominated. The governor-general became empowered to choose "front-bench" members of both Houses to form cabinets, whose advice he could refuse to accept in special circumstances.

The governor-general was charged with special responsibilities similar to those laid upon provincial governors, and could issue

---

[1] See p. 506, footnote 1.

[2] See *Report of Joint Committee* (Session 1933–34), Vol. I. pp. 19–22.

[3] The Council of State being permanent, one-third of its members retiring every three years ; the Assembly was given a maximum duration of five years.

ordinances to deal with them. Should the working of the constitution break down he was empowered to take over the whole administration. If all went well there would be no occasion to invoke the emergency powers which it may be said resembled those of the President of the United States.

The Act reasserted that matters involving sovereignty were unaltered but, while the ultimate supremacy of Parliament over British India remained, the powers of the secretary of state at the India Office were nearly all transferred to the Government of India. In view of federation a Federal Court, with appeal to the Privy Council, was created, and an Act of 1934 had established a Reserve Bank. Indians had been made eligible for King's commissions in the Indian Army in 1918, later to become equivalent to Dominion commissions; and with the Act of 1935 "Indianization" of the services in general was made systematic.

The new reforms did not give British India full representative government, for legislation was not the prerogative of a popularly elected chamber and was subject to veto. While the provision of safeguards was unknown in the different circumstances of previous Dominion evolution in the British Empire they were, to quote Sir Tej Bahadur Sapru at the Round Table Conference, "really intended in the interests of the responsible government that we are establishing at the centre and not to strengthen the hands of British control over us," a view with which the Moslems and minority parties concurred. But the Act had opened the way to complete self-government and a federated union of All-India with Dominion status, provided that Hindus and Moslems sank their communal differences, and the Princes, coming to agreement with British-Indian politicians, were prepared to sign their instruments of accession.

In July 1937, after the elections, provincial autonomy was established. Gandhi, maker and dictator of a " peaceful " revolutionary Congress, had discarded his policy of non-co-operation for what might be described as the Trojan Horse method to obtain independence; and in eight provinces (with a clear majority in five) Congress ministries were in power under the orders of the Working Committee.

Social betterment headed ministerial programmes,[1] Congress and non-Congress alike. The ministry of Bombay grappled with its industrial problems, but found that Prohibition caused serious financial difficulties. In Rajagopalachari, Madras had a premier of outstanding ability and force of character. Among the non-Congress governments the unionist ministry of the Punjab worthily upheld the administrative traditions of that province.

But for the display of Congress totalitarianism, against which the Moslems strongly reacted and bitterly resented, provincial autonomy could hardly have augured better for the future.

The Indian States. The extreme contrasts in the size and general conditions of the States, Hindu, Moslem and Sikh, have already been described. The political situation in Indian India at the beginning of 1939 may be summarized as follows :

While the Viceroy was pressing for early federation to set the seal upon the 1935 constitution, Congress was fomenting violent political agitation against States' autocracy, from Kashmir to Travancore, with some success—but with the deplorable appearance of militant communism in some of the larger States.

The autocratic rule of a hereditary prince could still inspire, as in the brave days of old, the devoted loyalty and pride of his subjects. While interest had grown in social services and free education, highly progressive States were considering political changes in the light of the new constitution for British India; and representatives of historic dynasties had already taken the decision to turn, in varying degrees, from the ancient order of Oriental government. Two examples may be given.

As early as 1894 the Nizam of Hyderabad recognized the right of the people to share in the framing of laws and to representation. The Nizam's council in 1938 consisted of a president (also presiding over the legislative council) and twenty members. Of these seven

---

[1] See *Indian Politics*, 1936-42, Coupland, pp. 26-166, for a detailed examination of the working of the provincial governments.

were unofficial, made up of two elected by the landed interest, two by the pleaders of the High Court, and the remainder nominated from among the residents of the State.[1]

In 1938 the Maharaja of Cochin applied the principle of ministerial legislative responsibility to an electorate of all tax-payers and those who had passed the school final examination or its equivalent. Certain "nation-building" departments were brought under the administration of a minister chosen from the elected members of the legislative council; and the executive authority of the State was declared to be exercisable by the ruler of over a million subjects [2] only through the *diwan*, or that minister.

India and Federation.

The central government was still, at the close of 1938, in a transitional stage between the Montagu-Chelmsford reforms and the political and economic union of the new constitution. There was no immediate prospect of federation with a strong central government. None of the princes had signed the necessary instruments of accession. They were still weighing the effect of an irrevocable decision upon their direct relationship with the Crown and their recognized rights, now threatened by Congress hostility. Other difficulties had emerged. Only the Liberal party, whose veteran leaders had lost all influence in Indian politics, defended the Act of 1935. The two great political parties in British India opposed the federal scheme as laid down in the Act, though for different reasons.

The Congress party voiced their objection to nominated representatives from autocratic States sitting in the central legislature with the elected members from British India. But stronger opposition was raised to the retention of finance, defence and external affairs—the keys to complete control—as reserved subjects. The orthodox

[1] 14,436,148 of whom 12,176,727 are Hindus, 1,534,666 Moslems, 544,789 Animists (tribal) and 151,382 Christians (*Census of India*, 1931, Vol. XXIII., Government Central Press, Hyderabad Deccan, 1933).

[2] Hindus 780,484, Christians 334,870, Moslems 87,902, etc., Literates form 46 per cent. of the male and 22 per cent. of the female population (3.37 per cent. in all), the highest in India (*Census of India*, 1931, Vol. XXI., Cochin Government Press, Ernakulam, 1933).

Hindu Mahasabha[1] while representing the aims and traditions of the Peshwas took, however, a longer and more realistic view than that of Congress, the "National" but predominantly Hindu party.

While Moslems throughout India strongly resented Congress claims to represent all Nationalist opinion, the Moslem League saw in federation Hindu control at the centre with the accession of the preponderating Hindu States. They countered it with the conception of a union of Moslem interests that might extend beyond the North-West Frontier, a reaction diametrically opposed to Indian unity. This was to take definite shape in 1940 as the determined Moslem League policy of Pakistan,[2] which meant independent rule in specified areas of the sub-continent.

Light had thickened over political India; and the house, which Holkar had described when Victoria was declared *Kaisar-i-Hind* as then "built from a vast heap of stones each stone in its right place from roof to basement," was now divided against itself by deep suspicion and mistrust. This was the situation when the war which was to bring disaster to European civilization broke out in September 1939.

We now know that India had a great homogeneous culture indigenous to her soil, whose highest expression flourished on the banks of the Indus. Since those far-distant days three influences have shaped her history. Two came by invasion through the north-west passes, the third came from over the sea. The Indo-Aryan descent upon the country gave India the development of her ancient and most powerful culture, the religion of Brahmanism and the concentration of caste, her deep philosophy and the idealism of Hindu art.

The Muhammadan conquests from Central Asia brought the doctrine of universal brotherhood in religion and the civilization of Islam to become an established institution in the country; but also to create the communal strife which has existed with varying intensity for nine hundred years.

The third great influence was originally introduced by the traders

[1] Founded in 1928 to preserve Hindu orthodoxy, it became a political body similar in organization to Congress and the Moslem League.
[2] See pamphlet, *The Pakistan National Movement*, C. Rahmat Ali (London, 1933).

of a European Power. The British, by enforcing over the peoples of India an entirely foreign guardianship and rule of high efficiency and absolute integrity, gave the sub-continent political unity, peace in the stability of order and impartial justice between Indian and Indian.

These influences have been manifested by great empires in, or dominating, the sub-continent—the Maurya and the Gupta, the Mogul, and the British.

With the passing of the British Empire of India [1] the sub-continent stands in the dawn of a new era. The immediate problem facing Indian statesmanship is to preserve the stability of order which its peoples have known under British dominion. The fearful alternative would be the chaos which followed the fall of the Mogul Empire.

[1] Announcement by Prime Minister, Mr. Attlee, in House of Commons, 20th Feb. 1947, "by a date not later than June 1948." *Hansard,* No. 42, 1947, cols. 1399 *et seq.*

APPENDIX

CONGRESS DECLARATION OF INDEPENDENCE

The original Independence Day Pledge of 26th January 1930 is to be found in Pandit Nehru's *Autobiography*, pp. 601, 602. The following text of the Declaration is as given in *Constituent Assembly for India*, by Professor Gangulee, pp. 296, 297.

THE DECLARATION OF INDEPENDENCE AT THE PLENARY SESSION OF THE CONGRESS AT LAHORE, *March* 1939

" We believe that it is the inalienable right of the Indian people, as of any other people, to have freedom and to enjoy the fruits of their toil and have the necessities of life so that they may have full opportunities of growth. We believe also that if any government deprives a people of these rights and oppresses them, the people have a further right to alter it or abolish it. The British Government in India has not only deprived the Indian people of their freedom but has based itself on the exploitation of the masses, and has ruined India economically, politically, culturally and spiritually. We believe, therefore, that India must sever the British connection and attain *Purna Swaraj* or Complete Independence.

"India has been ruined economically. The revenue derived from our people is out of all proportion to our income. Our average income is 7 pice (less than 2½d.) per day, and of the heavy taxes we pay, 20 per cent. are raised from the land revenue derived from the peasantry, and 3 per cent. from the salt tax, which falls most heavily on the poor.

"Village industries such as hand-spinning have been destroyed, leaving the peasantry idle for at least four months in the year and dulling their intellect for want of handicrafts ; and nothing has been substituted, as in other countries, for the crafts thus destroyed.

"Customs and currency have been so manipulated as to heap further burdens on the peasantry. The British manufactured goods constitute the bulk of our imports. Customs duties betray clear partiality for British manufactures, and revenues from them are used not to lessen the burden on the masses but for sustaining a highly extravagant administration. Still more arbitrary has been the manipulation of the exchange ratio, which has resulted in millions being drained away from the country.

"Politically, India's status has never been so reduced as under the British régime. No reforms have given real political power to the people. The tallest of us have to bend before foreign authority. The rights of free expression of opinion and free association have been denied to us, and many of our countrymen are compelled to live in exile abroad and cannot return to their homes. All administrative talent is killed, and the masses have to be satisfied with petty village offices and clerkships.

"Culturally, the system of education has torn us from our moorings, and our training has made us hug the very chains that bind us.

"Spiritually, compulsory disarmament has made us unmanly, and the presence of an alien army of occupation, employed with deadly effect to crush in us the spirit of existence, has made us think that we cannot look after ourselves or put up a defence against foreign aggression, or even defend our homes and families from the attack of thieves, robbers and miscreants.

"We hold it to be a crime against man and God to submit any longer to a rule that has caused this fourfold disaster to our country. We recognize, however, that the most effective way of gaining our freedom is not through violence. We will therefore prepare ourselves by withdrawing, so far as we can, all voluntary association from the British Government, and will prepare for Civil Disobedience, including non-payment of taxes. We are convinced that if we can withdraw our voluntary help and stop payment of taxes without doing violence even under provocation, the end of this inhuman rule is assured. We therefore hereby solemnly resolve to carry out the Congress instructions issued from time to time for the purpose of establishing *Purna Swaraj*."

CHRONOLOGY

1905–1910. Lord Minto Viceroy.
1907. Beginning of terrorist political action.
1909. Morley-Minto Reforms.
1910–1916. Lord Hardinge Viceroy.
1911. Delhi the new capital: Bengal reunited.
1914–1918. World War to Armistice.
1916–1921. Lord Chelmsford Viceroy.
1918. Influenza epidemic.
1919. Montagu-Chelmsford Reforms.
    Gandhi became national leader and established the political power of Congress.
1919–1920. Waziristan Campaign.
1921–1926. Lord Reading Viceroy.
1923. Indian Tariff Reform began.
1926–1931. Lord Irwin (Lord Halifax) Viceroy.
1930. Civil Disobedience: Red Shirt Movement.
1930–1932. Round Table Conference.
1931. Irwin-Gandhi pact.
1931–1936. Lord Willingdon Viceroy.
1934. Bihar earthquake.
1935. Quetta earthquake.
    Government of India Act passed.
1936. Lord Linlithgow appointed Viceroy.
1937. Constitutional Reforms established in British India.
1938. Maharaja of Cochin inaugurated the principle of ministerial responsibility in an Indian State.
1939. Second World War began.

BIBLIOGRAPHY

A Constitutional History of India from 1600 to 1935, A. Berriedale Keith, 1936.
The History of the National Congress (1885–1935), B. P. Sitaramayya (Madras), 1935.
Social Service in India, Ed. Sir E. Blunt (H.M. Stationery Office), 1939.
A Nation in Making, Sir Surendranath Bannerjea, 1927.

Young India, Lajpat Rai, 2nd Edn. (New York), 1917.

India in Transition, H.H. Aga Khan, 1918.

The Heart of Aryavarta, Earl of Ronaldshay (Marquess of Zetland), 1925.

The Story of my Experiments with Truth, M. K. Gandhi, trans. M. Desai, 2 vols. (Ahmedabad), 1927, 1929.

India's Case for Swaraj, Mahatma Gandhi, 2nd Edn. (Bombay), 1932.

Jawaharlal Nehru: an Autobiography, 1936.

The National Income of British India 1931–1932, Dr. V. K. R. V. Rao, 1940.

The Indian Problem (1942) and *Indian Politics* (1943), R. Coupland, D.Litt.

Constituent Assembly for India, N. Gangulee (1942).

A SHORT CHRONOLOGY

OF THE PERIOD COVERED BY THIS VOLUME

B.C.

c. 3250–2750. Civilization peak in Indus valley.

4500–1200. Conjectural range of dates Aryan invasion.

c. 563–468. Mahavira and Gautama, founders of Jainism and Buddhism.

c. 518. Darius I of Persia annexed Indus valley.

327–325. Expedition of Alexander of Macedon.

c. 321–184. Maurya imperial dynasty; Asoka, *c.* 274–236.

c. 220–A.D. 180. Andhra kingdom.

c. 184. Bactrian invasion.

c. 58. Saka invasion.

A.D.

c. 89–226. Kushan empire.

318–470. Gupta imperial dynasty; Samudragupta, 326–375.

c. 470–528. White Hun empire.

c. 550–750. Chalukya dynastic supremacy in Southern India.

606–648. Harsha, N.E. Indian emperor.

711. Arab invasion of Sind.

c. 973–1150. Second Chalukya kingdom.

c. 973–1220. Chola kingdom of the south.

1001–1030. Invasions of Mahmud of Ghazni; Punjab annexed, 1021.

1030–1160. Ghaznavid dynasty.

1173–1326. Hoysala paramountcy in Deccan.

1175–1206. Muhammad Ghori.

1206–1287. Slave kings of Delhi.

1290–1320. Khalji dynasty.

1320–1414. Tughlak dynasty.

1347–1518. Bahmani kingdom.

1358–1565. Vijayanagar kingdom.

1398–1399. Invasion of Timur.

1414–1526. Lodi dynasty.

1469–1539. Nanak, founder of Sikhism.

1498. Vasco da Gama landed at Calicut.

1526. Panipat I.

1526–1712. Mogul dynastic empire from Babur to Bahadur Shah I.

1556–1605. Akbar emperor.

639

A.D.

1605–1613. Establishment of Dutch and English Company factories.
1658–1707. Aurangzeb emperor.
1673. French founded Pondicherry.
1674–1680. Sivaji (*b.* 1627) king of Maharashtra.
1690. Calcutta founded by English Company.
1714–1818. Rule of Maratha Peshwas.
1738–1739. Nadir Shah's invasion.
1742–1754. Dupleix, governor at Pondicherry.
1748. First invasion of Ahmed Shah Durrani.
1757. Plassey decided British supremacy in Bengal.
1760. Wandiwash extinguished French power in India.
1761. Maratha Confederacy broken at Panipat by Afghan army.
1764. Battle of Buxar; British defeated Mogul alliance.
1774–1785. Warren Hastings, first governor-general (Regulating Act, 1773).
1783. Anglo-Maratha Treaty of Salbai.
1799. Capture of Seringapatam and death of Tipu Sultan.
1817–1818. Third Maratha War and deposition of the last Peshwa.
1823. Ranjit Singh (*b.* 1780, *d.* 1839) extended Sikh kingdom to Peshawar.
1835. Bentinck's " British Education " resolution.
1848–1849. Second Sikh War; Punjab annexed by British.
1856. Oudh annexed.
1857–1859. The Mutiny.
1858. Government of India Act; end of H.E.I.C.
1885. First meeting of Indian National Congress.
1914–1918. World War to Armistice.
1920. Gandhi, national leader for Swaraj.
1935. Government of India Act.
1939. Second World War began.

Kanishka   Andhra Dynasty

Demetrius

Eukratides

Gold piece
of
Claudius
                        Copper Token
                        Coin of
                        Mohammad
                        Shah
Coin of Horse Sacrifice Tughlak   Vijayanagar
Samudragupta   Empire

Jahangir-Portrait   Jahangir
                           Zodiacal Mohr

East India Co.   Rupee   Mohur
Half Pagoda Madras   Bengal   1835
18th cent.

Mohur
1835

INDIAN COINS
Key